Attack at Dawn

Reliving the Battle of Narvik in World War II

Ron Cope

Published by Clink Street Publishing 2015

First edition.

ISBN: 978-1-909477-97-1
Ebook: 978-1-909477-98-8

Dedicated to my granddaughter Naomi and her generation.

Contents

Acknowledgements

I have to give a big thank you to my publisher 'Authoright' for achieving exactly what they said right from the start. A highly recommended team for first time authors.

Imperial War Museum (Collections and Research Department). Audio Recordings Code Numbers as below:

Cope 11586, Pulford 10610, Bourton 10746, Cheshire 16304, Robinson 11286

Proof Readers: My sister in law, Jacqueline Vickery for her considerable support between 2010/15 and Laura Pallett in 2014. They both did a sterling job correcting my many mistakes and keeping me focused. Alison, my wife for her patience over the six years. She can now have her breakfast room and conservatory back, well that is after the HMS Hunter book is published.

John Warburton-Lee, Ralph Brigginshaw, Geirr Haarr, Peter Mitchell (submerged.co.uk), Bob Pearson and Trevor Baker for their fantastic support, now considered friends.

My squash playing partner for many years, Tom Currie, who was there in the beginning when I decided to put pen to paper. Throughout, he has given me outstanding encouragement.

My Dad's sisters, Auntie Marion and Auntie Vera who will be very pleased to see their brother's story finally written.

Leo Styles (Australia), Keith Greenslade, (Australia,) Lorry and Lucy Tirchett (Malta), Peter Michell at 'submerged.co.uk', Bill Sanders, Hans Houterman (Holland www.unithistories.com) Ian McCleod, Carmel Vassallo (Malta) Nicola Mulryan (Norway) Harry Rogers and Les Smale both of whom have passed away since I started my book.

The additional contributions from; Daryl Harries, John Avery, Mike Newton, Ted Stiles (Canada), Rosemary Barnes, Mike Stanner, Petra and Hakon Kristensen, Dominick Penrose, Gytha Lane-Morrow, Lesley Hood-Bourton, Olwen George, Catherine Mason, Heather McAlpine, Jacqui Harris, Lance Kennedy, Gill O'Rourke, Borg-Anna Sanders, Peter Siddall, David Woolley, Tony Quinn, Alexandros Kopsahilis, Fidelma Rogers, Tony Rogers, Kate Kennedy, Norma New, Di James, David Taylor, Anna Reid, Jill Smith, Richard Smith, Danielle O'Brien, Dr Grafton Maggs, Len Brigginshaw, Andrew Cuthberton, Tore Eggan.

Denis Darmanin, John Mizzi, Paul Aquilina, Mary Leavey, Carmel Grima, (All Maltese Citizens).

National Archives at Kew and Her Majesties Stationary Office. Nick Grant at Ian Allan Publishers for giving permission to reproduce quotes from Peter Dickens book.

Shropshire Star, Express and Echo (Exeter) Oystermouth Parish Journal, Sunday Express (1980), Daily Mail (20th April 1940), Western Morning News, The Packet (Falmouth), Navy News, Times of Malta, Malta Independent, Salford Advertiser, Carrickfergus Times, Middlesbrough Gazette.

If I have forgotten anyone, please forgive me but by all means make contact and the error can be corrected.

Author's Preface

This book is not intended to mislead readers into thinking it is a serious work of naval history. I leave that to those with far more professional abilities than I would claim to have. However, I believe it should be considered as being the first definitive record of accounts from those who were actually involved in the First British Battle of Narvik. It comprises their own experiences regarding how they managed to survive after the battle and also escape capture by the enemy. I cannot vouch that all the accounts are fully factual, although from the sheer volume that I have been able to gather, there must be a lot of truth.

However, I can definitely confirm the crew members of the 2nd Destroyer Flotilla were there and during the ensuing years were still able to describe what they had witnessed. In addition, I have to accept that the information that has been provided by the crew members' families and friends, passed on either verbally or recorded on paper or tape, is indeed true and correct.

As a mark of respect to the Norwegian people, I would like to point out on the front cover although I have written the phrase "First Battle of Narvik", in actual fact the first battle took place the day before. This was 9th of April 1940 when the German Navy arrived and was confronted by, two First World War Norwegian coastal defence ships, 'Eidsvold' and 'Norge'. The Norwegian Captains having stood their ground the two ships were eventually torpedoed and sunk in the fjord. This resulted in 282 Norwegian sailors losing their lives. However, during the rest of the book I will refer to the First Battle of Narvik as happening on the 10th of April 1940.

Foreword

By Ralph Brigginshaw, Signalman, HMS Hardy

As a remaining survivor of the Battle of Narvik, I was pleased to be asked by the author, Ron Cope, to write a 'Foreword' for the events described in this book.

After joining the Royal Navy in 1935 at the age of fifteen with initial training at HMS St Vincent and a period aboard HMS Rodney and HMS Warwick, I was very pleased to be drafted to HMS Hardy, the leader of the 2nd Destroyer Flotilla under the command of Captain Warburton-Lee [Captain D], in early 1939.

After war broke out we served for a while in the Mediterranean and the South Atlantic, based at Freetown. In February 1940 we were suddenly and urgently ordered to return to the United Kingdom. After a short leave we were then sent north and eventually arrived in Scapa Flo.

From there the author then explains the action and aftermath when five destroyers of the Royal Navy eventually met ten larger destroyers of the German Navy. This was in the snow covered fjords of North Norway in the early hours of the 10th of April 1940; as related by members of HMS Hardy's ship's company.

I would like to thank Ron for all of his work and patience in bringing this story to life in a very interesting book.

Crawley, Sussex
January 2015.

Prologue

After the battle, two Norwegian men were walking along the road overlooking the fjord near Narvik. One was a former medical corps soldier. They were searching to see if there were any poor souls from the aftermath that may have been swept ashore. After a while they saw two bodies on the rocks below. When they reached them they found that one was a young German sailor and the other had an HMS Hardy identity tag. He was Hugh Mantle from South Wales who was aged eighteen. Both killed or drowned in action. Their bodies were taken into Narvik for identification and burial.

You could just imagine those two Norwegians' thoughts at the time, "What a pointless waste of two young men's lives."

April 1940.

Introduction

My interest in the sea began very early in my formative years and this, along with my Dad's stories of his time in the Royal Navy, probably later led to my following in his footsteps.

The nearest popular seaside towns to Manchester were either in North Wales or the Lancastrian resort of Southport. As a youngster I remember being taken there on a number of occasions, travelling either on the train or by Charabanc or 'chara' as it was then known. These trips were usually on Bank Holidays or 'Wake Weeks' with my Gran Sarah Ann Murray, her sister Auntie Lizzy (Whewell) and other family members. All the passengers would be in a happy frame of mind because it was holiday time. En-route there would be sing songs and copious bottles of beer drunk by the men on the back seats.

However, the highlight was a week's holiday on the Isle of Man, staying at Mrs Youdall's small hotel in Douglas. Before arriving there with my parents, sister Edith, and brother Cyril (fourteen months older), plus a number of our extended family, I had the first opportunity to test my sea legs. I was about four years old and the voyage by ferry was not to my liking: I was sick for most of the time! Although, happily, on arrival at the port, the smell of smoked kippers were soon forgotten and the holiday began in earnest.

It must have been an enjoyable time, but in addition to the experience of sea sickness, another memory that comes to mind is of an incident at the boating lake on Douglas promenade. Cyril and I had been able to talk our Dad and Mam into buying us toy sailing yachts, which we were able to push by a rod into positions of manoeuvrability around the lake. Unfortunately, after awhile, having thought I had managed the skill of utilising the direction of the wind, I became too ambitious. This resulted in my stretching too far into the imaginary ocean and consequently I fell fully dressed into the water. To this day I can still recall going under, struggling for breath and then people around the side of the lake appearing in a panic and trying to haul me back onto dry land.

We can all remember frightening events in our younger years which are forever ingrained in our minds. But my experiences were not as life threatening nor was I in a situation as dangerous as having to fight by oneself for survival. As you will read later this was the case for many of the sailors in battles at sea.

These relatively minor incidents on the Isle of Man would soon become irrelevant to me, when my Dad became the proud owner of a motorbike with a side car and then later a Wolseley car. These cars were used by the police in the TV programme 'Fabian of the Yard'. Looking back now it was obvious for nostalgic reasons that Dad as well as Mam (although this was in the war years) always hankered to return to Devon. This will be become clearer later. Suffice to say, that in the 1950s after the war, similar to my parents, people were beginning to enjoy many improvements in their lifestyles. Package holidays abroad came later but in the meantime, with improved roads and the ability to own your own transport, they were able to go further afield.

The journeys down to Devon and Cornwall from Manchester, although long and tiring, provided me with opportunities to visit the August Bank Holiday's 'Navy Days'. The crowds were absolutely enormous. Remember this was the 1950s so Devonport Dockyard would then be full of all types of warships and submarines on show. Even better you could join the queues to go on board for a guided tour around the vessels. The smell of machinery oil, galley cooking and men living in close quarters was unique. There were also brilliant displays around the dockyard and on the lawns in HMS Drake barracks. Frogmen in large tanks waving as you stopped to look in awe. That is if you were not frightened of the divers in masks. And to top it all, the marvellous Royal Marine band marching up and down, in precise formation, going through all their stirring repertoire of tunes.

With my Mam on Plymouth Hoe 1952. Destroyer entering harbour. In thirteen years time I would be doing the same procedure. *Ron Cope Collection.*

On one occasion we spent some time visiting one of Dad's old shipmates, Harry Lambert, in Plymouth. Harry and his wife put us up for the night, it was a little crowded and I had to sleep on a camp bed in the lounge. I have vivid memories of Dad and Harry reminiscing about their time during the war in the Navy. I pretended to be asleep not wanting to miss their conversation about what were to me at the time some amazing stories.

I am sure that all these events and memories in my earlier years went towards forming a close interest in not only the Royal Navy but also in its impressive history. Like most boys reaching their teenage years, my life outside of school consisted of playing football and then in the summer months cricket. We would kick a tennis ball around the road, stopping to let the odd car go by. A goal would be scored when your accuracy skills enabled you to hit the telegraph pole or street lighting post. Time passed quickly and before you knew it, light failing, it was time to go back home.

Unlike today, where it appears that a considerable amount of time is taken up by staying indoors, with computer games or watching the unlimited number of television programmes. Then there were only two TV channels and they did not begin till four o'clock in the afternoon with 'Watch with Mother'. Finishing around ten o'clock in the evening but not switching off until 'God Save the Queen' ended. So we had to make our own entertainment or fantasise about being Duncan Edwards and winning the Cup or Gary Sobers hitting sixes out of the ground. Or playing 'Monopoly' or practising flicking cigarette cards against the bedroom wall before the next day at school when we had to be on top of our game. Otherwise we could end up losing a lot of our most precious collection. (The object of the game was to flick one of your cards on top of your opponents, then you win all the cards laid on the floor.)

There were no 'health and safety' issues in the Junior School, the teachers had gone home, before disagreements resulted in us sorting out our differences by a good old fight. We walked relatively long distances to and from school in short trousers without being escorted by a parent.

The big day came at the age of eleven when I moved to the 'grown up' secondary school. I felt this was a big step but it was not long before I settled into the new regime. However, it would be at least another year before I was given my first pair of long trousers. At least they were brand new, rather than 'hand me down' jumpers and shirts from my older brother Cyril.

Around this time, in my early teens, I had moved on from reading the comics 'Beano' and 'Dandy' to the more sophisticated editions of the 'Lion' and 'Eagle'. With regard to the latter, once in awhile it printed a feature on its namesake the famous aircraft carrier HMS Eagle. Little did I know or could have imagined that within a decade I would be serving on her as a young, twenty-two year old Petty Officer.

Throughout my childhood the words 'Narvik', 'Hardy', 'Warburton-Lee' and 'Mrs Kristensen' sprung up on a regular basis not only in the immediate Cope household but also within the extended family. I was born seventeen months after V.E. Day, in 1946, but from an early age I remember on many occasions my father, Cyril, reminiscing about his time served in the Second World War. In 1936 at the age of eighteen he had joined the Navy, which will be covered later from his memoirs. This meant that he was a career enlisted sailor rather than those who later became known as 'Hostilities Only' or H.O.s.

However, most of Dad's 'sea stories' usually returned to the early stages of the War when as a twenty-one year old torpedo rating he became involved in the First Battle of Narvik. In fact he was part of the forward torpedo tubes team which fired the first salvo into the harbour of Narvik. Looking back, it is obvious that this experience was so traumatic that it left him unable to forget the memories right up to his death in 2003. His passing away came four months after my mam, Edith, had died. They had been married for sixty-four years. As you will see in the latter stages of the book, in the early years of their marriage, they had to endure trauma and grief together.

When the subject of 'Narvik' was broached, normally when others enquired about his personal experience, I recall Dad was never boastful; in fact, the word 'magnanimous' comes to mind. I remember at social occasions or family gatherings that once strangers knew he had been involved in this momentous event, they wanted to know more. This would then trigger his apparent 'photographic memory' leaving his listeners mesmerised by his recollections. Right up until his passing away he could still recall the names of shipmates, even where they came from, and of course the sea battle fought at the time in a little known Norwegian fjord, as if they had happened yesterday.

There were two other events in my life which reinforced an understanding for the effect the 'Battles in Narvik' had on my Dad. These were both related to my joining the Royal Navy in 1964. Firstly, I had to go through the process of naval training and then my initial draft to HMS Devonshire, a newly built guided missile destroyer. I quickly found out that this was 'serious business'! It was not long before I realised that to survive you had to be physically fit in body and sound of mind, taking the bad with the good in your stride. Even though we were not then overly involved in any theatres of war I rapidly appreciated what my Dad and his comrades had had to endure twenty-four years previously. I began to understand the importance of discipline and team work, attributes adequately described later on in this account.

Prior to enlisting, probably influenced by my Dad's more favourable naval anecdotal stories, at the age of just seventeen, I began to give consideration to what I then thought would be a 'jolly life on the ocean waves'. I had left school at fifteen against the advice of Mr Evans, the Headmaster at my secondary modern school 'Wellacre' in Flixton on the outskirts of Manchester. In those days jobs were much easier to come by and parents had a greater influence on coercing you into employment. My father to his credit had the foresight to recognise a trade in electronics was the way forward for the future. Hence, in early 1962 I began working for the 'Fred Dawes Company' in central Manchester as a TV and Radio Engineer apprentice.

It was a cold December day in 1963 that I gathered up the necessary motivation or should I say 'guts' to visit 'Admiralty House' in the city centre. This was a time known as the 'swinging sixties' not only musically but also because of a thorn in the side of the Government called the 'Ban the Bomb' movement. It was in a climate of the so called 'Cold War' with differing philosophies of west and east – 'Capitalism and Communism'.

The first interview did not go well to say the least. The elderly gentleman who interviewed me was in fact a very 'senior' non-commissioned officer attached to the Naval Recruiting Service and had obviously had a distinguished career in the Second World War. On his lapels were the golden insignia of 'crossed gun turrets' with two stars below. Initially, I thought it would be wise to 'get him on my side' so looking very interested I enquired what they stood for. He explained he was a Chief Gunnery Instructor. However, I later learnt to my grief on numerous occasions that Chief G.I.s were seen as only 'Third to God', the 'Second to God' being the Master at Arms, known affectionately as 'The Joss man'. These authoritative figurers were not to be taken for granted and if so it was at your peril.

The Chief began doing the preliminary paperwork. He enquired about my age, if there was parents' permission, my school attainments, present employment, leisure pursuits and an ability to swim. He finally asked if there were any other members of my family who had been in the armed forces or were still serving. I felt quite confident by now especially when I explained my father had been a serving member of the Royal Navy in the Second World War.

Then the crunch came, Chief 'Nasty' looked directly into my eyes, his voice raised a few decibels and he said, "A bit of advice to you laddie, go away, smarten yourself up, find a barber and get rid of that fucking 'ban the bomb' badge on your jacket"!

I walked away feeling downhearted. However, whilst the situation at my place of employment began to improve, with an increase in pay and providing more 'on job' training, I continued to dwell on a need for a more exciting and challenging lifestyle.

So it was a month later, 'tail between my legs', wearing my 'Beatles fashionable jacket' and conventionally groomed haircut, I went back to see Mr Chief 'Nasty'. He seemed surprised. He took out the original paperwork, at least he hadn't ripped it up. Without a smile he gave me test papers for numeracy and literacy and showed me to a small room. I found the questions quite straightforward, quickly returned them and a thought did pass my mind that surely they weren't that desperate for 'canon fodder'. Finally, he said, "OK, we have marked the test papers and they were good. Can you come back in a week for a medical?"

Arriving once more punctually, wearing clean underpants, although apprehensive about tales from mates describing the intimate process heard from their fathers or uncles in the past. The doctor with a thin, grey face was older than Mr

Chief 'Nasty' and quickly asked me to undress. However, he then had me lying on a hospital type bed. "Please sit up with your legs over the end of the bed." At which point I noticed he had in his hand what looked like a small wooden hammer.

I started to cringe and my eyes began to water in anticipation of what was to come. However, relief came quickly as he began to tap both my knees. "Please stand up." He took hold of my testicles with his cold hands and 'ordered' me to cough twice. On completion, the worst part was over and within a minute I would be out of the grip of 'Doctor Death'. Having gathered my underpants I was asked to read the letters in sequence on a board about ten feet away. Then he explained that the next part of the medical check was for 'colour perception' purposes, which was required to assess which branch I would be suitable for in the Navy.

I will explain that, depending on the results, those with no problems are able to become what are known as 'bunting tossers', which is the Yeoman branch of the Communications Department. It is of no use to the Navy if you are unable to differentiate between colours of the many associated flags used at sea to visually transmit messages to accompanying ships. However, on a more personal note it was my intention to continue developing a career in electronics. This also required an above average level of colour perception to enable one to distinguish the different colours on relatively minute components such as resistors.

Back in full clothing, it was back to Chief 'Nasty'. He began in what I felt was a subdued manner. I started to wonder if the doctor had told him there was something wrong with parts of my anatomy. He indicated that he had remembered from the previous interview that I had mentioned my father had served in the Navy during the war. He went on, "Can you remember the ships he was on?" I replied, "Yes there were many; even a submarine – but the most important one was HMS Hardy." Chief 'Nasty' then appeared to change into Chief 'Friendly'. He replied, "There were two in the war which one was he on?" Feeling proud that he had queried this, without taking a breath, I said, "At Narvik in Norway, his Captain received the first Victoria Cross of the war." Showing no evident emotion in his voice, he replied, "Oh yes."

The rest of the interview went along the lines of, "The Navy are very interested in recruiting young men who have an aptitude for maintaining and repairing today's complicated equipment. Unlike in my day when for us 'old sea dogs' it was more about spanners and grease". To my surprise, Chief 'Friendly' shook my hand and informed me that there was a new entry level similar to Artificer Apprentices, for those with fewer academic qualifications which also took into account my present age. He finished by saying, "It will require you to attend a three day intensive 'Naval Board' in Portsmouth. If you are accepted then a letter will be in the post providing the relevant details."

To this day I do not know if my final acceptance into the Royal Navy was influenced in any degree by way of empathy shown because of my Dad's distinguished service history. However, what became a fact is that although I eventually served twenty-three years in the Royal Navy, my father, Cyril Cope, in his ten years' service, had been involved in far more exciting and traumatic action at sea than I ever was. Well, I also had excitement but in a different way! But that will have to wait until my next book.

Thankfully, my Dad left behind audio recordings and written accounts of his naval experiences, not only to his immediate family but also at the request of the Imperial War Museum. Prior to my father's death he gave me copies of the audio recordings. At the time I was heavily involved in my second career as a probation officer. However, in my spare time I managed to play back all six tapes. I was now fifty-five years old but memories came flooding back. There were parts I recalled and others I had forgotten. However, what struck me was that at some stage this was 'a story that needed to be told' for future generations.

In 2008, by now I had become semi-retired and on visiting my younger sister Linda at her home in Exeter I was finally able to go through my father's memorabilia. It then became obvious from his documents that he himself had intended to write a book about his exploits. Unfortunately, because of his substantial involvement between 1970 and 1996 as the founder member and Honourable Secretary / Organiser of the '2nd Destroyer Flotilla Association of Narvik 10th April 1940' he was unable to complete the task. By this time the Association had had to be disbanded, not only due to his own health problems but also because of the gradual passing away of most of the elderly members.

After considerable research, I was able to make contact with a substantial number of people personally associated with the five destroyers, 'Hardy', 'Hunter', 'Havock', 'Hotspur' and 'Hostile'. With the result that I received additional emotive and interesting accounts of those involved in the moving story of the 'Battles of Narvik', April 1940. In which their brilliant destroyer commander Captain Bernard Warburton-Lee (D2) was posthumously awarded the first 'Victoria Cross' of the Second World War.

In addition I have included extracts attributed to previous authors who have completed comprehensive research into the subject matter. I have also drawn on my own experience in the Royal Navy to visualise what life was like on those ships at the time.

In writing this book, it has always been my intention, rather than just presenting a historical account of the warfare strategies, that it should predominantly focus on narratives provided by those brave sailors who were present in the epic events on the 10th April 1940, many of whom were young men and without experience of war at sea. Secondly, and just as importantly, I wrote it in memory of my father, Torpedoman Cyril Cope.

In 1990, I accompanied my father to the 50th Anniversary of the Norwegian Campaign in Narvik. The British Government was represented then by the Defence Secretary Mr Tom King. At the memorial ceremony he acknowledged the fact that if those ten modern German destroyers had not been sunk in Narvik then they would have returned to their home port. Then, subsequently, been let loose in 'foraging packs' in the English Channel at the time of the Dunkirk evacuations. This would obviously have had a devastating effect on the imperative task of returning the troops safely back home and drastically changed the course of the war.

In producing this book I never for one moment thought that in ensuring my father's account would be accessible to a wider audience I would be going on a long and fascinating journey, where I have had 'many a cheer and many a tear'. It is definitely the truest account of a story never previously fully related by those sailors and their families involved in the First Battle of Narvik and the years following the event.

1

Cyril Cope: Torpedoman

In 1990, my Dad, Cyril Cope, was interviewed at his home in Exwick, Exeter by a curator from the Imperial War Museum in London. The audio tapes are still in the museum's historical records and are accessible to the public. Subsequently, I contacted I.W.M. in 2010 and they kindly sent me C.D. copies and with these added to Cyril's other personal audio tapes and written accounts, I have been able to form the basis for this book.

Rather than write this chapter as a question and answer version from the I.W.M. interview, I have summarised Dad's part of the conversation during the interview where he explained a part of his life before joining the Royal Navy and his experiences on enlisting.

"I was born in Salford, Lancashire in 1918 and was the middle of twelve children in the family. (Lucy, Bertha, John, Lily, Bill, Harold, Cyril, Ruby, Ronnie, Marion, Muriel and Vera.) My father had served in the Army in the First World War. When the war was over he first became a tram conductor in Manchester before moving to buses. I left school at the age of fourteen to become an apprentice electrician at 'Erskine and Heaps'. I had always had an idea to join the Services. Because of my father's own involvement in World War One, he wanted me to go into the Army. But I had always preferred the Navy.

"Where I worked there was an elderly chap who was a naval pensioner. During our lunch breaks, he used to tell me some fantastic stories about his time at sea. As well as about his son, who was also in the Navy at that time. He kept advising me and eventually convinced me that I should go into the Navy. So at the age of eighteen, that's what I did.

"On the 25th July 1936, having received my papers and railway ticket, I arrived at HMS Drake Barracks in Devonport, Plymouth. This was for 'Basic Training'. Initially I was homesick especially having left my brothers and younger sisters, but I took to the training with no problems. As long as you were able to take the discipline and do as you were told, it made life easier. I had thirty chaps in my class, the majority took to it, but you had one or two who were resistant to discipline. They seemed as though they didn't want to be there at all. In fact a couple decided to desert and instead of going back north from Plymouth, went south to Cornwall, but were soon picked up.

"I and my four brothers had always had discipline at home from our father. So there was little change. I always did what I was told and behaved myself. The way I looked at it, in the Navy, especially in the later years, I always thought the right way. I accepted discipline because I realised it would help me do the job I had to do in the Navy. Making it easier, which it did. I thought that the way the Navy dealt with me was very fair. I never had any qualms or got into trouble throughout my time.

"There were lots of things that you didn't like but you just got on with it. When we finally went to war, in fact you appreciated the discipline aspect, otherwise you would be lost. In a team of men, perfection was crucial. If you had one man who didn't want to do what he was told, the whole team would be in a mess.

Torpedoman Cyril Cope. Wedding Day 1938. *Ron Cope Collection.*

From my Dad's naval stories I had some idea of the ships he served on in the war. However, to verify these I had to apply for his service records. The section 'Personal Description' at entry to the Navy surprisingly showed that my father, in 1936 having just turned eighteen, was recorded as being 5 foot 5 inches tall with a 32 inch chest. All I can conclude from this was that during his boyhood days he was somewhat malnourished. Thankfully by joining the Navy and his subsequent training, this was quickly reversed. By the time I came along after the war and was able to remember, he was at least 3 inches taller and whilst he was never a barrel chested man, 32 inches seems a quite unbelievable measurement. Perhaps a sign of the times in the 1930s. However, they got the colour of his hair and eyes correct!

On completion of Dad's basic and seamanship training, in April 1937 he was drafted to HMS Lucia, a submarine depot ship, for nearly two years. During his time on board he was promoted to Able Seaman. In January 1939, it was back for further training at the 'Torpedo School' HMS Defiance in Devonport. Thereafter, he was drafted to HMS Hardy, a Plymouth based ship. However, the ship in dockyard hands, he was temporarily seconded to the Submarine Maintenance Ship, HMS Maidstone. Where better to put into practice his recent introduction to torpedo warfare?

After this short spell, finally in June 1939, Cyril, then having returned to HMS Hardy, sailed with the ship to join the Mediterranean Fleet. By now there were growing concerns of an impending war. Cyril, along with some of his other younger shipmates, was probably feeling apprehensive, yet they were all still looking forward to their first taste of leaving home waters to see a different part of the world. Not knowing that they were about to embark on a journey which would live with them for the rest of their lives.

2

The Captain

Bernard Armitage Warburton-Lee was born in 1895 at the family estate of Broad Oak, which was then in Flintshire, North Wales. Having been the family home since 1672, when Phillip Henry Lee, a Presbyterian minister, lived and preached there, Broad Oak borders both the county of Shropshire and the now county of Gwynedd, Wales. Bernard's ancestors were a mix of Scottish, English and Welsh; although Bernard, much like his grandson John, without doubt saw himself very much as a Welshman foremost.

In the 19th century, the Warburton-Lees had become a well-respected family involved in magistracy and land agency. Moreover, by the time of Bernard's birth, the family were respected within the local area for being financially secure and community focused. Indeed, Joseph Warburton-Lee, Bernard's father, was appointed to the distinguished position of High Sheriff, and then to Deputy Lieutenant of Flintshire. Interestingly, whilst it appears that the family were involved in many outdoor pursuits, no references to engagement in either sailing activities or connections with the sea have been found – understandably, the family did not exactly live close to the coast.

The youngest child of a large, happy family environment, Bernard was enrolled as a residential pupil at Malvern Link Preparatory School in Worcestershire in 1906 at the age of eleven. Despite being even further from the coast than the family home, it was probably here that the first seeds were sown towards his parents deciding that he was destined for a life at sea. In those times, the British Empire was still globally influential, and so had the largest naval presence in the world. Hence, at the age of thirteen, Bernard became a pupil at the Royal Naval College, Osborne House on the Isle of Wight, situated far away from his family – but nearer to the sea.

It is without doubt that for Bernard Warburton-Lee his two year spell at Osborne House was the first step towards becoming an independently minded person. Considered to have both the necessary intelligence and motivation to go on and fulfil his increasing ambitions to become a Royal Naval Officer, he was also a very competitive young man in regard to his choices of sporting pursuits. Maintaining a high level of fitness would be important to Bernard for the rest of his life.

Note: Originally Osborne House was bought by Queen Victoria and Prince Albert in 1845 as a retreat away from the royal court life. On the death of Queen Victoria in 1901 the new monarch King Edward VII presented it to the nation. Hence in 1903 part of the estate became a junior college for the Royal Navy.

In 1910, Bernard (now aged sixteen) became a cadet at the Dartmouth Royal Naval College, in order to further his knowledge in seamanship. Crucially, this period would have offered him opportunities to finally be on the water: for example, by participating in rowing whalers and sailing a dinghy up and down the River Dart.

From my own experience on the staff at Dartmouth in 1976–77, I witnessed the cadets being put through a very stringent and physical daily routine. In the early 20th century the training was without doubt more intense and the expectancy of coming through unscathed was lesser. Testament to this way of life came from a BBC documentary in which one cadet stated: "You can have my body and mind but not my soul". As such, it was to Bernard's credit that – under both physical and emotional pressure – he passed, coming top of his term, in 1912. His service records (beginning from the 15th June, 1908) describe both his ability and professional knowledge as 'very good', with additional comments from his Captain describing him as both 'zealous' and 'promising'. This assessment indicates that, even at this age, Bernard displayed an apparent loyal endeavour to serve his country.

It was on the 15th January, 1913 that Bernard joined his first warship, HMS Hyacinth, as a Midshipman. Initially, the 'light cruiser' was stationed in Cape Town, South Africa. A year later, the First World War began. Thus, in 1914, Bernard quickly had his first experience of war at sea when 'Hyacinth' was involved in operations against the German Navy.

In 1915, at the ripe age of nineteen, he was promoted early to Sub Lieutenant and shortly after, if only for a short spell, joined the torpedo boat 'Cherwell'. Then, in early 1916, he spent over two years on the 'M' Class destroyers 'Mameluke', 'Mischief' and the 'W' Class 'Wrestler'. He was assessed as having excellent ability: without a doubt a more than capable officer. This led to further promotions to Acting Lieutenant; then, on the 16th April, 1918, to Lieutenant. He was 'Mentioned in Despatches' for his services whilst on board the destroyers. This was his first long-term experience with destroyers, which were smaller and built for agility and speed. For those young officers looking for a potentially fast track route to their own command, and also being adventurous, ambitious and possibly impatient, this would have been seen as an ideal way forward.

Captain Bernard Warburton-Lee in formal naval uniform. *John Warburton-Lee Family Archives.*

It was whilst Bernard was playing his part in the war effort on 'Wrestler' in 1917 that he received the tragic news that his brother, Phillip, aged 24, had been killed on the front lines at Passchendaele. Phillip was an Army Captain in the Royal Field Artillery and at the start of World War One was sent to France. Subsequently, he was invalided back home, but later posted to Gallipoli. The ship taking him was torpedoed in the Mediterranean. In 1916, Phillip was transferred to the Royal Horse Artillery where at first he fought in the Somme, before his death on 11th October, 1917. This must have been a traumatic moment for Bernard, and probably had a profound effect on him for a long time after.

So far, the only blot on Bernard's 'copy book' happened just over a year after his brother's death, on the 30th October, 1918. At this time, still serving on the 'Wrestler', he was the 'Officer of the Watch' on the Bridge when the ship collided with the battleship 'Conqueror'. The Board of Enquiry came to the conclusion that he was "To blame for not keeping a sufficiently good look out, knowing that the course steered led him towards the battleship". Fortunately, the Board took into account his impeccable record: Bernard received a caution with the comment "To be more careful in future". This incident did not have an adverse effect on Bernard's career prospects: upon leaving the 'Wrestler' in the April of 1921, his commanding officer described him as follows: "very good executive officer, handles men well, fond of sport, takes an interest in the ship's company, has done a great deal for the efficiency of ship".

Research into the next stage of Bernard's earlier years suggests that he was now working towards being appointed to command a destroyer. During a well-earned spell ashore, he had to complete necessary courses in gunnery, signals and wireless transmissions, as well as a short stay on HMS Marlborough. Further evidence comes from his service documents, on the page entitled 'Special Reports': 'To be noted as a candidate for command of a Destroyer, March 1924'.

Bernard's grandson John Warburton-Lee, looking back over his grandfather's life says, "Naval life was not all hard work. He enjoyed several postings to Malta where he could pursue his passion for sport. By now he had become an accomplished tennis and racquets player and greatly enjoyed cricket and polo. He was a good horseman and the fast aggressive game of polo suited him well; although he always felt he could have been much better, if he could have afforded the better ponies.

"Service life in Malta offered many other opportunities. When not on the summer cruise, or doing local training, life was filled with midnight picnics, sailing, pageants and glamorous dinners. Bernard loved all of it."

Bernard Warburton-Lee's motto could have been, 'work hard – play hard'. It was during one of his spells in Malta that in 1923 Bernard, then twenty-eight, met Elizabeth Swinton, much younger, nineteen years old, touring with her father. His grandson John continues, "From his letters to her, it was obvious that the good-looking bachelor was instantly smitten."

Elizabeth Cambell-Swinton, to give her full name, came from Cringletie, Peebleshire, Scotland, born into a distinguished family, her father, George, being a retired Army Officer.

In November 1924, he finally got his wish, being appointed commanding officer of the destroyer HMS Tuscan in the 8th Flotilla of the Atlantic Fleet. However, this was destined to be short-lived, when he was promoted to Lieutenant Commander and in turn moved on to the destroyers 'Sterling' and 'Walpole'. During this eighteen month period, his service records were signed off twice by a certain Captain Tovey. He described Bernard as an exceptional officer in every way, commenting on his qualities of leadership, his excellent influence on others, his tactfulness, as well as describing him as a well-read, strong character.

In 1924, Bernard and Elizabeth were married at St James' Church, Sussex Gardens, London. They decided to settle in the Hampshire area, in order to be close to Portsmouth, and as such began their married life at Soberton Mill in Swanmore. They then had a son whom they named Phillip, after Bernard's brother.

In May 1926, Bernard found himself involved in a completely different type of deployment. At the time of the nationwide 'General Strike', he was required to lead a naval detachment to guard the 'Vickers' shipyard at Barrow. After this experience, Bernard returned to what he did best and enjoyed the most of his command of HMS Walpole. Having gained more valuable experience, he left the ship in April 1928 for shore side. His service records show that he had "Good influence and leadership. Plenty of initiative and go".

After a year ashore, Bernard returned to sea duties as Lieutenant Commander of HMS Vanessa. In April 1929, his ship was part of the 2nd Destroyer Flotilla attached to the Mediterranean Fleet. This environment at the Malta Naval Base meant that his ship was able to partake in naval exercises without the interruption of inclement weather. Just over a year later, Bernard's promotion to Commander came through and he returned to Britain. Subsequently, he completed a year-long Staff Officers' course at the Royal Naval College, Greenwich. Then, in May 1932, he went onto the Staff College at Camberley. After a short spell of being the officer in charge of HMS Centurion (a First World War battleship used as a target ship), he once more found himself back in Malta. This was in April 1933, when he became the commanding officer for the 'Sloop', HMS Bryony, described as a 'despatch vessel'.

Although officially part of the Mediterranean Fleet, 'Bryony' was in essence a small vessel used for transporting the Governor of Malta and other dignitaries around various ports in the Mediterranean. This was 'peace time', and in true Royal Naval tradition, Britain naturally wanted to 'show the flag'. It must have seemed a dream appointment for Bernard: he could put to use his considerable seamanship and managerial skills without the stress which comes with commanding a warship.

Note: The Bryony's log shows that between 1919 and 1933, the ship was the Governor of Malta's official sea going transport around the Mediterranean. From the time Bernard took over his duties the ship visited many prominent ports of call.

During Bernard's stays in Malta he became a close friend of fellow polo team player Lord Louis Mountbatten. Both had similar careers on destroyers. In 1928 Louis was the Signal and Wireless Officer for the 2nd Destroyer Flotilla and then in 1931 Fleet Signal and Wireless Officer. During 1934/36 Louis became the Commanding Officer for the destroyers HMS Daring and then Wishart. Louis' appointments also took him to the Mediterranean.

By the time of the Spanish Civil War in 1936, Bernard was well regarded by those in high command in the Admiralty as an exceptional destroyer Commanding Officer. In July of that year, he was promoted to Captain of HMS Witch.

Note: In the late 19th century, the Spanish naval base at Ferrol needed to be rebuilt and a number of major British shipbuilding companies became involved. At the outbreak of the Civil War there remained a residue of British workforce and concerns were raised for their wellbeing. HMS Witch was sent commanded by the newly promoted Captain Warburton-Lee.

Upon being promoted to Captain, Bernard must have thought that he had finally reached the pinnacle of his career ambitions: without any major hiccups, he was now well-bedded-in to the family of destroyers. However, in 1939 (after completing a tactical course in Portsmouth the previous year) he was finally informed he was to command his own destroyer flotilla. This must have been one of the most celebratory moments in his life.

This was on 28th of July, 1939, one month after his friend Lord Louis Mountbatten was appointed to command the 5th Destroyer Flotilla. As a matter of interest Lord Louis' ship was HMS Kelly, which was sunk on 23rd of May, 1941, which was made into a famous old film starring Noel Coward, 'In Which We Serve'.

Lieutenant Bernard Warburton-Lee. 1918. *John Warburton-Lee Archives*

Bernard took up command of 'Hardy' and the flotilla of nine 'H' Class ships on the 28th July, 1939, at the time 'Hardy' was stationed in Malta. One wonders whether it was a coincidence that Bernard's past mentor, now a Rear Admiral (given the task of 'working up' the destroyer flotillas to peak efficiency) was none other than 'Jack' Tovey. The Rear Admiral would have arrived in Malta in early 1939, and probably had a say as to who should be appointed as the future flotilla's commanders. Tovey became known as one of the great sea commanders of the Second World War; undoubtedly, a man of such a long distinguished naval career would have had sufficient insight to recognise those subordinates, like Bernard Warburton-Lee, who were capable of rising to his own high standards.

Further insight into Bernard's time as Captain can be found when one listens to interviews with some of his crewmen, provided in the Imperial War Museum archives and other sources.

One such testimony came from Cyril Cope. Upon being asked whether or not he liked Bernard, Cyril replied: "As a Captain, yes! Part of our training would be towing forw'd to aft (bow to stern) with another ship or they would tow us. A difficult manoeuvre, but out there in the 'Med' it was very rough at times with warm weather.

"There were things like that which made you resentful. All ships carried out exercises making smoke, black smoke from the funnels, white from canisters on the fo'c'sle and on the quarterdeck. The white smoke was deadly, it had a sickly taste, and if the ventilators were left open on the fo'c'sle the messdecks got full of it and it took days to clear. I was never popular nor the Captain for doing that.

"But by God, he managed to get us to do it, until it was just right. Not only on 'Hardy', but the other four ships in the flotilla. They probably resented it more than us because it was our Captain telling them what to do. We used to talk amongst ourselves. Why are we doing this or that? However when war started and we had to take part in the Battle of Narvik, I suddenly realised how helpful it had all been."

Cyril was also asked: "What do you think of the 'Hardy' to serve on and Warburton-Lee's disciplinary approach?"

He immediately replied: "To an extent it was a happy crew, we Torpedomen and Asdic ratings shared a messdeck. We all got on well together. Captain Warburton-Lee was a stickler for keeping fit. Even on the Equator he would have us running up and down the deck from the fo'c'sle to the quarterdeck. It was a common sight to see nearly the whole ship's company running around the ship, up the ladder on the starboard side to the forecastle, down the one on the port side, along the iron deck to the quarter deck, round this and back again, time after time. All this, even on the Equator in a temperature 100 to 120 degrees, sometimes fully dressed in our whites.

"After the run we would do physical jerks on the iron deck, this being the hottest deck due to having the boiler room and engine room underneath it. Mind you, he would do it himself and on the quarterdeck he would do his press-ups. He was also very much a disciplinarian, which once again may have been resented by some of the crew. But when it came to being in action, that discipline and fitness came in very handy. Without this, none of us in any of the other ships could have managed to do what we did. The only thing we did not do was jump over the side for a swim, and I am sure the skipper would have had us doing that if there had been no sharks around!

"Being the leader of the flotilla, our ship had more officers than the other four ships; the extra ones being the Torpedo, Gunnery, Asdic, Signals and Paymaster. The latter being the Captain's Secretary. We also had an Engineer Commander. The Torpedo Officer was Lt Heppel, the Paymaster was Lt Stanning. Both these officers figure prominently in the story to follow. I hope that you will understand that because of having this staff of specialist officers, our ship's company were expected to do much better than the others during the various exercises. Our Captain made sure we did.

"Although it was very hard work for all the ship's companies involved, we had cause to be thankful in later months for the way he made us train, and the way he pushed us to perfection at our various jobs. The battle which will be unfolded to you tested us all to the utmost and I'm sure that as you read about it you will agree, that all we went through during our training off the coast of Malta, held us in good stead during and after the battle."

Bill Pulford appears to go along with Cyril's opinion. Here, Bill describes his impressions after joining 'Hardy' in January 1940, where he found a relatively "happy crew and a strictly run ship by a fastidious Captain. There was good camaraderie between the lower deck and officers. Captain Warburton-Lee was not aloof, but he kept himself to himself as much as possible. I liked him and I think everyone else did. There is always a faction that thought Warburton-Lee was a slave driver, but 'hells bells' we were on his ship and there was a war on! He never bullied, but we knew he was the Captain. When he was about he never failed to speak to anyone. He chose his own men as much as possible; he demanded the best and he got the best.

"When we were in harbour – and that was not often – if there were any 'Submarine Warnings', we would always go out first. The only time we would get a full night in was if 'Kelly' (HMS Kelly) was also in. This was because Warburton-Lee and Lord Louis Mountbatten were the greatest of friends. The two Captains would get together and we'd expect a quiet night. However, he was always there, four hours on, four hours off, and the mere fact he was there kept us there. If he could do it, we could; that's all there was to it. The only time I knew him to be apprehensive was before we went into action at Narvik, wondering how the men would react the first time in action. However, he said to his Secretary (Paymaster Lieutenant Stanning) after the first opening engagement, 'My fears were unfounded'."

Bert Mason also gives his personal impressions of the 'skipper', Captain Warburton-Lee: "Our skipper was a real task master, intent on maximum efficiency and many times I fell foul of him when he was taking his walking exercise on the upper deck adjacent to the torpedo tubes. Seeing something secured that displeased him, he would blast me with verbal abuse, saying something like; 'Tied up like a bloody bunch of flowers' etc. I lived in mortal fear of him."

Cyril gives another personal example of the Captain's leadership qualities. "One day I was on the torpedo tubes with one of our crew, a chap renowned as being a 'scruffy fellow', who had no razor blades. As we were spending so much time at sea, the canteen ran out of them. Those of us that had blades were OK, but this fellow wouldn't think of borrowing one from even his best mates. He was determined to go unshaven.

"Anyway, we were brightening up the brass work on a scorching hot day, then the Captain came along the iron deck going towards the Bridge. As he passed he looked at me. I was always clean shaven and wearing clean overalls; I was entirely different to my mate, so it stood out. Having looked at me first and then the other chap he said, 'When did you last have a shave, is it about time you had a shave then?'

"The instant reply was not very convincing, 'I can't Sir, there are no razor blades in the canteen – they've run out.'

"'Well Cope here he had a shave, he's all right. Right, just wait here a minute.' Off the Captain went returning shortly. 'Right, there is a new blade. Go to the wash room and get a wash and shave. I don't want to see you like that again, unshaven.'"

However, there were other sides to Captain Bernard Warburton-Lee's temperament. Bert Mason recalls that in January 1940 there was a partial change of crew on board 'Hardy' in Devonport. "We exchanged a few of the ship's personnel. One of those joining was 'Tubby' Cock, the new Chief Buffer, so called because he was an enormous rotund man. He was told by the skipper, Captain Warburton-Lee, to return to the barracks, but apparently replied: 'I'm here and here I will stay'. And stay he did." This illustrates an example of where Bernard would be seen as a fair minded person, who could listen to other people's determined viewpoints and be persuaded. This was especially so in 'Tubby''s case: his Captain could see a character with courage and unique man-management skills. These assets would be much needed when the going got tough; 'Tubby' lived up to his 'skipper''s expectations.

One, if not the only, remaining 'Hardy' survivor is Ralph Brigginshaw. Now aged ninety-two, he describes his time as a nineteen year old Signalman (who kept watches on the Bridge) in a letter dated June 2012: "When we were on duty on the Bridge we were always kept on our toes. I am sure all the Signals staff liked him."

However, a final testimony to Bernard as Captain of the 'Hardy' comes from Walter Mitchell, then a Seaman 'Gunner', as recorded in his local newspaper: "Captain Warburton-Lee was a leader amongst men; the finest man a man could wish to serve under. I am proud to have sailed under him, and 'Hardy''s crew. Well if I ever have to go into such action again, I hope it is with a crew like that. They were fine."

3

Outbreak of War

"Little did our ship's company realise when we left Plymouth in June 1939 that our two and a half years' commission on the Mediterranean station would be cut short by the actions of the little man with the Charlie Chaplin moustache. Our ship's company had commissioned 'Hardy' early in June knowing where we were bound for and for how long. Before leaving on our journey, a group from a 'Historical Society' presented the Captain and ship's company with the last letter written by Admiral Lord Nelson to Captain Hardy before the 'Battle of Trafalgar'.

"There we were then, en route for Gibraltar. 'Hardy' was the leader of the 2nd Destroyer Flotilla; our commanding officer was Captain Bernard Warburton-Lee. He was the senior officer in charge of the flotilla, which consisted of nine destroyers whose names began with the letter 'H'. At this time however there were only five ships going on this trip, the other four would be returning to England for refitting and to give leave.

"Our trip across the Bay of Biscay to 'Gib' was uneventful. We started the usual settling in routine, getting the ship clean and tidy or as the saying goes, 'All shipshape and in Bristol fashion'. The ship's company got to know each other better, friendships were formed and plans made for runs ashore in 'Gib' which some of us managed, though we were only there for one night.

"There was the usual 'taking the Michael' out of the newly trained crew on their first experience at sea. A young seaman was asked by his 'Killick' (Leading Seaman) to go and find a 'long stay'. Off he went, wanting to get in his 'leader''s good books, to the upper deck lockers. He stood there for half an hour waiting patiently without wanting to interrupt the Chief Bosun's Mate. When at last he was told, 'OK Skin, you've done your stay long enough you can go now. (The term 'Killick' originates from the past term for a heavy weight utilised as a small anchor. This could have been a stone or rock but since taken on by the Navy as jargon for a Leading Hand's. Therefore he would have on his left arm for his badge of rank, a single anchor. Whilst 'Skin' is a term used by older seafarers for a sailor looking too young to grow a beard.)

"However, these attempts to put inexperienced ratings in their place didn't stop at other parts of the ship. A Stoker working tirelessly in the hot, sweaty environment of the boiler room started asking too many questions. This led to the Chief Engine Room Artificer telling him to go to the engineers stores for some 'Elbow Grease'. Again this chap took the request at face value, probably rushing away thinking;- 'That's a new type of lubricant they never told me about in training'. You couldn't blame him, in 'plumbing' terms it sounded quite plausible. When he got there, the Leading Stoker in charge looked at his mates, then after a minute they all burst out laughing, much to the young man's chagrin." These accounts come from my Dad, Cyril, parts of which he told to me over the years.

2nd Destroyer Flotilla in Gibraltar. 1939. *Ron Cope Collection.*

One of the ship's company, who joined in Devonport in July 1939, who would probably have been known as 'Skin', was Charles Cheshire aged eighteen. He, like many naval recruits in those days, came from a background of having been in the care of a Children's Home. Charles, who originated from Stafford, describes his sad upbringing. "My father was a chauffeur and gardener, his work took him to various places and we ended up in the East End of London. I went to eight different schools but when I was eleven my parents split up. I was sent to an orphanage at Frodsham in Cheshire. It was very strict but it left me in good stead, I was a lot more confident for my age. I was in a job where I had to look after myself, it was a 'Toolmakers' and I worked in the warehouse for twelve months. I left the orphanage at fifteen and the place I was living was quite close to the Manchester Ship Canal. I used to spend a lot of my spare time down there, watching these merchant ships go back and forth. I decided to apply for work on one of them.

"They wrote back to say I would have to do six weeks' training down in Tilbury. Now I didn't care much for that part of it, leaving and going down there. So I applied to join the Royal Navy and wrote to the recruiting office in Manchester. I went for my interview and asked him, 'Shall I get a ship straight away?' He said, 'Yes.' Which suited me fine, I thought that's what I want. Plus I was naïve as I didn't realise that all shore establishments were called 'ships'. I was sent to Rosyth and it was a ship, the old 'Majestic', which in its time was the third largest in the world, only the 'Queen Mary' and 'Normandie' were bigger. It had been re-named RN Training Ship HMS Caledonia.

"I started in 'Communications' with semaphore and signal flags. It was very strict, more than the 'Home' – no smoking or drinking and in the first six weeks, we weren't allowed ashore. But the food was very good and on the mess decks we had to 'sling' our hammocks, which prepared us for going to sea. I then went to a 'Boys' Training Ship' and accommodated at Devonport until eighteen when I commenced my 'Man's Time'. It was then I joined my first ship the 'Hardy'. My job was Shipwright's Mate assisting the Chief Shipwright, CPO Harper from Devonport; it was one of the best jobs: no watches at sea. The Chief had to be available to go to other ships in the flotilla, so if there were any problems, I went with him.

"One of my first jobs was the Captain's writing desk in his sea cabin, it had a flap on it which came down towards you, and the hinges and support needed replacing. At sea on the 'Hardy', if when we went to action stations or did a practice shoot, our job was to go around the ship, especially down in the officers' quarters, taking down anything that might drop down with vibrations from the guns going off. We would work on anything made of wood like the boats that wanted repairing; make parts and fit them. I had two 'Action Stations', depending if it was either surface or aircraft. Now, for surface action I was in the wheelhouse, on the ship's telegraph but for anti-aircraft action I was on a machine gun on the port wing of the Bridge."

Cyril: "When we left 'Gib', we turned east into the Mediterranean, setting course for Malta, which was to be our base for the rigorous 'Work-Up' programme necessary for making our ship and ourselves into an efficient fighting unit. This would take time of course, but we had plenty of that. That's what we thought! When a ship is re-commissioned, when you go out to a station, whether it is the Mediterranean or Home Fleet, you do the 'Work-Up' period which lasts two to three months.

"We started our practice drills as soon as we entered the 'Med.': Gunnery, torpedoes, and depth charge exercises for hour after hour. Later on it would be for day in day out, night in night out, never knowing when we would be returning to harbour. This was only the prelude. A warship with a new crew needs a couple of months' working up to attain a high standard of teamwork efficiency. To enable the ship to take part in any battles with the enemy whenever and whatever time they may take place. It is very hard work for everybody concerned, energy sapping and soul destroying because the drills are repeated time after time until the Captain is satisfied that the ship's company is one hundred per cent efficient in all departments.

"As I have previously tried to explain, discipline plays a major part in all the phases of running a ship, especially in time of war. There is something the majority of men take to easily and the longer one serves in the forces the more one gets accustomed to it. Of course there are always the 'odd men out' who don't like discipline and can never get used to it. The ones with a chip on their shoulders, the ones who make it harder for the rest of the team to reach their peak. As you will read later we reached our goal regardless of our 'odd men out' who of course must remain nameless.

"There was another example of naivety, not only concerning the younger ship's crew, but also older sailors having their first visit to Malta. A couple of days before arriving, the Petty

Officer Gunnery Instructor passed the word around the ship that he was looking for volunteers to take part in 'The Annual Maltese Dog Hunt'. This was intended to help out the locals in reducing the amount of stray dogs on the island. As expected, this led to a lot of volunteers, wanting the authorisation to practise their gun firing abilities. The next day the P.O.G.I. had many names put forward, including a couple of young officers. At about 1000 hours they were instructed to muster at 12 noon on the quarterdeck, in the correct dress for shooting practice.

"Well, you've never seen anything like it, for us who were in the know, in my case by chance, able to witness the event. At least twenty smartly attired men, wearing boiler suits, khaki belts and gaiters and polished boots turned up. However to their embarrassment rather than being given a rifle as they expected, they could only hear a roar of laughter from most of the ship's company as we came around the corner onto the iron deck. It takes a while but you learn quickly about the matelot's bizarre sense of humour."

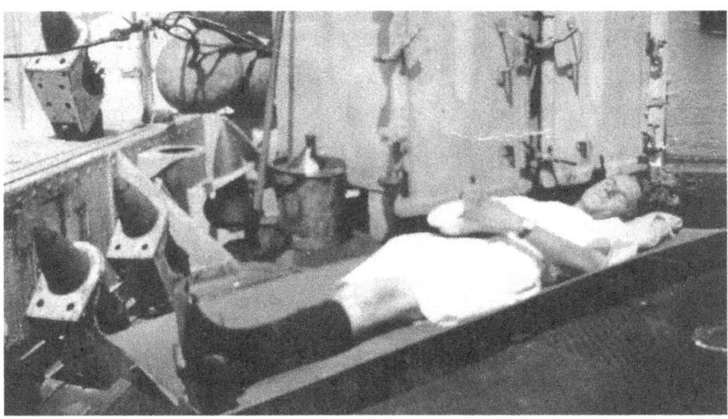

Cyril has a Make and Mend, probably Malta in 1939. *Ron Cope Collection.*

Traditions carry on, as I fell for it on my own first visit to Malta in 1965. I am sure those now presently serving in the Royal Navy are still being asked to join the annual event: although 'political correctness' may now prevent this from happening.

Cyril continues, "The weather at this time of year in the 'Med' was sunny, dry, and very hot. Malta was no exception; it was lovely there, ideal for swimming, sunbathing and drinking 'Blueys' in the many bars on Sliema Creek. The 'Blueys' being bottles of local ice cold beer. (So called because the background colour of the label on the bottle was blue.) We could only take part in these pleasant pastimes during our short spells in harbour, and believe me they were few and short. Small taxi boats called 'Dyhajsas' (pronounced 'Dysoes') would come alongside the ships, as a means for a short cut from the dockyard. These vessels were elegant and colourfully built on the same lines as Venetian gondolas. Once arriving at the jetty you took an outdoor type of lift up the steep rocky cliff face to enjoy the delights offered in Valletta."

I personally recall the 'Dysoes' when visiting Malta in the 1960s, so I could picture in my mind when Dad relayed the following story. It was a fact that some sailors returning to their ships late at night on a Dyso, in an inebriated state, having spent all their Maltese lira, took to jumping off the vessel to swim the remainder of the journey. The Dyso-men were obviously not at all pleased with losing their fare and over the years this caused a lot of animosity between them and 'Jack'.

Most of the sailors' – first and probably – last port of call in Valletta was Strait Street, infamously known as the 'Gut'. Here Cyril reminisces about one such evening ashore in the 'Gut'. "There was the usual scene of 'matelots' letting off steam, and the normal banter between ships' crews, Army and RAF chaps. It was quite early so no one seemed overly intoxicated.

Past stories and jokes were exchanged. I remember one old 'salt' a three badge 'Killick' getting a laugh. He related a story of when he was last down the 'Gut'. His mates were drunk then and one of them going back to the bar to top up accidentally tripped over the bar owner's dog and on doing so his reaction was to splutter out some kind of expletive. This was not taken too kindly by the landlord who shouted out in his wonderful melodious Maltese broken English: 'Why you kick my dog and call him "f..k off" when his name is Fido!' Apparently, on that occasion everyone was amused, took it in their stride and thus another potential bar brawl was avoided.

"During July and August, we spent most of the time at sea on exercises, firing guns at targets towed by other ships, and anti-aircraft guns at targets towed by Aircraft. The torpedoes would have 'dummy heads' and every time we fired them in practice, we had to go out in a whaler to pick them up and bring them back to the ship. Then we set to cleaning and polishing them, to prepare them for the next shoot and put them back into the tubes. We did this during the day and the night off Malta, because we would never do enough nor do it right. Thank goodness we didn't have to bring the shells and depth charges back as well.

"Time went quickly for us in Malta, with plenty of work on the ship, enjoyable runs ashore; down the 'Gut' in Valletta, the bars of Sliema Creek, or Vittoriosa front, and swimming in Buigi Bay with ice cold lemonade to follow. Very soon this came to an end; – too soon for us. It happened like this. There had been many buzzes (rumours) about war with Germany being imminent. Those of us who had been in the service during the 1938 crises thought the same thing would happen again. We would be standing by on a war footing for a week or so, then a peace treaty would be signed and we would be back to normal, but alas this time we were wrong.

"On the evening of Tuesday 29th August, my pals and I were drinking in our favourite bar in Valletta. At about 2100 hours a 'Naval Shore Patrol' came in the bar saying that all naval personnel had to return to their ships immediately. This happened all over the island and of course all army and air force personnel had to return to their barracks or camps as well. This made us think a bit, things must be bad for them to round us up like this. It became serious when we arrived back on the ship.

"Once on board we started changing the dummy torpedo heads for the live ones, all practice ammunition was sent ashore, the 'ready use' lockers at the gun positions were filled with live ammunition; we checked the search lights, the depth charge racks and throwers; the Gunners checked their guns. The officers started to pack their portmanteaus with best uniforms, swords, cocked hats, capes and other special items for sending ashore. 'This must be the real thing,' said the older and wiser ones.

"The following day we left Malta fully prepared for war should it commence. We had not been at sea long when the Captain spoke to the ship's company. He explained the reason for the emergency, and left us in no doubt that we would soon be on active service. He said our present task was to make for the entrance to the 'Dardanelles', wait for a large German grain ship coming through from Russia via the Black Sea and shadow it without being seen. Closing in as soon as war had been declared and either capture it or sink it. Providing it did not stay in 'Neutral' territorial waters, which it may well do in the hope of reaching a friendly port.

"We reached our destination, meeting up with another of our destroyers HMS Grafton. Evidently quite a few Royal Navy ships were out on patrol doing similar jobs. With all ships in their respective positions we waited. Sunday

September 3rd started as a lovely day, very hot but quiet and peaceful; we held our church service as usual on the quarterdeck. The Captain spoke more than on previous occasions, the emphasis being on prayers for ourselves, our ship, and most of all for our families at home if war started. After church I went up to the Lewis Gun and search light platform to sunbathe and get my head down, having had the middle watch (midnight to 0400). I was feeling rather tired, but I didn't sleep much. I kept thinking of my family at home, wondering what they were all doing and thinking about this terrible moment of time.

"We knew that 1100 hours was the deadline. That we could expect some form of announcement on the radio shortly after that time, but I couldn't bring myself to go down to the messdeck to listen to the radio. I waited and hoped for a miracle. A few minutes after eleven o'clock a messmate called Atkins came excitedly up to the platform saying, 'It's on, we are at war with Germany.' Then we heard the Quartermaster, piping that lower deck will be cleared after dinner. This was duly done and the Captain told us officially of the 'Declaration of War'. The 'Articles of War' were then read out by him, we then gathered round a map of the Mediterranean area on which quite a lot of little flags were pinned. Each of these flags represented German merchant ships which were at that moment in various 'neutral' harbours. Also, where Italian ships were berthed in case they came into the war. Our job would be to hunt them down when they left harbour. At that time there were no German warships in the Med' except for U-boats of course. The latter would be our main targets if and when we located them.

"So you see we were in the fight right from the start, and well prepared for whoever came along to have a go at us. We never found out what happened to the grain ship; perhaps another of our ships took care of it. We were soon on our way to Alexandria to take up convoying duties. Our trips with conveys of merchant ships took us to Malta, Gibraltar, back to Malta, and then on to Alexandria or Port Said. It was a hard task at the start, getting the merchant ships to keep station. They would wander off course, go too slow or too fast, make too much smoke by day, or show lights at night. Our destroyers were like sheep dogs rounding up a flock of sheep. If we lost a sheep during the night, or in a thick mist, one of the escort would have to drop back to look for it, then shepherd it back to the flock.

"There was one consolation at that time, as mentioned we only had U-boats to contend with, as regards being attacked. There were no Dive Bombers or E-boats to watch out for. Nor, the Italian Navy to think about. All that was to come later for some of us but at that time we had no inkling of what would be happening in the 'Med' in the months ahead. Not that our ship would ever see it of course. She was to depart from the scene, long before the real battle in the 'Med' started in earnest.

"We convoyed through September into October 1939. We took our place with the mightiest Naval Fleet ever anchored at Alexandria, waiting for the Italians to enter the war on the side of the Germans. During one of our convoy trips from Gibraltar, one of the ships in the convoy, a large French Troopship full of Senegalese soldiers, collided during the night with another ship. The Troopship was badly damaged in the bows, and had quite a lot of casualties including some French officers and mules trapped down below decks. We escorted this ship into Malta where it could be repaired.

"The big problem was how to free the French officers and the mules as they were trapped between steel bulkheads which were so close together that it would take Oxy-Acetylene equipment to burn away the steel. This would of course mean a slow agonising death for them. The mules could be shot to save them any further pain but what about the officers. After many ways had been tried to free them and meetings of those concerned I believe they were given a revolver to shoot themselves! We saw this ship again on one of our convoy trips. It had a concrete wall down the now sloping bows. That collision was our only mishap in all the convoys we escorted.

"We had been hearing of losses in ships, especially small ones in home waters; ships that we all knew with perhaps old shipmates on board. What had happened to old so and so, we would say to one another, and we would wonder how many of our old shipmates had been lost in action. Realising that these losses in ships might lead to destroyers being recalled to England for convoy duties we thought that our turn had come. It happened during a convoy run from Alexandria to 'Gib' via Malta.

"We received order to proceed to Malta at full speed and on arrival filled up with oil, water and food. Leaving as soon as possible, and once again at full speed proceeded to Gibraltar. We and our other four ships tore into Malta Harbour, got what we came for, and tore out again, leaving behind lots of mail which had been brought alongside just as we were ready to shove off. We thought that this is it, we are heading for home. On arrival at 'Gib' the same thing happened again. Just enough time to fill up with oil, water and food, then out once more. 'Where to go?', we all wondered. We hadn't long to wait for the answer. On leaving the 'Straits' (Gibraltar) we turned south. We certainly couldn't be going to England that way unless someone had moved it while we had been away.

"Very soon the Captain gave us the reason for our sudden dash westward. We had to rendezvous with the 'Ark Royal' and 'Renown' somewhere in the South Atlantic. They also were on a secret dash from home waters. This was the start of the now well known 'Force H'; the fleet the Germans were always looking for. They even said many times that they had sunk it. Older readers may recall the broadcasts of Lord Haw-Haw (the late William Joyce). He claimed the sinking of 'Force H', in a lot of his broadcasts from Germany.

"On our way south, we had to take a look at the coast around the Canary Isles. U-boats were suspected of using bases there, and might well intercept 'Ark Royal' and 'Renown' when they passed that way. We had a good search around but found no bases. We stopped and searched some Spanish vessels but found nothing of interest to us. On meeting up with the 'Ark Royal' and 'Renown' we set course for Freetown on the West Coast of Africa.

Able Seamen; 'Shiner' Wright, Billy Wearen and Andy Whearty. 1939. *Jacqueline Harris Collection.*

"This was to be our base for the mission we were to undertake during the next two months. We did not know at the time what that mission was. On arrival at Freetown, we were met by a score of native canoes, some loaded with fruit and coconuts, others with dark skinned natives who wanted us to throw coins into the water so they could dive after them. They never missed a coin.

"Looking towards the shore we could see there wasn't much of a village there. A jetty made of wood, a few small buildings. Then further on a small village with sizeable buildings. Beyond that again, we found later during our wanderings, the jungle with its tiny native villages. These were typical African Kraals, mud and grass huts.

"For entertainment we played football or hockey, on very hard dusty pitches in temperatures up to 120 degrees; drank beers which were also hot and cost 'five bob' a pint (five shillings or now twenty-five pence – expensive in those days), or we could have a nice cup of tea or lemonade at a little canteen run by some English ladies who lived nearby. They were grand old girls and we were very thankful for what they did for us. We could also go for a swim to a lovely little beach southward along the coast; travelling there in a large open lorry. The driver being one of the local African natives. There was no speed limit in that part of the world and the journey was hair raising. On the beach we would change into our trunks surrounded by a large group of native children and grown up girls. As soon as we started to undress they would start laughing their heads off. The more we tried to cover ourselves up with our towels the more they would laugh. You would have thought that they had never seen a white man before.

"We used to enjoy our swim and game of football on the beach. We also enjoyed watching the fishermen bringing their nets full of fish out of the sea onto the beach. Then would begin a sorting and sharing out of the catch. What a terrific noise they made, everybody talking at once, arguing like hell, and us expecting a fight to break out any minute. Whole families joined in and it was fun to watch. Everything turned out all right in the end though and off they would go with their share of fish, which strange to say they used to hang up outside their huts till it was dried hard and hundreds of flies buzzed around it and then they would cook it.

"Don't get the idea we were on our holidays. We spent many days and nights at sea with the 'Ark Royal' and 'Renown' searching for the exclusive 'Graf Spee', the German 'Pocket Battleship'. At that time was doing quite a lot of damage to our fleet of merchant shipping, which we relied on to bring vital supplies to Britain from the Far East. Apparently we had lost a lot of ships to this lone 'wolf raider', and we were part of a plan to trap and sink it, to put an end to the run of success it had enjoyed for so long.

"The 'Ark Royal', 'Renown' and our five destroyers would sail many miles into the South Atlantic. The 'Ark' would fly off her planes to search an area of ocean approximately 250 sq. miles. We would keep sailing on, the planes would return, refuel, and fly off again, after we had travelled another few miles. This we did for many days. Our oil, fuel and water supply was replenished by 'Ark Royal' or 'Renown' whilst under way. We could also get bread and other food from them. This increased our range of travel quite a bit and enabled us to stay at sea for longer periods than we would normally have been able to do with our limited oil, water and food storage capacity.

"During our periods at sea on this mission, we still did a lot of exercises. We were never short of practice and the planes from 'Ark Royal' came in very handy for A.A. Firing. We also did quite a lot of P.T. Exercises on the upper deck to keep fit. We grumbled at all this, as servicemen usually do, but it certainly kept us fit and on our toes. It also helped to pass the time away, because time at sea can be very tedious when there is not a lot to do. On a small ship there is no room for recreational facilities; perhaps a few books, a game of Uckers (Ludo with complicated rules), a game of cards but no gambling. We didn't in those days have Tombola and we certainly didn't have film shows on the ship. Comforts for the troops had not reached us, nor were they ever to. I remember we had the crossing the line ceremony. That was a bit of fun but did not last long enough. We all received a certificate which was very well made out. I think Lieutenant Stanning did these. On them it mentioned that this was the first 'Hardy' to cross the line in time of war. Those are the few things we could do in our spare time.

"When we were not on watch or at action stations, of course we could write letters home, but that wasn't easy to do because our letters from home had not caught up with us from Malta and on top of that our letters had to be censored by the officers. It was a job knowing what to write about. Let's face it, who of us likes to have their intimate letters to wives and sweethearts read by another person. I don't suppose the officers liked having to read the letters but the job had to be done and we could not blame them. There was one story that went the rounds of the ship about one officer making remarks about passages in a rating's letter. We were furious about it but as it could not be proven; there was nothing we could do about it but just hope that this particular officer did not read our letters.

"We must have travelled thousands of miles in our search for 'Graf Spee', and at one period we were steaming along a line parallel with the Equator. This line started on the West

Coast of Africa and finished in South America, on the Brazilian Coast. Each vessel had so many miles to patrol in one direction, and then turn back on its tracks. This went on for days and we never saw a single ship, not even our opposite number, as we turned back at the end of each run. By this time the 'Ark' and 'Renown' had left us to forage further south without an escort. Ours was a lonely vigil and with the hot sun beating down on us by day, the messdecks like ovens at night, it was no picnic. Water became scarce and what drops we had tasted warm and of chlorine. Baths were limited for everybody just at the time when we could have done with a bath every day because of the heat, which caused us to sweat so much.

"There was one amusing moment whilst we were searching for the 'Graf Spee'. I was on watch on the Bridge. Torpedo Lieutenant Heppel was Officer of the Watch. He saw what he thought was a light a long way off through his binoculars. Thinking it was the 'Graf Spee', he decided to change course and put on speed towards the light. The Captain was down in his cabin and must have thought, 'Hello, what is happening here?' He dashes to the Bridge and says to Heppel: 'What have you put up speed for?' He replied, 'Oh, there's a light over there straight ahead, Sir. It's a ship, it's got to be a ship.' 'OK,' says the Captain, who stood there saying nothing. However it turned out to be a star, low down on the horizon. We had been chasing it but not getting any nearer. He played hell with Heppel, who never lived it down. He reminded me of it when I visited him down in Cornwall. We had a laugh. 'Do you remember when I was chasing that star?'"

Cyril mentions George Heppel. He was born in 1912 and had joined the Navy as a cadet when he was fourteen years old. He came from the Portsmouth area, and by the time of

Narvik he had been a Lieutenant for six years and was aged twenty-seven. He had specialised in Torpedo Warfare and therefore was the Torpedo Officer on 'Hardy'. As 'Hardy' was Captain (D) with overall command, this meant he would also have responsibilities for overseeing the other ships in the flotilla. He had joined the ship in June 1939, so was well established in his professional status. George becomes an inspirational character in the book and earns great respect from his subordinates.

Continuing with Cyril's experience chasing the 'Graf Spee': "After about three weeks of this patrol we got a break. It would be about the 13th of December, signals were received saying that 'Graf Spee' had been sighted far to the south. News of the battle between her and our three cruisers, 'Exeter', 'Ajax' and 'Achilles' started to reach us. We headed South at top speed out; but had to call in at Pernambuco, a port in Brazil, for oil and water. Our other ships 'Hunter', 'Hotspur', 'Hostile' and 'Havock', having joined us from their patrol positions, we were now in a hurry to get to the scene of the action."

An enlightening account regarding the end of the chase to find the 'Graf Spee' was mentioned in Able Seaman 'Gunner' Dougy Bourton's interview with the Imperial War Museum at his home in 1989. Obviously, not all the ship's company were fully conversant with information from the command. Or others like Cyril may have forgotten about certain aspects of their experiences at the time of the interviews.

Either way Dougy Bourton was adamant that the following did occur. "It has always been a source of concern to us survivors of 'Hardy', that as we travelled South till we arrived at the mouth of the River Plate, after the Battle of course, we were informed by our Captain, Warburton-Lee, that if she didn't leave harbour, his orders were to go in and torpedo her where she lies. Although that would have been breaking all sorts of neutrality, he informed us, that if that was the case, then we would go in and torpedo the 'Graf Spee'. This has never been acknowledged by anyone. Efforts to get information from the Admiralty never brought any recognition of the facts: it was always a puzzle to us as to why this happened."

Back to Cyril. "We reached Pernambuco early on the morning of the 17th of December. The authorities there gave us twenty-four hours in harbour to take on oil and water. They even allowed us to go ashore for a few hours, which some of us did , enjoying a few cool drinks in the bars and stocking up with fresh fruit, especially pineapples, then heading back to the ship. It had been a very welcome break for us.

"By this time the 'Graf Spee' was due to leave Montevideo harbour, where she had been allowed in for seventy-two hours to land her wounded and make repairs to the damage done by our cruisers. The time having expired, the ship was expected to leave harbour and try to get past the net of British ships waiting for her.

"The Commanding Officer, Captain Langsdorff, on the order from Hitler, decided to scuttle the ship, which he did outside the harbour in sight of the British ships. As we arrived back on board our ship the local newspapers came out with the news of the scuttling. We thought this is it, the job's finished, off we go home, or at least back to Freetown. But no we still had got the 'Altmark' to search for. This ship was a German prison ship of ill repute, having on board a great number of merchant seamen taken from ships sunk by 'Graf Spee'. It was not until a few months later that the full story was told of the terrible conditions under which these prisoners were kept on the 'Altmark'. I only wish we could have found it during our search, it would have lessened the long and bitter weeks those men had to endure.

"The Admiralty expected this ship would try to get back to Germany, so a full scale search was put under way in the same areas we had searched for 'Graf Spee'. It was like looking for the proverbial needle in a haystack but we got on with the job. Also, of course there were still a lot of enemy merchant ships in harbours in South America. They were just waiting for the chance to slip out unnoticed and try to get home. We knew the names of these ships, their cargo and in which ports they were. It only needed any one of them to get up speed prior to leaving, and our agents ashore signalled the Admiralty and they passed it on to us. Not many tried to leave, I might add.

"The search for 'Altmark' went on till after Christmas. We had then been at sea for many weeks, with just the one break at Pernambuco. Once again we were running short of oil, water and food. We received our Christmas dinner for New Year, a fleet oil tanker bringing it out to us when it came to replenish our oil and water, which we took from her while we were steaming along.

"A short while after this, we received orders to give up the search for 'Altmark' and proceed to Dakar in French West Africa to recuperate, as our skipper put it!

"This visit lasted three days and we all managed to get a run ashore, where we were able to drink pints of champagne at the pavement bars. All along the dockside at Dakar there were huge mounds of ground nuts reaching as high as thirty feet. We called them 'monkey nuts'. Quite a few handfuls went into our lockers. They were never missed out of a few millions and we enjoyed them. Our stay in Dakar at an end, we wondered what lay in store for us next. It had been a good tonic for us after the rigours of the past few months, but we knew that lots more work had to be done. So it was with great surprise when on leaving harbour we turned North and the Captain cleared lower deck to inform us that we were heading for Gibraltar, staying there just long enough to take on food, oil and water, then proceeding to Plymouth. There would be no shore leave in 'Gib' because we would not be there long enough to even get cleaned.

"Our next stop would be Plymouth. Everyone was pleased to hear this news, knowing it would mean few days' leave for us, much sooner than we had ever thought possible. When we last saw Plymouth breakwater, our two and a half years' commission had been cut to seven months.

"So with hearts much lighter, faces more cheerful, we continued to Gibraltar, stopping now and again to board and search ships but never finding any Germans or supplies on them. Our short stay in 'Gib' was uneventful except for the weather, which was to change for the worse as we left harbour for the last leg of our homeward journey.

"Gales started very quickly and as the wind was coming from the cold North, we were running into it. The sea was very rough and this was before we reached the 'Bay of Biscay'. As we ploughed into the Bay the wind blew much stronger, the sea became a cauldron of high waves and deep troughs. We had to reduce speed because the strong heavy seas on our bows started to buckle some of the stanchions on the forward messdeck. Bulkheads had to be shored up with timber. It was the worst weather we had encountered in any of the seas or oceans we had travelled. I had been on destroyers before the war on Irish Sea Patrol at the same time of the year as this; it was bad in the Irish Sea but nothing compared to this. I had also been in a submarine both ways across this same Bay but this trip really beat the lot.

"We still had to keep our 'Watches' on Guns, Torpedo Tubes and Depth Charges and walking along the iron deck was very tricky, even when using the life lines which were always rigged in rough weather. These are long steel ropes running the length of the iron deck on each side of the ship with rope ends fastened to them by a ring which would move along the steel rope as you walked along. They were at a convenient height for even the shortest of chaps to hold on to and no doubt these lines saved many lives on ships as small as ours.

"The battle which will be unfolded to you, tested us all to the utmost and I'm sure that as you read about it you will agree, that all that we went through during our training off the coast of Malta held us in good stead during and after the battle."

4

Calm Before the Storm

Cyril Cope like the rest of the ship's company was in high spirits, looking forward to returning back to the ship's base in Devonport and a spell of leave. However, little did they know that when next their ship left Plymouth Sound, it would never return. Neither would many of their present ship's company and others who were to join them on their next big adventure.

Cyril had planned to see his wife Edith and family in Salford. But he almost did not make it. "I was on duty on the forward set of torpedo tubes, and as it was so wet and cold, I was wearing quite a lot of clothes, also my sea boots. For a fraction of a second I let go of the handrail on the tubes; the ship chose that moment to roll heavily to port. A huge wave came on board washing me down towards the ship's side. My feet went between the deck and the bottom guardrail into the water. I managed to catch hold of the next guardrail and hung on like grim death, as the ship righted itself. Two of my messmates, who were holding on to the lifelines, grabbed hold of me and pulled me back. That was a near thing because if I had gone overboard, the ship could never have stopped to pick me up.

"There was one thing we could be thankful for in having this rough weather; we knew packs of U-boats were operating in and around the Bay of Biscay, especially at the approaches to the English Channel. As a matter of fact, the Captain received signals from the Admiralty that some were waiting for us to leave the 'Bay'. The German agents in Spain at that time were very efficient and even Spanish fishing boats were well equipped to send word to Berlin about shipping in the area. We knew that this rough weather was bad for our trip home, though it maybe was also bad for U-boats, and a successful attack was nigh impossible. All the same we kept a good look out and everybody was on their toes. This was one journey from which we intended to arrive home safe and sound.

"Once out of the Bay, the sea and the wind eased a bit. We got quite a few contacts on our 'Asdic' but didn't have to drop any depth charges. The sight of 'Ushant' then Eddystone Lighthouse thrilled everyone on board. We were nearly at journey's end. Passing through the breakwater into Plymouth Sound was always a wonderful moment on any Royal Navy ship, even in peacetime, especially for the ratings whose homes were in Plymouth. This time for us and our ship it was fantastic. The view of the Hoe, the flag of the Commander and Chief, Plymouth at Mount Wise. The standing to attention on the upper deck, whilst the courtesies were carried out between our ship, Mount Wise and other ships, brought a lump to many a throat. Home were the seafarers, home at last after packing a lifetime of history into seven months.

"One week's leave was granted to each 'Watch' while in Devonport Dockyard. We didn't think it was enough really after being away seven months and with so much time spent at sea; but there was a War on, it had to be fought and won and somebody had to get on with it. Also, destroyers were badly needed for Convoy work and for screening the big ships when they put to sea. Our resources at sea were put to the limit because of the ever increasing numbers of U-boats and by the building up of the convoy system, which was getting larger week by week as more merchant ships became available; so we just had to grin and bear it as the saying goes. A few days' leave was better than none at all.

"Besides having minor repairs carried out on the ship whilst in the dockyard, we were also fitted with some new equipment which countered the magnetic mines and torpedoes the Germans were now using on a large scale. This consisted of large cables running around the whole length of the ship and connected to an electrical supply. This demagnetised the ship and so prevented the detonator in the mine or torpedo from being operated by the electrical circuit which was produced by the permanent magnetism of the ship's hull. This magnetism is something that all metal ships have. This method of counteracting these deadly weapons was called 'degaussing' and it had taken our boffins quite a while to find it. In the meantime, we had lost quite a few ships which we could ill afford to lose.

"The necessary work on the ship completed, our leave at an end, we once again left Plymouth. Some of our old ship's company had left the ship, others had taken their places. Among them some lads under the age of eighteen were coming to sea for the first time. Another was the new Chief Bosun's Mate (known as the Chief Buffer) George Cock. He was called 'Tubby' to the rest of the ship's company, being a barrel shaped chap weighing over twenty-four stone. Very cheerful and helpful to all of us."

Bert Mason, known at home by his Christian name Arthur, was born and bred in the village of Maesbury in 1913. He was educated at the local council school. On leaving school he became a shop assistant at an Oswestry drapery firm.

However, because of ill health, he later found farming work. In 1933 his health had obviously improved, so he joined the Royal Navy at the training establishment HMS Vivid. His first ship was HMS Rodney before going on to complete a torpedo and electrical course at HMS Defiance in Devonport.

By the time Bert became one of the crew of 'Hardy' he had served on a number of other ships, including in 1936 an interesting spell on HMS Stork. The ship was based in Penang, Malaya (Malaysia) and did surveying duties around the Siamese (Thailand) coast. Hence, by the time Bert arrived on board 'Hardy' he was considered to be an experienced and important asset to the ship's company, which as you will see proved to be so.

Bert Mason begins by describing his role on board. I was a Leading Seaman and a Leading Torpedoman. LTO for short, and my job on board was the care and maintenance of the after set of quadruple torpedo tubes. I was classed as Number One of the tubes. This was my 'action station', cruising and general work station. The tube crew also formed part of the Depth Charge watch keepers. We could change positions very quickly. The Number One of the forward tubes was a Welshman. Able Seaman Joe Sweetland, also a LTO. Joe came from Tonypandy and we were close mates. Sadly at a later date, Joe was lost on HMS Hecla, a destroyer 'Repair Ship', when she was sunk whilst on passage in the South Atlantic."

Another proud Welshman was Leading Seaman Alec Hunt, aged twenty-three but would have been considered a veteran. He joined up in 1933 for Boy Service at HMS Ganges, where he must have excelled, as he became the 'Button Boy' for the 'End of Training' ceremony.

Note: Rather than try to imagine the bravery of the event I recommend readers to log onto 'YouTube' to see an actual representation.

Alec was born into a family with a long tradition as crew for the 'Mumbles' lifeboat in South Wales. His grandfather was a survivor of an 'appalling 1903 disaster'. From a young age, it seemed inevitable that Alec was destined for a career at sea. By the time he was drafted to 'Hardy', he had served on five warships. He had also received injuries from an incident on the aircraft carrier HMS Eagle. Other than seven months spent in Drake Barracks, he was 'sea-going' between 1934 and the beginning of the war in September 1939.

The 'Oystermouth Parish Journal' had a feature on Alec. The article was written by 'Graff', the son of Glyn Maggs, the landlord of the Victoria Inn, who recalls, "A few weeks before the first wartime Christmas, Park Street lad, Leading Seaman Alec P. Hunt returned home on leave. [...] Alec was a very handsome young man with a ready smile, and a wit to match. Needless to say, he captured all our hearts! In view of his long period of overseas service, leave entitlement had built up, as had his back pay. He enjoyed every day of that long leave to its full. Many nights were spent with family and in the wonderfully warm environment of the 'Vic' bar. And what nights they were!

"Although only a few months into the conflict, a wartime spirit was establishing itself. Locals, servicemen home on leave, soldiers from the Mumbles batteries, sailors [...] would seek each others company and share an evening of fellowship. [...] Alec's leave shot by and all too soon, it was time to go back to war. There was that wonderful last night! All Park Street crowd were there! [...] In a packed bar room, at the end of the evening, Alec stood on one of the tables and sang a farewell song. He jumped down and there were handshakes, embraces and, the inevitable, flood of tears. The women were even more upset.

"But there was a last gesture! Such a simple one, but one which was to trigger off a string of events that became the subject of great conjecture and debate for many years to come. Alec climbed up on to the wall seat [...] and with a piece of chalk wrote on the wooden picture rail: 'L/Sea A.P. Hunt RN'. Before dawn on the following day, Alec made his moving, family farewell and, with thick head, was on his way. With traditional kit bag shouldered, he made his way down a dark, sleeping Park Street to catch the early Mumbles Train. This was the first stage of a tedious journey, in troop packed trains, to join his new ship: Destroyer, HMS Hardy."

Early into my research I had contact with John Avery whose father Frederick 'Gordon' Avery was a Stoker on 'Hardy' and survived to tell his story. Gordon, as he liked to be known, was born in 1915 at Oreston, Plymouth. On leaving school, he initially worked for a major tomato grower before moving on to employment at a local bakery. John takes up the story. "His mother was widowed, leaving her with five children, so the two eldest boys joined the Navy to help support the family." On completion of basic and engineering branch training Gordon was sent to his first ship 'Hardy'.

In the meantime, from John Avery I also learnt that there was another new crew member who at that time had joined the ship. This was Stoker Frank John Good, known as 'Jack'. He had briefly served at the end of WW1 and then became a member of the Royal Naval Reserves (RNR). This required him to complete one week familiarisation training each year. Aged thirty-seven at the outbreak of World War Two, when mobilisation took place in 1938, he, like many sailors on the five destroyers in the 2nd Destroyer Squadron, was recalled back into active service.

All the information about Jack was provided by his granddaughter Anna Reid with the help of her mother, Marie Florence, Jack's daughter. Here Anna points out, "Initially Granddad was only called up for a few weeks and was then sent home. This was at the time of the 'Peace in our time' speech by Neville Chamberlain in September 1938."

Jack Good was born in 1901 in the Camden area of London. Between the wars he worked at the Bethnal Green hospital in the laundry department, where he met Caroline Emily. They were married in 1929 and Marie Florence was born later that year. In 1937 he moved to Brentwood Hospital where he was employed in the science laboratory.

Similarly to Gordon Avery, Jack, although badly wounded, also survived the forthcoming event of the Battle of Narvik. This led to both of them and their families forging a close friendship for many years to come, as you will read in later chapters.

There was another new member of the ship's company who joined in January 1940, previously mentioned in 'The Captain' chapter. This was Leading Torpedoman William 'Bill' Pulford from Wavertree Liverpool, also known on board by some as 'Scouse'. He was the natural 'comedian' in the 'Torpedoman's and Asdic Operators' mess. His mother died when in child birth, leaving him to be brought up by his grandparents. His grandfather wanted him to become a butcher, so on leaving school at fourteen he became a butcher's errand boy. He joined the Navy in 1934 at eighteen and did a complete career change, training first in seamanship then as a Torpedoman. As previously outlined this required the additional role of also being an electrician.

Hence, when Bill arrived on 'Hardy' he was a well-qualified and relatively experienced rating. On board the ship he was not only a crucial member of the forward torpedo tubes crew but also the 'Low Power' specialist. This included the maintenance for the electrical systems to the main armaments, both torpedoes and the gun control systems.

Those ratings qualified in electrics would now be known as electricians, but at this time in the Navy they were called a 'Wireman' up to the rank of Petty Officer. It follows that those ratings repairing and maintaining were then called 'Wireless Mechanic', up until 1943 when they became known as 'Radio Mechanic'. Probably because the equipment was a relatively modern technology it required a more highly trained sailor, therefore he was able to rise to the rank of Chief Petty Officer. However, destroyers are smaller vessels with fewer crew members, therefore in the case of 'Hardy' the Telegraphist would be trained both as user and maintainer.

It appears that initially, some of the new additions to 'Hardy' had been drafted to Malta. However, probably because of the urgency of the Admiralty to start the operations in Norway, priority was given to fully manning the warships involved. Unfortunately, it appears that whilst 'Hardy' got their full complement, someone down the line forgot to inform them that they would need 'Arctic' clothing, rather than their previous issue of tropical kit. I am sure that if they could have foreseen into the future, their preference would have been to go to the warmer climes of the Mediterranean.

In the meantime 'Hardy' went back to sea. Cyril explains, "After passing through boom defence at the breakwater, we turned West in the direction of Land's End, rounded this and headed into the Atlantic, through St Georges Channel into the Irish Sea. Once again we started our 'working up' routine, practising on the guns, torpedoes and other exercises. The older members of the ship's company soon got into the swing of it but for the new chaps it took some time.

"It was many weeks before the Captain was once again satisfied with the efficiency of the ships' companies of all five ships. Our destination from Plymouth was Greenock (Scotland). We anchored in the river and during our stay there saw the largest merchant ship ever built. It passed close to us on her way out to sea to start her maiden voyage, which took her to America and to the start of a career which was to take her all over the world as a troopship. This giant of a ship was the 'Queen Elizabeth' and our ship looked like a tiny model alongside her."

Bert Mason recalled the event in more detail: "A few of us were standing on the quarterdeck when Chief 'Tubby' Cock pointed out a large two funnelled liner in the gloom of the wintry day. He told us it was the 'Queen Elizabeth' just up from the builder's yard. No-one believed him but a week later all the national newspapers were splashed with enormous headlines 'Queen Elizabeth arrives safely in New York, having crossed from UK in record time!" Then I realised that I had seen the two 'Queens' commencing their maiden voyages as way back in 1936, I saw 'Queen Mary' come up the Clyde from her builder's – John Brown of Clydebank. On her way she grounded slightly."

Cyril and his messmates, having just been on leave, appeared to want to save their pennies. "Nothing exciting took place in Greenock and after a couple of weeks we left for Scapa Flow, our large Naval Base in the Orkneys. The majority of our ship's company had never been to 'Scapa' before, but we had heard quite a lot about it from those who had. We found it was just as they had told us, a cold bleak, desolate place with snow clad hills, isolated farms with their small stone cottages, a few cattle but plenty of sheep. At this early period of the war, there was very little else ashore. Nothing worth going ashore for really. I don't remember anybody from our ship going anyway.

"We carried on with our exercises and spent quite a lot of time at sea acting as a screen for the Battleships and Aircraft Carriers which were part of the large fleet based at 'Scapa'. The fleet which at that time waited patiently for units of the German Battle fleet to leave the safety of their harbours in a bid to get at our vital convoys coming across the Atlantic. This was to happen eventually and we ourselves met up with two of them, but more of that later."

About this time in their travels, Bert Mason provided an amusing story regarding the ship's 'organ'! "Nearly every Sunday we would have a church service, even at sea, if it was quiet enough. The pipe always went out: 'Prepare for'ard mess decks for Church Service'. To supplement it and the singing we had an old dilapidated organ which always had to be rigged up for the Paymaster Lieut. Stanning, the Captain's Secretary, to rasp out some strange gurgling sounds; accompanied by the lads attempting to co-ordinate with the sailors' hymn, 'For Those in Peril on the Sea…'"

"The organ was kept in the tiller flat. And every Sunday it was the bugbear of a Leading Hand and two (ratings) to get it up and transport it across the iron deck to the for'ard mess deck. Then after the service the reverse procedure. But one evening on leaving the Clyde our 'Buffer' standing aft near the depth charge rails, called a couple of depth charge crew over and told them to open up the tiller flat hatch and get the old organ up. 'What for?' they asked. 'Just do as I say and ask no questions!' was the reply.

"This was done while a couple of lookouts peered around the after superstructure in case anyone came sauntering aft. It must be remembered that the officers' cabins were aft, but as we were leaving harbour most of them were on the Bridge. The next thing, 'Over the bloody stern with it' and over it went. The last I remember was seeing it floating away down the Clyde in the wake of the ship's propeller stream barely visible in the late winter evening! 'Tubby' called us together and swore that if anyone leaked out anything about what had happened, he would flog the living daylights out of them. We all grimly swore to secrecy.

"Sunday came and it was harbour routine. The pipe rang out in the forenoon, 'Rig for Church in the for'ard mess deck!' Three men opened the tiller flat and after a vain search reported to First Lieutenant Mansell that, 'The organ wasn't there!' He said 'Surely it must be' and went to look for himself. In the end he had to knock sheepishly on Captain Warburton-Lee's cabin door to say we had lost the organ! The Skipper was outraged and quickly told 'Number One' (First Lieutenant, to clear the lower deck and search for the organ. Then the pipe, 'Clear lower deck, every man on board, search for the organ!'

"Down in the boiler room, engine room, store rooms, magazines, between decks, the upper deck – the search went on. The Chief 'Buffer' Cock organising with a will, but eventually the search was abandoned. Somehow the service did not seem the same now that the old music box was not there. We missed it. Little did we know then, that there were not many more services to come!"

The term 'Buffer' relates to a Non-Commissioned Rank. In this case Chief Petty Officer 'Tubby' Cock was the intermediary between the seamanship ratings and the First Lieutenant.

Another main character is Lieutenant Commander Victor George Mansell, the First Lieutenant on 'Hardy' since June 1939. Victor was born in 1905 in Portsmouth and entered the Navy at the age of thirteen. I have little information about his early years and I can only presume he went through the usual education and training at Royal Naval colleges. However, the information I do have shows that he was promoted to Lieutenant in 1928 and Lieutenant Commander in 1936. All in the normal time progression expected. On joining 'Hardy', it appears that somewhere along the line he had become a specialist in Anti-Submarine warfare. However, his experience at sea and rank led to him becoming second in command on 'Hardy'.

Cyril goes on to mention another humorous incident. "We encountered many U-boats on these trips, a few of which were sunk but not by us; although there was one which we were certain we had sunk. It happened like this. We were out on one of our trips with the fleet, when we got a definite contact on the 'Asdic Set'. 'Hardy' and another of our destroyers went into the attack dropping depth charges from the 'Racks' astern and also from the 'Throwers' on each side of the ship. The attack went on for hours. It was like a game of cat and mouse. All of a sudden a large patch of oil came to the surface. This could mean one of two things; the U-boat was badly damaged or her Captain was trying the old trick of blowing oil out of the boat. All upper deck personnel on our ship were told to keep a good lookout for debris, although this couldn't be positive proof of a sinking. He could also blow bits of uniform or anything else out of the torpedo tubes to fool the hunters.

"A shout went up, 'There's a sailor's cap in the water.' As it passed along the ship's side, one rating fished it out with a boat hook and gave it to Lt Heppel, who ran up to the Bridge to show it to the Captain. When he took it from under his arm, it was found to be a cap with 'H.M.S.' on it. Moreover it belonged to Lt Heppel's writer and servant, a chap called 'Harold Trigger'. It had fallen off his head when he was leaning over the side looking for debris from the U-boat. You can imagine what a laugh that brought forth from all hands on the upper deck.

"We sat over that U-boat for nearly twenty-four hours hoping for proof of a sinking. We used up practically all our depth charges and we saw a lot more oil come to the surface but we left the area not knowing for certain that the U-boat was finished off, so we could not claim a victory.

"Towards the end of March we received sudden orders to proceed to the Shetland Isles, so off we went, 'Hardy, 'Hunter', 'Hotspur', 'Hostile' and 'Havock', everybody wondering what was in store for us; plenty of 'buzzes' as usual, but not one near the truth. It's a good job we can't foretell the future."

5

A Day on the Mess Decks

For non-nautical readers I think it would be a good idea to give you a picture of life on board the 'H' type destroyers. I spent a lot of time trying to obtain the 'As Fitted Profile' drawings of the ships' compartments. Eventually, I managed via the modelling book 'British Destroyers. 'A'–'I' and Tribal Class', by Les Brown, the next best, a plan of the external superstructure. However, 'Hardy' had an extra gun, midships and a different forward mast configuration.

It is worth noting that the rates of pay for Junior Rates at this time depended on whether they had joined up before 1925, in which case they were on a higher rate. Also for every three years over the age of eighteen Petty Officers and below were awarded a badge (stripe), a maximum of three. These badges were worth 3d a day. So a 'three badge man' earned 9d a day. There were also extra earnings for those entitled to a daily tot of rum (over twenty years old) but who abstained, this amounted to 3 pennies (20 shillings to the £ and 12 d in a shilling).

Therefore, as an example, the weekly pay rates up to Leading Hand were as follows:

Boy Sailors	8 shillings and 9 d (43p) on completion of training
Ordinary Seaman Rate	14 shillings (70p)
Able Seaman Rate	22 shillings and 2 d (£1.11p) (Joined after 1925)
Able Seaman Rate	25 shillings and 6 d (£1.28p) two badges (Joined after 1925)
Able Seaman Rate	31 shillings and 6 d (£1.60p) two badges (Joined before 1925)
Able Seaman Rate	33 shillings and 3 d (£1.66p) three badges (Joined before 1925)

In 1940, the civilian average weekly pay (six days x ten hours a day) for a craftsman was £5 and a labourer £4. Although, service men did receive free food and lodgings, albeit not hotel standard. 'Source www.winksworth.org.uk'

Kit Muster at Boy Training, HMS St Vincent, Gosport 1935. Ralph Brigginshaw is the blond lad. *Ralph Brigginshaw Collection.*

Ralph Brigginshaw, then a nineteen year old Signalman on 'Hardy', tells me, "As a matter of interest regarding pay, at St Vincent (Boys' Training establishment at Gosport) we had to line up every Thursday and collect our pay. This was 1 shilling and 6 pence and a bar of 'pussers' soap. The balance of the money was put in a Post Office account for us."

As a matter of interest, at that time a pint of beer at today's prices would be 9 pence, a bottle of wine 33 pence, a packet of crisps 1 penny, a gallon of petrol 27 pence, a first class stamp 1 penny, a Ford Popular car £80 and the average house £750.

First, the scene is set at sea; the ships are sailing through gale force winds and driving rain. The seas are rough and darkness has fallen. The ship's company when on operations cannot be at action stations all the time, so they are stood down to two watches, 'Cruising Stations', for periods of six hours at a time. The Junior Ratings' (Leading Hand and below) accommodation areas are spread around the ship but all are one or two decks below the iron (upper) deck and most are forward. They are numbered, from the bows to aft, Mess 1, Mess 2, Mess 3 and so forth. The further you are up for'd the more motion can be felt and on a destroyer the deck can go up and down by well over 25 feet in very rough seas. When the keel hits the bottom of the waves the force causes a violent shudder which oscillates throughout the ship's superstructure but in particular for'd. I can confirm this having served on frigates which were similar in size to the old destroyers.

Here I will explain how one of No 4 Gun Crew situated on the after part of the ship (quarterdeck) negotiates the journey when he comes off watch for a well-earned rest. His aim is the Seamen's No 5 Mess, his 'haven', although not quite as you would imagine it. Here the 'Gunner' has to move slowly to a vertical iron ladder down to the open iron deck and walk forward about thirty-five yards, past the two sets of torpedo tubes and the whaler davits. In mountainous seas this is a treacherous path with only guardrails to hold on to. Although by doing so you are obviously nearer to the side of the ship, where any incoming seawater will be at its most powerful swell. (As you have just read about in Cyril's close encounter where he narrowly escaped going overboard.) However, if as is the case here, the ship is at a state of readiness for action then the guardrails would have been released in order to allow the firing of the torpedoes. Thus, making his journey more dangerous.

The 'Gunner' would be wearing Wellington boots over a boiler suit topped by a soaking wet oilskin coat. Having managed the passage on the wet slippery iron deck, he would have arrived at a steel screen hatchway. This would require him to unlock the bulkhead door's heavy latches to a compartment directly below the Bridge structure. Walking to the starboard side he would come to a passageway, not much wider than three feet. There would be various compartments along the passage as he continued walking for'ard. These included Transmitting Station (TS), then the 'Wireless Office' and the Junior Ratings' washroom with a sliding steel door (no baths or showers as we know them). It is here that the 'Gunner' could finally discard most of his wet attire and dry his cold body. The compartments deck would have a number of galvanised 'dhoby' buckets scattered around in which to put wet clothes.

He would now be about to enter No 5 Mess, which is not at all welcoming at first glance. The deck head is low but he would still have to stoop lower to avoid touching the slung hammocks where his messmates were probably absorbed in deep dreams, some snoring but none in tune. A vision from the story of the 'Black Hole of Calcutta' would come to his mind, but at least now he would be feeling warmer if not yet fully dry. In fact anyone who has experienced little outside air circulating in their home can imagine the amount of condensation formed in the messdecks, from wet clothing and so many men's bodies.

There were metal lockers bolted to both of the ship's sides, port and starboard in twos, one on top of the other with a stowage rack above for kit bags or suitcases. Each sailor would have a personal key. Space would be at a premium so the lockers were not large, in fact you wonder how on earth the sailors might have managed to place all their kit and personal belongings into them. On joining the Navy the recruits have numerous 'kit musters'. The kit needs to be set out and ironed to the exact same size as that shown in an example provided on a picture hung up in the messdeck. The idea being that this would allow all the kit to smartly fit into the regulation size lockers.

A part of the mess would be partially lit for those able to eat their 'scran' or participate in any other nocturnal activities. However, this would be by way of a small lamp masked by blue paint on the deckhead, all 'scuttles' with blast protected glass and their 'deadlights' tightly secured, so it would be almost total darkness.

There were scrubbed wooden tables on both sides and each constituted a separate mess. The nearest was No 5 Mess and the next No 4 Mess, which was the torpedo crew's and Asdic operators' mess. Then came the central circular support of No 1 Gun, and for'ard of that structure were Nos 3, 2 and 1 Messes, No 1 Mess being the furthest for'ard where the compartment began to narrow towards the bows of the ship.

The stench would be unimaginable with restricted air flow causing unpleasant aroma that would consist of uncontrolled flatulence, cigarette and pipe smoke, both stale and new. If that wasn't enough the foul smell of unwashed sweating bodies, plus dirty and wet clothes and of course vomit in buckets, the result of those sailors who had not yet or never would gain their 'sea legs'. Not all food items would have been devoured. Today's 'Cook of the Mess' had managed to make a large 'Manchester Tart', left in a 'dixie', the remnants of which would be going stale by the minute. There would be one bonus though, an ongoing hot water urn to brew a well-earned mug of tea accompanied by a daily tot of 'nectar' from the last remains in the 'rum fanny'.

Note: Naval Terminology:

'Pusser' slang term for anything belonging or attached to the Royal Navy. Originates from the word 'Purser' (continues to be used for an officer title in the Merchant Navy).

'Dhoby' comes from those sailors in the past who were deployed in the Far East naval bases. It is a Hindu word sailors adopted for meaning washing clothes. I will not need to explain what the terms 'Dhoby Dust' or 'Dhoby Itch' mean.

'Scran' is food.

'Scuttles' are portholes or circular windows for those who enjoy the delights of cruise holidays.

'Deadlights' are hinged metal flaps clamped over the scuttle on the order to 'Darken Ship'.

'Lamps' are electric bulbs.

'Cooks of the Mess' would be two mess members from a duty roster. They would be detailed for the week and excused forenoon (0800–1200) work at their normal part of ship.

'Manchester Tart', ineloquently known on board as 'Manchester Slut', was a 'clacker', or as we would say, pastry crust, with a thin layer of jam over a thick layer of lemon flavoured custard. The top of the pie has a sprinkling of desiccated coconut. The term 'clacker' is now used by men in the public arena when they say, "Wow, look at the legs on that bit of clacker".

'Dixie' is a large mess tin cooking dish or pot.

'Rum Fanny'; this needs a more in depth explanation. It is an oval shaped vessel with a handle used for holding the mess rum ration. Initially it originated in 1867, to provide canned mutton as an alternative to salted meat in a cask. However, sailors took a while to get used to the method because around this time a young girl named (Sweet) Fanny Adams had been murdered and her body dismembered. The sheer coincidence resulted in Fanny's name living on in a completely unintended way.

These are just a small selection of sailors' extensive slang words, to allow the reader to understand that in the Navy they have their own vocabulary. It can take years before a sailor will become fully conversed with all the content.

If any readers are interested in learning more Naval slang and usage then I recommend the book written by Rick Jolly called 'Jackspeak'.

Ralph Brigginshaw, to my knowledge the only surviving crew member of the 'Hardy', confirms the dining arrangements and the living conditions: "We had no special cold weather clothing and did the best we could. As regards hammocks we were issued with these and took them with us from ship to ship. Fortunately, we managed to find enough hooks to hang them on, even with the extra crew. But it made the messes quite cramped and a job to turn in between the night watches."

The dining arrangements, termed 'Canteen Messing', gave each Mess the responsibility for ordering their own weekly issues of tea, sugar, cocoa and milk. Depending on how long the ship had been at sea there was also a daily issue of bread, margarine, potatoes and meat. Although bread would normally only be baked on board when in calm seas and under normal ship's routine. (In other words not cruising or action stations.) Otherwise, they would only have bread available in harbour or when alongside a depot ship. If there was no bread then in order to sweep up the gravy or soup it was back to the notorious 'ship's biscuits'. These delights were kneaded cakes of flour, baked with the least quantity of water as possible and then stored below. Until such times as required for emergency rations, when they would emerge in the company of the wheat eating beetle called the 'Weevil'.

As you would imagine fresh fruit and vegetables would not last long at sea, so the appointed 'Cooks of the Mess' would have to rely on the tinned source. However, to the hungry sailors this could prove to be an untimely problem. The tins were stored in a locker between the mess decks. Access was from the heavy lid at the bottom of the locker. In times of rough weather the tins could escape and be found floating around in any water that had made its way inboard. This could quickly result in the labels becoming detached from the tins. Thus, this often resulted in a frustrated 'Cook of the Mess' trying to make a soup and opening what he thought was a tin of peas only to find it was a tin of rhubarb. It was not long after that the idea of labelling was discontinued and the contents were 'branded' on the top of the tins.

Finally, when the 'Cook of the Mess' had got together all the ingredients for the next meal, off he would go to the main galley for Petty Officer 'Cook' Richard Richards and Leading 'Cook' Charlie Sadd to supervise and complete the final task. As one sailor was heard saying to his mate, making sure he was in ear shot of the ship's cook, "Did you know the Chefs' training course has the most difficult exams in all the Navy?" Of course the cook hearing this started to feel his 'standing' with his peers was about to be raised rapidly on board the ship. But he was quickly brought down to earth. "Yeah, no one's passed it yet."

In crammed mess decks on operational duties, there would be little the men could do about tidying up their living quarters, gash (naval term for rubbish) accumulated; cigarette packets, nutty wrappers (toffee papers), crusts of bread, tea leaves and old newspapers or magazines. This would have to wait until calmer weather when it could be 'ditched' over the side. However, when 'dream time' came and they would finally arrive in port or anchor off, as night follows day there would be an immediate order for First Lieutenant's 'rounds' of all the Junior Rates' mess decks. Or the more daunting prospect of Captain's rounds. The saying goes in the Navy, "If you can't take a joke, why bother joining up?"

However, they would now be in harbour, mess decks cleaned and tidy having had First Lieutenant's rounds. It was the 4th April, 1940, a Tuesday evening, the first of two days' rest for the ships' companies of the five destroyers. Although, for some it was still 'turn to', such as the watch keepers and those doing crucial repairs or maintenance on weapons or below in the engine and boiler rooms. Not many men ventured ashore to the desolate landscape of the Shetland Isles, especially at this time of the year. However, it did not stop the energetic Captain Bernard Warburton-Lee, as you will see in his last two letters to his wife Elizabeth.

Here again I will try to put together a scenario showing how those members of the ship's company, off watch, were relaxing whilst believing there was something afoot at command level. As I have explained, on 'Hardy' the gun crews were in the Seamen's No 5 Mess and the Torpedo Crews and Asdic operators were adjacent in No 4 Mess. Nearby were the Signalmen and Telegraphists and the Stokers' mess decks. Many of the men would be writing what would be possibly their last letters home for a while.

The letters sent home were usually mailed from the ship when arriving at the next port of call. This meant that there could be a considerable number of mail bags dispatched containing letters written over a long period of time. In those days, the General Post Office service, unlike today's standards, was a slow process. The Forces' post whether sent locally or from abroad went via G.P.O. London. After the war it was called British Forces Postal Service (B.F.P.O.).

In No 5 Mess, in order of seniority, starting with the Leading Seamen, there were Alec Hunt, 'Captain' of No 2 Gun, and his opposite number Frank Edwards, Ron Cockayne, in charge of the T.S., and Edward Plant 'Captain' of No 3 Gun (midships). One of them, normally the most senior in time served in that rank, would be nominated by the First Lieutenant as the 'Killick' of the mess, with the overall responsibility for discipline and the general running of the mess deck.

Leading Seaman Ron Cockayne had written a letter home stating he was in No 3 Mess. This would have been in the same vicinity of No 5 Mess, for'd of the ship. Therefore, taking into account that the Seamen and Gunners department was the largest on board, it is obvious that there was a need for more than one mess, probably another aft of the ship.

Ron Cockayne, aged thirty-four, was born into a long line of gamekeepers beginning with his great great grandfather on an 'Estate' in Cannock Chase, Staffordshire. His father Henry, also in the same type of work, moved with his family to Ruabon, Denbighshire, where Ron was born. Coincidently, this was not more than ten miles away from where Captain Warburton-Lee was born. Ron, at the age of just fifteen, joined the Navy as a Boy Sailor in 1921. By now his family was living in Bridgnorth, Shropshire. He completed his training at HMS Ganges in Ipswich and one year later joined many other Boy Sailors on HMS Hood.

Ron was fortunate to be aboard, for in the following year the battle cruiser, as the flag ship with other warships in the squadron, went on a ten month 'epic' deployment around the world. It was known as the 'Empire Cruise' although sailors in the squadron later termed it as the 'World Booze Cruise'. Obviously for the likes of Ron and his fellow Boy Sailors it must have been a wonderful introduction to life in the Royal Navy in peacetime. Blissfully unaware of what was to follow in 1940.

Ron later went on to serve as an Able Seaman and then Leading Seaman in other ships where he gained further qualifications and experience in the 'Gunnery' branch. Although sometime during his naval service he had become a proficient gymnast. In 1931 he met and married Sarah Ann Ford from the Spring Hill district of Birmingham and they had their first child, Jean, almost two years later. Sarah Ann remained living at her mother's home and this was where Ron would return for his leave periods.

Leading Seaman Ron Cockayne. *Provided by daughter Jill Smith.*

Having completed his service time, Ron left the Navy in 1936 and enrolled for the Royal Naval Reserve for four years. Prior to this he had gained the professional qualifications necessary to become a Petty Officer. The family were still living at Sarah Ann's mother's home and he found employment with a local 'Brass and Copper Foundry'.

However, with the situation in Europe rapidly deteriorating in 1938, as previously mentioned, the Government began the mobilisation of reservists, some of whom were in their forties. So it was that Ron then aged thirty-one, after just twenty-seven months of having returned to 'civvy street', found himself back at the barracks in Devonport. Prior to this, as a reservist he had completed ongoing training and so he continued in his former rank of Leading Seaman. However, he would have required further familiarisation courses to become a competent operator in charge of the T.S. section for the gun systems on destroyers.

In addition, as previously outlined in his naval background, he had formed an interest in gymnastics. Probably since no longer a 'spring lamb', he moved on to become an instructor in the sport. According to his family, Ron had been privileged to be involved in the training of the young sailors for a pre match exhibition of gymnastics at a F.A. Cup Final at Wembley Stadium. However, for whatever reason, he was unable to attend this memorable occasion. It appears that Ron was not your average type of sailor.

Subsequently, when 'Hardy' returned to Devonport in January 1940, Ron became another new crew member to join the ship. This must have been an uncertain and anxious time for him, having to leave Sarah Ann who was heavily pregnant with their second child.

Then there were the Able Seamen; firstly, 'Dougy' Bourton (No 4 Gun), who was one of many others in the ship's company that hailed from South Wales. Dougy, born in 1920, came from Ebbw Vale. Here he explained his upbringing to the interviewer for the Imperial War Museum archives in 1989. "I was born in the mining valleys. As I grew up the financial conditions were grim. My father was an unemployed invalided former miner. We were a family of four. Although I fought hard to get into the Grammar School and did well there, it became obvious in 1936 that somewhere along the line I had to go to sea. This was not because of a desire to become a second 'Nelson'; but purely from an economical standpoint. I applied for a First World War cruiser which at the time was moored in the River Thames." (Royal Naval Training Ship.)

Dougy having had a grammar school education, in 1939 was eligible to take the HET Entrance exam to become an officer. There were two ratings on 'Hardy' that became eligible whilst in the Mediterranean. However, because his date of birth fell in April, he was unable to go home until later. He did finally return for the Mock exam but volunteered to go back out again to 'Hardy'.

Returning back to the other Able Seamen in the 'Gunners' Mess deck, there was also Dougy Bourton's pal and fellow Welshman Stan Robinson (Gun Operator Director). You will hear more from Dougy and Stan later as they go into action and relate their attempts at survival. Another mess mate was John 'Jack' Hay, born in the Everton district of Liverpool. Jack, as he was known, came from a seafaring background. His father was a merchant seaman, then later worked at the 'Tate and Lyle' sugar company on the docks. Jack had always wanted to join the Navy and enlisted as soon as he was able.

On completing training in 1936, Jack was initially drafted to HMS Hunter. By the time he joined 'Hardy' at the age of twenty-one he had already seen action. This was when 'Hunter' was mined during the Spanish Civil War. He was a proficient and very successful boxer representing the ship in competitions and it is said, "Worth a wager".

A Kirby man, Able Seaman Andrew 'Andy' Whearty's action station was also as a T/S Operator supervised by Ron Cockayne. They sat next to each other on high stools at the gunnery control desk. Andy was a close pal of Dougy Bourton. After the battle had ended, although from different parts of the ship, their friendship would bring them together again, unfortunately under tragic circumstances that time.

Able Seaman Jack Hay. *Provided by nephew David Taylor.*

In No 5 Mess there was also Geoff Bailey from Pontnewynydd. Like Dougy Bourton and a fair number of other crew members, he came from another of the South Wales mining villages. Geoff's father also worked at a local colliery and Geoff was one of three sons and four daughters. He left school at fifteen and first worked in an office at the colliery before he was old enough to enlist in the Navy. Subsequent to completing his training at the age of eighteen he joined HMS Royal Oak. This was just before the war began. However, as fate would have it, luckily he left before his nineteenth birthday, since history records that the 'Royal Oak' was torpedoed at anchor in Scapa Flow with the loss of 810 sailors. This was just one month after Geoff had departed. Whilst he felt great sorrow for his former shipmates killed, he was not to know what lay in store for him when he eventually joined his next ship, 'Hardy'.

Note: Between the start of the Second World War in September to December 1939 there were 128 sailors below the age of 17 killed in action. Most of those, 115 in total, lost their lives when HMS Royal Oak was sunk. I must emphasise these statistics are not confirmed.

Continuing with the members of No 5 Mess, others included Henry Lang (No 2 Gun crew), Walter Mitchell, Billy Wearen, George Matthews from Streatham in London (all three No 3 Gun), Les Smale (Gun Operator Director) and Arthur 'Shiner' Wright.

Walter Mitchell, known by his family as 'Mick', was aged nineteen and had volunteered to join the Navy just nine months earlier. Prior to this Walter had worked as a shop assistant. He came from Laverton in Worcestershire and was the youngest of eleven children. Walter's parents Abel Henry and Sarah Elizabeth had five sons, one of whom was already in the Army when the war started, serving as a Farrier

Sergeant in India. The remaining three brothers, because they were in 'Reserved Occupations', working on the land, were not called up for active service. His sister in law Betty Mitchell, now aged ninety, explains, "Walter enlisted because he was young, bright and very modern."

Billy Wearen's great niece Jacqui Harris, having found the website 'submerged.co.uk', contacted me in an attempt to find out more information about her great uncle. Many years ago I seem to remember my father mentioning a shipmate on 'Hardy' who had originated from the same area of Salford. When Jacqui sent what information she had on Billy it rang a bell. It is one of those moments of many when in hindsight I could have made notes. Billy was born in 1919 and his birth certificate obtained by Jacqui showed the registrar's Sub-District office to be 'Greengate', Salford and coincidently in the vicinity in which Cyril had worked before joining the Navy.

Able Seaman 'Gunner' Geoff Bailey. *Supplied by Mike Stanner on behalf of the Bailey family.*

Above left: Left to Right: Able Seamen; 'Nobby' Clarke, Andy Whearty, 'Shiner' Wright and Les Smale. The Mediterranean or West Africa. 1939. *Les Smale Collection.*

Above right: Ordinary Seaman Hugh Mantle on completion of Naval Training. Aged eighteen the youngest on 'Hardy'. *Daryl Harries, on behalf of the Mantle family.*

Billy enlisted in the Navy in 1937, a year after my father, and joined the 'Hardy', when, as part of the Mediterranean Fleet, she returned to Malta in July 1939. Before long, as usually happens, the crew members quickly got to know if someone arrived on board with a similar accent and background to themselves. As for example, those crew members who hailed from the Valleys of South Wales, or Devon and Cornwall.

However, Billy Wearen, possibly in his early childhood years, for reasons unknown, was given up for adoption by his mother Veronica Wearen. The 'Birth Certificate' states Veronica was a restaurant 'Kitchen Maid' living at Albion Street, Salford, but there was no mention of the biological father.

Subsequently Jacqui's Great Grandmother adopted him, but none of the family knew when or why. Before Billy joined the Navy, he worked in a local Wool Mill as a 'Fettler', cleaning machinery and sharpening the cutters. He became an Able Rate relatively quickly. I am unsure which gun crew he was attached to, but it may have been No 3 Gun, midships. Jacqui Harris will explain a little more about Billy shortly.

Les Smale came from the Devon village of Stoke Canon. He was fifteen when he joined as a 'Boy Seaman' in 1935 at the 'Ganges' training establishment near Ipswich. Prior to embarking on 'Hardy' at the beginning of the war, he had already served on the battleships 'Queen Elizabeth' and 'Rodney'. He was the third oldest of four brothers, one was also in the Navy and another was serving in the Army, whilst the youngest was still at school. As you will read later Les not only became a prominent character in the Battle of Narvik but, similar to Dougy Bourton, his narrative has provided an important contribution to the book.

Although Les was only twenty there were even younger members in the mess. Ordinary Seamen Hugh Mantle aged eighteen (probably No 3 Gun) was one of seven brothers and sisters and left the family home in the Welsh Valleys village of Pentwyn. The 'Hardy' would have been Hugh's first ship, same as another young Ordinary Seaman Harold Davenport who came from Blackburn.

Austin McNamara and Tom Watson (No 1 Gun) were from Bolton. Austin's 'sea boot stockings' that he was wearing would eventually go to the other side of the world and became an heirloom kept by his proud family up until the present day. The saga of which will be told fully in a later chapter.

There was another Able Seaman on board, whom I found out about by chance. This was Walter William White from Exeter. I became aware of Walter after I had contacted the

Exeter newspaper 'Express and Echo' regarding the 70th Anniversary of the Battle of Narvik. Subsequently, the newspaper kindly printed a feature regarding my father Cyril's and Les Smale's involvement in that epic battle. To quote, "The recent stories in 'Nostalgia' relating to Devon sailors involved in the Second World War, 'Battle of Narvik' have brought back bitter sweet memories for Lily White. Miss White, ninety seven, who lives near Belmont Park, has good reason to remember the sea battle well."

Walter was Lily's older brother and had joined the Navy at the age of sixteen. So at the age of twenty-eight he would have been an experienced crew member when he joined 'Hardy'. Walter's action station was 'Ammunition Supplier', which tells me he was probably a general seaman working in other parts of the ship, rather than employed as a member of a 'Gunners' team. So I am uncertain as to which mess he belonged to. However, Walter was to survive to fight another day but tragically died before the end of the war.

Of Able Seaman Charles William Stocks, I have even less information. However, from what I have been able to retrieve, Charles came from South Elmsall in Yorkshire and joined the Navy at the age of seventeen. I have grouped Walter and Charles together because having both survived the Battle of Narvik, they jointly went on to serve in another ship, but in a different theatre of war.

6

Make and Mend

Alec Hunt, the man from the Mumbles with 'a ready smile' would have had no problems settling into his sixth ship. Since returning from leave, he had not felt sorry for himself and got on with his life. As you can see he had written a letter home to his 'mam' with important news.

29th March 1940

My Dear Mam,

Well here I am again mam, dropping you a few lines, I hope you are not worrying too much as we have been to sea for quite a long while, as a matter of fact mam, we even forgot it was Easter last week, as we had a rotten trip, and believe me mam if I wasn't so fed up in my life, the only thing that cheered me up, was your two letters. I had three from Rose and a parcel from Vera, I had a parcel from Annie and a letter from Fred yesterday. So I have not done too bad for mail, have I?

And to tell you the truth I enjoyed the parcels of Welsh-Cakes, but as usual mam, we share and share alike, and we had a decent old feed between the crowd of us, that doesn't mean to say that the food is no good, far from that, it is very good indeed, we have nothing to grumble about at all, in that respect, but you can guess what it is like to have a parcel from home mam, it goes down well.

Well mam I hope this is not going to hit you too much, but I would like to get married, I would like to bring her home next leave if it is alright with you mam, and then you can judge her then, but I seem to be quite contented when I am with her, she has no parents, and I thought it a good idea to get married mam, of course if you don't consent, I don't think you will do that though as she is a very good kid, although a little older than myself. I bet you do not know what to make of this mam, do you, but I always knew myself if the right one came along I would not mess about, as I don't believe in that, and I truly think that she will be a good wife to me, so what is your verdict mam????

I have not told any of the family yet, as I want you to know all about it first, so will you let me know mam, as soon as you can, because I would not like her to get things, as she is doing at present for nothing, because I would not go against you mam, but I would not think of it again.

Well mam after all that I have not got much news, but I will write you a long letter on Sunday. I hope you are feeling your feet again, and that the weather is helping you along now, so will close now mam, with all my love.

Your loving Son Alec
God Bless you mam.

Leading Seaman 'Gunner' Alec Hunt, from a family of the 'Mumbles' Life Boat crews. *From great nephew Keith Greenslade's Collection.*

In the Signalmen and Telegraphist ratings' Mess 6, the chatter at that time could have been about the latest films they had seen or wanted to see the next time they were home. Alfred Hitchcock's first attempt at directing a film in the USA was a great success. It was adapted from Daphne Du Maurier's 1938 novel 'Rebecca' and had won an 'Oscar'.

There would also be lots of banter and heated conversations regarding their favourite football teams. In 1939, Everton had become champions of the First Division, followed by Wolverhampton Wanderers, Manchester United were fourteenth and Chelsea just managed to escape relegation. In May 1938 Preston North End were the previous year's F.A. Cup losing finalists but then made a come back the following year and won the Cup beating Huddersfield 1-0. It was the first televised final, not that many of the sailors were able to see it live, most having to wait later to see it on the newsreel at the cinema. The BBC commentator said, "If there's a goal scored now, I'll eat my hat". Seconds later Preston scored and he kept his promise.

In May 1939 the two finalists were Portsmouth and Wolverhampton Wanderers. The 'Wolves' were clear favourites having scored nineteen goals in the five Cup games and were second in the league. By contrast, Portsmouth struggled in the relegation zone. Yet, Portsmouth won with a resounding 4-1 victory. It would have been a trigger for much ridiculing, from the 'Pompey' crew members and those predominantly from the Midlands and North of England. However, with the start of the war in September 1939, after only three games being played, further matches were suspended, when Arsenal were top of the league.

There are five sailors in No 6 Mess whose names will appear in the following chapters. Signalmen Ralph Brigginshaw (as mentioned), 'Ginge' Turner, Bernard Kennedy, Telegraphists 'Ned' Sparkes and Victor Gould. In fact Bernard, known as 'Bern', was from Cwmbran, another recruit from the mining area of South Wales. He joined the Navy at the age of fifteen. Although his niece Pat Ofield, however, recalls that Bernard, "Altered his birth certificate, and noticeably so, in order to join up before he would have been allowed. I have the birth certificate and it always made me smile. He was so keen to join the Navy and see the world." As a local newspaper reported years later, "He used to enjoy reading adventure books but little dreamt that the true story of his later experiences would be just as exciting."

In his letters, survivor Ralph Brigginshaw recalls: "I had already made my mind up at the age of seven or eight that my future was at sea. Probably due to all the 'salty tales' from members of the family, and when one of my cousins came home in his bell bottom trousers, that was it. I started work as a farm hand which meant getting up to herd the cows in, to arrive at the dairy by 5-30am. I had to give that up after 3 months, as I had problems with wearing 'Wellies' which were swelling my feet up. My next job was a storeman, come odd job man for a builder in Swindon. I joined St Vincent six weeks after my 15th birthday." I remind readers of the point raised regarding the limited space in messdeck lockers, see the photograph of Ralph and the classes' efforts at a 'kit muster'.

Similar to Geoff Bailey, Bernard Kennedy's first sea going warship was the 'Royal Oak' and he also left before it was sunk in September 1939. It may have been that they had first met in the short time they were on the battleship. Although they were employed in different parts of the ship, it could be that on recognising they had the same melodious accent from the Welsh Valleys, they became friends. It must have been fate that the two joined 'Hardy' around the same time, for Bernard would later go some way to save Geoff's life. Bernard was a proficient swimmer having learnt in the 'deep pond' at Cwmbran clay pits. Like Jack Hay, Bernard was also a keen boxer both before and after joining the Navy.

Victor Gould, aged twenty, was a Fleetwood Grammar School pupil. He joined up at seventeen, following in the footsteps of his father, who had also been in the Navy during the First World War. Victor would be at his action station in the wireless transmitting room, below decks, throughout the ensuing battle.

In the Stokers' mess, talk could have turned to the usual gripes about life down below in the engine room or boiler room, complaining about the builders of the ship. Two had just finished a long spell in the boiler room. A fictitious comment could go along the lines of: "Bloody manufacturers this is the second time we have had to fit that steam pipe". There was no sign of sympathy from their messmates. Then these sailors being in a mechanical trade, the conversation moved to cars, as one Stoker mentioned his uncle had his own business and had just taken ownership of a brand new Vauxhall 'Twelve'. "He must have a bit of money because it's a luxury car, cost him

£215 and on top he had to pay £9 purchase tax. He's really pleased because it's got semi-servo brakes, no draught ventilation, independent springing and a synchro-mesh gear box; and listen to this he reckons he gets 30 miles to the gallon!"

Not all the men were interested in what was going on at home. It could have been too depressing. So they took to playing 'Uckers', a modified game of Ludo, developed over the years by sailors to make it more tactically interesting. The counters can be piled up to become 'blobs' and, depending on the amount piled, will dictate what is needed to challenge to get past the 'blobs'. However, a 'mixy blob' negates the need to have to challenge. The Fleet Air Arm had their rules and terminology complicating the game even further. In some mess decks they had manufactured an Uckers board which was built into the surrounding furnishings. The games became very competitive and could end up being very noisy events, with a mixture of so called 'industrial' language.

The newer ships, built in the mid 1930s, had their own SRE (Ships Relay Equipment) installed which connected a tannoy system around the ship. This enabled radio programmes to be wired to mess decks which could then be temporarily disabled for command or general ship's announcements. However, BBC News or musical programmes were only available depending on the communications department being able to tune into the appropriate stations.

One of the mess members was Stoker Harry Rogers, who came from Middlesbrough. Harry, like many young men in his area, worked for a local firm, called 'The Cargo Fleet Iron and Steel Works'. The conditions were harsh and laborious and as Harry said, "killed most men of that time before their sixtieth birthday". So at nineteen years of age, Harry enlisted in the Navy in 1936. He believed, 'tongue in cheek' that joining up – "saved my life!" However, as you will read,

Harry, after the Battle of Narvik and subsequent incidents in WW2, aptly deserved his nickname Harry 'Houdini'.

In the Torpedo and Asdic ratings' mess, one of the tables was being utilised for a very competitive card game called 'Euchre'*, pronounced ju-ker. Most of the other sailors found the 'mind boggling' rules for this 'trick-taking' game hard to follow. However, the two pairs of players competing at that time were from either Cornwall or Devon and had been introduced to the game by their forefathers.

Along with Cyril, other mess members from the 'Torpedo' branch included Bert Mason, Bill Pulford and Tony Hart. However, research into Bobby McAtamney proved to be particularly fruitful. In fact, Bobby McAtamney's daughter Kate Kennedy was one of my first contacts and this gave me considerable impetus to continue the search for more of 'Hardy's' crew members or their families.

Bobby, aged twenty, was one of six brothers from Carrickfergus. Interestingly, all served in the war, resulting in them becoming known as the 'Fighting McAtamneys', representing the Army, Navy and the Air Force. As events aboard the 'Hardy' progressed, Bobby played an important part in the rescue of a very popular crew member. Other mess members of the 'Torpedo' branch were Bill Pimlett, Jimmy Lee and Joe Sweetland.

My father, Cyril, was also writing home to my mam. Due to what followed the next day the letter was not sent nor was it retrievable. However, I think it was on our trip to Narvik in 1990, over a beer or three, that he was able to recall most of the contents of his letter. Hence, this is not exactly what was written in the letter, but as he told me.

* *Note:* There are a number of websites explaining how to play Euchre.

Dear Edie,

At the moment I have been advised to write this letter to you and give it to a pal. Hopefully, it will not need to be sent. I think about you all the time and worry about you expecting our first baby. Should this letter be sent and reach you, then be assured I did my best. If it works out that I don't return, I am very very sorry for you and our child.

All my love as always with fondest memories
Your Husband, Cyril xxxxx

The Chief and Petty Officers' mess would not be so crowded as the Junior Rates' messes. Some, who had been on duty when 'Up Spirits' had been piped at 1130, would be enjoying their daily allowance of rum in the early evening. This would give them a 'boost' from a hard day's work and an appetite, if they needed it, before supper. It was equivalent to today's treble pub measure at 60% ABV and as a privilege POs and CPOs could have it neat, unlike the Junior Rates. The reason being that Junior Ratings' rum was mixed with two parts water and half a gill of rum known as 'Grog'. The term originated from Admiral Vernon, who introduced it in 1740. He always wore a distinctive long coat made out of 'Grogram' cloth. He could not be missed when he came on board because of the coat. When he appeared the sailors would say "Here comes old Grog".

A fact unbeknown to the serving sailors at the time was how much priority the Royal Naval Command placed on the need to preserve the ongoing stocks of rum during the war. For the Western Royal Naval Regional Area it was stored in an underground slate quarry called 'Carnglaze Caverns' at St Neot, Cornwall. To this day the caverns are open to the public and the first of the three caverns is still referred to as 'The Rum Store'.

The Chief and Petty Officers' mess had a full time 'Messman', a privileged place to work. The right man would be chosen by the Mess President, having been advised by a senior Chief, possibly the Coxswain or Chief Bosun Mate. More often than not the Messman would be an older rating, known for being reliable and able to keep confidences. His duties would involve not only collecting the rum issue and meals but also cleaning out the mess in the forenoon as well as returning for regular general tidying up. This evening whilst he was carrying out his duties, one of the Petty Officers wanted to show his gratitude, by giving him a tot of 'neaters'. Totally against 'King's Regulations and Admiralty Instructions' of course, but sometime rules are there to be broken.

Tonight four Chiefs had been challenged by the Petty Officers for a very competitive 'games night', which included cribbage and dominoes. Two of the Petty Officers were Maltese and trying to get their heads around the scoring for cribbage. However, 'Tubby' Cock, having now settled into life on board his latest ship is all for it, being a self proclaimed expert at the card game. Chief Stoker Edward Stiles, a very popular and well respected member of the ship, was probably sitting quietly concentrating on his seagoing hobby. This was making brooches out of gold wire and mother of pearl with the ship's name painted on in fine print. He sold them to the ship's company as presents for loved ones at home. From their proceeds he gave a percentage to the ship welfare fund, to purchase things such as football strips and other items of sporting gear that were not provided by the Navy.

Edward Stiles aged thirty-eight came from Plymouth and had been promoted to 'Chief' in December 1938. He was one of three brothers whose father was a tram conductor, a job in which Edward was also employed prior to joining the Navy. Early into my research I had a post from Mike Newton, Edward's grandson. He pointed out that "all the 'Stiles' of this era were either Royal Navy or Merchant Navy men". By now Edward was another experienced senior rating, not only responsible for the engineering part of ship but also the Divisional Chief for the second largest department on 'Hardy'. This required him to take charge of the watch rota system for no fewer than thirty-three Stoker Junior Ratings, as well as being responsible for their discipline and welfare issues.

Edward was married to Violet (nee Miller) and they had two daughters, Violet and June, now aged fourteen and nine respectively, and a son, Edward, age seven. They had recently purchased their own home in Newton Abbot by taking out a mortgage. Subsequently, I have had additional contact with other family members, which will be mentioned in a later chapter. Suffice to say, that because in those days deployments to foreign stations could be as long as three years, Edward spent long spells away from his young family.

A Petty Officer Stoker had just come off a twelve-hour stint down in the boiler room replacing a faulty steam pipe. He was still sweating and sorting out his oil ridden overalls. However, the rest of the mess noticed he looked relaxed and was smiling. They knew he had achieved his task. Two Chiefs and a Petty Officer were in a corner of the mess discussing what news they had been able to gather regarding the ship's future destination, as all three were in regular ear contact of officers who would possibly be in the know. Another Petty Officer sitting nearby quietly reading a book was George Quinn. George probably had reasons to be quiet as he was the secretary to the Paymaster Lieutenant Stanning and probably knew more about what was going on than most of the other senior rates.

Chief Stoker Edward Stiles. A popular crew member on 'Hardy'. *Mike Newton and Ted Stiles Collections.*

They were joined by a Chief 'Tiff' (Artificer) who to their annoyance butted straight into the conversation when it was getting interesting. The 'Tiff' told them about his wife who had just signed an agreement with the 'Gas Department' in Fore Street, Plymouth. He was really pleased that for 6d (old pennies) a week rental the new gas cooker was all enamel with free installation and maintenance.

One of the four Petty Officer Stokers on board was Aubrey 'Bill' Woolley who had joined the Navy in 1923, so he was now an experienced member of the Engineering branch. His service records (now in the hands of his son, David) revealed that, in 1933, Bill had served on HMS Byrony when Captain Warburton-Lee was in command. Bill would survive the Battle of Narvik but by the end of the year he would be invalided out with tuberculosis.

On board were eight Maltese crew members, employed in the wardroom, including the already mentioned above Petty Officer Stewards Joseph Lewis and Anthony Xuereb. The remainder, in a separate mess probably not too far from the wardroom, were Leading Stewards Antonio Briffa and Joseph Micallef, Assistant Cooks / Stewards Carmelo Aquilina, Casha Gaetano, Emmanuel Fabri and Anthony Ronayne.

The reason that 'Hardy' had a large number of officers, stewards and cooks was because as flotilla leader the ship not only had a 'four ringed' Captain but also an increased number of officers on board. Captain Warburton-Lee had his own steward and cook, whilst the officers included Commander Engineer Alan Coe and two Lieutenant Commanders, Victor Mansell and Russell Gordon-Smith. There were in addition another eight junior officers and five of warrant ranks. This complement of officers was substantially more than the other four ships in the flotilla. In fact, although the 'Hardy' was initially designed for a crew of 178, on sailing from the Shetland Isles there were 197.

This compared to 'Hunter', which although designed for a complement of 145 actually had 157 on board. Presumably, figures for the other three ships in the flotilla would have been similar, with just two Officer Stewards and a single Officer Cook. As such, estimates for the total number of Maltese crew members in the flotilla was between twenty and twenty-three. This highlights the importance of Malta and its attachment to the Royal Navy in World War Two.

Two of the Maltese crew members on board 'Hardy' were Toni Briffa, his grandson sent a photograph of his grandfather in naval uniform. The second, subsequent to my having a feature in the 'Maltese Times', was Anthony Ronayne. Anthony similar to his countrymen, was a courageous young man, who at the age of nineteen voluntarily enlisted for service in the Royal Navy at the outbreak of World War Two not knowing what the future outcome would be for himself or the allied forces in their fight against Nazism. HMS Hardy was his first ship. Officer Steward Anthony Ronayne would survive the battle, however, in his account he describes the extraordinary circumstances which required his family having to make arrangements for a 'Remembrance Mass' in his honour at their church.

The talk in the Maltese mess deck at some stage would certainly have come around to the weather. This time of the year their island would be basking in warm sunshine. They were now in the northern parts of Scotland. However, what they did not know was that their destination was going to be a lot colder and dismal.

The officers' accommodation was aft of the ship, which included Captain Warburton- Lee's 'Harbour' cabin. My thanks go to John Warburton-Lee, the Captain's grandson, for allowing me to publish the last two letters the Captain wrote to his wife, Elizabeth. In fact there were more in the family's memorabilia, as the Captain seemed to write as often as possible to Elizabeth. However, I first need to explain that as you would expect Captain Warburton-Lee as the overall commander for the 2nd Destroyer Squadron would have been made well aware of the future battle plans from his superiors at that particular moment in time. This was probably unknown to the rest of the squadron's sea commanders and their crews.

Irrespective of this, it appears that throughout the lead up to the potentially dangerous situation that Captain

Warburton-Lee was about to put his men that his letters home showed he remained calm and was able to continue to consider personal and domestic issues at home. The flotilla now in harbour, the Captain and the crews of the ships were taking advantage of a short period of rest and recuperation. At the end of this, the first letter to Elizabeth, he either makes an incredible prediction or his obvious intellect had logically worked out the strong possibility of the outcome.

4th April

Darling One

Today about three quarters of the usual gale, so Geoffrey and I proceeded ashore in sailing boat (all motor boats being bust) and after some adventures we landed on the beach. We walked over bogs in wind and rain such as I cannot remember it was so cold that we felt inclined to cry! When due to come off, the boat went to the wrong place and we got stuck up for an hour, finally had to wade across a young river and so back to the ship. It took 20 minutes before I could get any feeling into my bones – now after bath I feel grand and that it was well worth it!

I have been thinking more about your employment to keep you amused and about Soberton.

The war is going to intensify quite soon, it will I think be long and gory and by the end of it I doubt if we shall have much left. Again after the war I may want to or have to leave the Navy and we shall be poorer than we are now.

At the present Soberton is a fairly expensive place for its size – quite a lot to keep up, though there are corresponding amenities.

If we wanted to change into somewhere smaller, everyone else will be doing the same thing, so anything nice would be unobtainable.

All this brings me to the conclusion that really Soberton does us very well and it would be a pity to leave it. But to keep it we shall have to try and make some part of it pay – farm a bit of it – grow something. Now is the time to experiment because;

1. War is the time when agriculture has the best chance of paying.
2. Any form of business would help you for petrol and taxis perhaps.
3. At the moment we have enough money to put into any scheme and it wouldn't matter much if it paid or not.
4. We have the farm buildings to start on.

The only thing I can think of at the moment as possibilities are:

Pigs – but here we have the snag of obtaining food.
Chickens – rear them, kill them and dress for the table. Advantage of this is you only have the part of the year.
Vegetable Growing – using frames or houses and heating them adequately.

I imagine that winter lettuce or perhaps sea kale would pay and not be too luxurious for wartime.

Anyhow if you want a job why don't you go and do a farming course. Much more likely to do good than most others and might stand us in good stead. You wont manage heavy work, so don't try – but agricultural college stuff is necessarily clearing out the pig sty's.

Give all this a think over and let me know what are your reactions.

Don't forget the war is going to start quite soon. I am going to start it.

Your own Husband

About supplies via GREENING, we can't get any fresh vegetables or fruit – any how of course it's a bad time of year fallow, nor fresh fish except herring very occasionally. If you think it worth while sending any supplies, in small quantities, you could go in GREENINGS refrigerator and keeps indefinitely. Do not bother about it if's a nuisance or if you think it not worth while.

Captain Warburton-Lee, at the beginning of his letter, mentions being accompanied ashore by Geoffrey. This was his secretary Lieutenant Paymaster Geoffrey Stanning. Then aged twenty-eight, the son of a clergyman, Geoffrey was educated at Marlborough College in Wiltshire. At the age of eighteen he joined the Navy, however, due to his short sightedness, he became a member of the 'Supply / Writer' branch. By the time he had been appointed to 'Hardy', he had served a number of years at sea, including the cruiser HMS London (which became involved in the evacuation of British citizens, during the Spanish Civil War).

Back on shore duties in 1937, Geoffrey completed a linguist course in German, which intriguingly required him to spend six months in Germany. He becomes a prominent character in the following chapters of the book and plays a significant part in the forthcoming action. He also had an opportunity to use his newly acquired skill of the German language, albeit not directly with the enemy.

Captain Warburton-Lee, as you have read was a devoted husband and family man, here he writes his last letter to Elizabeth.

Hardy 5th April 1940
Darling,

I have been telling you repeatedly that you won't hear from me for a bit. I think now that it is really so. Today, we had a really lovely day – the sort that one gets in the extreme north just now and then.

We had a paper chase and ran up the local mountain – which was lovely – after it was over!

I wrote to Bertram today, said he could have my boat for £150 if he said so quickly. I don't suppose he will.

If war should spread to these parts, I feel sure that boats will become as valuable as gold and more so. Nowadays there is always an extreme shortage of boats, wherever operations are going on.

Lewis went to explore the local metropolis today but didn't find much. Not even fish which is funny. Not any signs of ADIE thou he must be about somewhere.

Will you please order me a dozen 2lb pots of Coopers marmalade, to be delivered to Greening and address to me C/O him. Hawleys or anybody will deliver it on board if you telephone order.

Good night Darling one, I love you.
Bernard

The 'wardroom' is where the officers had their meals and spent most of their recreational time in harbour and off watch. There are conflicting views as to where the name 'wardroom' originated. One suggests that in the far past it was known as the 'Wardrobe Room'. In fact the lower deck sailors, similar to 'Cockney' slang, still refer to it as 'Wardrobe'. It is said the term was derived from the days where officers kept their spare wearing apparel. More intriguingly, it was also where loot secured from enemy ships would be stowed. The second suggestion, less likely, was because the wardroom in action stations was converted into an emergency sickbay with an operating table and necessary equipment; hence, 'Ward Room'.

The Captain was only present in the wardroom by invitation of the President, who was the Executive Officer/First Lieutenant. On 'Hardy' it was Lieutenant Commander Victor Mansell. He was responsible for overseeing the general running of the wardroom. He appointed other officers to be members of the wardroom committee, delegating them to various responsibilities. These included a 'Wine Member' to look after bar stocks and officers' bar bills. A 'Treasurer', to keep the mess accounts. A 'Secretary', to be responsible for recording the wardroom mess minutes at meetings and the 'Entertainment Member' to arrange social functions.

In harbour the officers would be required to wear formal evening dress or 'mess dress' on formal occasions, at either 'white tie' or 'black tie' events. Each evening at dinner, if wine is served, a toast would be made depending on the day of the week.

Monday	Our ships at sea.
Tuesday	Our men.
Wednesday	Ourselves. (Because nobody else is likely to bother.)

Thursday	A blood way or sickly season. (To ensure a quicker promotion.)
Friday	A willing foe and sea room.
Saturday	Wives and sweethearts. (May they never meet.)
Sunday	Absent Friends

Note; the parts in brackets are the 'tongue in cheek' remarks provided by a past Royal Naval officer not serving on HMS Hardy or involved in the First Battle of Narvik.

By 2014 women had been serving at sea in the Royal Navy for over twenty-one years. Therefore the Ministry of Defence taking into account 'cultural changes', decided that officers at the traditional Saturday evening toast were now required to state "Our families". The Tuesday toast was also changed to "Our sailors".

7

The Storm is About to Begin

All those crew members named in the last chapter are factual characters but in an imaginary setting, now we return back to reality. The crew are about to learn their destination and the reasons why they are going there. Cyril Cope begins, "On arrival at the Shetland Isles after a journey which was quite uneventful, we could do nothing but wait and see what sort of a job the Admiralty had lined up for us. Oh yes, we knew something was in the wind because of all the comings and goings of Senior Officers to and from our ship. Also, the Captains of our other four ships were coming on board for meetings with Captain Warburton-Lee.

"One night, during the first week in April, we set out from these Isles which were so much like the Orkneys, cold, barren and windswept, not realising that we were going to end up in a far worse place than this and in conditions much more trying than we had ever encountered before. During that night we rendezvoused with our 'Battle Fleet' from Scapa. Once again, just like he had done on other missions, the Captain told us the reason for our secret journey. We would be escorting some 'E' class Destroyers to the coast of Norway. These ships had been converted to mine laying ships and their job was to mine the entrances to fjords in Norway. It was thought that the Germans were about to invade this Scandinavian country and the mining was meant to stop German warships or troop ships from going up the Fjords to attack the various ports or at least to make it hard for them."

That same week there were other ships leaving harbour, but they were not British. In the 1970s my father, Cyril, had met a number of German veterans from the Battle of Narvik at arranged 'Reunions' in both London and Bremerhaven. They were from all ranks and one of them was Korvettenkapitan Karl Smidt who was in command of' 'Erich Giese'. She was also on her way to Narvik, as all will become clearer. However, their past adversaries were now friends and mementoes were exchanged. Amongst many gifts presented to Cyril as the Honourable Secretary was a diary, kept by Karl Smidt, of the events leading up to and during the battle. Here is the beginning of Karl's diary translated into English, other parts will be interspersed in following chapters.

Korvettenkapitan Karl Smidt, 'Erich Giese'. *Cyril Cope Collection.*

APRIL 6 1940.

DEPARTED FROM BREMERHAVEN TO NARVIK WITH TWO HUNDRED AUSTRIAN ALPINE SOLDIERS ON BOARD

Cyril continues, "They had had their guns and torpedo tubes taken off, replaced by rails along their sides with mines installed. They were in line and we were either side for protection. The Captain cleared lower deck and told us we were going to the coast of Norway called the 'Leads' escorting these destroyers to lay mines off Norway. He then said: 'Now I will tell you why we are going to do it. Iron ore ships can come down the coast from Narvik, they then normally come out into the open sea. But German iron ore ships don't do that. They come out of the fjord and go through the "Leads", which are still inside Norwegian territorial waters, a neutral country. Therefore it has been planned to mine the entrance to the "Leads"; so German ships can't go in there and risk being "blown up", forcing them out into open sea, where our forces can attack them, outside the territorial waters. That's the plan. Now when the destroyers have laid their mines, it will be a new minefield and not charted. So we need to remain in the area for 48 hours watching out for and warning neutral shipping.'"

Les Smale, in his written account, gave a more detailed explanation of the reasons for 'Operation Wilfred' (as it was to become known). "Germany imported over 40% of her iron ore, some 9,000,000 tons, from Sweden. During summer months it was imported via Lulea in the Gulf of Bothnia and the Baltic Sea. Lulea became ice bound during the winter months and the ore was transported by train to the ice free port of Narvik in Northern Norway. Ships were able to travel South of Narvik by way of a deep water passage, within

Norwegian territorial waters, known in Norwegian as the 'Indreled' or 'Inner Leads'. It was also being used by blockade runners proceeding to and from the outer oceans. For about a thousand miles therefore they had the protection of Norwegian neutrality. Churchill, as First Lord of the Admiralty had long advocated mining what he described as the 'Covered Way', in order to force enemy ships out of neutral waters where they could be intercepted."

"Hitler can make war for only a year if he is denied supplies of Swedish iron!"

So wrote Fritz von Thyssen, one time personal friend of Hitler, to Winston Churchill.

Cyril continues, "On approaching the Norwegian coast, the escort of battleships, aircraft carriers and cruisers left us, proceeding southwards in search of any German units which might be coming towards Norway in support of an invasion force. We and the rest of our flotilla carried on with the mine layers to the objective. The weather at this time was uncomfortable, bitterly cold, sea rough and snow beginning to fall heavily. The coast came into view through swirling snow and mist. The mine layers set to work and we patrolled between them and the open sea, watching and waiting for any interference from the enemy. On completion of the laying each ship took up a position near the minefields to intercept and warn any neutral shipping about the newly laid mines. This was in accordance with 'International Law' and as we had to stay there for forty-eight hours, it was going to be a long wait for us.

"The heavy snowstorm which we were having to contend with was a blessing in disguise. It helped to shield us from the prying eyes of the enemy above and below the waves, but it meant that we had to keep an extra special lookout for the neutral ships. Darkness soon arrives in that part of the world, not that we had seen much daylight with such a snowstorm raging. On watch on the upper deck, it was terrible cold and although we wore blue suits, jerseys, duffel coats, scarves, balaclavas, gloves, sea boots with sea boot stockings and a couple of pairs of ordinary socks, we still felt it and like all service men the world over complained about their miserable lot in life.

"We patrolled up and down all day and into the night without sighting any neutral ships. On the 8th April at 2000 hrs, suddenly we received signals from one of our destroyers asking for assistance. She was being attacked by two German heavy Cruisers further along the coast. As our flotilla set off to the position she had given us we had the mine laying destroyers trailing behind. They had to come with us because without us they would be unprotected. We couldn't go at full speed because of the heavy seas and snowstorm. When we reached the spot all we found was wreckage from Glowworm and started to hunt for survivors. We found none nor did we see any sign of the two enemy ships, although we searched for quite a while. By this time we had been joined by 'Renown', the Battle Cruiser we had escorted during our force 'H' mission in the Atlantic. We then took a course which the Admiral in Renown thought the enemy would take. He had assumed command of all ships present and his ship led the ten destroyers in line ahead.

"The Glowworm had intercepted the German units which were on their way to Narvik. It first sighted 'Dieter Von Roeder' and engaged it with gunfire, hitting it and setting it on fire. This ship broke off the fight and disappeared into the mist. Then the cruiser 'Hipper' attacked 'Glowworm' hitting her several times. 'Glowworm' got in some hits on 'Hipper' and finally rammed it. 'Glowworm' sank almost at once with few survivors who were picked up by the Germans, but the Captain of 'Glowworm' went down with his ship. The 'Hipper' had been so badly damaged by 'Glowworm' that it had to return to Germany and took no further part in the Norwegian invasion."

There is a thorough account of this sea battle between 'Glowworm' and 'Hipper' in Geirr Haarr's book 'The German Invasion of Norway – April 1940' (pages 93 to 95). However, here is a summary of the last moments of the 'Glowworm' and the brave parts played by both opposing Captains, Lieutenant Commander Roope and Kapitan Heye as that described here by Geirr.

"Whether 'Roope' also intended ramming the cruiser or if the ensuing collision happened fortuitously will never be ascertained, in spite of the legend. Torpedo Officer Lieutenant Ramsay, the sole surviving British officer, later told his rescuers that neither the helm nor the emergency rudder was manned at the time, and so the destroyer's turn towards 'Hipper' was probably accidental." Geirr Haarr adds, "Glowworm was going down quickly and Lieutenant Commander Roope gave the order to abandon ship. Legend has it that at the last moment, Lieutenant Commander Roope shook every hand of every man around him. At 10:24 GeT, 'Glowworm's' boilers exploded and she slipped under; the abrupt stop of the siren causing an eerie silence in spite of the storm.

"Having searched briefly for 'Mechikergefreiter Ritter' and not yet under way, Kapitan Heye felt obliged to assist the British sailors struggling for their lives. He gave the unprecedented order for 'Hipper' to heave to, downstream of the drifting survivors. In spite of the danger of British ships showing up at any time, he stayed for over an hour rescuing survivors. Lowering of boats was out of the question, but all personnel on deck, including some soldiers, helped to pull the frozen, oil-soaked British sailors up by ropes and ladders. The oily, icy water exhausted the British survivors. Many grabbed the ropes thrown at them but could not hold on and drifted away. Lieutenant Commander Roope was seen in the water helping his men to the ropes. Finally he took hold of a line himself and was pulled some distance up the side of the cruiser. To the horror of British and Germans alike, just before reaching safety, he let go and fell back into the water.

"From a crew of 149 on board 'Glowworm', forty men were pulled out of the water. Several were wounded and at least two later died. The rescued men not in need of medical attention were given dry clothes, cigarettes and hot coffee. They were questioned, but only a few were willing to say much. Kapitan Heye learned little more than the name of the destroyer and that she had belonged to a squadron of three more destroyers and possibly one or two larger ships, bound for Lofoten. None of the survivors appeared to have any impression of the larger tactical picture and expressed surprise to have encountered a German cruiser at sea."

'Mechanikergerefreiter Ritter's rank was equivalent to that of a Leading Seaman. Ritter was washed overboard when both ships collided.

Finally, returning back to Geirr Haarr's authoritative research (page 96): "It was only on the repatriation of the 'Glowworm' survivors after the war, when Lieutenant Ramsay was interviewed by the Admiralty, that the order of events came to be known in Britain. As a result Lieutenant Commander Roope was posthumously awarded the Victoria Cross, Lieutenant Ramsey received the Distinguished Service Order and Engine Artificer Gregg, Petty Officer Scott and Able Seaman Merritt the Conspicuous Gallantry Medal."

Given these facts, then in effect Lieutenant Commander Roope would have been the first recipient of the Victoria Cross in the war, rather than Captain Warburton-Lee.

Now the 9th April, Cyril recalls how, "I had taken over the middle watch at midnight on the forward torpedo tubes. This was my action station until the torpedoes had been fired. After that I had a repair party to go to. This was in the Engine room where I would be standing by to carry out repairs to anything damaged by enemy action. My watch, if nothing happened, would finish at 0400.

"In the Royal Navy during wartime, when at sea it was always the practice in our ships to close up at action stations just before dawn and dusk when at sea. The reason for this I will explain. If a ship encounters an enemy ship at that period of time when the sun is either rising or setting, the ship nearer the rising or setting sun can be seen much sooner and more clearly than the one furthest away. Consequently it can be attacked before those on board have sighted the ship in the shadows with drastic results, if the aim of the gunners on the attacking ship is good.

"At approximately 0345 just as the first rays of the sun began to break through the snow filled sky heralding a new day, we were surprised to hear shells whistling over the ship and seeing them drop into the sea not very far away. The alarm bells for action stations ran throughout the ship and as the men came running to their action stations, rubbing the sleep out of their eyes, I looked out to the horizon on the starboard side and saw the two German heavy cruisers, with red flashes coming from their guns. These two ships were 'Scharnhorst' and 'Gneisenau', which had been in company with the ten destroyers we eventually encountered the following day at Narvik. During our search for 'Glowworm', the destroyers slipped past us and managed to reach Narvik that night on 8th April.

"They were low down on the horizon and were steaming in the same direction as we were. As we were nearest to the rising sun they had spotted us before we spotted them and they had the advantage of opening fire first. Luckily for us their gunners were not on target. Our crew, not knowing that we were being attacked, thought this was just the usual 'stand to' and they were moaning and groaning at being turned out on such a cold morning. They were probably thinking how nice it was going to be to be able to get back to their hammocks in the warm mess decks. They soon had those thoughts dispelled when they too heard the gunfire and saw the shells falling not far from the ship.

"Within the space of a minute or two all our action stations were fully manned but as the range was far too great for our guns to reply, we could only wait until the range was shortened. There was not much chance of this happening as the guns of 'Renown' had a much longer range than the enemy ships. They were travelling away from us at a far greater speed then we could manage in such rough seas and in the blinding snowstorm. The enemy knew that by running away and keeping out of range of Renown's guns, we in the destroyers could not hope to fire at them with either guns or torpedoes. We had both sets of torpedo tubes trained on the starboard beam and the guard rails down ready for firing the torpedoes.

"At the time I had the headphones on and heard the order to go to the guardrails and cut them down. This was to allow the torpedo tubes to slew into position from fore and aft. The guardrails were held up by the spun yarns, so I had to get out my knife and cut them free. The guardrails were designed so they then just swivel and fall down taking the wires with them. So down that little chase I went to the guardrails three times to try and cut the spun yarns; but the seas were so heavy, the waves were coming over onto the upper deck. Every time I went to the guardrails to do this, I was drenched, absolutely soaking through. However, once done, then all of a sudden I got the order to go back to the guardrail to put them back up."

German Alpine Troops disembarking. 9th April 1940. *G.Haarr Collection.*

KARL SMIDT

APRIL 9 1940. AFTER A STORMY SEA-CROSSING ARRIVED AT NARVIK WITH 10 GERMAN DESTROYERS. SOME BOATS TIED UP IN THE HARBOUR OF NARVIK, 3 IN OFOTENFJORD ANR 3 AT ELVEGAARDMOEN. THE ALPINE TROOPS UNLOADED IN THE MORNING..

Signalman Ralph Brigginshaw: "I happened to be on the middle watch (midnight to 0400) when we met the two German ships. We were bouncing along astern of the 'Renown' and I was on the Bridge with an 'Aldis' lamp to keep in touch with the destroyers astern of us. We opened fire, which didn't do a lot of good, except that it cheered us up a bit in all the rough weather. It certainly wasn't the sea for torpedoes."

Dougy Bourton: "I was the 'Loading Number' on No 4 Gun and we were firing at such extreme range that the guns were elevated so high that at times I was on my knees forcing the shell and cartridge up hill at an angle of 45 degrees to get it into the breech. The weather was atrocious so much that we couldn't fire No 1 Gun, so that we had to bring up their crew aft, with the ammunition parties. But eventually the 'Scharnhorst' had been hit several times, and the 'Renown' had only suffered very minor damage. The 'Scharnhorst' and 'Gneisenau' took off and made their escape."

Cyril and the other Torpedomen's efforts were in vain: "We waited and waited but the weather was against us. It was impossible to close the range and the Admiral in 'Renown' realising that the destroyers could not maintain the high speed for much longer signalled Captain 'D' (Warburton-Lee) to abandon the chase, leaving 'Renown' to carry on alone. We had no misgivings leaving it to the battle cruiser because we knew that she was more than a match for the two German ships. Very soon the ships of 'friend and foe' disappeared from our sight in the thick blanket of snow and mist. The mine laying destroyers left for home escorted by 'Hostile', but we in 'Hardy', having received signals from Admiralty to proceed to Vest fjord, which led to the iron ore port of Narvik, set off with the other three ships."

Here is an explanation by Cyril about the strategy of 'destroyers in battle'. "When a flotilla goes into battle to make a torpedo attack on the enemy ships, you go in line ahead as fast as you can go. When you get into range you swerve off to port or starboard and fire all your torpedoes. So as we then had five destroyers in the flotilla that's eight torpedoes on each firing at the enemy. That means there was a chance that one might hit. Not necessarily hit, because that would be lucky. The idea was to make their ships turn away and not be able to fire their guns at your own battleships or cruisers. All of us who manned the tubes were hoping we would be able to get near enough to mount a torpedo attack because five destroyers each with eight torpedoes to fire, going in at high speed towards the enemy would be a wonderful sight. A sight not seen since the 'Fleet Battles of the First World War', and given a certain amount of luck, some of the forty torpedoes might find the target."

Lieutenant Stanning was among the decision making officers. "At about 1130 we got a message from the Admiralty ordering us to take three ships and attack Narvik the same evening. So far as I can remember very little information was given as to the forces which might be in Narvik except that one or two ore ships had landed soldiers. This was exciting though it did not look a very difficult proposition and taking 'Hotspur', 'Havock' and 'Hunter', we set off up Vest Fjord. 'Wash' (Captain Warburton-Lee's nickname) immediately began issuing orders for the attack which was to start about 2000 the same evening; as we could not get there much before."

At this point it was decided to muster the Landing Parties on the five ships, kit them out, provide them with food rations and weapons. Leading Seaman Bill Pulford, Torpedoman Cyril Cope and Able Seaman 'Gunner' Dougy Bourton tell their stories; some of the following were recorded at their homes for the Imperial War Museum by the interviewer Conrad Wood.

Cyril: "After a 'council of war' it was decided to proceed up the fjord at 12 noon, engage shore batteries, any German units encountered, then attack Narvik, landing men ashore to capture the town."

Dougy Bourton recalled, "It had been decided to make arrangements for the possibility of sending a landing party ashore in Narvik. The Gunnery Officer Lieutenant Clark, one of the most brilliant officers of his time, who was as I understand a prize winner at 'Whale Island' (Gunnery training establishment in Portsmouth). A really top class man, and recognised as a future Admiral, no danger! He told us from the top of No 3 Gun (midships) that he only wanted volunteers, therefore if anybody wanted to withdraw, you were completely at liberty to do so, nothing would be taken against you. He ordered, 'All volunteers take one pace forward', and all the company took one pace forward. He said, 'That is what I expect of the "Hardys", prepare to land, after the battle we'll see what we can do to the German Army.' Anyway we steamed away from the fjord and out of sight."

Dougy Bourton was correct in his estimation of Lieutenant Edward Keats Urling Clark's attributes and potential for higher positions in the Navy. Edward was twenty-nine years old and married Lorna Bell in 1937. They had just had their first child, a son. At Dartmouth he immediately impressed the training staff. He was top of his term in examinations and was rewarded by becoming 'Chief Cadet Captain' and then awarded the 'King's Dirk'. As an Acting Sub Lieutenant, during further training his examination results led to him being awarded 'memorial prizes'. He was described as "having a brilliant brain and a zest for athletics and a priceless gift of leadership qualities".

Promoted to Lieutenant, Edward served on HMS Keppel in the 'China Station', where he had his first experience of destroyers' capabilities, required in action. Returning to England in 1936, he completed gunnery courses, after which his career continued with distinction. Subsequently, he was sent to HMS Warspite as the second Gunnery Officer before returning as the Gunnery Officer on another destroyer HMS Hardy. This appointment indicates how highly he was regarded by his superiors. Captain Warburton-Lee wanted the best and maybe had influenced Edward's appointment to his ship.

Note: A tribute written by a 'Brother Officer'. "There is no doubt that Urling Clark was a great man. With his brilliant attainments he might have already achieved fame in another walk of life. He read widely and was a keen student of music and the arts. But he chose the Navy and entered into his life with all his matchless vigour. That in his short career he had time to leave his mark on it is a tribute to his exceptional professional ability. That he is mourned as the best and truest of friends by a wide circle of officers is a tribute to his fine character and splendid qualities". [...] 'The Times' – Friday May 3rd 1940

Bill Pulford provided a more down to earth, 'tongue in cheek' account of his involvement in the 'Landing Parties': "I was Leading Seaman in charge of the Lewis Gun Platoon (machine gun), I was detailed off to go ashore and try and retake the town and Lieutenant Commander Mansell was the officer overall in charge. I was taught as a Leading Seaman, having a humorous attitude I suppose, that boats always flew 'White Ensigns'. When I knew I was to be in a whaler to land, I went to the flag deck and cadged one. I thought well if I go this goes in with me."

A few weeks later, Bill talked to a newspaper reporter, admitting that he had little knowledge of Lewis guns and his platoon consisted of eight Torpedomen with just two guns, as well as demolition charges. However, he managed to catch hold of the Petty Officer 'Gunnery Instructor' (P.O.G.I.) and received a three day course condensed into about an hour. From this he was able to lecture his team, "with the aplomb of a man who knew everything there was to know about such things."

Having stocked up with chocolates and cigarettes from the canteen, Bill continues, "This was to create a friendly feeling towards the natives and, should the need arise, to stretch our own rations. Later on Lt Heppel came down to the mess-deck to give us a pep talk. When he had finished, the ship's SRE was switched on to broadcast Vera Lynn singing, 'It's a Lovely Day Tomorrow'. If only she knew."

Bill's saga concerning his 'small boats ensign' will not end until the 1980s, when it arrives at an appropriate resting place.

Cyril was one of Pulford's platoon but as you will see later, he got a pleasant surprise. "We got ready for the job, I was detailed for the Lewis Gun Section and as the weather was so cold we put on as much clothing as we could wear. We collected one blanket, three days' food rations, which consisted of bully beef, ship's biscuits (not fancy ones), tea, sugar, tinned milk and what sweets or chocolate we could scrounge from the NAAFI canteen.

"We didn't have enough rifles to go around so we torpedomen had 'cutlasses'. Torpedomen always had 'scabbards and cutlasses' tied by lanyards to the funnel where they were at the ready. This was something we practised when doing our 'work up' in the 'Med' in case we were needed for boarding other ships. Goodness knows what we were supposed to do with them; I could never envisage having to use one. 'Gospel Truth.' During this time Lt Stanning and Lt Heppel went to a pilot station."

Geoffrey Stanning got an unexpected invitation: "'Wash' sent for me while I was having lunch and said he was thinking of calling at the pilot station at Tranoy to see if that was occupied by the Germans, or whether they had any information that might be useful to us. I wanted badly to ask if I could go and do this, and was just about to when he said which boat would I like to take, so there was no need. We decided that I should go in the skimmer, as it might be possible to escape fast in it if the place was occupied by Germans. The motor boat would have been better but it had an accident just before we left Scapa and had no propeller or rudder.

"The skimmer, however, decided not to take part. For one thing the steering wheel had broken off, presumably in the morning's activities, and for another it refused to start in spite of the united efforts all afternoon of all the talent in the ship. I was not so very sorry when we found that it would not go, as I should have certainly got wet again and it certainly looked rather small and shelterless if anyone started firing.

"We arrived off Tranoy at about 1600 and clutching a chart I got into the starboard sea boat. Just as I was going, 'Torps' (Torpedo Officer Lt Heppel) came and suggested that he might come too which I was only too glad of his considerable moral and physical support. We landed on the nearest point of land and told the boat's coxswain to go round to the pier which we could see in the little harbour. We walked on rocks covered with seaweed and once I slipped and put my foot into water up to the knee which was annoying.

"We could see the inhabitants, mostly men, coming down to the pier, but there did not seem to be any Germans as they were all strolling along in the most nonchalant fashion. After getting fairly near to them we found we were on an island separated from the land by about fifty yards of sea, so we had to call up the boat again and go to the pier in it. We went ashore at the pier and walked up to the crowd of about twenty to thirty men and boys, some of whom spoke English to a certain extent. We asked them whether they had seen any Germans and they said they had seen five German destroyers going towards Narvik that morning; when asked how large they were they said: 'Larger than that one', pointing to 'Hardy'.

"We suggested one of them might like to come and pilot us to Narvik, but their refusal was definite and unanimous. I then unrolled my chart to ask them one or two questions, but found I had brought the small scale chart of the lower part of

Vest Fjord. I must have picked up the wrong one from the desk on the Bridge in my hurry. So, we drew pictures in the snow of Narvik and its harbour and, as we had a Signalman with us, sent him to make a signal to the ship (as we thought) 'Wash' would need pacifying if we stayed much longer.

"Another man then said he had seen a submarine go up towards Narvik and that he was sure the place was mined. A small boy said he had seen six destroyers not five as the other man had said. It never crossed our minds then that they could have been six and five, making eleven in all. They asked if we intended to attack Narvik and when we gave a non-committal answer, said we ought to go and get some more ships before we tried. On our way back I saw we had four ships with us and found that 'Hostile' had arrived. When we got on board we explained the situation to 'Wash' and discussed the thing thoroughly in the chart house.

"It was a most thorny situation. We had been told to attack Narvik and therefore must do so unless there were urgent and very strong reasons against it. Although the Admiralty obviously had no idea how strong the enemy forces were in Narvik, to ask for further instructions would be delaying the operation to an unreasonable extent; and we also had a feeling that possibly our operation at Narvik had been timed to fit in with some other undertaking further down the coast, and any delay on our part might possibly prejudice someone else's success or even safety. But whether the Admiralty would consider the extremely grave risk of five modern destroyers justifiable in view of the new information seemed doubtful. On the other hand, our information was not necessarily reliable and as the Admiralty had given us specific information, it was reasonable to suppose they knew better. We already had experience of the unreliability of local information when we were in the South Atlantic; when one day we ('Hardy' and two destroyers) were variously reported as two tankers and a submarine, six destroyers and two cruisers. Someone reminded 'Wash' of this.

"Poor 'Wash' was in a quandary. If he decided to attack the place and failed, perhaps with the loss of several ships, he would be told by the Admiralty that he was mad to go in when he knew there was considerable opposition. If, on the other hand, he had decided to withdraw, he would be asked why he did so on unreliable information of small boys when the Admiralty had given him specific intelligence which he should have had no reason to doubt. He spent a most unhappy half hour in which, to my mind, he more than earned his V.C."

In the meantime Cyril and the expectant Landing Party platoon were getting themselves sorted out. "We had finished our packing and only had two more things to do. A last letter home just in case, to be left with a pal, then a cup of neat Navy rum to cheer us on our way. Everybody was ready for the off, we queued at the galley for the rum. My mess mate Tony Hart, whom you will be hearing of again, was first in the queue. I was second, Tony drank his, I drank mine, but before the next chap could get hold of his cup the 'Officer of the Watch' came in shouting, 'No more rum Chef the orders has been changed, the job's off till midnight!' I staggered down to the mess deck with my pack and not having had any sleep for forty-eight hours, got my head down on a mess stool and slept until the next watch, which was the 'First Dog' at 1600 hours, not long really, three and a half hours."

Geoffrey Stanning, with his colleague officers, was in the vicinity of the charthouse: "We all waited about, quite unable to help him as it was a decision which he alone could make and that without encouragement or advice from us. He decided, as we had been hoping, to go on with the operation. I went straight away to cypher a message to the Admiralty. In which he gave the information 'Torps' and I had obtained at Tranoy and said he intended to attack at dawn, high water. The reason for the postponement was partly that we had spent a fair time off Tranoy and though there was still time to get up to Narvik that night, it would be much better to go up before dawn and get there when there was more chance of surprise.

"We made off down the fjord with a view to convincing any hostile observers that we had indeed gone away to get some more ships, as we had been advised at Tranoy. Soon after we got under way, we sighted what was obviously a submarine on the surface, but it turned out to be a small fishing boat; it gave us a few minutes' excitement though. I don't think the operation orders were changed to an appreciable extent, but the ships were given the gist of the situation as it now was and told the new time of the attack."

Narvik harbour late 1930s. *G.Haarr Collection.*

This was an ideal time, before returning back down the fjord, for Captain Warburton-Lee to devise his 'Tactical Plan' which would then be passed on to the commanding officers of the other four destroyers. These were sent in separate signals.

1. Ships are to be at action stations from 0030. When passing Skredneset Hardy will pass close to shore and order a fine line of bearing. Thereafter ships are to maintain narrow quarter line to starboard so that fire from all ships is effective ahead.

2. Germans may have several destroyers and a submarine in vicinity, some probably on patrol. Ships are to engage all ships' targets immediately and keep a particular look out for enemy who may be berthed in inlets.

   On approaching Narvik, Hardy, Hunter and Havock engage enemy ships or shipping inside harbour with guns and torpedoes.

   Hotspur engage ships to northwest of Framnes, and the Framnes battery if firing. 'Hostile' assist on either targets. Prepare to make smoke for cover and to tow disabled ships.

3. If opposition is silenced, landing parties from all ships except 'Hotspur' make for Ore Quay unless otherwise ordered. Hardy's First Lieutenant in charge.

4. Details of batteries as in Admiralty message on p.p. 42,43.

5. Ships are to operate Asdics whenever possible and attack any submarine.

6. Additional signal to withdraw will be one Red and one Green Verey light from 'Hardy'.

7. Half outfit of torpedoes (four) to be fired unless target warrants more. Destroyer depth settings to be used. (6ft and 8ft, alternate torpedoes.)

8. In order to relieve congestion of movements all ships when turning to fire torpedoes or opening are to keep turning to port if possible. Watch adjacent ships, keep moderate speed.

9. Additional communications. Set watch on:
   a) 2800kc/s on remote control.
   b) Fire Control Wave. (For concentrating firing; not used).

Note: British destroyers unlike their opponents had not yet been fitted with voice radio. This circuit was operated on by a Morse key on the Bridges and used for rapid manoeuvring and action signals, usually in the form of groups from the Fleet Signal Book.

These Tactical Orders by Captain Warburton-Lee were later seen as concise, thorough and clear instructions, when taking into account the up to date intelligence available at the time. Although, those highly qualified and well read in naval warfare strategies may suggest some probable deficiencies were omitted.

8

Signals Passed Between D2 and The Admiralty

Throughout the 9th of April, signals were sent back and forth between Captain Warburton-Lee, the Admiralty and senior officers at sea in the battle groups. Although there are too many to repeat here, for those wishing to have a full account of these communications, I recommend Peter Dickens' book, 'Narvik: Battles in the Fjords', Chapter Three. For now it is sufficient to state that the following two significant signals are ones which the crew members would always remember.

As stated in the previous chapter, Captain Warburton-Lee had sent a signal to the Admiralty, which read, 'Norwegians report Germans holding Narvik in force, also six destroyers and one U-boat are there and channel is possibly mined. Intend attacking at dawn – high water = $1751/9^{th}$'. The reply from Mr Churchill, First Lord of the Admiralty, was as follows: 'I leave it to you to decide what action to take. You are the sole judge, but whatever you do, I shall back your decision to the limit'.

Note: There was a hidden code for the terminology in signals learnt by naval officers. If the Junior ranking officer sent a signal to his superior with the wording 'Intend', unless otherwise 'counter ordered', it would be done; and the Junior Officer is not seeking a reply. Hence, naval custom was, in signals you never state 'Propose' when you can 'intend', and never request for guidance.

Paymaster Lt Geoffrey Stanning described the feelings around the ship from brother officers to the senior and junior rates: "I went down to the wardroom and we gossiped for sometime as there was a lull in the cyphering activity, and I had not very much to do. But there was no chance of getting any sleep, which we all badly needed as if I went to my cabin someone was certain to come in and want something. Aquilina (Carmelo Aquilina from Malta) the wardroom cook managed as usual to produce quite a reasonable supper and we all felt much better after it. Almost before I had finished 'Wash' sent for me. He was still worried about going into Narvik and wondered what the Admiralty would think of his taking the risk or alternatively of the delay in attacking the place.

"The ship's company would have been desperately disappointed if the attack had not come off and I told him this; we talked for some time and then went up on the compass platform. It was about 2130 then, dusk and very clear, and calm. We were steaming up and down on the side of Vest Fjord near the Lofoten Islands and were then on the Northern leg. It was very still and we could see the snow covered peaks on each side of us quite plainly; it made the whole thing seem completely unreal and very awe inspiring.

"'Torps' (Lt Heppel) came up while we were on the Bridge and said he had been on the messdecks explaining the situation to the ship's company, which was the sort of thoughtful thing he would do. I soon went down and talked to various people on the way down, including some telegraphers (who of course knew more of the situation than most of the ship's company). They were full of life and it was encouraging to talk to such resolute people. I lay down in my bunk at about 2230 and slept a bit but was wide awake when I was called at 0015. The ship's company went to action stations a few minutes later and I went up to the Bridge. We were still going up Vest fjord.

"I was busy for a time installing the Petty Officer Writer in the charthouse with the cyphers which were in my suitcase with a weighted bag, and with paper and pencil to take a narrative which I would pass by voice pipe from the compass platform."

The Petty Officer Writer mentioned was George Quinn born in 1914 in Chudleigh, Devon, the son of a retired Royal Naval Officer. On leaving school George worked for NAAFI offices before joining the Navy in 1933. He had served on the battleship 'Rodney' and within six years promoted to Petty Officer. He was married to Cristina Ellen, who had just given birth to their first son, Michael. On 'Hardy' George would have been in charge of the daily running of the general administrative department known as the 'Ship's Office'.

However, returning to the tense and apprehensive atmosphere at command level, George had one more extremely important departmental responsibility, that of Secretary to Paymaster Lt Stanning. When the Captain received or wanted to send highly classified wireless signals (to either the Admiralty in London or to other ships), Lt Stanning would copy the messages and pass them onto George Quinn for encryption or decryption.

Here, George's youngest son, Tony, takes up the story. "Being re-countable directly to Lieut. Stanning, he worked on the signals and was first to hear that they were moving on to make an attack on Narvik. He knew this, a number of hours before the rest of the crew on board. He had to keep it to himself and was 'terrified', knowing the fjords situation."

It appears George Quinn was referring to having to decrypt the signal from the Admiralty at 1130 on 9th of April ordering the ships to attack Narvik that same evening.

Lt Stanning started to sense the forthcoming tension on the Bridge. "It was snowing by this time and it took ten minutes to get from forward to aft with all one's clothes on, on the very slippery decks and including climbing over the torpedo tubes trained outboard. When I got back to the Bridge we were just going to alter course to turn up Narvik fjord. Just after we had altered course in the very poor visibility, we almost ran aground either on some ice projecting from the beach or the snow covered beach itself. 'Torps' saw it first and by that time it seemed inevitable that we should run ashore but the ship began to swing just in time and we got away with it; I thought it was the beach and not ice.

"The visibility got even worse a little later and it began to snow faster or rather the flakes got bigger and we had to reduce speed from fifteen knots to twelve and had a fog light burning. Alterations of course and speed were passed by W/T (Wireless Telegraphy) using quick manoeuvring procedure. Pilot (Navigator – Lt Commander Gordon-Smith) seemed to be quite happy about his position and everyone else had confidence in him, though he could not possibly have been blamed if we had gone aground. I took soundings for him for a bit while Midshipman Pope was doing something else and then took Asdic bearings of the beach until a cypher arrived."

Desmond Montague Pope aged nineteen was the only Midshipman on 'Hardy'. This was his first full time appointment. However, he would have been on board the ship predominantly for sea training purposes. Desmond from Taunton in Somerset was a Royal Naval Reserve (RNR) junior officer having enlisted in May 1937. At the beginning of the war I am sure he never thought for one moment that he would quickly become involved in such a momentous sea battle.

Geoffrey Stanning by now has decrypted the signal. "This was a message from the Admiralty giving 'Wash' full liberty of action and assuring him of full Admiralty support. Also, telling us that two Norwegian coast defence ships might be in German hands. The message was very heartening though we did not bother much about the last part about the coast defence ships. Shortly afterwards we got another message which came in very mutilated and incomplete, so that at first I could de-cypher none of it.

"As it was marked 'Immediate', we thought it might be second thoughts on the Admiralty's part and possibly telling us to call off the operation. So it was very worrying not to be able to do it. However, we got another version soon after and I found it was ordering us to count up the Germans in Narvik and their guns and their stores and everything that was theirs. This message looked like a joke and certainly caused some amusement but it would have been kinder to refrain from making a signal which was obviously not really essential at such a moment."

Returning to the time when action stations had been ordered, Cyril Cope provides his usual vivid description of the dramatic events that followed: "We ploughed our way through the blinding blizzard of freezing snow to the entrance of Vest fjord arriving at midnight, dead on time. All hands were at action stations, all machinery except main engines stopped – nobody was allowed to make noises. We even had to talk in whispers, and we weren't allowed to move about unnecessarily. Every action station exposed to the cold, bitter weather had a 'Dixie' full of hot tea or coffee, with plenty of rum in it. I'm afraid most of us were too excited and intent on our surroundings to drink much of it."

Cyril reminisces: "There we were: five small, silent, ghost like ships, steaming steadily but surely up a narrow fjord, each ship enshrouded in mist and snow with just a blue light showing on the after mast for the following ship to steer by. We, in 'Hardy', had no one to follow."

9

Transit the Fjord

During the hazardous four hours' journey to meet with their enemy, it was crucial the five destroyers kept in contact by wireless telegraphy. Once more in my father's documents I found a copy of the W/T log recorded on board 'Havock'. There was no mention as to where the copy came from. But it may have been provided by one of the officers or telegraphers on board at the time and my father was given it at one of the Narvik Association's reunions. 'Havock' was fourth in line and most of the signals orders were sent by Captain Warburton-Lee (D2). These were to all the four ships identified as D F (Destroyer Flotilla). The Captains of the ships would have relayed their messages or replies in 'Morse Code' via the Bridge Telegraphist. What follows are the communications once the flotilla started their journey, deep into the fjord.

0044 (Time) 2nd D F from D2 – Proceed at 12 knots.

Lt Stanning had other responsibilities to consider. "I then went aft again and instilled into Mr McCracken that he should dump the safes aft in an oil fuel tank if anything happened. This sounds rather as if I had some premonition of disaster, but that was actually not the case as I had given up trying to think what was going to happen to us and was not in the least worried. If I had stopped to think, I should have remembered that disaster always overtakes me when I have no premonition of it, and never when I have."

0106 2nd D F from D2 – Proceed at 20 knots.
0146 2nd D F from D2 – Proceed at 12 knots.

At this point there appeared to be another vessel ahead. 'Hardy' went 'hard a starboard'. This resulted in the ships getting out of line in a disorganised manner. Shortly afterwards a ferry lit up like a Christmas tree came out of the fog: 'Hostile' had to rapidly veer off. It seemed at the time that she may have had to navigate her own way to Narvik.

Cyril, like his shipmates either on the upper deck or below, feeling tense and control of their destiny out of their hands: "We relied on the skill of our Navigating Officer, Lt Commander (Russell) Gordon-Smith to take us safely to our destination. Everybody knew that a trip up the fjord (even in daytime under normal conditions) without a local pilot would be dangerous and a tricky operation. But to succeed under our present conditions would require a miracle. Our miracle was having such a brilliant gentleman, like our Navigator Gordon-Smith in charge of the job. For make no mistake, it was his skill, not the Captain's that controlled our passage up the fjord."

0215 Hotspur from D2 – Are you alright.
0216 D2 from Hotspur – Yes, you are just out of sight.

The ships now moving out of line, D2 was particularly concerned about 'Hotspur''s re-positioning.

0221 2nd D F from D2 – My course and speed 075 degrees, 12 knots.

Cyril: "As I have said, the fjord was narrow in parts and at times it seemed so easy to jump ship, or even throw spuds at the shore batteries wherever they were. We were using 'Asdic' to help in the navigation. This gave us soundings off the sides of the fjord, because most of the time we could not see the sides or anything in front of us. The snow coming down was too thick."

0232 Hotspur from D2 – I am about to pass Hamnes Holm abeam to starboard.
0233 D2 from Hotspur – In touch.
0234 2nd D F from D2 – Turn in succession to 095 degrees.
0239 Hotspur from D2 – Are you in touch.
0240 D2 from Hotspur – Yes.
0242 2nd D F from D2 – Good luck, let them have it.
0249 D F from D2 – Make your call signs if in touch.
0250 Call signs.

In fact, visibility, in naval terms, was one and a half cables, equivalent to 300 yards. I would also add that Cyril's involvement in the 2nd Destroyer Flotilla of Narvik Association, a rapidly growing membership in the 1970s, meant that contact information of other crew members was passed on to him. One contact address provided was that of Bill 'Ned' Sparkes. An appropriate surname as it happens because up until I joined the Navy those working as Radio Operators were still referred to as 'Sparkes'. After the war, Bill had emigrated to the United States. In 1978, Cyril wrote to Ned at his home address in Michigan. Although it took a while to receive a reply, Ned described his role in the engagement as a Leading Telegraphist on 'Hardy': "Concerning that fateful morning, we in the rest of the 'Radio Department' were too busy to know what transpired in other parts of the ship. Our biggest problem was finding our way up the fjord in the snow storms. We did this by getting 'radio bearings' from the radio stations 'ROST' and 'Bodo' – and area projections from them. In the time itself I was in charge of the second Radio Office and would take over if the Main Office went out of action, which eventually it did."

Note: After the war, because of the rapid technological advances, there was an increased procurement of complex radio and electronic cryptographic equipment on board ships. This led to the Royal Navy deciding to have two separate departments. These were the 'Communications' branch, which included both radio operators and yeoman of signals, and the 'Radio Electrical' branch, responsible for the maintenance of equipment. However, during the Second World War, Telegraphists like Ned Sparkes had to perform both tasks.

Moving on, Les Smale described the moments before going into battle: "My particular action station was as a member of the Gunnery Directions Crew, with a duty to operate the Cross Level Unit. Since the close proximity of the fjord shoreline on either side made the unit inoperable, I was ordered out of the 'Director' to become a 'Bridge Messenger' and as such was in a 'ring side seat' as it were, to see all the action that was to come."

The 'Fire Control System' for the guns, as it was known; the Cross Level Unit was a means of measuring the roll of the ship in order to put on a line correction for the way the Guns would be thrown off, due to the roll of the ship. You measured the angle and this put in a counter-angle to bring the Guns back to a datum. You look through a telescope which is at right angles to the line of site of the Guns. So as the ship rolls, say ten per cent, you bring datum line onto the horizon and gave the information into the line direction to the Guns.

For those readers wanting more information about the 'Fire Control System' see Dickens' book, page 169.

It is worth clarifying for readers that 'Hardy' had five gun turrets, being the Lead Destroyer (D2), unlike the other four ships, which had four gun turrets. The guns were numbered, forward to aft as one to five. In 'Hardy' Nos 1 and 2 were on the forward deck, No 3 amidships between the two funnels and Nos 4 and 5 at the stern.

Able Seaman Stan Robinson's action station was also in the gun 'Director' as the 'Trainer' number. "I was responsible for keeping the target from port to starboard, then the men on the other side controlled the depression and elevation."

Cyril continues, "The snow also gave us a problem with the guns and torpedoes. It kept piling up on them, the breech blocks froze up, the traversing gear on the tubes got blocked up and this would cause a problem when we came to turn them onto a port or starboard bearing."

The Royal Naval warships still had the older type of torpedo tubes, which could only fire in one position, i.e. 90 degrees outboard from their normal steaming site of fore and aft. However, the more modern German destroyer's tubes were able to be placed into various firing positions. As the story unfolds, will this make a difference to the end game.

Bert Mason, some days before going into the fjord, realised he had a dilemma. "Since the previous sea action on training our after tubes, I noticed they had become exceedingly stiff as if freezing up. The Training Numbers were having a hell of a job getting them to move. I had searched underneath for any grease nipples and applied a grease gun where I could use it. I called the Chief Engineer Artificer, to see what he could make of it, but he was useless! All I got were some sarcastic remarks that we did not know our jobs. Throughout that long night it was a constant worry for me that if we got a quick order to train starboard we were in trouble!

"On we steamed through the dark, 'Arctic' night, closed up for action stations, huddled around our weaponry; foremost tubes trained to starboard; after tubes trained to port, firing cartridges inserted but 'ready' pushes withdrawn. No noise, no talking, just the gentle swish of water against the ship's side. Above us and aft was No 4 Gun's crew, closed up and as silent as the grave.

"Then somewhere near, a flicker of sparks and we immediately jumped into action. Below, in his little galley, our Captain's Maltese cook 'Guiseppe' was endeavouring to cook his Master's supper. In seconds his 'Charley Noble' chimney was dismantled amid a deck plate screwed over the hole. The next minute he was out through the after door wondering why his galley had so suddenly choked up with smoke and fumes and his Captain's supper was in ruins. Just too bad for the 'old man'.

"Occasionally we sighted a jut of land in the middle of nowhere; now and then a tiny blue flash of a signal for the next ship astern, otherwise total blackness. A whispered message came through – 'we are fifteen minutes from Narvik'. Nerves were getting tensed up and straining our eyes we could just make out a snow covered shoreline and what looked like a scuttled merchant (ship) partly lying on its side."

Rumour had it that Captain Warburton-Lee not having had a hot meal for over twenty-four hours, called up his cook to the Bridge with his request for a hot meal. Sadly he had to accept sandwiches.

Les Smale having been detailed off as messenger on the Bridge applies full concentration to his new duties. "The orders were to sink all ship's targets and needless to say everyone was 'on their toes' the whole time. It began to snow pretty heavily and we couldn't see either shores and this made navigation much more difficult. It was bitterly cold and where we were moving around in a vain effort to keep warm, we were forming circles of ice on the deck. Twice, rum and tea were brought around and did we need it? Generally a quiet atmosphere surrounded the ship as was only to be expected in such a tense situation. Once in particular, when the Gunnery Officer Lt Clarke passed around that we were going to pass a shore battery, everything was particularly quiet; with no one saying a word and only the wash of the ship to stir the apparent peace."

'Hardy' had an open top Bridge, leaving all the officers and men more exposed to the atrocious weather conditions than those in other parts of ship. Cyril points out, "The chaps at the guns were also having problems, even bringing red hot pokers out of the galley to thaw out the breech blocks. This packed snow caused us some trouble during the battle which was to follow. The tactics of our Captain and Navigator were as follows: to pan up the fjord as silently as possible, at such a speed as to enable us to arrive at the entrance of Narvik harbour as the dawn broke. In this way we hoped to catch the enemy still turned in and fast asleep."

During my spell on the staff at Dartmouth Naval College in 1977, I remember the Officer Cadets being emphatically reminded that 'one of the first principles of war is surprise'.

0330 2nd D F from D2 – Turn in succession to 080 degrees.

Cyril continues, "I have already mentioned that dawn in that part of the world came up at approximately 0345. We arrived outside the harbour entrance at 0350, once again on time. Through the swirling mist and snow those of us on the upper deck, by now frozen stiff with cold and immobility for nearly four hours, could just see the inside of the harbour."

Peter Dickens (page 56) describes, "Gordon-Smith of Hardy, and the navigating officer of the 'Diether von Roeder', both advised their Captains to turn towards Narvik Harbour having calculated that they were in exactly the same position at exactly the same time, 0340. The Hardy however, was somewhat to the south and west of her dead-reckoning position, perhaps owing to an over correction for the flood stream and some leeway from the now north easterly wind. The two ships turned course 110 degrees and kept perfect station on one another, at the most one and half miles apart and probably less, totally unaware of the fact."

0342 2nd D F from D2 – Turn in succession to 110 degrees.
0344 2nd D F from D2 – Am steering for entrance of Narvik harbour.
0346 2nd D F from D2 – Form on a line of bearing 280 degrees.

Geoffrey Stanning: "Just as the Pilot (Navigation Officer) was convinced we were there, we saw land on our port bow and more land ahead as we went on but it turned out not to be Narvik but a small inlet to the South West. We turned and went out again and went further up the main fjord, keeping the land on the starboard hand in sight. Up to now we had seen no sign of civilisation at all and what was more extraordinary, no sign at all of Germans as we had thought they would have had a destroyer patrolling the lower part of the fjord or at least a submarine anchored in the channel.

"We thought we had either passed the patrol in bad visibility or else there was none there. Several people even thought Heppel and I had got hold of the wrong end of the stick at Tranoy and that there really were not many Germans at Narvik and hopes began to revive, of a landing party.

"I suddenly remembered it was my birthday and I believe 'Wash' would have sent down a bottle of champagne, but for the fact that just at that moment we saw a fishing boat lying off a small wooden pier on our starboard hand; that looked more promising and a moment later we saw a headland on the port bow which Pilot thought must be the North side of the harbour entrance. It was!"

0350 2nd D F from D2 – Proceed at 6 knots.
0352 2nd D F from D2 – Turn together 20 degrees to starboard.
0356 2nd D F from D2 – Hostile in touch.
0359 2nd D F from D2 – Turn together 30 degrees to port.

Nineteen year old Able Seaman 'Gunner' Geoffrey Bailey is part of No 2 Gun, for'd just below the Bridge. Having been fortunate enough to have avoided being a casualty on his first ship 'Royal Oak', he starts to feel the tension rising in himself and those around him. "The snow had cleared and it was getting light, we could see where we were. The fjord at this point was very wide and we increased speed a little bit, I didn't see any sign of life ashore. The fjord widened into a sort of bay. Like a hunter approaching the lion's den, we crept warily forward to what was obviously the entrance to the harbour."

0405 2nd D F from D2 – Stop engines.

Having reached their destination this order was given to confirm the correct bearing to proceed.

> 0406 2nd D F from D2 – Proceed at 10 knots – turn together 40 degrees to port.

Les Smale was in hearing distance of the Captain and his officers on the Bridge and recalls: Just about 0400, in the vicinity of the harbour, we made for what we thought was the entrance and only stopped just in time when we realised that it wasn't. After a little scout around eventually we found it and the plan had been to fire on the enemy from the entrance. We were all very surprised when the 'Hardy' began to lead the division into the harbour itself. It seemed to be so cheeky and yet here we were doing it!

> 0408 2nd D F from D2 – Stop engines.
> 0410 2nd D F from D2 – Go astern.
> 0411 2nd D F from D2 – Stop engines.

Gunner Dougy Bourton, calm and alert, remained near his No 4 Gun mounting. "The only thing of any interest at all, as we approached Narvik, was that we went through the wash of a very large ship. We wondered what it was and we rolled quite considerably. So we were all on our toes waiting because we had been standing at action stations all this time. We had been fed soup or hot tea laced with rum, as we got nearer Narvik. This would have been close to four o'clock and the scene was as if you were looking at a stage, curtains were parted and you saw the whole harbour displayed, like a theatrical battle.

"I was the 'loading number' for No 4 Gun. I stood alongside the tray and pushed the tray forward, which contained the shell and cartridge. The cartridge was about three foot long, made of brass, with a base of 6 to 7 inches, narrowing down to 4.7 inches, where it entered the breech behind the shell."

0412 2nd D F from D2 – Turn together to 010 degrees proceed at 10 knots.
0413 2nd D F from D2 – Point ship to 010 degrees.

Back to No 2 Gun and Geoff Bailey: "Our 'faces' set, the 'gunlayer' with his eyes on the gunsights, AB (Jack) Hay ready to shove a round into the breach, the two loading numbers standing by with the second round in their arms and myself with my eyes glued to the range dial, my ears cocked to catch the slightest order from the Bridge. We were ready for heaven knows what, the whole German fleet for all we knew."

Loading numbers were probably AB Henry 'Jock' Lang and Acting Leading Seaman Frank Edwards, either way they are confirmed as part of No 2 Gun team. As previously pointed out the Captain of the Gun was Leading Seaman Alec Hunt.

0415 2nd D F from D2 – Turn together to 010 degrees proceed at 10 knots.

Cyril Cope described that moment. "Through the swirling mist and snow we could just see inside the harbour. We stopped engines and waited for the other four ships to catch up with us. Everything was fine up to now, everybody present, no alarms sounded by the enemy. 'What is to happen next?' we think. Two ships ('Hotspur' and 'Hostile') are detached to engage shore batteries at Framnesodden. We alone glide silently into the harbour. The other two ships ('Hunter' and 'Havock') waited outside, across the harbour mouth, just clear of the entrance."

0416 2nd D F from D2 – Proceed at 6 knots.
0418 2nd D F from D2 – Turn together to 90 degrees.

Geoffrey Stanning saw a merchant vessel at the entrance of the harbour and more shipping inside. "I saw a man walking up and down amidships in the supposed British ship and asked 'Wash' if I should hail him and ask where the Germans were. He said, 'No, we don't want to wake up the Germans in the town'. The town was at least half a mile away, we knew, but the silence was so uncanny that we felt we were bound to wake someone up if we spoke loudly."

0422 2nd D F from D2 – Am entering south side of harbour.
0423 2nd D F from D2 – Am turning to port follow me round.

Geoff Bailey recalled, "We swung gentle to port and nosed our way into the harbour, it was full of ships flying the Swastika. I saw a small sailing boat with a couple of people in it, I felt like shouting to them to scram before they got hurt. I looked through the gun port and lying between them was a German destroyer making a beautiful target for our torpedoes."

0424 2nd D F from D2 – Proceed at 12 knots.
0426 2nd D F from D2 – Alarm bearing 010 degrees.

Cyril looks out to starboard from his position on the forward tubes. "There is a large British iron ore ship (RMS Blythmoor). It was obviously heavily laden, because she was so low in the water. As we came close we were able to look down on her, we could see there were two German sentries, one aft and one for'd, with guns. However, on seeing us glide towards them they scampered down hatches. They didn't fire their guns, didn't raise an alarm, Captain Warburton-Lee brought the 'Hardy' alongside the merchant ship with our engines just ticking over. This obviously allowed the Captain and others on the Bridge to take a good look into the harbour."

0428 2nd D F from D2 – Am turning to port, standby to fire, torpedoes starboard side.
0429 2nd D F from D2 – Near ship is British.

Les Smale witnessed a similar view and says, "There was already one ship run aground on our starboard side as we went in but there were plenty more good ones about for us to sink. Merchant ships were small fry at that moment. We were looking for destroyers and a submarine. All our guns had been unfrozen with hot oil on the way up and were loaded ready for anything. Everything seemed to be still very quiet and peaceful but that was all changed a few minutes later when we suddenly sighted a destroyer's bows, showing from behind a large whaling ship.

Dickens (page 60): "All peered intently, and none more than Heppel (Torpedo Officer) who knew that his torpedoes would be called upon the moment a target was sighted. He had trained his forward tubes to starboard and the after mounting to port so that his reaction could be instantaneous; enemy speed zero, safety pins out of the whiskered pistols, impulse cartridges inserted, stop valves open. Someone breathed, 'There they are!' and the Chief Yeoman broke out the battle ensigns already furled at the two mastheads." The Chief Yeoman was 'Arthur Campian'. Unfortunately, I have no more information about his whereabouts after the battle.

10

The Enemy Caught Asleep

Cyril and the team on the torpedo deck swiftly forgot about the icy conditions and started to realise they were fast approaching their first experience of battle with the enemy. Cyril, headphones clutched tightly to his ears, becomes gripped with excitement. "On our starboard side we saw a wonderful sight, especially to a trained gunner and torpedoman. An array of merchant ships of many nations, all taken over by the Germans by this time. Not that we stopped to ask mind you. In line with the sights on my tubes I could see two merchant ships, bow to stern, with just enough gaps in between to see an oil tanker with a German destroyer tied up to her, with fuelling pipe lines still attached. I looked to my right to see two more German destroyers, about 500 to 600 yards apart.

"The order came over my head phones; 'Cut the guard rails.' I went with my seaman's knife and did what was asked and confirmed to the Bridge. Then, next order, 'Stand By to open fire on foremost tubes'. Forget what else, but the 'oiler' ('Jan Wellem') and destroyer ('Wilhelm Heidkamp') first, then any of the other ships. The Captain must have decided not to fire the guns, but to keep it as a surprise attack with torpedoes only."

Geoffrey Stanning recorded the initial action from the Bridge. "We drifted past the merchant ship with engines stopped. Someone suddenly said 'there they are' and 'Torps' asked permission to fire torpedoes at two destroyers which we could see alongside each other in the middle of the harbour with their bows towards the town. He fired four torpedoes at them and 'Wash' ordered twenty knots and helm (coxswain in the wheelhouse) to take us round the ship in the entrance and out of the harbour."

Cyril, similar to some of the other shipmates' accounts, had the advantage of access to documentation long after the battle took place. (For example, by eventually knowing the names of the enemy ships involved and those hit by their torpedoes.) Unlike Geoffrey Stanning, and other officers whose formal accounts had been requested by the Admiralty and therefore recorded shortly after the events.

Cyril continues, "Away goes our first torpedo, I could see it pass between the two merchant ships. There is a big flash and bang, up went the destroyer ('Wilhelm Heidkamp'). No time to cheer, away go the other three torpedoes, you could clearly see them making their way through the same gap. They were also direct hits, thinking that's part of the job done. The only destroyers at that time not hit were the two being refuelled ('Hermann Kunne' and 'Hans Ludemann')."

Geoff Bailey: "I heard the swish of the D.C. tin fish as it left the tube, for a second I saw its wake and then a terrific roar as the German destroyer blew up. She had been hit in the magazine, pieces blew hundreds of feet in the air and then we opened up with our guns. It was like hell let loose."

Geoffrey Stanning, "As we gathered way, 'Guns' (Lt Clark, Gunnery Officer) sighted more destroyers alongside the quay and got the guns on to them. Just then I saw one of our torpedoes hit the bow of a large merchant ship astern of the two destroyers we had fired at. A split second later there was an almighty explosion from the direction of the first two destroyers (we could no longer see them) and I knew that 'Torps' had made a good shot.

"After the first large explosion there were many more which showed that magazines must have been hit and what must have been thousands of rounds of ammunition began to explode in the air which made a proper fireworks display. That was good beyond all expectation but even at that moment we could not help thinking with horror of the loss of life we must have caused for they were large destroyers, though we could not identify them precisely."

Peter Dickens (page 61) in researching for his book, interviewed both Lt George Heppel and Cyril Cope. He states: "Never fire torpedoes in penny numbers, was a principle well imbued in Heppel and although it was theoretically impossible to miss a stopped ship at such a ridiculously short range he launched three in a narrow fan. On the foremost tubes, Torpedoman Cope's duty was to ensure that the drill went without a hitch, which he did; but being a man of acute awareness of his surroundings he also saw the targets."

With regard to torpedoes Nos 2 and 3 they in turn were sent on their way. It appears No 2 hit the German destroyer 'Anton Schmitt' directly in a compartment adjacent to her main magazine. Cyril vividly recalls "It just blew up and the concussion and shock waves put out of action a third destroyer nearby ('Hermann Kunne')."

Bill Pulford, like Cyril, one of the forward tubes crew, in his interview with Conrad Wood for the Imperial War Museum in 1989 was still able to give a descriptive picture of the first torpedo hitting the 'Wilhelm Heidkamp'. "At 0420 Narvik ceased to be a little unknown town in Norway and suddenly burst out into history of the world; because here one almighty explosion occurred. The first torpedo struck the after part of the first German destroyer, it struck the after magazine. We saw the after gun leave the ship altogether, curling through the air, it did a complete U turn and landed on the fo'c'sle of its own ship. Another torpedo struck her and the ship went down."

The moment arrived to which Bert Mason was not looking forward. "Suddenly, the order from the Bridge, 'All tubes, ready starboard'. This was the dreaded moment and I knew we were in trouble. Our four 'Training Numbers' were struggling desperately to get the tubes around 180 degrees. (Port beam to Starboard beam.) At the same time the foremost tubes were firing and all their torpedoes gone. With that all hell broke loose, as our five 4.7 inch guns opened up on targets that became visible. With our communications man screaming his head off, 'Ready Starboard! – Ready Starboard!' I felt completely helpless; but then the men from the other tubes saw our predicament and quickly set to pushing like hell to get those obstinate tubes into position."

By now Cyril and the rest of the foremost tubes crew were feeling very relieved. "On that never to be forgotten morning at Narvik, we were lucky; our tubes were trained on the engaging side. Our mates on the after set of tubes had theirs trained to port. Due to the hard packed snow and ice on the traversing gear, they were finding it hard going, time was passing. Our guns had by this time opened up on the ships and shore batteries. Our crew ran to the assistance of our mates, with two men on each of the tubes' handles, the rest of us were pushing like mad on the back end of the tubes."

Bert again takes up the story of the ongoing struggle. "A split second before they locked into position and I was knocking in the 'ready pushes' the T.L. (Torpedo Officer – Lt Heppel) in the 'torpedo control unit' had his fingers on the firing switch and the first torpedo shot out, causing the tubes to whip and the 'fish' to slightly graze the protecting stanchion. Then the tubes locked and two more missiles followed leaving us with one."

Cyril, adrenalin flowing, goes on to describe the damage caused by the three aftermost torpedoes. "We were again lucky because the force of the torpedo leaving the tube caused it to move towards the bows and hence the locking position. Goodness knows what would have happened if it had pushed the opposite way. One target hit was a large railway jetty used for iron ore wagons to unload into ships' holds. Up went the wooden trestle logs, sleepers, train lines, wagons and iron ore. Oh, what a mess! You've never seen anything like it, we really started to cheer then, we acted like children at a pantomime."

Les described those exhilarating moments: "There was a terrible explosion together with a vivid semi-circular white flash of stars twinkling around the edge. If one could forget what that explosion contained, it could be described as being extremely beautiful. But when one thinks of sleeping men being killed outright – then it's different – perhaps though, even if they were enemy. Simultaneously with the explosions we gathered speed and opened fire with the guns."

0439 2nd D F from D2 – Am turning to Northward.
0441 Havock from D2 – Come fire Torpedoes.

Cyril, with his apparent gift of a 'photographic memory', vividly recalled the ongoing action. "We were firing heavily at targets so close it was impossible to miss, but we were not getting anything back from the enemy. So we started our engines and slipped out of the harbour, telling other ships ('Hunter' and 'Havock') to go in and have a crack. This they did, firing their guns and torpedoes – then out again."

0442 D2 from Hotspur – Nothing to Northward.

As mentioned, 'Hotspur' and 'Hostile' were initially detached to engage any possible shore batteries and cover their three sister ships making their attack. At this stage the whole brave mission was carried out with the strength of the enemy unknown. Hence, because of the damage inflicted, due to an unsuccessful response battle plans had to be rapidly modified.

Dougy and the rest of the gun crews, who also had high levels of adrenalin flowing through their veins, described 'Hardy''s retreat. "We fired at everything which flew a German flag or 'Red Ensign' (British Merchants), everything then was a German ship and we did a colossal amount of damage. It was so close, all we did was train the guns, didn't have to apply any range because the range was so short. The amount of return was negligible except the odd army gun which was firing but generally speaking the Germans took off."

Geoffrey Stanning remained at his position on the Bridge. "There were signs that the Germans were beginning to wake up as they were beginning to fire out of the harbour but it seemed to be only small stuff; as it was tracer we could see it coming. Not that anything we could do would stop it hitting us if it wanted to, but it was comforting to see. The Germans were firing blindly out of the harbour and we were firing blindly into it and it all seemed rather comic; as the two sides were within a mile of each other but neither could see each other."

Geoff Bailey: "Guns on the 'Nazi' merchant ships opened fire, but it was ineffective and we didn't have a scratch. We concentrated our fire on two more destroyers lying at anchor. We scored several hits by this time. We had turned around until we faced the mouth of the harbour with our accompanying destroyers coming up astern. We came out of the harbour and swung around and slowed down for a breather."

Stanning: "That was the end of the first attack and we began to form up to do some more. The two ships sent up to Rombaks Fjord had come back by this time and reported that there was nothing there so this time there were five ships to do the attack. We wanted to keep close to the entrance to make sure that nothing came out."

0444 Hotspur from D2 – Fire your torpedoes into the harbour.

By the time the first three ships had moved out of the harbour, 'Hostile' was already sending salvos at the enemy. Dickens (page 66) describes the determination and ingenuity to get their targets. 'Hostile' stopped engines. "The gun-direction telescopes were opaque with snow that could not be wiped clear fast enough, but over open sights it was hardly any easier to aim. Spotting fall of shot was almost impossible so 'blind ladders' were used, groups of three salvos fired rapidly, with an 'up' 400 yard correction between each; then the same with a 'down' correction and so on. Steady nerves and good drill resulted in the 'Diether von Roeder' being hit twice, seriously, while the 'Hostile' remained unscathed."

0448 Hotspur from D2 – Stop making smoke.

As set out in Captain Warburton-Lee's 'Tactical Plan': "Prepare to make smoke for cover and to tow disabled ships." This was cover for 'Hardy', 'Hunter' and 'Havock' on retreating from the harbour. Thankfully, there had been no need for 'Hotspur' to tow any of her sister ships. After the 'Hotspur' had cleared her funnels with smoke, Captain Warburton-Lee told Commander Layman to fire torpedoes into the harbour.

0456 2nd D F from D2 – Report number of torpedoes fired.
D2 from Hotspur – Four.
D2 from Hunter – Eight.
D2 from Havock – Five.
0459 D2 from Hostile – None.

In fact, 'Havock' had sent an incorrect number, as they had fired three and five left over. In the meantime the five destroyers had formed a disorderly circle continuing to engage the enemy as each moved into position at the harbour entrance.

Cyril's own feelings of jubilation were probably echoed around the ship especially for those sailors on the upper deck able to witness the success of their endeavours. However, it became short lived. "The visibility had got very bad again, so we withdrew down the fjord. I thought Oh God, we have done it – it's over for us!"

Geoff Bailey and the rest of No 2 Gun crew had got their breath back, "We were in high spirits, and not one of our ships had a scratch. When the last of our ships came out, we increased speed and with guns blazing went back into the harbour, which by now looked to me like a harbour of sinking ships."

Bert gave his version of the swiftly unfolding events. "In a matter of minutes we were well clear, out in the open fjord and a chance to assess any damage the 'Hardy' had received. There were no casualties as far as we knew, but we noticed a few shell holes in the after funnel. 'Tansy' Lee (Able Seaman James Lee) one of our number, picked up a small shell lying nearby. He quickly dropped it and kicked it over the ships side, as it was 'red hot'.

"For us, the Torpedomen, we thought it was all over as we retreated down to the entrance of the fjord. I was wishing we could have got rid of that last 'fish' so that we could stock up a complete new outfit when we got back to base. It was not to be! Our Captain had decided to go back in again, leading the others in the flotilla to give them a chance to fire their torpedoes."

Geoffrey Stanning was still on the Bridge. "A fair amount of small stuff was being fired at us out of the harbour but was not doing any harm. It did seem a wise precaution to put on tin hats and we all did so; but after a short time I noticed that everyone had laid them aside again. We circled in front of the harbour, again firing guns at the enemy flashes, when we saw them. The enemy by this time was firing heavier stuff which we knew must come from the damaged destroyers and we were anxious to know what damage had been done; as we had heard a good many more heavy explosions but could see nothing of the result."

0501 2nd D F from D2 – Report damage to enemy seen.
0503 D2 from Hotspur – Two merchant ships sinking.
0504 D2 from Hostile – Merchant ship and Destroyer observed to be hit by 4.7 shell.
0505 D2 from Hunter – Five torpedoes hit, damage to enemy Destroyer not observed.
0506 D2 from Havock – Destroyer hit by 4.7 shell.

Peter Dickens (page 68): "To these reports could be added the Hardy's torpedoing of a destroyer and a merchant ship, but the combined reports do not begin to convey an impression of the havoc actually wrought. It is no wonder that the action was continued, and that Warburton-Lee told the 'Hostile':

0507 Hostile from D2 – If you can find suitable warship target, send four torpedoes in.

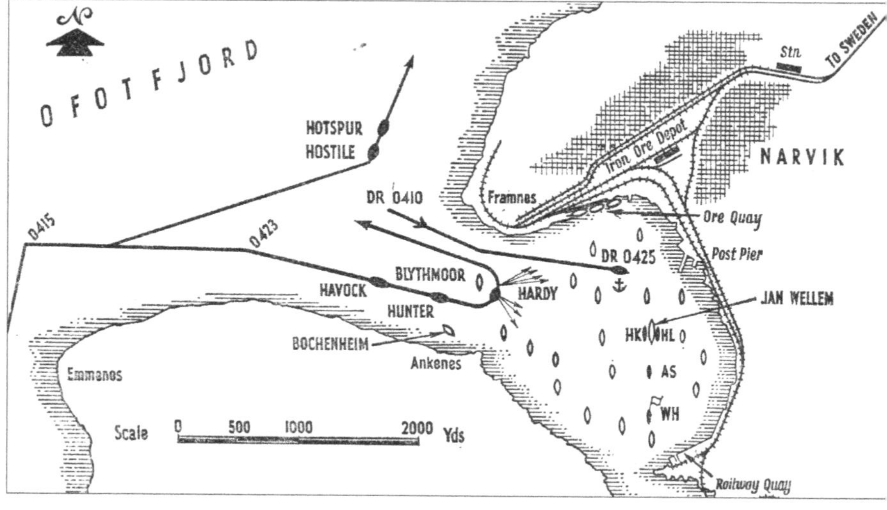

Diagram by unknown survivor of the First Battle of Narvik. *Cyril Cope Collection.*

"It is fairly clear from this signal and his own actions that in spite of the Admiralty's order to sink German merchant ships, Warburton-Lee considered their warships to have first priority."

The other four destroyer Captains were under no obligations to follow the Admiralty's order as it had not been made specific in Captain Warburton-Lee's 'Tactical Plan'. The outcome therefore was that 'Hostile' followed 'Hardy' by prioritising the German warships. 'Hotspur' and 'Hunter' treated all cargo vessels as legitimate targets if no enemy warship was in their sights, whilst 'Havock' was known to have avoided British cargo vessels.

0509 2nd D F from D2 – Look out for torpedo tracks.

Commander Wright, the Captain of 'Hostile', must have been frustrated waiting for the right opportunity to release the torpedoes. He probably wanted to finish off with another attack on 'Diether von Roeder', but unknown to Commander Wright, in the previous engagement his salvoes had hit a fuel tank resulting in a raging fire in one of her boiler rooms. However, the disabled 'Diether von Roeder' managed to release all its torpedoes in the direction of its adversaries.

11

Second Attack

Dougy Bourton: "While we were reforming outside the harbour, some torpedoes were fired at us from inside the harbour. All ships did their utmost to avoid them; two passed under 'Hardy' but did not explode. This was probably due to our degaussing gear."

Torpedo Officer George Heppel, just over two weeks after the battle, wrote a report giving his professional opinion, which wasn't far wrong. "After a time the ships in the harbour started ineffectively to return the fire and Hardy withdrew outside the entrance followed by Hunter and Havock who had fired torpedoes after Hardy. Hotspur then attacked with torpedoes from just outside the harbour entrance and all five ships were engaging the harbour and a small battery on 'Franmnesodden' with their maximum power.

"During this period a number of torpedoes, possibly a dozen were fired at us from the harbour and ships did their utmost to avoid them. Two, however, ran under Hardy and the escape must have been due to the success of the D.G. (De-Gaussing) equipment or possibility that contact torpedoes were set too deep in the confusion."

Narvik harbour after attack by 2nd Destroyer Flotilla. *Cyril Cope Collection.*

Wilhelm Heidkamp took first torpedo hit from 'Hardy'. G. Haarr Collection.

The Germany Navy had two models of torpedoes, a battery driven type on their U-boats, and an 'internal combustion' version on destroyers. Both types utilised a 'magnetic pistol' to detonate the warhead. It was designed to explode below their target, causing an increased level of damage. However, at Narvik, as the Germans were later to discover, their innovative device became inoperative, as it was affected by the earth's magnetic field. Especially at the higher latitudes in that part of the world.

This was a stroke of luck for the 2nd Destroyer Flotilla. Fortunately, the Royal Navy had previously discovered these problems and decided to keep to the substantially tested and trusted 'impact pistol' torpedo.

Note: The ineffective German torpedo proved to be an obvious advantage to the 2nd Destroyer Flotilla. Whilst the Royal Navy's Mark IX torpedo, of a simpler design, it was to prove up to the job. So much so, that probably because of its success at Narvik, it not only remained an effective weapon during the Second World War, but was also used by the Submarine Service for another thirty years. This was probably down to the Royal Navy, unlike their adversaries, having previously spent a long period completing development trials. Especially being, thoroughly tested in areas of high altitude. There is a suggestion that the German Navy's usual efficiency on this occasion was let down by the pressure above, to make sure their torpedo development programme was kept secret.

By now 'Diether von Roeder' was a defeated foe and for her the battle was over. An ammunition locker was hit and the contents ignited. A salvo had hit into a messdeck and started a fire for'd, a number of sailors were killed. An injured man rushed on to the upper deck covered in flames and luckily survived. He had been spotted by an officer who pushed him over the ship's side, the officer then jumped in himself and pulled the man out. Another hit destroyed a turret, killing all the gun crew. Her demise came when a compartment near to the after magazine received a direct hit which required the magazine to be rapidly flooded. Finally, she lost her main electrical power supply.

However, Captain, Korvettenkapitan Holtorf had managed, with serviceable engines, to manoeuvre his ship to another mooring, the 'Post Pier'. Securing her aft with the bows anchored facing directly out to the harbour entrance. A clever move if his intentions were to make his ship a smaller target should the enemy decide to make another attack.

0514 2nd D F from D2 – Stand by to follow round again, keep a sharp lookout for torpedoes.

Cyril's moment of jubilation came abruptly to an end. "Then over my headphones came a message from the Captain. 'We have just done a good job but I think we should go back and do a bit more – perhaps this time we can stay.' Both our tubes crew by this time had trained them fore and aft, there was still one more torpedo left in the after tubes. Having done this we were free to join our Repair Parties."

0515 2nd D F from D2 – Stop making smoke.

Geoffrey Stanning: "We went on circling the entrance for some little time and then withdrew, whether by signal or unanimous decision to have a rest I can't remember. All ships reported no damage, no casualties and 'Hostile' said she still had a full outfit of torpedoes, presumably because she had been up Rombaks Fjord. Mansell came up to the Bridge and said we had a small hole in the after funnel and said that three torpedoes had definitely gone under us. We felt very pleased and in high spirits."

0520 Hostile from D2 – Have you fired any torpedoes yet.
0521 2nd D F from D2 – Proceed at 20 knots.
0522 D2 from Hostile – Intend to fire torpedoes when going round this time.

Commander Wright not knowing that the 'Diether von Roeder' had changed her position was still optimistic that 'Hostile' would be able to send her torpedoes in to finish the job. However, irrespective of moving out of line from his sister ships, his search was in vain.

It appears, as seen in the signal below, that at this stage Captain Warburton-Lee was becoming impatient with his fellow officer.

0530 Hostile from D2 – Follow round, don't go the wrong way each time.

Diether von Roeder hit twice by shell fire, at an angle on the quay. G .Haarr Collection.

Cyril described the 'Second Run' as he saw it: "We approached for our second attack at a fair speed, entered the harbour, rounded the merchant ship which we had not sunk yet – in case it blocked the entrance. We opened fire with all guns at the shore batteries and at any shipping left afloat. The other four ships followed us in doing the same. By this time the Germans were well awake and doing a lot of firing. But they were firing skywards. I was stood next to the 'First Lieutenant' (Lt Commander Mansell). I thought 'this is funny they are not firing at us'. I said to the 'First Lieutenant', 'They think it's a bloody air raid Sir'. Everybody laughed, including Jimmy the One." (Royal Navy jargon for the Executive Officer / First Lieutenant.)

Les' observations were slightly different. "We re-entered the harbour; they were ready for us. I should say, some of them were firing H.A. and other L.A. (High Angle / Low Angle elevation). The Germans didn't know if they were under surface or air attack. It was a crazy sight which greeted us this time round. With stems, sterns, funnels and masts sticking up all over the harbour, making the graveyard of the ships sunk in the first battle. But for the grimness of the situation it was almost an amusing sight. There was more gunfire from what appeared to be shore batteries and they were firing ammunition fitted with tracer. So that you could see it coming towards you – sometimes it exploded in flight, while others went off on contact with the water.

"Glancing over the ship's side I noticed that there were explosions erupting from the water at various places around the ship, which threw up black clouds of smoke. I thought they might be controlled mines but I don't know for sure. We came out of the harbour again without casualties but with a well earned scar – a two inch hole in the foremost funnel."

It had been almost an hour since the action had begun and it occurred to Captain Warburton-Lee that due to poor visibility (unlike the first attack) there was little more to gain; so he decided to withdraw his flotilla back into the fjord.

It appears that about this time a long overdue signal was sent to warn the remaining German destroyers not in Narvik that they were under attack. This was sent from the 'Hans Ludemann', which when the action began was being re-fuelled and had managed to slip away from the 'Jan Wellem'.

12

Dilemma: Do We Go in Again?

Geoff Bailey, rightly, felt their job had been done. "No 2 Gun turned its fire on a 'howitzer' on the foreshore, which was worrying us. A few rounds finished that one off. We fired on the remaining merchant ships as we came around and scored hits on them and then came out of the harbour a second and last time, as we thought."

Having come back out of the harbour after the second attack you could not blame the relatively young officers, flushed with success, from feeling invincible. However, it was now time to take stock of the situation to allow Captain Warburton-Lee to make an informed decision. Once more, as on the occasion of entering the fjord the day before, there were discussions with his officers. Stanning again seems to be more specific about how the decision to re-enter or not was decided. Probably, this was because it was one of his responsibilities, on behalf of the Captain, to take notes as an official record of battle events.

However, there appears to be an unreliability of accounts after such a fast-paced, adrenalin-fuelled event, when the memory is never one hundred per cent efficient.

Stanning in his account writes, 'Wash' then said that he thought perhaps we ought to withdraw and asked us what we thought. The answer was unanimously in favour of going in again and for the following reasons:

1. We did not know what damage we had done nor what forces of the enemy were left. As all guns had ceased firing very early into the second attack it was possible that all opposition had been silenced. It would be ridiculous to withdraw in the face of no opposition at all and if there were any enemy forces left we ought to try and estimate their weight and report it.
2. At the same time 'Wash' was anxious that no one should get torpedoed but it was pointed out that so many torpedoes had been fired at us already that there could not be many more to fire.
3. 'Hostile' had fired no torpedoes at all so far and 'Wash' wanted to let her have a turn.

George Heppel recorded, "Visibility closed down again and after this part of the engagement ships withdrew. Torpedoes remaining were signalled to Captain (D2), together with the report of damage, which was nil. The situation was then reviewed. We had five good ships, 'Hostile' with her full outfit remaining. This meant that on our most unfavourable intelligence of the enemy strength that we would have to fight one or possibly two ships on patrol on the way out.

"Opinion was divided but the Gunnery Officer and myself were in favour of a last attack with 'Hostile's' torpedoes. The reasoning being that we should have to meet the patrol in any case and our success up till then still held out the possibility of our attack being more than a raid by gaining permanent control of the fjord. Captain (D2) decided on the attack and ships were formed in a loose line ahead and steamed up past Ankenes again. Each ship opening fire in turn and 'Hostile' firing torpedoes."

Cyril appeared able to regain his composure, after having experienced the previous encounters. "Out we came again, still undamaged and feeling on top of the world. We steamed down the fjord about the same distance again, when over the head phones came a similar message as before. The Captain announced, we did more damage, but we are going back in again, but this time we are staying. 'Landing Parties' get prepared."

This led to a dilemma for Cyril, the torpedoes on the forward tubes having been fired, he would now be able to go to his next action station, in his role as an electrician for the 'Repair Party Station' in the engine room. Presently, he was a 'communications number', because at this stage there had been no damage incurred. However, as you have read another duty he could be called upon to do was that of the 'Landing Party' team. As it happens, the events that are about to follow made this irrelevant.

In the meantime Cyril's thoughts now were about returning 'whence they came'. "So another quick turn around and back for our third attack. This time we didn't go into the harbour, there was too much damage and blazing oil on the water. Also the merchant ship near the entrance was sinking, very nearly blocking it. Enemy guns were still firing and this time our wireless aerial came crashing down."

Dougy Bourton: "The two attacks we went through, the only thing we had was a two inch hole in the after funnel, a piece of paint flew off and it cut my 'Gun Layer' and made a tiny cut on the side of his nose. We were laughing like hell, to say he had been wounded in action. This was a source of great amusement to us."

0544 2nd D F from D2 – Proceed at 20 knots.

The ships were initially in line but Captain Warburton-Lee, in an attempt to be more fruitful in engaging the enemy, allowed the ships to zig-zag at will. The enemy were in a better position to see their targets than the five destroyers, with the harbour still full of smoke and the dense mist having re-appeared. As previously mentioned by Lt Heppel, 'Hostile' was able to finally fire her torpedoes. 'Hostile' at the end of the line fired four torpedoes into the 'unknown' but received a hit herself.

Les Smale: "We were all quite happy and very pleased with our work, but when the Captain ordered yet another attack we weren't quite so keen. It was getting very hot in the harbour and they were ready for us this time, but if the Captain went, we went. For the third time we entered the harbour and they were more than ready. After seeing the effect of our own torpedoes, I know, there was no one not anxious to see the effect of one of theirs on us. Each time one came towards for us 'Full speed ahead' was ordered and we turned towards it, to present as small a target as possible. On one occasion we had just evaded one, only to run into the path of another.

"I honestly believed that my heart stopped beating as I held my breath, together with everyone else; as we waited helplessly for the explosion to occur. But it never came despite the fact that it passed right under us and the general belief that the German torpedoes were all fitted with 'magnetic heads'. If they were, then we owe our lives to our 'deguassing' gear.

"With that thrill over and two of our 'foes' burning and the shore batteries silenced, we turned from the harbour for the last time. The wreckage in the harbour would have to be seen to be believed, so I can make no attempt to describe it adequately, other than to say it was immense."

Cyril and other crew on the upper deck were starting to wonder where will all this end? "My pal Bill Pimlett dropped to the deck. I watched him crawl for'd on his belly. That was the last I saw of him. He was killed shortly afterwards at his 'Repair Party Station'."

Dougy Bourton remained at his gun at the after end of the ship, waiting for the command to provide a 'sitrep' (situation report). "The ships had regrouped, and the Captain had decided to make one last attack. This we felt was pushing it, we were not happy about this because by now of course, everybody in the area were well and alive and we knew now that this was going to become troublesome. Anyway, we went in and did a third attack, blasted everything, as I said that looked like a German ship, whether they were sinking or floating. We came out, formed line ahead and set off down the fjord."

Geoff Bailey at the for'd end of the ship provides his account of the third attack. "We still had a few 'tin fish' left so in we went again and fired these at the pier and jetty; at the same time narrowly missing being hit by one ourselves fired by one of their crippled destroyers. Luckily it passed underneath us. By now the harbour was in chaos and when we came out there was hardly anything left in the harbour which hadn't either been sunk or badly damaged by shell or torpedoes and we felt quite proud of ourselves – but not for long."

13

Retreat into the Fjord and to Open Sea

Geoffrey Stanning: "'Wash' himself suddenly sighted what looked like a cruiser and two destroyers coming towards us from the direction of Rombaks Fjord. They were obviously enemy ships and we opened fire at each other simultaneously. Whether it did us good or harm that the visibility increased just at that moment I don't know but if it had kept down for few minutes longer we might even have collided with them."

0553 2nd D F from D2 – Withdraw.

Stanning continues, "'Wash' ordered the signal to withdraw red 'Very light' and thirty knots; Clark (Lt Gunnery) protested that we were hitting them and wanted to stay and have a crack at them. But just at that moment two more ships appeared ahead and Cross (Lt Signals) said 'Birmingham'. The distance was about four miles, I should think. I looked at them through glasses and caught sight of hoods on the funnels and knew they were not Birmingham's whatever else they were. We had 'Jane's' on the Bridge, so I looked it up in that, found they were large German destroyers and convinced 'Wash'. It looked as if we were in a tight corner."

These were 'Wolfgang Zenker', 'Erich Koellner' and 'Erich Giese', which originally were sent to Herjangsfjord awaiting their turn to be refuelled by 'Jan Wellem'. They had mustered as much speed as was possible to catch up with their adversaries.

First Lieutenant Mansell recounts the moment and a further surprise. "As we crossed the entrance we suddenly saw a large German ship with two destroyers coming down the fjord towards us. It seemed as if it was time for us to go and a red rocket to be fired. We raced away down the fjord firing at the enemy astern of us. Suddenly we sighted two more ships ahead. 'They're our cruisers' said someone, but they weren't, they were two large German destroyers. We were caught between two forces and 'Hardy' and 'Hunter', the two leading ships were coming under the fire of both."

0556 2nd D F from D2 – Keep on engaging enemy.
– This was the last signal made by Capt D2.
0558 D2 from Hostile – Three Destroyers leaving harbour.
0559 Signal passed in by Hunter. No reply from Hardy.
– Only Hostile and Havock making call signs.

Les Smale: "As we passed the harbour entrance, with our guns facing aft and firing a few 'farewell' shots, we felt to a certain extent relieved. But when, all of a sudden, 'Alarm Bearing Red five degrees' was ordered we were all taken by surprise. There was no need to look, for we knew in a moment that we had met the enemy once more and to his advantage. He must have been waiting for us."

George Heppel: "As 'Hardy' cleared the entrance three enemy ships were seen coming out of Herjangs or Rombaks fjords and the signal to withdraw and increase speed to 30 knots was immediately made. Each ship in turn engaged this unit with 'A' arcs open and must have caused considerable damage. 'Hardy' made smoke, fire was returned from the enemy's foremost guns but 'Hardy' was not hit.

"The leading ship of this unit seemed very large and in error was reported as a cruiser. All our ships were steaming westward at thirty knots when two large ships were sighted coming out of the thinning snow ahead, at a range of five or six thousand yards. It was thought possible that they were some support for us, possibly including 'Penelope'. As they turned we made the challenge but both ships opened fire, I think on 'Hardy'."

The two German destroyer ahead were the 'Bernd von Arnim' and 'Georg Thiele' anchored in the Ballangen Bay also previously awaiting their turn to be refuelled.

Stanning: "The two Germans ahead turned to port and opened fire and we engaged them, leaving the other three to our rear ships. I think it must have been at this moment, when we were taking on the two ahead and 'Wash' wanted the others to go on with the other three, that he made his last signal: 'Keep on engaging the enemy', but I don't remember it being made. We also had an enemy report. We were being hit by then and evidently doing them some damage, but they were uncomfortably accurate and I felt several hits forward. Then there was a tremendous explosion on the Bridge."

Heppel: "'Hardy' replied with the foremost guns and turned to port; the after group (guns) shifted target from the enemy on the starboard quarter as soon as it could follow director. The range was now short and becoming shorter at a rate of about forty knots and 'Hardy' began to be hit hard. The right hand enemy ship shifted target from us as our other ships engaged him, but I am quite unable to give any account of the subsequent fire distribution either side."

The 'Hardy' having manoeuvred out from the third attack, as previously mentioned, Cyril had other tasks which required him to be on his toes and prioritise. "I didn't go immediately down to my alternative action station, the engine room, but stayed near the tubes with my headset on in case I received an order to 'make smoke' from the canisters at the stern. I was facing aft as we tore away from the harbour, so I didn't see the German ships straight away. The first I knew was when I heard shouts on the Bridge through the headset, 'Ships on starboard quarter, three in number!' The Captain had spotted these ships and he immediately ordered 'Open fire'. They were near enough to be recognised as enemy ships. They returned our fire.

"We kept course down the fjord. All we could do was fire our after guns, and then a chase took place at thirty knots, full speed. We had not gone very far, I think Narvik to Ballangen, about twenty miles. When all of a sudden through the mist and swirling snow, two big ships crossed our bows. The Captain thinking they were two of our cruisers signalled by 'Aldis lamp' 'Are you the Cleopatra and Penelope?' They did not reply – just let go with full salvoes. These were the 'Georg Thiele' and 'Bernd von Arnim'. The 'Hardy' being the lead ship took the brunt of it and one of the salvoes hit the Bridge. At this moment we started to be hit very heavily forward and we began to turn to port; at the same time, making black smoke from our funnels. This helped to cover the actions of our ships in line ahead – astern of us."

Geoff Bailey went on to describe a few minutes in his life which were to be forever etched on his memory. "As we came out of the harbour for the last time we saw two grey ships approaching head-on at full speed. We thought it was more help, as though we had needed it. We were mistaken; it was help all right, but for the enemy in the shape of two destroyers heavily armed. 'Enemy bearing right ahead!' I bellowed, I almost lost my tonsils doing so. Our guns were still pointing to the harbour and we lost precious seconds in bringing them to bear on the enemy.

"Jock (Able Seaman 'Gunner' Henry Lang) looked around the gunshield as the enemy came at us at full speed. 'Now we are for it', he murmured, 'You're telling me', I replied, as he slew around on his gunlayer's seat and gripped his gunlayer's handles and stared at his pointer intently. Looking at him gave me confidence. All of this was happening in seconds and then came the enemy's first salvo, CRACK, CRACK! They landed either side of us, sending spray high into the air and then we fired our guns. The enemy's second salvo came over. I saw a flash, felt the ship shudder."

The First Lieutenant, Mansell's duty at this stage was to roam the ship to feed back information to the command. "Everything seemed to go satisfactorily until we were coming out when the first time I realised anything was amiss was a heavy burst in the fore mess deck. I took the place of Able Seaman Naylor (wounded) on the port winch until I could get a relief, as there was a hoist half way up and gradually slipping back.

"When I got relieved I went aft to see what other damage there was and found the ship under very heavy fire, with practically the whole of the starboard side of the 'galley flat' (including the T.S.) demolished. Wounded men were coming to the fore 'dressing station' in fair numbers. I went out the port side onto the iron deck and found bursts dropping all around the ship which was steaming at high speed with all guns firing. I then went forward again on to the mess deck to see about the wounded and the ammunition supply which was being carried on."

Bert Mason: "This time it was different as we had been caught in between German destroyers that had been anchored out of sight up another fjord. Shells were screaming down around us and our Bridge was receiving direct hits. There we were our tube crews totally helpless, hoping for some order to come from the Bridge. One minute our engines were revving up to full speed; the ship twisting and turning; flag signals hoisted at the yard arm; then just as quick, hauled down again. Apparently, a signal had been sent from one of the ships in the harbour about the British attack."

Only Geoff Bailey was able to recall the traumatic moments of what happened next to No 2 Gun crew. "I didn't realise at the time that we had been hit. I heard someone scream. I gripped my range dial wheels more tightly to prevent myself from screaming, our loading was great. Everyone kept shouting and praying, 'Please God help us.' 'Get that ammunition up here' was the last words he ever uttered, there was a great roar, and a blinding flash and I was flung up against the gunshield and felt a burning sensation on my face. I put my hand to my face and felt warm blood coursing down it. I pulled myself erect and then noticed my hand was shattered. I wanted to faint, but couldn't. I looked around; everything seemed to be on fire, the deck was a shambles."

Dougy Bourton: "They opened fire and hit us immediately; they couldn't miss. We made smoke, covering our ships. The three on our starboard quarter engaged with the ships astern. I can remember the first salvo – it hit us on the starboard side. There they were firing on the starboard bow; I remember feeling our ship moving sideways through the water, just pushed sideways. They hit us again several times, blew away the Bridge – awful mess – and slowly but surely it was evident to me something drastic had happened because the ship was losing way and slowly moving to port."

Les Smale remained on the Bridge as the salvoes came in, described that moment. "For an instant, shells were crashing into us. I found myself at the bottom of the ladder behind the wheelhouse and was thrown flat on the deck by a shell which blew off the steel door on the port side. I was protected by the barbette support of the director; fragments of the door or shell injured the two signalmen who were with me. I put them into the Navigator's cabin and dived into the Captain's cabin myself."

From Les' recollections and at a later date those provided by Ralph Brigginshaw, it appears that Ralph was probably one of the two Signalmen placed in the safety of the Navigator's cabin. Below the Bridge was the wheelhouse, aft of which was both the Navigator's cabin (port side) and, adjacent, the Captain's sea cabin (starboard side).

Charles Cheshire the young man brought up in a Children's Home who was determined to have a life at sea was at his alternative action station in the wheelhouse. Under the circumstances, no one would have blamed him at this moment for having had second thoughts about his decision to join the Navy, due to what happened next. "You couldn't distinguish whether it was our guns going off or we were being hit. We couldn't see what was going on; the 'dead lights' were down. The Coxswain had come off the wheel and was just sat down at the back of the wheelhouse. What had happened I don't know, whether it was a blast or what I don't know, anyway he was dead. From what I could see there was not a mark on him.

"It wasn't long before the lights had gone out; in fact, I found myself in the Captain's sea cabin, which was at the rear of the wheelhouse. It was while I was in there that I could see small holes coming up through the floor. A shell had burst below and shrapnel was coming up. I thought, well I'll get out and went next door to the Navigators' cabin, where he kept all his charts. But the lights had gone I got on the wheel but there was nobody on the Bridge at that time anyway; they were either dead or wounded. As far as I could see it wasn't answering the helm. I couldn't see where we were going anyway. The compass was a gyro compass, what was called a 'strip compass'; I suppose there was a film inside with all the degrees. We had lost power and that had gone out. The magnetic compass, well you couldn't see that because there were no lights, but there was nobody up there to give orders."

Les continues, "Another salvo crashed in and something hit my head but I wasn't hurt. Self preservation I guess took me to the port side – but just as I got to there the Telegraphist came out of the wheelhouse shouting that the Coxswain was dead."

Walter Mitchell, still only nineteen (who nine months before was employed as a shop assistant) was one of five in No 3 Gun crew. Luck on his side, he managed to survive the salvoes which also hit the midships gun turret and its platform, just aft of the flag deck. He lived to be able to tell his story to a local newspaper, the 'Evesham Journal', which in my opinion was a somewhat banal description of the events and did not take into account the horrifying scene the young sailors had to face. This is an extract from the newspaper:

"He escaped with only a minor injury – nothing more than a small surface wound from a spent piece of shrapnel. Mitchell and his comrades had been firing their average of more than ten rounds a minute, until the Captain of the gun crew was injured from the first shell which fell on the platform. Mitchell, who was the 'load number' moved over to take his place and less than a second later another shell exploded almost on the spot where he had been standing and killed three of his comrades. This second shell put the gun out of action. 'I will always believe in future that "He who hesitates is lost", he confided'."

I cannot say for certain the names of those other four in No 3 Gun crew with Walter Mitchell. Although, seventy-two years later with the help of Les Smales, it is possible that the 'injured' Gun Captain was either Leading Seaman Edward Plant, who in fact died in the action, or Able Seaman Hugh Argent who was wounded and survived. There remain three courageous young sailors killed who I have been unable to account for, two of which were probably part of the gun crew, Seamen Hugh Mantle and George Matthews, and Able Seaman Billy Wearen.

Stan Robinson recalled the moment they were first confronted by the attacking enemy destroyers. "The Germans' technique of gunnery was superb; they fired over, they fired over and then they hit. They always hit with the third salvo. It wasn't long before they were hitting us left, right and centre." He adds that when the end of the battle came, "The Germans were firing from point blank range, about 300 yards away. That's why they had some direct hits on us, especially on the Bridge, so we couldn't get out of the way to abandon ship."

Geoff Bailey was severely wounded but alive, when horror confronted him again. "Jock was lying on the deck, I recognised him by his coat, his head had been blown off. Lying up against the guardrails was AB (Jack) Hay with a terrible wound to his head. The Captain of the gun lay sprawled on his side, his face a mass of blood. Where were the others, had they all been killed? I got down on the gun deck. A German destroyer passed at that moment firing like hell. Shells were thudding into the ship's side, screaming overhead, it was – hell with a vengeance."

Coincidently, Jack Hay, the boxer with potential, had also formed a relationship. David Taylor, Jack's nephew who provided the previous information about Jack, explains, "My mother Hilda was Jack's younger sister; she was aged sixteen when Jack was killed. His parents, Lawrence and Mary, my grandparents, were unaware that during the 'Hardy' refit at Devonport in January 1940, Jack had married a Plymouth girl called Violet Ruby Bedwell." David goes on to tell the remainder of the story in a later chapter.

Geoffrey Stanning, feeling stunned, gradually regains consciousness, sees utter destruction and bodies covered in blood all around the Bridge; a never to be forgotten sight he would remember for the rest of his life. "I found myself coming down and falling on the gyro compass and ended up very much in the same place as I had started, about half way between the Asdic set and the gyro compass. Lt Cross had been at his desk (W/T Remote Control Station), Clark on the starboard side of the Bridge forward, 'Wash' by the Asdic Set and Gordon-Smith behind the gyro compass. 'Torps' I thought had been somewhere about too.

"I had the same sort of feeling of shock that one has if one is carrying a tray of very valuable china and drops it. 'Wash' was now lying on his back, breathing, but with a terrible wound on the side of his face and another in his side. Pilot (Gordon-Smith) was lying on his face, down the step-down from the compass platform and was kicking. There was no other sign of life at all. I remember thinking that the Bridge had suddenly got very dirty and there was a frightful smell of cordite fumes; both compasses were broken and I think the chart table had gone."

Able Seaman Thomas Watson, like his messmate Austin McNamara from Bolton, was described later by his local newspaper as "the 'Range Finder' on the Bridge, he was very lucky as there were a number either killed, or injured with shrapnel wounds". In 2012, I wrote to the newspaper to see if they would print my letter, where I explained I was trying to contact Thomas or his family. But to no avail.

Geoffrey Stanning, who was in shock, put his mind to prioritising. "I had a feeling of loneliness and it seemed as if I must be the only person alive in the ship at all. But the ship was steaming at speed and making for the southern shore and I suddenly came to and realised that unless something was done about it at once we should be on the 'bricks'. I think I probably hailed the wheelhouse and got no reply, for I suddenly came to the conclusion that I should have to go down there myself. I must have been standing on my right foot because I put my left foot to the deck and found something had happened to it and I could not walk on it; I remembered the terrific jerk of the explosion. On the way I rolled Pilot over on his back in the narrow alley by the torpedo control instruments and left him as comfortable as I could.

"Sliding down the ladder to the wheelhouse, I found it a shambles, saw some debris of bodies about but don't remember seeing the Coxswain's body or anyone else's. I turned the wheel to starboard and rather to my surprise it felt as if it was still all right. The ship had been darkened of course and there was nowhere to look out and see what affect the wheel had had but luckily the iron cover of the centre square window was hanging and by pushing it open I could look through. The ship had answered the helm and was swinging so fast to starboard and towards the enemy that I put some port wheel on, and then had another look. For what seemed like some time, but could not have been more than a minute or two, I went on steering the ship down the fjord having to hop to the square window and lift up the flap to look through at intervals to see where we were going."

At this point I take you to another paragraph in Peter Dickens' book (page 80), where he captures that moment most brilliantly and aptly. "Step by step, each time splitting the difference, Stanning achieved a roughly steady westerly course. The impression was growing on him that he was quite alone in the ship, but after what seemed to him a long time but could not have been more than a minute or two, his 'Man Friday' turned up in the form of Able Seaman Smale and Stanning hobbled and hoisted himself up to the bridge."

Geoffrey Stanning, who let us not forget, was the Paymaster, not a specialised seaman officer, continues with his account. "Then Able Seaman Smale appeared in the doorway and I told him to come and take the wheel and that I would go back to the compass platform. I think he must have been one of several ratings who took shelter in the chart house, and that he was the first to come to his senses and decided to go out and see if there was anything to be done. I was more than glad to see him, especially as he had been my servant (messenger at call) and I knew what a reliable chap he was."

Cyril described the damage caused by the enemy to 'Hardy': "The shelling had done a lot of damage to our forward guns, they hit the Bridge, killing Lt Clarke the Gunnery Officer, Lt Cross the Signals Officer, mortally wounded the Captain, and severely wounded Lt Commander Gordon-Smith. The only man who could move around was Lt Paymaster Stanning. They kept on pounding us and we turned to port so that all the hits that were coming in were on the starboard side.

"The next to be hit was the wheelhouse; Chief Coxswain Heal who was on the wheel, was killed. A nice chap, liked by all the ship's company and his death was a vital blow to the ship at that moment of the action. In the meantime, the T.S. (Guns Transmitting Station) had been hit; this is the part of ship where the guns were controlled from. A shell had come in through the 'Canteen Flat' hit my pal Bill Pimlett in the middle of his back, the chap I last saw going forward on his belly.

"It then entered the T.S. and severed the legs of the two operators who were sat on high legged stools. Then it exploded blowing up the table which housed all the controls. The other two operators sitting opposite didn't get a scratch. They carried their two mates out onto the iron deck, putting them on their 'stumps' against the funnel and gave them a cigarette. The next vital place to be hit was the Torpedomen's mess deck which housed the gyro compass and Asdic cabinet."

Tragically, one of those killed in the T.S. was the man who had dedicated part of his life to the sport of gymnastics,

Leading Seaman Ron Cockayne, the Royal Naval Reservist, who had had to leave his pregnant wife Sarah Ann and their seven year old daughter Jean. In a later chapter you will read about the birth of Sarah Ann's second daughter named Jill and how by chance, after seventy years, I was able to make contact with her.

The other operator next to Ron Cockayne in the T.S. was Able Seaman Andrew Whearty, who as you will read, died later.

Dougy Bourton, the ex grammar school pupil from Ebbw Vale, although appearing years older than his age, moved a step further up in maturity. "You don't have fear when these shells come over. We were so trained, call it being 'brain-washed'; there's a hole in the end of a gun, you put a cartridge in it, you close the breach, somebody pulls the trigger or presses the pedal. You do it automatically; it's not until afterwards, that 'whirring' that went over, could have been a fifteen inch shell, you think 'Christ!', what would it have done on this gun deck: it would have torn the ship in two. So, actually at that time, I can't honestly say that I felt afraid, because things happen so fast. It's like looking at a picture; the adrenalin is flowing certainly when the enemy is in sight."

Les Smale, another young man from a village in Devon who seems to have been born to a life in the Navy, put his fear to one side. "I, for no reason I can explain, went into the wheelhouse and took over the wheel from Lieutenant Stanning, the Paymaster, who said he was going back to the Bridge. The wheelhouse was a shambles. It was not till I was actually on the job that I realised the danger I was in but consoled myself by thinking that, 'if this was my day, then it was my day'. I felt better.

"I couldn't make contact with the Bridge and my repeated calls through the voice-pipe of, 'wheelhouse to Bridge' were unanswered. I was left to my own initiative as to what I should do. Looking through the gaping shell holes in the wheelhouse side, I could see for the first time the German ships. There were five of them, two ahead and three to starboard."

In the meantime, another officer on the Bridge at the time is alive and well enough to continue his emergency duties. George Heppel, 'Torps', survived the direct salvoes and this would prove to be a most fortunate stroke of luck that enabled him to go on and play a crucial role in future events, more ways than one.

George had been at the back of the Bridge when it was hit and was saved by the 'trunk' of the director. "I was hit by two small splinters from what must have been the hit in the wheelhouse when I was at the after end of the Bridge. Leading Signalman Reed reported to me that everyone on the signal deck and in the wheelhouse was out of action. I wrongly assumed that the wheel was out of action too, so I ran aft to get the ship under control from there. Judging from 'Hotspur's' damage my assumption had good grounds but unfortunately I was wrong." George made his assumption having later learnt about 'Hotspur's' dilemma in having collided with 'Hunter'.

The First Lieutenant Victor Mansell: "Heavy impacts were being felt and Nos 1 and 2 Guns were put out of action by direct hits, ammunition was supplying to No 4. I went aft again and found the galley flat full of steam and smoke and when I got outside, the ship was slowing up rapidly and heading for shore. It was reported to me that the main steam had gone and then I got a message that everyone on the Bridge had been killed."

Geoffrey Stanning: "I was thankful to have 'Smale' on the wheel and be able to go back to the compass platform (Bridge) and see what the situation looked like from there, where one could see what was happening. When I got back, I don't think I gave any helm order immediately, as we were going on down the fjord. But I realised that something would have to be done in a moment as we were getting nearly abreast the German ships. I looked forward and saw that both Nos 1 and 2 Guns were completely out of action, although some of the after guns seemed to be firing still. The question was whether to try and rush past the Germans or whether to try and ram them, which I knew, were probably the proper thing to do next.

"Then I remembered about the other ships and went to the starboard side of the Bridge to look and see what was happening to them. I don't remember ever seeing them as I had just got to the side of the Bridge, when what seemed like a whole salvo seemed to hit the engine and boiler room and a cloud of steam came up. The ship began to slow down and I came to the conclusion that the entire engine room department must have been wiped out; actually only one man was wounded by that salvo which I regard as altogether miraculous. Steam must have been let out in so many places at once that there was no question of anyone being injured by escaping steam."

George Heppel was out and about but found that he had to do another 'lungs bursting' sprint. "I was about to steer by main engines when I found that the ship was still under control from forward and so I ran forward again, found Able Seaman Smale at the wheel, who said he was still getting helm orders. I went to the Bridge and found that the Secretary had given the last order. I cancelled it at first in order to take the ship down the fjord, although we were losing our way. He told me that he, and I think, Lieutenant Fallwell from the director, had decided, as main steam had been lost and damage was most severe, to beach the ship."

14

Beach or Not

Geoffrey Stanning, notwithstanding being an injured man, was in a quandary as to his next move. "There was no one alive to be seen anywhere and I felt absolutely alone; it seemed to me that there could not be more than about twenty people left alive in the ship. There was no one to send to see what was happening and it sounded as if the ship was no more use. We still had considerable way on and I came to the conclusion that the best thing to do would be to put the ship ashore. In parenthesis here I would say that I was more than worried afterwards by having taken this decision and was not convinced I had done right for some time. The considerations which I did, or ought to have weighed seem to have been as follows and there is no doubt that I thought of some of them at the time, though unquestionably not all.

1. "The ship was no more use as a fighting unit and there seemed to be hardly anyone left alive in it.
2. "It is wrong to put a ship ashore in enemy territory where he might be able to get at the considerable amount of secret gear in the ship, not to mention ciphers and codes.

3. "I did not know how to sink the ship myself, and quickly; if I undertook to try this I thought I should have to do the work almost entirely myself and I knew I could not get very far with my injured foot.
4. "I thought there was a reasonable chance of my being able to destroy a great deal of stuff with the aid of Smale, who knew at any rate where a good deal of my stuff was, and if we were ashore it would take the enemy some time to get at us, more than if we were drifting about in the fjord.

"I think most of these four considerations were in my mind as well as the most potent one of all – self-preservation. So, I decided to put the ship ashore. There was not much time to be lost, as the ship was losing way fairly quickly but I wanted if possible to reach some houses a few hundred yards from the shore so that we could take shelter; one of them was hit by a shell as I looked and set on fire. This may have been an outbuilding of Mrs Kristensen's farm. I put '10 of port wheel on' to bring the ship gently towards the shore and just after Heppel appeared; it was a long time before I discovered what had been happening to him and I wondered what had become of him between the time of the Bridge being hit and the time he re-appeared.

"When Heppel arrived on the compass platform, he found me there and roughly the following exchange of views took place:

"Heppel, 'What are you doing?'

"Stanning, 'Going on the bricks'.

"Heppel, 'You can't do that, midships-starboard 20'.

"Stanning, 'I think I put my elbow in the voice pipe as Smale never got the order'.

"Stanning, 'We must; we won't go anymore'.

"Heppel, 'What d'you mean?'

"Stanning, 'Well you bloody fool, there's no more steam!'

"I felt extremely bad tempered and irritable."

Heppel later stated, "I concurred at once and ordered 'port twenty' on to the shelving beach and I accept shared responsibility for this step."

Bill Pulford was at his action station with the 'Repair Party', in charge of the aft electrical switch board. Any electrical equipment or lighting damaged during battle would have to be isolated, as well as re-directing supplies from the 'forward' switch board to other 'after' services still workable. "I went up deck for a breather and to see how things were going. I saw 'Hunter' coming up astern of us. She had been hit and was on fire forward. Her No 1 Gun was a mass of flames. We were sustaining hits then. These five German destroyers having challenged them, they replied by opening fire, so we knew we had our work cut out.

"Our two foremost guns were engaging, but we had to alter course to port a shade to bring our after gun battery back into a bearing gunfire position. I was still aft at the time when that shell hit the main steam pipe. Then everything stopped, engines stopped, dynamos came off the switch board indicators and all lights went out. My first indication then was towards the steering motors. I thought the 'after' power switch board had gone, so I had to try and arrange power supplies from the for'd to the steering motors, so we could steer the boat."

The electrical system was run on what was called a 'Ring Main', which carries the power around the ship. Should a dynamo or its appropriate section of the Ring Main become damaged, then the interlinking fuses automatically blow. This then isolates the damaged section. Consequently, the loss of the steam will result in the engines becoming ineffective, halt the dynamos from turning and then losing the ship's electrical power. This obviously leaves the ship disabled and presents a winning advantage to the enemy.

In the meantime, Cyril was in a position to see how the action was affecting the other ships of the flotilla. "I was watching this ship (Hunter), as she was the next in line, suddenly receive a direct hit on what seemed to be her bottom as she heeled over on the turn."

The accounts provided by Hunter's crew members regarding their own experiences of the 'First Battle' and the eventual sinking of their ship will be told in my next book. However, subsequently Cyril was to be told, "Hunter had been hit by salvoes in the engine room and her steering gear had been put out of action, and as she had slewed away out of control the next ship in line the 'Hotspur' had rammed her."

Cyril explains the desperate plight confronted by 'Hardy': "The room for manoeuvring was limited; we could not get past the two groups of enemy ships. Their guns were larger than ours and although we were hitting them hard we were getting more in return. I had gone down to the engine room as soon I saw 'Hunter' get hit and when I realised we were being hit forward."

Whilst the five destroyers' guns were 4.7 inch, the Germans' guns were the equivalent of almost 6 inch.

By now, Bert Mason, still feeling helpless on seeing 'Hunter' in "dire distress on fire and sinking", recalls, "Then from the Bridge came an order, 'Light a smoke float – aft. After a quick word with the others, I armed myself with a box of matches and dashed aft. On reaching the quarter-deck, I could see No 5 Gun firing astern, the Warrant-Gunner, Mr McCracken standing near and the decks awash from fire hoses. I crawled on my hands and knees below the gun muzzle and as I reached the smoke float I could see black smoke pouring from our funnels. I knew I had to get the smoke canister working quickly to make an effective screen."

White smoke has to mingle with black to allow it to cling closer to the surface of the water.

In the meantime, Les Smale was still at the wheel. "We were close to the shore so I steered a course that kept us as close as I dared and hoped we wouldn't go aground. In a little while contact was made to Lt Stanning on the Bridge and he ordered, 'Hard a starboard, we are going to ram'. I felt fit for anything now but almost immediately it was cancelled by 'Hard to port, we're going ashore'. I put the helm over to port. Just as we were about to go aground the Midshipman (Pope) came into the wheelhouse shouting, 'You're going aground...you're going aground' – and ran the engine telegraphs to full astern. It had no effect as the engines had lost steam due to the hit in the boilers and it was because of this loss of power that Lt Stanning had changed from ramming the enemy ships to taking the 'Hardy' ashore."

By now, Bert was desperate: "Everything was wet I could not get the damn thing to ignite. Through my mind, there was one thought; when this was all over the Captain would want to know why we had not obeyed orders to ignite a smoke float. Again, I was being plagued over the thought of the torpedo tubes coming around so slowly and considered we might have missed a chance with the remaining torpedo because we had moved off target. He was sure to delve to the bottom of things! Giving up, I started making my way back to the others. Things had gone strangely quiet. When I got by the 'Gunner' McCracken, he turned and said 'It's all over'. I said 'Why'. He answered – 'We're aground'."

First Lieutenant Mansell: "By this time there was much damage inside the ship, and many would say that they only escaped because all hammocks were slung and stopped splinters from flying about. Two more guns went out of action leaving only one firing."

The mess decks had to have all movable items (such as personal belongings including hammocks and bedding) well stowed away as these could cause damage or injuries in a battle. As well as clogging up emergency pumps that assisted in keeping the 'water tight integrity' of the ship. In fact, new procedures were changed to the extent that the 'Chief Shipwright' and his team would complete rounds of all parts of the ship to make sure that this was the case and report back to the First Lieutenant. The mess decks were also utilised for holding 'First Aid' or 'Damage Repair' parties. The author would add that the above procedure was applied in his time in the Navy and may have been different in 1940.

Bill Pulford: "I got down to the after switch board, it was dark and a voice from up top bawled out, 'Abandon Ship Below!' I don't know how I felt then, this wasn't an exercise. Although we had exercised abandon ship dozens of time in the past, this was for real. My stomach sort of hit the deck. Anyhow, what brought me together was a voice from above bawling out, 'Get the wounded out, we have got to get the wounded ashore'. I thought hell 'wounded' that means we are in shallow water. My first thought then was to put the depth charges to 'Safe' which were aft."

In hindsight Cyril believed, "The enemy may have been concentrating on 'Hardy' because we were the 'Leader' of the flotilla. We certainly took most of the initial punishment but then it was the turn of 'Hunter' and 'Hotspur'. During the latter stages our other two ships ('Havock' and 'Hostile') were able to make their escape down the fjord. This is not meant to reflect on the bravery of our comrades in the other two ships; they fought as well as we did, doing a lot of damage to the enemy and suffering casualties against odds far too great for such small ships. If any men who took part in the battle on those ships ever get round to read this story, I hope they will believe me when I say how pleased survivors from 'Hardy' were when we heard that their ships had escaped down the fjord."

In my next book, I explain how both 'Havock' and 'Hostile' were able to continue to play major roles in the aftermath of the 'First Battle'.

By now, with all torpedoes gone, Cyril had arrived at his next port of call. "When Bill Pimlett left me, I tried to get a response from the Bridge. When I heard nothing (there was nobody alive up there to hear me) I decided to go to my next action station in the engine room. Here I had my bag of tools, and my job was to stand by in case there was any electrical damage. I was with the Engineer Commander [Alan Coe] and the Warrant Engineer [George Coggan] for five minutes when the engines packed up.

"We all looked at each other and the Commander said 'this is it, we have had it'. He told me to go to the upper deck and find out what was happening. The ship was gliding towards the shore. I went up the ladder, and as I opened the hatch, the First Lieutenant was bending down to open it. I noticed that he had smoke coming from his pistol and I thought, 'Good God, he's gone off his head and shot somebody! I was about to drop back down the ladder when he said, 'Cope, tell the Engineer Commander it's every man for himself, abandon ship'. I went down the ladder fast, gave the message, and led the way back up the ladder with the officers and the engine staff following."

Irrespective of the pandemonium all around them, the torpedo crew make one more effort to strike at the enemy.

Bill Pulford, who was still aft sorting out the necessary procedures that he had been trained for, now moved forward. "The searchlight platform was all twisted – gone! A voice called out 'Pulford give me a hand, there's one torpedo left!' It was Lt Heppel at the after 'tubes' which were jammed."

Bert Mason then became involved. 'Out on the upper deck there was some activity around the after torpedo tubes. The Torpedo Officer, along with some Torpedomen was preparing to fire the remaining torpedo, which they did. Whether he intended ditching it to prevent it falling into enemy hands or whether he hoped it would hit one of the enemy destroyers patrolling some distance away, I cannot say. But within some ten minutes the defenceless 'Hardy' was again being shelled, causing more casualties."

Les Smale, when looking back on events, believed that during the ensuing battle a report had come to the Bridge that a fog lamp on the flagstaff had shattered and fragments had jammed the breach of No 5 Gun. This led to No 5 Gun ammunition being fed up to No 4 Gun to allow it to continue firing, probably as a last ditch attempt, at the enemy.

Bill Pulford: "Towards the end of the action, when 'Hardy' had lost all power and had suffered severe damage and many casualties – I heard a voice from No 4 Gun bawling out for more ammunition. Mind you the language wasn't too clever. 'We're still firing and fuck all is going to stop us, we're going on until we have got no bloody shells.' There were volunteer ammunition supply parties going around to all the magazines, getting the shells and trying to get them up to No 4 Gun."

Returning to Cyril's account: "The next main damage to the ship – another salvo hit the two forward guns, killing some of the men. Then No 3 Gun, which was between the funnels – was completely wiped out with all the gun crew killed. The Captain of the gun crew was probably Leading Seaman 'Gunner' Edward Plant, the other six members of his crew were all young sailors, some of whom had come onto the ship for six months before going on to 'Officers Training'. One had a 'Bachelor of Science' degree and another 'Bachelor of Arts' degree."

I have not been able to substantiate the credibility of these so called 'young sailors' being on board for 'Officers Training'. However, Les Smale believed the salvo which destroyed No 3 Gun was also the one that hit the Bridge, the main steam pipe and a whaler.

Nineteen year old Dougy Bourton at No 4 Gun appeared to want to take the enemy on single handed if need be. For his brave actions he was eventually awarded the Distinguished Service Medal. Here Dougy describes the last attempt to inflict damage on the attacking German destroyers. "In the meantime we carried on firing and we fired as they passed us. One of these ships ran aground on the other side of the fjord, but we were too busy to bother about it. But eventually, our ship had stopped; we carried on firing at the ships belting down the fjord, still firing at us.

"Then we heard the order 'Abandon Ship'. There was one funny happening during this time in which the 'Gunner' and myself took part. The gun crew had gone to look for ammunition and I was firing on my own at the time. The 'Gunner' Mr McCracken (Warrant Officer), who was the 'Officer of the Quarter Deck', stuck his head through the hatchway and said, 'Can I give you a hand'. So I told him in pure 'navalese', 'Go away and get some more ammunition', which he did, to my surprise, because it wasn't the least bit polite at the time.

"They threw shells up through the hatchway, I had cartridge cases up there, so I carried on firing, still on the starboard quarter the ammunition finally ran out. I fired the last two shells, they were for ordinary practice, made of cast iron filled with sand, but I knew if it hit then it would shatter and still cause a lot of damage. I was firing low at the water line of the ship at deck level, so as to cause as much damage as possible.

"Eventually the last round fired off, the Torpedo Officer came up and shouted, 'Bourton lower the "Ensign"', so I told him, 'Well can't we get more ammunition to carry on Sir'. He said, 'No! That's an order, lower the "Ensign".' So I hauled the seagoing Ensign, the tatty one on the 'gaff', which was immediately above the after gun deck. I tied it to the guardrail and left it there."

Thirty-nine years later, Dougy Bourton would meet the Captain of 'Georg Thiele', namely Korvettenkapitan Max Wolff, at a joint reunion of the British and German veterans of the First Battle of Narvik in Bremerhaven. By now Max was a retired Admiral. Dougy recalled, "I remember one conversation with him. He heard about me firing Hardy's gun. He said, "Doug you were firing at me and I was firing at you." I said, "that's correct Max." He replied, "It's a good thing we were bloody bad shots." Which I thought, just about shows the idiocy and the futility of the whole thing we were engaged in." In a later chapter Dougy recounts more of his meetings with other German veterans who took part in the battle on that fateful day, 10th of April 1940.

Back to the aftermath of battle, and First Lieutenant Victor Mansell, who realised he was now the senior officer on board. "At that moment, No 3 Gun was hit and put out of action, I went up to the Bridge and the ship was ashore. No 4 Gun was still firing. I went down and sent up a party to bring up the Captain and Navigating Officer who were still alive, and then went aft. Lieutenant Heppel reported there was one torpedo left and I gave him orders to fire it. No hit. No 5 Gun was out of action and No 4 Gun's ammunition supply had failed. The ship was under heavy fire from three German destroyers at close range and I gave the order to Abandon Ship."

In collating information from various sources, it has to be expected there will be conflicting accounts, especially taking into account the relatively short time between the Battle's beginning and climatic end. As previously pointed out, the memory is never 100 per cent reliable. Obviously the crew members had gone through an extremely traumatic experience but still in the back of their minds was the thought of self survival.

15

Abandon Ship

As already described, one of the badly injured sailors was nineteen year old 'Gunner' Geoff Bailey, one of seven children, from a South Wales coal mining community. On abandoning ship the predicament faced by the able bodied crew was apprehensively dangerous, but for those suffering from wounds it was even more so. Geoff, having witnessed the carnage around him, started to come to his senses. Geoff recounts, "I was not alone on the gundeck as I thought, for the 'Trainer' came around the gun and asked me if I was all right. I nodded my head. He grimaced, 'That's a bad un', he murmured. I looked down on the upper deck; men were struggling to get the boats out. We were going down very slowly I noticed and we were near the shore. I heard someone shout, 'Abandon Ship'."

Another man who had witnessed death all around him was Walter Mitchell. Once No 3 Gun had been put out of action he walked for'd, making for the Bridge to receive further orders. Obviously this would not have been easy because of the extent of the damage caused by the salvoes. He would have made his way down to the next deck where the starboard whaler had been wrecked by the salvoes. Then, by steel ladders up to the next deck, which was the flag deck and finally to the Bridge. The scene on his transit must have been unimaginable, there were many bodies scattered around dead or dying, including the injured Signalmen Brigginshaw and Turner, as it was this part of ship that had suffered most of the damage. When Walter had managed to arrive at the Bridge, he heard the order "Abandon Ship".

Paymaster Lieutenant Stanning believed that there was still more to be done before going ashore. "At that moment we reached the shallow water and the ship grounded so gently that no one knew at first – even those on the mess deck – that she had gone aground. People at the back of the Bridge then began to come to life again and several signalmen got up as I made my way to the back of the Bridge. I was rather appalled to see that they had already started to abandon ship and was absolutely astounded to see the number of men who poured out.

"The first thing in my mind was to destroy the cyphers and the A/S (Asdic) cabinet and Bridge Set (External Receiver) and I was terribly afraid that everyone would jump overboard before I had time to get people to do all this. I did not know then that almost all the officers were alive and unhurt and I had forgotten and lost sight of Heppel, who had gone to fire his last torpedo at the enemy. He fired it and it hit nothing except a guardrail stanchion as it was going over the side. I scrambled up the flag lockers and called people by name to come and help me.

"I sent a message to Mr McCracken, by the 'Chief Stoker', who I thought could help him, to throw the safes aft into the oil fuel tank outside the Captain's cabin. I told Midshipman 'Pope' to get the naval cyphers out of the chart house, put them in the weighted bag and throw them overboard as far aft as he could. 'Pope', incidentally, had acted with promptitude just before; when he saw the ship was going aground, he rushed to the wheel house from wherever he was and put the engines to full speed astern, not knowing there was no steam.

"Mansell then came up and said that the Asdic cabinet had been blown out of the ship and he confirmed that the set on the Bridge had been destroyed. (This was at that time newly introduced secret equipment and it was crucial it did not end up in German hands.) The doctor was on the Bridge attending to the Pilot. Mansell said the Telegraphist in the R.C. hutch (Remote Control) on the Bridge was pinned in, but Midshipman Pope got something and levered it open and let him out. Mansell then said he wanted to get the motor boat out and went down from the Bridge on the starboard side to help but the after thread of the davit was twisted and we could not turn the boat out. It was full of holes in any case and had no rudder or propeller."

First Lieutenant Mansell reported, "I went forward to see about the books and Asdic cabinet (this had been wrecked by a direct hit just outside it). Paymaster Lieutenant Stanning was organising the destruction of the books which were put in a weighted bag and dropped over the stern, which was probably in deep water. Surgeon Lieutenant Waind was attending the Captain and Navigating Officer. Mr McCracken the Gunner and I had been ordered by the Secretary (Stanning) to dispose of the secret chest in the office aft and this he did by dropping the contents into an oil fuel tank under the Captain's cabin." This was stated in Lt Commander Mansell's narrative for the Admiralty and is now kept in the National Archives at Kew.

Meanwhile, Stanning, limping around the upper deck, was still trying to find a sea worthy vessel: "We then turned to the 'skimmer' which is kept the other side under No 3

Gun deck (midships) and has to be man handled under the torpedo davit normally, so it was not easy to get out. All we wanted was something which would float to take the rest of the wounded ashore in. I sat down with Coe (Commander Engineer), to unreel the wire for the torpedo davit.

"A moment or two later, I looked up and saw the 'Pilot' coming down from the Bridge alone, looking an awful sight but to my surprise apparently more or less all right. He sat down beside me and lighted a cigarette. I went on unreeling the wire but a moment later Pilot suddenly began choking and I thought he was dying as he then lay quite still. I got someone to put him in the narrow cross passage where he would be out of the way. We found the 'skimmer' could not be got out as the stanchion (upright post fixed to the deck structure) supporting Number 3 gundeck was badly bent and the boat could not be got past it. Mansell said he had a Carley float which was floating quite well and he would be able to take the wounded ashore in that. I think the enemy had been shelling the ship sporadically all this time and I remember seeing several shells hit the beach not far from our men going ashore who were going in a thin black stream up the snow. But now the shelling got more intense and we decided to 'abandon ship' finally."

There appears to have been a number of attempts by crew members to negotiate the 'skimmer' into the sea, as you will now read.

Dougy Bourton, having had to be ordered from his 'beloved' gun turret, made his next move towards survival but before then he had to endure the sight of carnage all around him. "Then there was the cry 'Abandon Ship' all over the ship. As I walked for'd, the First Lieutenant came back to the portside of the Bridge and shouted for volunteers to go up and help down the wounded officers. I crossed to the starboard side and carried on up a ladder, which was in a hell of a condition. I got on to the back of the Bridge which was a shambles. The Gunnery Officer Lt Clark, I could only identify by the fact that he wore a pair of skiing boots with black clips on the front that was all that was left of him. The Signal Officer Lt Cross was lying on his back with his eyes open, looking up to the heavens, he was dead in the centre of the Bridge."

Bert Mason provided his observations on the initial reactions to the order 'Abandon Ship'. "There was pandemonium. Some men were already in the water swimming away from the ship. Most of the tubes crew were tugging at lines, securing 'Carley floats' and it was here that my razor sharp trusted seaman's knife came in handy. I undid it on its lanyard around my waist, I slashed binding after binding whilst the others carried anything that would float and dumped it over the side. Then my attention was attracted by a young Asdic rating, Able Seaman Hillier. He was screaming, moaning, crying and gibbering; he was in a terrible state. Two of us got hold of him and shook him but it was no use.

"Down below in the water sat in a craft we had just launched, were the ship's Chief Electrical Artificer and Chief Purser. They were paddling away from the ship's side and when we shouted for them to wait for others, they just ignored us. We thought of chucking Hillier over the side, in the hope he would clamber into the raft, but the other two in it were moving away. Later on Hillier's body was found washed up on the beach, drowned. I am sure with a bit more cooperation from the two in the raft, we could have saved him. I still think about it."

Dougy: "The Captain had been pulled to the back of the Bridge on the port side. He was actually clinging to the side of the Bridge and pointing to the shore, obviously telling everybody to make for the shore, he eventually laid back down."

Les remained at the helm. "I didn't feel the ship ground. I think I stood there at the wheel in a dazed condition for two or three minutes, until someone came by shouting 'Abandon Ship'. I walked (they were not firing at us now) out to the point five machine gun deck and helped two injured signalmen into the sea boat. The whaler was full to overflowing, with no one at the falls to lower it. Someone did come along to perform this duty and took a turn at lowering it as for a normal boat's crew of seven, whereupon the boat went down with a terrific rush and capsized. A Carley float was in the water by now, full of survivors and I remember shouts of 'anyone got a knife?' None was forthcoming; it was needed to cut the paddles free. Some men were beginning to reach the beach and I noticed that the swimming distance was not all that far, and that one could wade half the journey.

"Being a fair swimmer I decided I would stay and help where I could do so. I took off my duffel coat and oilskin and went to the Bridge to give a hand as necessary. The Bridge was in a terrible state with the following casualties. The Captain seriously wounded in the head and arm and unconscious; Signal Officer – dead; Navigator – suffering concussion; Paymaster – with foot injury. I with the 'Middy' (Midshipman) released the Telegraphist from his remote control post, the door of which was jammed shut.

"We then assisted the doctor to bandage the Captain and then put him in a 'Robinson' stretcher (a sort of wrap round affair to prevent the patient falling out) and lowered him to the fo'c'sle deck. We then got the Navigator clear of the Bridge and destroyed what books we thought might be of use to the enemy before finally leaving the Bridge ourselves."

Stan Robinson, from his action station in the Gun Director above the Bridge moved rapidly. "We had already grounded then, all the firing came from the starboard side. All we had to do was clamber over the Bridge down in the port whaler. So I climbed down the ladder to find the port whaler was so badly damaged it sank straight away."

When asked in his interview for the Imperial War Museum "How frightening was it in the Battle?" he replied, "Terrifying, and the average age of the crew was twenty-four. I think the youngest man aboard was eighteen and the oldest the Captain, forty-three."

Dougy: "Then I found the Navigator, who was my particular boss on board, because I was one of four 'Quartermasters' and I had to assist the Midshipmen with chart corrections. A very fine officer was Lt Commander Gordon-Smith. He was standing in a daze, his skull was fractured, I can't add to that. He seemed to be unconscious on his feet. So I'm walking him to the ladder at the back of the Bridge, turned him round, put his hands on the ladder, helping him climb down and his feet and legs moved and finally got him down to the upper deck. I sat him there and someone came along with a cloth or something to try to wipe some of the blood from his face.

"In the meantime, I found they had brought one of our particular shipmates up, Able Seaman Andy Whearty. He had been a good friend of mine. They laid him on the deck. He had been in the 'Transmitting Station'. He was very badly wounded from the waist down, the 'Transmitting Station' table had been blown open and he was badly carved about."

In the Communications Department was twenty year old Victor Gould from Thornton in Lancashire who had been in the Navy since the age of seventeen. He survived to be able to tell his story to the local newspaper 'Fleetwood Chronicle' (dated 3rd May 1940). "As a First Class wireless telegraphist he was in the transmitting room throughout the action," Victor explained, "Outside, it was bitterly cold and a snowstorm was raging when 'Hardy' entered Narvik. Having no time to get excited, the noise of explosions came from the bay. The transmitting station was put out of action through power failing, and a shell that burst in the boiler room brought great clouds of steam from the funnels. The Germans were still pounding the 'Hardy' as she drifted to the beach. When the order to abandon ship was given, the crew jumped into the water and made for shore. We were under fire and just after we had reached land, one member of the crew, somewhere about my own age, who had not been married long, was killed by a shell."

We return to Ned Sparkes, who as Leading Telegraphist would have been one of Victor's mentors. Ned, having been trapped in the small radio office by a buckled steel door, was not given an opportunity to go to his next action station, the Main Communications Office, because of the ship being grounded. "I saw nothing of the action. After swimming ashore, I met up with a bunch of the crew and a friend of mine. This was Leading Seaman Mason. He had the 'Ensign'. Don't ask me how he came by it: I don't recall."

Bert's account of the 'Battle Ensign' will be told later. However, in the meantime he mentions, "When the 'Abandon Ship' order was given, the 'Battle Ensign' flying at the after mast was hauled down, indicating we had surrendered. The Germans sportingly ceased firing on our now helpless boat."

Nineteen year old Walter Mitchell, although probably still in shock, described his next move to the reporter for the 'Evesham Journal'. "When we got that order to leave the ship we slipped over the side into the icy water, and we were then still under fire; but the (German) destroyers soon drew off. We had to swim 200 yards and wade another 100 through that icy water to reach land. It was the coldest bath I have ever had!"

As previously stated by Dougy Bourton, it was he who hauled down the 'Ensign', around the time Bert was aft making a considerable effort to ignite the smoke screen canister. It is important not to confuse the small boats 'Ensign', which Bill Pulford had taken from the Flag Deck, with that of the 'Ensign' on the stern gaff, which is much larger.

Bert continues, "Joe (Sweetland) and I remained together and as the shelling had ceased the general panic subsided. There were a few men left and we were a bit reluctant to go over the side. I think it was then that Gunner McCracken collared me and said he wanted me to help him inside the 'Ship's Office'. He seemed so cool and relaxed as if he were on an everyday job. Pointing to an oil fuel tank cover he said he wanted it opened which was no trouble. He then handed me a bunch of keys; he said one fitted the ship's safe and I was to go through them, one at a time, until I got the safe open.

"We succeeded and then he told me to hold out my arms carefully and take every single paper as he got them out and dumped them in the fuel tank. Midway through this operation he came across some money; £1 notes, ten shilling notes, two shilling pieces and then put them in his pockets. I remember thinking, 'He could have given some of it to me!' But under the circumstances it did not seem much use. The job completed, he banged the safe shut whilst I dropped the lid on the tank."

Bill Pulford, from his account, was also involved in the task of dealing with confidential material, however, a different version to that of Bert Mason's. "'Give us a hand you chaps.' It was the Gunner, Mr McCracken who had the remainder of the confidential books and wanted them thrown over the side. So 'Torps' and I got together and we pitched what was left of them over the side, so they wouldn't get into the hands of the enemy. I then left 'Torps' and made my way forward to the port side, which was the sheltered side. I realised then that we were still being fired at and men running aft with shells."

I would add that Lieutenant Heppel did not mention his involvement in this episode in his report to the Admiralty. However, as you will read shortly he did become involved in destroying confidential material after the ship was finally abandoned.

From the conflicting accounts I have received, only to be expected in times of battle, there appears to be uncertainty as to how many safes were on board. In my view there were at least three safes on board and as the ship was flotilla leader with Captain 'D' probably four. Access would be delegated to officers including those of Warrant Officer rank. These personnel would be the 'custodians' for the keys. This was a precaution so that in times of battle or other unexpected circumstances there would be at least one additional delegated custodian.

For example, I presume Lt Paymaster Stanning was the main custodian of the safe in the ship's office. However, as previously mentioned, he not only had other duties to contend with but was also injured. Therefore, I also presume that Mr McCracken was the second custodian. It seems that this was indeed the case, as described by Bert Mason, and was where cash was kept for the daily running of ship finances. This was for both the ships' companies' fortnightly pay or any other incidental bills that needed to be paid, especially while away from home waters.

There was another occasion when a safe had to be dealt with, respectively the one in the Captain's 'Harbour' cabin. Substantiated from the information given by Lt Heppel in an interview with Peter Dickens for his book (page 102) and also in 1980 from a national newspaper. I quote Lt Heppel: "We had to get clear quickly because explosive charges had been set behind the safes, so that any confidential papers would be destroyed." These obviously relate to the flotilla's operational orders and other classified documents for 'Captain's Eyes Only'.

Diether von Roeder with sentry on Post Quay. *G. Haarr Collection.*

Cargo ship torpedoed by 2nd Destroyer Flotilla. *Tore Eggan Collection.*

John Avery relates how his father, Stoker Gordon Avery, was given an unexpected task before abandoning ship. "My father was called to the Bridge, just as the final few gasps of power allowed the steersman to ground the ship. Lt Stanning ordered my father to take the keys to the ship's safe and remove all coded books and documents, so they would not fall into enemy hands. The overhanging metal decking damaged in the explosion would not permit the safe door to open other than a few inches. My father went to the 'bilges' (depth of the ship in the engine compartments) and coated some rags in thick oily water and neat diesel oil. He rammed this into the safe, locked it again and then threw the key overboard."

It appears that the safe in question was in the Captain's 'Sea' cabin, which was just below the Bridge, rather than the previously described 'Harbour' cabin. Captains of destroyers and large warships did have both accommodation arrangements. However, the issue of the safes on board 'Hardy' presents an intriguing problem that needed further exploring. Hence, a short chapter to come will allow this to become clearer.

16

Enemy Try to Finish Off Their Prey

To summarise, the events unfolding at this moment in time showed that the 'Battle Ensign' had been hauled down, a normal practice in battles so as to make the statement: "We are not able to continue the fight". The Germans, as was the mariners' tradition, showed mercy towards their seafaring enemy. But in the understandable panic, in a furiously moving and obviously fearful situation, it appears on 'Hardy' there was insufficient co-ordinated leadership left on board. It appears that parts of the ship were doing their 'own thing' as a matter of survival. No 4 Gun continued to fire, having received new supplies of shells, and a torpedo was launched for what reason we don't know.

However, looking at this logically, the Captain of the German destroyer, now pouncing on his prey, must have been uncertain in his own mind as to how much damage had been achieved so far on 'Hardy'. As well as wondering how many more shells and torpedoes could be fired on his own ship. Subsequently, the German Captain, for the safety of his own crew and ship, had no alternative option but to recommence the battle. Whilst perhaps under these circumstances his decision was acceptable, what happened shortly after, in my view, was inexcusable.

Bill Pulford's recollections: 'Not far off the beach there was a small hamlet of four or five dwellings. When 'Hardy' grounded our first thoughts were of getting all the wounded that couldn't do anything at all for themselves, tied and strapped to anything that could float and prepared to get them ashore. Now, although the bows were on a deep shelving beach, the midships and where the torpedoes were, was very deep water. The wounded were lowered over the port side. Some of our chaps who were already in the water, were passing them and getting them ashore."

Bobby McAtamney, the young seaman from Carrickfergus, having got to the side of the ship, jumps to safety. He then saw 'Tubby' Cock also in the water, appearing to be in difficulty, so he dragged him to safety. They had a laugh about it afterwards. As Bobby said, "Tubby only floated because of his size."

In the meantime, Bill Pulford remains busy turning out the davits to launch the 'skimmer' to take the wounded Captain ashore. This effort was frustrated by another shell which destroyed the boat and killed most of those around it. Bill was knocked unconscious, and wounded in the leg and foot. When he came around, all the buoyant material on deck was being collected together and tied to the more seriously wounded who were then lowered over the side as gently as possible and towed ashore by others already in the water. Seeing a messmate clinging to 'a baulk of time', Bill decided to join him and slid down the falls into the "shockingly" cold water and struggled across the intervening 200 to 300 yards to reach shore. "We didn't have far to swim before our feet were touching the ground. When we had got all the wounded off the ship the order came: 'Every man for themselves!' Then, and only then, did I see men, myself included of course, leave the ship for their own safety and No 4 Gun stopped firing."

Stoker Jack Good, a veteran from WW1, was one of those severely wounded who ended up in the water. Here is an account, described by Jack's granddaughter Anna Reid. "As a London lad, he probably wasn't a very strong swimmer. So finding himself in the cold fjord waters in too many clothes, injured, having lost an eye and two and a half fingers and gained some shrapnel, he struggled to swim ashore. Apparently he kept thinking he was on land, only to find it was instead one of many rocks, and he sank back into the sea. He was just about ready to give up when Gordon (Avery), an all year round swimmer from Plymouth, grabbed him under the arm and swam him to shore."

There was another heroic attempt made in saving the life of a friend. As mentioned previously, Bernard Kennedy and Geoff Bailey became friends, since they had both had similar upbringings in the mining valleys of Wales. Lance Kennedy, the son of Bernard, who lives in Cornwall, made contact with me to provide information about his father's experience at Narvik which links with Geoff's account. Bernard, probably because he had survived with no injuries, was fully aware of events as they unfolded, unlike Geoff who was obviously traumatised and could not fully recall who was present at the event.

Here Geoff, having heard the ship was being abandoned, recollects the following daunting struggle to remain alive. "I clambered down on to the upper deck and caught a fleeting glimpse of our trainer jumping overboard. With the help of a seaman I got my coat and oilskin off. I got into a boat, which was lowered into the water.

"We started to push the boat away from the ship's side, but the inevitable happened, the boat being overloaded capsized and I was flung into the water. I went under and came up gasping for breath. I grabbed the keel of the boat, but a couple of other blokes had the same idea and the boat went under again. I gave it up and started to swim for it on my back. I had swum twenty yards when I heard someone shouting to me to stand up. I stood up; the water came up to my knees. I had been swimming like hell in two feet of water? All this time the Germans were firing at us and when I looked back I saw five destroyers circling around taking pot shots at us. It was great fun for them."

Lance Kennedy retells his father Bernard's story explaining how he was in the vicinity of the Bridge and the flag deck and amazingly came out of it uninjured. It seems that on abandoning ship he saw his pal 'Gunner' Geoff Bailey, "Had half of his hand blown away". He then pushed Geoff through 200 yards of icy "bullet ridden" water ashore.

Cyril arrives at his 'Abandon Ship Station', which was No 4 Carley raft on the port side, near the forward funnel. "Not all the men detailed for this raft arrived. There were about four of us, all the others including those 'boys' on the gun had been killed. But those few of us left, cut the ropes holding it, carried it to the side and dropped it overboard. One man of the party has the job of holding onto a line which is attached to the raft and he should tie this to the guard rail of a stanchion. Our man was the Petty Officer Telegraphist (Reginald Bonetta), he forgot to hold on to the line and our raft went floating away down the fjord. Believe me we called him some very uncomplimentary names in proper nautical language. The look on his face when he realised what he had done made us all roar with laughter. I think he must have expected us to throw him over the side. Anyway what had been done couldn't be undone and there was nothing left to do but swim ashore."

Les Smale is confronted with a predicament. "As I reached the fo'c'sle deck and had just taken up my coat to retrieve my valuables from the pockets, the Germans opened fire on us again and registered a direct hit on No 2 Gun, which was already out of action. I dropped flat and felt splinters of metal hitting my 'tin hat' which undoubtedly saved me from injury. The doctor (Surgeon Lt Waind) was injured in this and Chief Stoker (Edward Stiles) was mortally wounded. Having retrieved my valuables, we put the Captain, in his stretcher, over the side and into the water."

Bert Mason, where he recalls: "Just prior to this renewed shelling, voices from up on the Bridge were yelling at me to go up on the fo'c'sle deck just below them. They had the Captain lashed on a stretcher, lowering him feet first, and wanted me to grab him and lay him on the deck. As he came down, I saw that his head and face were in a terrible state. He was groaning and breathing heavily and as he breathed lumps of flesh on his face were moving in and out. I did not think of him as dying, but then the officers were rushing down and took charge. There were only about a dozen men left on the ship apart from the wounded. So I gave a hand to get them laid in position for taking off. The ship's doctor (Waind) was busy attending to them when a shell burst near and killed most of the poor fellows, the doctor himself being badly wounded in the arm.

"Then with the renewed firing we knew it was time to go! The officers dumped the 'skipper' in the water and dived in after him. He was dead when they got him to the beach. I was told that some of his last words spoken on the Bridge were "I shall never forget No 4 Gun crew."

Cyril tells his version of those few moments: "I was standing with Petty Officer West who was in charge of the torpedo tubes crew. He and I had served together before the war for about two years and we got on very well with each other. He should have also been on my Carley float. We both took a good look around the ship; it was a 'shambles'. All the boats except two were smashed to bits, one was the small motor boat we called the 'skimming dish'. Our Midshipman, Mr Pope and Chief

Stoker Stiles tried to get this boat over the side with the intention of using it to take some of the wounded ashore.

"Unfortunately the shelling by the enemy ships started again. We had a few minutes' respite which had enabled us to get the wounded onto the iron deck but now the shells were coming inboard once again. One hit the 'skimming dish' mortally wounding the Chief Stoker, and wounding others who were helping with the original wounded members of the crew. Including Surgeon Lt Waind who I noticed was standing next to Lt Heppel. That put paid to using the 'skimming dish'. This left the port whaler which looked intact."

Harry Rogers, although a Stoker by trade, during the battle his action station was that of 'ammunition supplier' to No 4 Gun. This probably meant he would have been one of the last to leave his post. On reaching the upper deck Harry was also one of those involved with getting the 'skimming dish' sorted out. During which he felt something 'bite' his back. The shore was not far away and Harry was a strong swimmer. He remembers walking up the beach and noticing blood in the snow. Then he realised that the blood was coming from him. He didn't remember much after that."

Walter Mitchell, now safely ashore along with some of his shipmates, took refuge in a number of chalets on the shore, "most of them deserted". They stripped off their already freezing clothes and dried themselves with curtains and other oddments left behind by the former occupants. "We had no means of making a fire and were almost frozen, but the fellows stuck it well; there were no complaints." However, in the back of their minds they were wary that the Germans would send an armed party to find them.

Stan Robinson, having taken the leap into the water, found himself, "Swimming for my life! We then got picked up by some Carley floats, they capsized so we swam ashore about

500 yards. I laid down on the beach, I couldn't get up, we were perished with cold. A big Norwegian civilian picked me up, and took me to this house."

Les is also getting close to venturing into the icy Arctic conditions. "Our only access to the water at this point was via the under fall, which still hung vertically from the 'Davit Head'. Shinning down, I paused on the lower block to take off my fur lined 'flying boots', before entering the water. I didn't get them off as the First Lieutenant came down the fall on top of me and I found myself in the water. One of the Signalmen, who was injured behind the wheelhouse, was still in the water and asked me to help him. I saw him ashore all right and then began to realise the cold was colder than I had ever experienced before.

"By now No 4 Gun had finished firing but the Germans were still firing at us and bits and pieces came flying over, calling for numerous 'ducks' under water, in an effort to dodge the danger. The First Lieutenant was now calling for help with the Chief Stoker (Edward Stiles). So I went to give him a hand ashore. I then went back to assist 'The Gunner' (Mr McCracken) to bring the Captain to the beach where almost immediately he died. I dare say he would have been happier, if he had known anything about it, if we had left him on board."

Charles Cheshire: "I suppose in five to ten minutes of being hit it was that bad that the order had gone out to 'abandon ship'. We'd been hit all down the starboard side, the land was to the portside, so I went down to the port whaler, which was inboard. I got on the forward end and a Stoker and I got this whaler out. It was already full of men. So when it came to lowering this boat, we had this Stoker on the after end and he hadn't been trained really to take the turns off the cleat, leaving one arm (davit) to lower, he took the lot out but it started to go down stern first. So I took mine off so it would level up. However, it crashed into the water, I thought I'm not going to get wet here. Since it was already in the water I went down the life lines. I got in, they took the hooks off and they let it go. It hadn't gone far before it sank on us, so we were all in the water.

"Now we were all well wrapped up. I had got an overcoat, plus an oilskin and sea boots. The first thing I did was get rid of the sea boots and eventually the overcoat and oilskin. I started to swim to the beach, I thought it was strange that people were walking and I am stuck here. Anyway, I reached down and there was ground, so I just stood up and walked the rest of the way. It was that cold I didn't feel myself touch the bottom. When I did stand up it was only knee deep. From there we made our way to a small house, where there was the survivors of the crew, the whole crew had made it there."

Cyril pins his hopes on the port whaler until disaster almost occurs. "As Petty Officer West and I looked for'd' along the ship's side we saw some of the wounded being put in the whaler. You have three or four men at each of the bow and stern falls to let it down evenly. Leading Seaman 'Jack Walters' was also in the boat. He was Coxswain and a mate of mine. As we watched I took off my overcoat and balaclava. Just leaving my blue suit, boots, belt and gaiters, ready for the swim ashore. I was just saying to PO West, 'it looks like we will have to swim for it Mick', when I saw the whaler go into the water with a rush. I thought 'Good God! Nobody will get out of that alive', but as the boat hit the water it landed stern first, then the bow end, and miraculously it stayed level. Unfortunately, those on the bow falls were 'Stokers' who weren't used to lowering boats. Instead of leaving a couple of turns of the boat's falls on the cleats and lowering slowly they took all turns off and just let the lot go when they started to lower it.

"The only casualty was Jack Walters, for as the stern end hit the water the tiller swung round hitting him on the buttocks, slicing a piece of flesh off one side. The rope lashing holding the tiller had broken with the force of the boat hitting the water. The shore incidentally was about three hundred yards away. It looked forbidding with its snow and ice clad cliffs sweeping up from a beach of thick snow, the air temperature at that time of the morning, 0630, was eighteen degrees below freezing. We could only hope that the water was warm enough to swim in without us getting cramp. On seeing the whaler was floating all right and ready for moving off with plenty of room for more passengers, I said to Mick the PO 'Come on there's our ride ashore'. I climbed over the guardrail, blew up my rubber lifebelt and dived in, Mick followed me."

Bert is also about to take his first hesitant step into an icy cold fjord. "I took my shoes off and tied them by their laces to my belt, made sure my life belt was inflated. I got hold of the ship's 'Battle Ensign' lying at the foot of the main mast, rolled it up and tied that to my belt. As I climbed the guardrails, I felt a blow on the inside of my left leg near my knee and realised that I had been hit with something. There was no time to investigate as more shells were coming on board."

Lt Heppel was well clad in warm rubber trousers and sea boots when he finally took the plunge so that the icy waters did not freeze on him. He was then able, by bullying them and swimming back each time, to induce two ratings who were clinging to the whaler's lifeline, very cold and frightened, to strike out for the shore. He describes, "A third I was unable to help because I was by then too cold. I left him and he died."

Stanning: "I went aft between the torpedo tubes and took off my oilskin and just then a shell burst on the 'Chief's seat' abaft the after funnel. I think this was what killed the Chief

Stoker. I jumped into the sea fully dressed except for my oilskin. I hate jumping into the sea and would never have done it if I had not been desperately frightened. My first concern was to swim away from the ship to avoid the shells and tried to calm myself by telling myself that there was not much of me above the water to be hit. I found I could swim quite well, especially as I had blown up my rubber life belt and thought I had about 200 yards to swim, but astonished when I touched ground about fifty yards inshore of the ship. I very soon found that I was quite unable to get along on my feet and made my way on my belly for the remainder of the distance."

Bert, hoping to swim to safety, once more came across an unexpected challenge. "Joe and I dived in the water together, struck out and in a few minutes we had reached a point near the beach where we could wade. Then from behind us we heard a cry for help, and looking back we saw Paymaster Lieutenant Stanning waving. We were undecided what to do, as we were suffering from the effects of the bitter cold water, but back we turned. We saw that one of his ankles was shattered. It wasn't so bad hauling him through the water but when we got to the beach and a high wall of snow at the water mark, it became really hard work. He was complaining bitterly at our rough treatment. Yard by yard we kept at him, supporting either side, he was quite a big man. Our objective was a wooden house about 400 yards away."

Here is Geoffrey Stanning's version of the event. "As soon as I reached the beach I realise I was being left behind and would never catch up the others or find where they had gone without help. So I shouted to two ratings ahead, both Torpedomen and they came and helped. There was about 100 yards of foreshore covered with rocks and pools; just the place to play if one was a child, but now it was sheer agony to me even with two men's help and I kept on begging them to go on and leave me as I felt I should never get anywhere. They were both fairly exhausted but they helped me along, urging and swearing at me. At last we reached the top of the beach and there was a path about fifty yards long and four feet deep in snow before we at last got to the road. The road was easy as the snow was trodden down but then there was another path deep in snow before we got to a wooden house about fifty yards above the snow."

Les, now ashore, is faced with his next aim for survival. "My first wish was to get circulation going again, so I stamped my way up through the snow to the nearest house, as had many others of the crew. Looking back, as I left the beach, I saw a ship upturned showing its keel, rudder and propellers and felt that it must be one of the German destroyers that we had sunk. Unfortunately, it turned out to be the 'Hunter', though I didn't know it at the time. Our own ship was on fire forward and rounds of ammunition of different calibres were exploding all the time."

Cyril, having hit the water, had a strange experience. "The time under water must have only been seconds but to me it seemed a lifetime. It is said that when you are face to face with death, in a situation like we were in, the whole of one's life passes before you. I had never believed in anything like that, although I was as superstitious as most sailors, but I can honestly say that the whole of my life passed through my head while under water. The only thing I could think of when I reached the surface again was the fact that my wife was expecting our first baby within the next few days. I pictured her listening to the BBC and prayed that the shock would not harm her or the baby. From that moment on I was determined to get home safe and get there soon. I then struck out for the whaler.

"Jack Walters saw Mick and me swimming for the boat and held his hand out to pull me into it. Having got me in safely, he held his hand out again to grab Mick, but before he could reach him the boat overturned. All those in the boat were now dumped into the water underneath the boat, evidently some shrapnel had 'holed' the boat, this had not been noticed when the boat was lowered into the water. There were about seven or eight of us in the whaler and when it turned over we found ourselves underneath, with an 'air gap'. There was swearing and cursing, then we ducked from under and lay across the keel.

"When a boat of this type is 'waterlogged', it does not sink but keeps on turning over and over. While we were lying across the keel it turns over and we all found ourselves underneath again. Once more we got out from under, some of the lads had had enough, and they swam towards the shore. Those left lay across the keel on our bellies, once again it turned over, under we went, out we got onto the keel for a third time, more lads left to swim for shore, leaving Lt Fallwell and myself on the boat. When we got pushed under again, he said, 'Right Cope I've had enough, I'm off', and away he went, leaving me on my own.

"Previously, I had seen shells dropping on the beach, so I was not that keen on setting off; even though I saw lots of heads bobbing up and down in the water swimming ashore. I thought I would just give it a little longer. However, lying on the keel I finally decided, it was time to go."

As previously stated by Bert Mason, he had witnessed the Asdic Operator Alex Hillier being wounded on board. However, Cyril was told shortly after the action that Hillier was also hit by a shell whilst he climbed out of the water and was instantly killed. Tragically his luck really ran out. Similarly to young Victor Gould's account, there were other instances of men making it to the beach, having to endure not only shells but also small armed guns' fire.

However, Bill Pulford, from his recollections, is adamant that the Germans had changed their target from 'Hardy' to the shoreline. "As we were scrambling up the beach, the Germans stopped firing what we call D.G. (in fact Direct Action Impact) shells at 'Hardy' and they transferred to shrapnel. As we were struggling up the beach to the 'hamlet' so to speak to these four or five houses 'fragment' shells were bursting overhead and I saw two or three chaps going down, struck by these 'fragment' shells. I know they were fragment shells because of the way they were scattering down on the water. They were not shell splinters, what everybody seems to call shrapnel, it was a proper shrapnel shell. Shell splinters are a completely different thing altogether."

Dougy, still looking after his wounded shipmate Andrew Whearty, gives his professional opinion regarding the German response. "The ship was, as we understood, on fire below; it was obvious there was no way we could hang about too long and having received the order to abandon ship, there was little else I could do. I found a wandering 'Stoker' with two lifebelts, so I took one, put it round Andy, slid him under the guardrail and dropped him into the sea. I had to jump in afterwards to be alongside of him. I waited for him to come up, so I could see where he was, then turned him round.

"We eventually got near the shore and I dragged him into the shallows. There was mud, snow and ice, the Germans were still firing at us. They were actually firing at the houses where the men were making to. But they didn't machine gun us, which was said at the time, and they did not shoot at us in the water whatsoever. But they did shoot up in land. Whether they were salvoes or not I didn't know but they did aim at the houses, or shelter where the men were making for.

This I can swear to. I am prepared to say, they were either ricochets from shells that went over the target, could be, I don't know.

"I had to wait for some considerable time for Andy to die. It was only when he said a few words to me, I said a few prayers that I could remember at the time, which was not a lot. These are my own particular memories, which I hang on to myself. He died then actually. So I dragged him a little further up the beach, buried him in the snow as much as I could, to make it look a little decent for him. I wandered up now, staggered up to the house, which I believe was about fifty to sixty yards on my right. To the house which belonged to Mrs Kristensen, she was there with her daughter."

In 1971, Mrs M. Ashton the sister of Andrew Whearty wrote three letters to Cyril, as a response to national and regional newspaper features. I include parts of her letters. However, after thirty-one years Mrs Ashton had not been able to ascertain where her brother was buried in Narvik. She was looking for final closure, "You must excuse my writing, shattered nerves, from the loss of three good brothers and also my husband in the war." She also added that she had seen a newspaper feature, "I recall that chap's name was called 'Taffy Bourton', I shall write to him today. I would like to have a chat with him.

"After Andrew 'passed on', I saw him. The way I saw him, he seemed to me as though the back had been smashed in. I also knew that Thursday morning he had gone, the bedside clock, as I woke up, straight dead on six o'clock. I did not tell my mother, I waited until she received the news of his death. He was the 'apple of her eye'. I had an idea he had a premonition of his death. He came on leave at Christmas, after the 'Graf Spee' affair, he mentioned the name of his Captain and remarked, I shall go with him, and I don't mean looking for glory. Yes they were all heroes and young ones too on the 'Hardy'."

Mrs Ashton explained that she had written to the 'War Graves Commission' and was disappointed to be told her brother's name was not known to be on a grave in Norway. She always believed Andrew's body was laid "side by side with Captain Warburton-Lee on the beach".

The Captain was left on the beach for his body to be dealt with later. Andrew Whearty's body, as described by Dougy Bourton, taking into account the chaotic circumstances, rightly out of respect was temporarily buried under snow. This seems to have led to Captain Warburton-Lee finally being put to rest in the Ballangen cemetery. Whilst Andrew's body, having been found later by the local community, although buried in the same cemetery but having no identification, meant that his grave, similar to a number of others, was marked 'A Sailor – Known Only Unto God'. Finally, Mrs Ashton: "I feel sad at heart most of them young boys lying in a nameless grave. I will go there one day."

Staying with the issue of the enemy deliberately firing shells and small gunfire at the escaping crew, in 2001 Maltese Steward Anthony Ronayne provided his account of the events when the ship was 'Abandoned' to a local newspaper in Malta, 'It-Torca-Pron'. Anthony, then aged nineteen, described, "Before jumping into the sea I took off all my clothes except for underwear. I then put on a lifebelt and jumped into the freezing water. In the meantime the Germans were firing from the shore at all those in the sea."

The newspaper article goes on to report, "While swimming he heard an officer shouting for everybody to swim ashore but a few seconds later this same officer vanished as he was hit in the head and drowned. As he was nearing the shore, he met Lt Fallwell who was almost exhausted and helped him to get ashore. Once on shore they noticed that there was a row of barbed wire. They went over to it and while walking they saw a small fisherman's hut and went inside. There was nothing inside except for a piece of curtain and Anthony wrapped it round him as he was freezing with cold. In the same hut there was a young sailor about sixteen years old who was holding one hand with the other which was ripped off his body, trying to put it back in place."

As I have already pointed out, on board 'Hardy' there were eight Maltese crew members. Anthony went on to say, "Together with Guzieppe (Joseph) Micallef and Toni Briffa we walked to safety. At one stage Guzieppe Micallef could not walk further and fainted. Along came some Norwegians and put some ice down his mouth to revive him."

It is possible that the person who had part of his arm severed was Able Seaman 'Gunner' Geoff Bailey. It could also have been Geoff who Harry Rogers mistakenly witnessed as a Chief Stoker having his arm severed. Harry's survival attempts are described in the next chapter.

Cyril having finally decided on self preservation in the icy cold waters gets involved in another anxious rescue attempt. "As I was about to shove off, I heard a cry for help from the ship. I looked around and about twenty yards away was this mess mate Tony Hart. Of course he was a 'non-swimmer'. Although you had to be able to swim in the Navy, he and I knew, he was one of those who used to always get out of swimming instructions. He had jumped overboard with a lifebuoy over his head, it was the Captain's special lifebuoy painted in white, with the name of the ship in gold enamel. Knowing Tony couldn't swim a stroke, and that if left alone he would just drift away with the current, either drowning or freezing to death, I slid off the bottom of the whaler and swam towards him. Just in time, the whaler turned over again.

"On reaching my mate, I grabbed hold of the lanyard attached to the lifebuoy. I told him to watch what I did, and do the same. I then started to swim with one arm and I think my legs, I say I think because by now it was impossible to feel my legs. I was without feeling from the waist down. Slowly I pulled Hart towards the shore. I saw another rating pulling some youngsters on the end of one of the whaler's oars, they could not swim. I also saw Lt Heppel go back a couple of times to help the non-swimmers. I think he was the last man to leave the ship side and he encouraged the rest of us to keep going, with his own feat of endurance and good humoured words.

"Not far from the shore, Hart started to babble, he kept on saying, 'God Bless You, God Bless You, my mother and father will never forget you for saving my life'. I let him carry on for a while then I got fed up with his ramblings, and said, 'For goodness sake shut up and try and help me by using your arm like I am.' I think at this time I was beginning to feel the strain and the intense cold, nevertheless I kept going, closing my ears to his thanks and praises. I managed to reach the beach, despite the shells coming over, and despite having to tow Hart. But on stepping out of the water I said to him, 'Right Tony you are as good as me on dry land, let's get walking.'

"With that I stumbled towards a trail of blood and discarded clothing which led up the cliff face, only then did I realise the reason for the discarded clothing, mine had started to freeze solid on me. I began to tear at my clothes, first my gaiters and heavy boots, these had been put on for the 'Landing Party'. Then at my blue uniform, leaving only my vest and pants on, I looked back towards Tony Hart he was still standing at the water's edge with the lifebuoy round his neck. I walked back to him and said, 'What the bloody hell do you think you are doing with that?' He replied, 'I am taking it home, my father will hang it up in his pub at Saltash'.

I said to him, 'Sod your father's pub, take the bloody thing off, get your clothes off quick before they freeze on you and let's get moving up there', and I pointed up the cliff face to where the last few of our survivors were climbing. I thought for a minute he was going to cry as I took the lifebuoy off him and threw it back in the water, leaving him to follow me.

"I started to climb the cliff and this time he did what I had told him to do, then he shouted, 'I am ok now Sid'. At that moment I knew that whatever had been wrong with him before, he was now the 'old Tony' I had known on the ship and on the many trips ashore we had been together. As we reached the top of the cliff we saw a wire fence with a road on the other side of it. Normally with my long legs I could have climbed over in one stride, but by this time my feet and legs were frozen beyond feeling. It was impossible to convey to them the message to lift themselves up, so I just leaned my stomach against the top strand and tipped over head first into the snow on the other side. Tony Hart followed suit and we lay there laughing at each other for a moment. Covered more by snow than clothes, we had to take our vest and pants off, as they had also frozen hard.

"We helped each other up and holding on to the fence we looked along the road away to our right. On the left hand side of the road we saw a chalet into which some of our shipmates were going. To our left a good way along the road we could see two more chalets, behind us the last two or three survivors were reaching the top of the cliff. 'Come on let's run and get the circulation back in our legs and feet', I said. I tried and fell flat on my face, my mate Tony and another chap who had just reached the top, laughed their heads off before picking me up. We shuffled along the road towards the chalet supporting each other, our legs and feet were like blocks of ice."

Sketch by war artist Terence Cuneo of 'Hardy' survivors climbing cliff to safety. By kind permission of daughter, Carole Cuneo.

There was one sailor who by all accounts was washed up on the beach, that was Stoker Henry Maxfield. Cyril Cope, on his first visit back to Narvik in the early 1970s, endeavoured to find and record all the known graves of those taking part in the 'Battles of Narvik'. He deduced from information given, that when local men found Henry's body, because he looked to be a man in his forties, wearing a boiler suit, they assumed he was a 'merchant seaman'. This led to confusion as to where his body was actually buried. Cyril, therefore, believed that Henry's grave was marked as such, rather than like his unidentified shipmates, whose graves were marked as previously mentioned, 'A Sailor – Known Only Unto God'.

17

Sanctuary found at Petra's

The property in which most the men were able to find sanctuary belonged to Hakon and Petra Kristensen. In 1972, they were invited as 'guests of honour' to a reunion in London for the '2nd Destroyer Flotilla Association of Narvik 10th April 1940'. Unfortunately, they were unable to attend the next reunion in Portsmouth two years later. However, on this occasion, as a guest of honour, the 'Mayor of Ballangen' in his speech passed on a message from the Kristensens. By the way the translation for 'Skogseth' is 'Farm in Forest'.

The Mayor began by mentioning that on the Kristensens' returning to their home, after the London reunion, their experience had "awakened the memories of bygone years". He then went on to describe the Kristensens' homestead.

"Near Grindfjord Ferry-Quay lies the small farm of 'Skogseth' in Vidrek. It has forty 'mals' of cultivated land and until recently food enough for four cows and a horse. Petra and Hakon Kristensen both cultivated the ground themselves by hand. The hardest work was the removal of the fir trees' roots. Mrs Kristensen remembers how her husband used to shake the last of earth from the roots because the soil was so precious. When the roots were dry they were burnt and the bonfire reminded Mrs Kristensen of a firework display as the nature of the wood caused so much spark and crackle. Later Petra Kristensen would again experience 'Fire and Crackle' but not from cultivating the land for life giving but the exact opposite, 'Death and Destruction'. It was early April 1940 and she was first to attend to the men of HMS Hardy which was sunk in Narvik."

The 'Mayor of Ballangen' continued to read out Petra's memories of that day on 10th April 1940. It is worth mentioning at this point that Hakon was a fisherman and at the time was away for a few days. This left just Petra and their seventeen year old daughter, Ruth, at home.

"It was morning and I heard firing in the fjord as I sat in the barn milking the cows. When I came out I saw warships in the fjord and German ships coming out of Narvik harbour. Up on the ridge behind the house was a large boulder which gave us protection when the shooting became severe.

"I banked up the fire so that the house would be warm when we returned and so we ran up behind the boulder. There was terrible shooting and we didn't dare to move until it had quietened down. When we returned to the house we saw smoke in many places, the door to our house stood open and smoke came out. We thought the house had been hit by the bombardment, we saw people who had swam in the sea and heard cries for help. We also saw naked men come up from the beach and walk towards our house. When we came in the house it was full of frozen naked sailors. In the oven I had left some wood to dry and the sailors had set fire to this causing the rooms to be full of smoke which was the reason they had opened the door.

"A youth cried and whimpered, 'my legs, my legs', he had frostbite. On a chair sat a badly wounded man who turned out to be the Chief Stoker [Edward Stiles]. A shipmate was holding him who said to me when I wanted to help, 'There is no hope he is hit in the stomach'. I thought we ought to get him to bed but the beds were full of naked men who had wrapped the bedclothes around themselves. In one of the beds sat two young boys weeping.

"The first thing we did was to find clothing for the naked sailors, as they were terribly cold. Those who had arrived first had already wrapped themselves up in the first and best they could find, bedclothes, tablecloths and ladies wear, including, the contents of the dirty linen basket. Survivors from 'Hardy' still kept arriving and soon the house, barn and outhouses were overflowing. The complete milk yield (30 Litre), freshly baked bread and everything edible was soon gone. This of course only helped a little for such a large number of men."

Charles Cheshire is not the first to have made it to the Kristensens' homestead. "Everyone was wet through, of course, there was six feet of snow ashore. Best thing to do was get the clothes off. From there I was a bit hazy as to what happened. There was a woman and a daughter there, everyone was getting their clothes off, wringing them out, I suppose trying to get them dry. But this young woman gave me a jumper to put on, I had nothing myself. There were others, they had newspapers wrapped around their feet and legs."

Geoff Bailey, like others, under extreme difficulties finally manages to find the sanctuary of Petra's homestead. "We walked for what seemed to be hundreds of miles when eventually we reached a house. I walked into the house and was racked with pain, trembling with chattering teeth and shaking limbs. I was freezing cold. The boys ripped curtains off the windows and grabbed any kind of clothing, undressed and put them on until the house looked like the backstage of a pantomime."

Bill Pulford: "When we got ashore, we made our way to these four or five houses. The first thing I had thrown into my hand was a cup of coffee by a young lady about eighteen years old. It was half full but it was enough to warm me inside. The house was chock a block with men from the ship and this lass, without further a do whatsoever, she stripped me and started towelling me as vigorously as she could. I thought no more about it, looking around there was four or five of us stood stark naked and ladies were there. They were giving us cups of coffee and drying us best they could, and somehow embarrassment didn't enter the field.

"We got dried and picked up items of clothing. I managed to get hold of a woman's jumper and skirt, other than these I had my underpants which I managed to keep. Shoes, I didn't have any because I had to swim ashore. It was then I realised I had been hit, I had two holes in my leg and they were bleeding."

Stan Robinson: "When I got ashore at Mrs Kristensen's home, I remember standing up and suddenly cutting off my uniform with scissors, which of course was frozen stiff. I was in a single bed then with another 'boyo', who had already had one lot, when he went down on the 'Courageous' previously. We were shivering so much with shock, cold and terror, we had been in the water half an hour you see. We were shivering so much we were actually knocking each other out of the bed. We had four hours of that."

Les Smale recalls, "I eventually reached the wooden house and there were two women there, a Mrs Kristensen and her daughter, doing all they could to make the survivors comfortable. The house was full of steam from thawing bodies. Personally, I was so cold and so exhausted that I could not take my soaking clothes off, though I knew I had to. The 'Yeoman of Signals' helped me out of them eventually and I wrapped myself in a black silk dress which I found on the floor.

"I was glad now that I had been unable to discard my boots at the bottom of the whaler's fall when leaving the ship for unlike most of the others I still had something to wear on my feet. Many made improvised shoes by cutting their rubber lifebelts and putting their feet in the two sealed ends. The most comical of all was the Canteen Manager (NAAFI employee, Mr Moore) who wrapped his legs around with newspaper. Then there was one who cut a hole in carpet; put his head through it and tied the two draping ends around his body with a piece of string."

Geoffrey Stanning, having been assisted by Bert Mason and Joe Sweetland to reach safety, describes vividly his initial impressions. "At first there seemed to be absolute pandemonium inside the house which was full of men and a stink of bodies, burnt cordite and wet clothes. The house was certainly full and in the two bedrooms upstairs, most of the early arrivals had dressed themselves in the clothes and bedclothes of the owners, Mrs Kristensen and her daughter. These two were now downstairs, tearing down curtains, uprooting carpets and mats to wrap sailors in. They also produced what food there was in the house and we almost all had a slice of bread and butter."

Bert Mason recalled the moment but had another priority in mind. "Eventually we made it and found the surprise of our lives. The house was crammed full of 'Hardy' survivors in all sorts of stages of undress, being warmed and thawed out before a great roaring fire and being given hot cups of coffee by the occupants, Mrs Kristensen and her daughter. I have forgotten to mention that when I reached the beach my boots were missing – laces may have broken when I jumped overboard – so I had made the journey up to the house in stocking feet."

Back to Paymaster Stanning. "We stayed like this for some little time, gradually sorting ourselves out and talking things over. My foot was getting extremely painful and I got someone to cut my boot off and the foot then swelled up like a football, as it had evidently been wanting to for some time."

Bert Mason: "The ship's Medical Officer, Surgeon Lieutenant A.P.B. Waind RNVR was doing his best to give treatment to the wounded. One man I noticed was Able Seaman Trigger (Harold Trigger) whose action station had been Bridge Communication Number. He had a nasty looking wound down his back. As we brought Paymaster Lieutenant Stanning in, the other officers grabbed him, sat him on a chair and used a knife to cut away his wellington on his injured ankle. They pulled the other one off and threw it on one side. Seeing that I had no boots I made a mental note of this."

Geoffrey Stanning: "I got hold of Dr Waind and asked him if he had made sure Pilot was dead and what had happened to 'Wash'. He said that 'Wash' was almost dead before he left the ship but had been brought ashore on a Carley float and died on the way. 'Guns' and 'Flags' (Gunnery Officer and Signals Officer) he said must have been killed outright; I had not seen them at all. Pilot he had not seen and did not know anything about him. Heppel was out somewhere and I sent a message to him asking him to go back to the ship, fetch Pilot and make sure all the books in the Captain's cabin aft ('Sea' cabin) were destroyed. After some time a message came that he had gone and that was a relief."

In the meantime, Bert Mason: "I went outside, took my overall off, wrung as much water out of it as possible and put it back on again. It was certainly chilly! But Joe and I had expended a lot of energy bringing in the wounded officer; our blood circulation was in excellent condition. I needed shoes badly so I sneaked over and pinched the good wellington discarded by Stanning and then managed to find another fairly good match."

Lieutenant George Heppel continued to show his outstanding leadership qualities, appearing tireless; probably working on immense levels of adrenalin pumping through his body. "When we got ashore the Norwegians took us into their little houses and dealt with the wounded and let people wring out their clothes. I did not have time for this and 'paddled' round all the houses [probably meant outbuildings] where our men were. A Norwegian doctor soon came to deal with the more serious cases and arranged a bus as an ambulance."

Dougy Bourton: "We just stripped the house of everything, anything to keep warm. Some people had taken their clothes off to swim ashore. I was fortunate because I was still in my boots and gaiters, but of course we were ready as 'landing party' to go ashore; to take on the German Army and Narvik. So they said."

Cyril Cope went on to describe the calamity. "The chalet we arrived at was a 'two up and two down' affair made of wood. The rooms were very small compared with rooms in our houses. It was owned by a middle aged lady and her daughter who was about seventeen years of age. On hearing the gunfire in the fjord and shells landing on the beach they had fled into the pine trees further up the cliffs. These ladies were very brave and helpful; no praise would be high enough to describe what they did for our chaps.

"There were over one hundred men in that chalet all as naked as the day they were born. We were huddled together in groups for warmth but the ladies never batted an eyelid as they passed to and fro among the wounded. We might not have been there for all the notice they took of us in our nakedness.

"After settling the wounded on what pieces of furniture there was, the next thing to do was 'call the roll' to see who was missing. My pal Bill Pimlett was not among the survivors. He was the chap who left me to crawl forward on his belly to his 'Repair Station'. After much enquiring I found out how he had died when the shell coming through the canteen hit him in the back, carried on into the T.S. (Gun Direction Transmitting Station), doing the damage which I have already mentioned. His loss was a sad blow to me and to the rest of the men in the Torpedo Department.

"As soon as we had thawed out we went upstairs to rummage in drawers, boxes and cupboards for clothing. Soon the place looked like a 'sales day' at some large departmental store, with clothes all over the place. But alas, we could only find women's clothes. Everybody found something to wear, except our Canteen Manager. He was over six feet tall, had flaming red hair, a large nose (hence nick named 'Beaky') and wore horned rimmed glasses. As he was also naked, he looked comical and every time he passed the other chaps they roared with laughter. Search as he did he couldn't find anything to wear.

"I had been lucky enough to find a pair of girl's knickers and a long bright yellow dress which almost touched the floor. I watched the Canteen Manager searching frantically for clothes and listened to the ribald jests and jokes thrown at him by some of the chaps, all in good fun of course. Finally, I couldn't stand it any longer, I took off the yellow dress and gave it to him, leaving myself with just the knickers, which were white and had no elastic in them. We were all in the same boat of course with just enough on to make us decent, for the journey we knew we would have to take, if we were to save ourselves and get to England."

Dougy: "We looked after the wounded, I found a young Welsh lad, Geoff Bailey, who had been a 'Sight Setter' on No 2 Gun and he had his right hand blown off. It was in tatters and I remember making bandages out of a table cloth and what I considered then a very neat sling to lash to his hand. To stop any bleeding I made up a patch for what was left of the finger and a huge bandage for his hand and the sling to lash it to his body. Our doctor, Surgeon Lt Waind was there, who had been doing a great job, although he had been quite severely wounded himself to his right arm and shoulder. But he still did marvels with his one arm."

As described and confirmed by those present, Geoff Bailey, during the many hours he was at Petra's homestead, never "murmured". For his courage he was awarded the Distinguished Service Order. Surgeon Lt Arthur Waind RNVR was also decorated for his dedication to duty under extreme circumstances.

Geoffrey Stanning seems to put to one side his own difficulties to reappraise the survivors' situation. "It was a very odd state of affairs as we obviously could not stay as we were forever, crowded in this house which the 'Kristensens' had now abandoned to us. Yet no one was in a fit state to go far for the time being and many had no boots. At the same time, we fully expected the Germans to send a party ashore from one of their destroyers to catch us, or else to send from Narvik for us but I knew this was a fair distance by road as there were two deep inlets between. As I was the only person who could speak German and as it was quite warm outside, I made my mind up to try sitting outside so that I could see what was happening and if any Germans came along I would be the first to negotiate with them.

Petra Kristensen's home. Circa 1983. *Provided by Bill and Borg-Anna Sanders.*

"Just as I was making my way outside, there was a big explosion from somewhere down the fjord and a column of black smoke rose over the mountains. We could not make this out and thought it must be our ships in action again. Actually it was 'Hostile' (in fact 'Havock') torpedoing 'Rauenfels'. We were also anxious to know the fate of the other ships as several of us, including myself had seen one ship apparently sinking at the turn of the fjord and I thought I had seen Germans lower boats to pick up survivors. We did not know till a long time afterwards that 'Hunter' was badly damaged and a few minutes later 'Hotspur' was hit and her steering gear jammed so that she rammed 'Hunter' and bowled her over. I was convinced that there were survivors from 'Hunter' and about forty turned up about a month later.

"It was quite warm outside and someone brought a sort of sleigh chair for me to sit on. I took all my clothes off and hung them round me and it was very satisfactory to see them and myself steaming in the sun's warmth. The ship was burning forward and 'ready use' ammunition was exploding at intervals; someone came up and said they had seen a man walking about on the fo'c'sle and we thought it might be either Pilot or a Stoker who was missing. It was the Pilot. On the other side of the fjord, I could just see through the trees, another destroyer – a German one – ashore and in much the same state as ourselves. There was no sign of life anywhere near her."

18

Rescue Mission

Cyril: "During the forenoon our officers held a conference to decide what to do for the best of all concerned. Something had to be done quickly for the wounded and the position of the rest of us would have to be sorted out, one way or another. Remember we had no clothes except the bits and pieces, or any boots or shoes, except for one man I will tell you about later. We were in a foreign country which had been invaded by our enemies. We did not know at that time how much of the country had been taken over by the Germans. One thing we did know for certain was that they were in Narvik which lay in one direction along the road passing the chalet. What we would find in the other direction we had no means of knowing.

"I talked quite a lot to Chief Stoker Stiles who had been severely wounded in the stomach by shrapnel. He was slowly passing away but was still conscious. It was hard to stand there telling him we would get him home and that he would be all right; when we knew there was no chance of him lasting the day out. He had been a very popular chap with all members of the ship's company and had been very clever at making brooches with the ship's name on, out of gold wire and mother of pearl. My wife, Edie, had one of these brooches and it is still as good as new, although it is over thirty years old.

"All the 'Hardy' survivors, other than one, finally managed to get ashore, climb the cliff face, and by either the 'Grace of God' or 'Luck', together found a place to re-group. However, further hurdles needed to be overcome before they were able to avoid capture and have any chance of being rescued."

George Heppel has no intention of forgetting the probable guilt he must have felt, for having left the badly injured Navigating Officer (Pilot) to his own fate. "The fore part of the 'Hardy' was ablaze from fire which, I think, started in the motorboat which was smashed; and after a time all the remaining 'ready-use' ammunition of the foremost guns started exploding; and in the middle of it all, the Navigator who had regained consciousness, had left the comparative safety of the place where I had left him and was wandering about. It therefore became necessary to fit out the expedition to go back to the ship at once."

It is a well known fact, that both in the past and the present Navy, those with a relatively long time in the Service have learnt never to volunteer unless under duress or the outcome was to their own advantage.

Bert Mason gives his version of what happened next. "It was then that Lieutenant Commander Mansell called us all together and said, 'Now when the Germans come for us we are only to give information about names and service numbers'. On no account were we to say what we did on board, for example, Asdics, signals etc. Joe and I decided that as we were in good physical condition and getting warmer all the time we would make a break for it and get away from the house. We knew Narvik was in one direction so we decided to go the opposite way.

"The two of us started our trek but I don't think we had gone six yards before we were confronted by Lieut. Heppel. He said, 'Ah! Mason, you are my senior Leading Seaman, the Navigating Officer is still on board, I want you to come back with me to rescue him.' Apparently he had been wounded in the head and made comfortable, perhaps lapsed into unconsciousness and in their last minute panic when the shelling had started again he was left on board. Now, having recovered, he could be seen walking up and down the quarter deck. Heppel went on, 'I will meet you down the beach in five minutes time.' I turned to Joe and asked, 'Are you coming?' He said 'No.'

"Still having the ship's 'Ensign' with me, I pushed it into the snow-bank, marked the spot, intending to pick it up later and made for the beach to find the Torpedo Officer already there. We selected a Carley float, pushed it out until it floated, jumped in and paddled away, detouring clear of the ship bows until we got under the stern and slightly on the port side. The for'ard part of the ship was on fire, burning fiercely, ammunition exploding sending myriads of sparks and burning debris into the air. Here we were comparatively safe and the only other worry was a German patrolling destroyer out in the fjord. Someone could easily have opened up on us with a machine gun, but they didn't interfere.

"Close up to the ship's side we could see the Navigator and he made no attempt to look over the guardrails. Our problem now was how to get on board as there was no hand grip of any sort and with the side straight it must have been a good seven or eight feet to the edge of the deck. I said I would try and jump for it, so standing on the edge of the float I leapt upwards, but with the raft being unstable all I managed was the edge of the upper deck with my fingers. I hung there a couple of seconds and as the raft had moved away slightly I fell back into the icy water completely submerged. The Torps (Heppel) dragged me back in, so it was back to square one – wet and cold. Torps then got desperate and called, 'Pilot throw us a line, throw us a line!' I said, 'There are life lines rigged from the after superstructure to the depth charge rails but I don't suppose he has a knife to cut them.' (These had been rigged up a few days ago when we were in stormy seas off the Norwegian coast.)

"It was then that my seaman's knife came in useful again and undoing it from my waist I handed it to the Torps and very carefully he tossed it on board over the guardrails. We waited for what seemed ages, and then for the first time the Navigating Officer appeared at the guardrails with a rope and started passing it over the side into our raft. I watched fascinated as he took the loose end and ever so slowly and deliberately secured it with a clove hitch. We now had means of getting on board. In the meantime a little rowing boat had turned up manned by a solitary man – Stoker Bowden. No questions were asked and Heppel told me to take the boat's painter and make it fast to the Carley float, which I did, or thought I did.

"The Torps then told me to climb on board first, and go to his cabin, search out any civilian clothes of his and get changed into dry ones as quickly as possible. With a bit of sunlight shafting into the cabin I soon stripped off my wet clothes and in their place I had dry underwear, socks, his best flannels, sports jacket and over that a kind of waterproof anorak. There was a nice pair of shoes but they were too pointed – they hurt my toes so I had to revert back to the wellingtons. Back on deck I found that they had got the Navigator into the raft – he was very quiet and I could see that he had been knocked about badly. Also, they had loaded the dinghy with blankets, cigarettes and a few bottles of spirits located in the wardroom stores. There were other things passed down of which I was unaware and it was not until many years later I found out what they were!

"I was now back on the raft with Heppel on board, saying he was going to destroy the Captain's safe with an explosive charge and we were to be ready to push off as soon as he came over the side. He was going to attach a TNT charge and fire it with a length of slow burning 'bickfords' safety fuse, giving us time to push off as soon as he came over the side for the last time.

"The next minute he was over and down the rope and looking over yelled at me, 'You bloody fool you have let the dinghy slip away!' Sure enough it had come adrift and was about two yards off. I said we could easily get it but he blurted out we had to get well clear as quickly as possible before the charge went off. And so we lost the dinghy and contents, but nothing more was said. Thinking back on it I wondered why I had been so careless in not making sure the painter was more secure, but then after being submerged in the icy water, my fingers may have been quite numb!

"We were well clear and near the beach when the charge detonated blowing a huge hole in the starboard side of the ship. Walking the Navigator slowly up to the house we handed him over to the Surgeon (Waind), thankful that the whole exercise had gone off without any mishap, except the loss of the dinghy. I never saw Lieut. Commander Gordon-Smith again and after a spell in hospital at Ballangen, he was spirited away one night along with others. This was by Norwegians across the fjord to Harstad, where he was embarked on one of HM ships back to UK. He never recovered from his injuries and died about four months later."

Lieutenant Commander Russell Gordon-Smith, for his outstanding courage and navigational skills in the Narvik raid, was awarded the Distinguished Service Cross (DSC).

Lieutenant Heppel wrote his account of the rescue a few weeks after the battle, here is his version. "It was at first difficult to find volunteers for the expedition back to the ship. The reason was that most of the men were chilled or wounded and even if well enough to go out were undressed in the warmth of the houses while clothes were drying. However, I found Leading Seaman Mason and Able Seaman Bowden who agreed to come and Able Seaman Slater followed, in a commandeered dinghy. The first two came down to the beach with me, where we found a Carley float from the ship and after towing it a couple of hundred yards up the fjord, in order to give the fore part of the ship wide berth, paddled it out to the ship.

"I do not remember very clearly but I think at this time the only enemy ship in sight was the one ashore on the northern side of the fjord and her consort standing by. The whole of Hardy's fore part was still burning with the 'ready-use' cordite and shells exploding but all was quiet and safe aft. We paddled the first float to the stern of the ship and hailed the Navigator, who was standing on the quarterdeck.

"He grunted a reply but it was clear that he did not quite understand what was going on. It was almost impossible to get on board without his assistance. Mason fell overboard in one attempt, in his second dip that day. But we made the Navigator understand that we wanted a line and threw an opened knife onto the quarterdeck. He managed to cut off a length and make one end fast to the guardrail but the manner in which he did this showed that he was not normal.

"With this help we got on board and started to collect stores to take ashore. A medical chest, shoes and clothing from my cabin, cigarettes and a little brandy from the wardroom, were passed down into the float and Slater's dinghy. Rifles and ammunition were ready to take ashore but it was decided to leave them on this trip and take only the comforts which were more immediately necessary. The Navigator was lowered into the float and Leading Seaman Mason and I went below to the Captain's cabin with a nine pound T.N.T. charge to destroy the safes. When we had placed it, I sent Mason on deck, and after a couple of minutes lit the fuse and followed.

"They were still not quite ready to shove off, but I climbed down into the float and we started to leave the ship. At first Slater tried to use the dinghy to tow the float but this was not a success, so I called him into the float, intending to tow the dinghy. Unfortunately, Slater, thinking the dinghy was made fast, threw the painter over the side and the boat drifted away up the starboard side of the ship, towards the place where the charge was about to explode. I therefore decided to leave it and we paddled towards the shore. The explosion occurred when we were about half way there and thinking that the dinghy had been sunk by it, I did not consider that it was worth while turning round to recover it. So we paddled ashore, where we were met with a stretcher on which the Navigator was carried to the makeshift ambulance which took him to Ballangen hospital."

Cyril: "We noticed that the Navigating Officer was badly wounded in the face, this had been done by shrapnel. He was immediately attended to by the Norwegian doctor who lived in a chalet not far from the one we were in. He had been helping our doctor (Waind) and the two ladies. The doctor did a wonderful job for our lads and as I said about the ladies, I will say about the doctor, no praise is high enough for him. I hope he survived the War and received some form of recognition from our Government."

Bert Mason's version was what he remembered right up until the 1990s. In all those following years he continued to think it was he that had let down his well respected leader Lieutenant George Heppel. However, later, readers will see that there were other items of a sentimental nature that drifted down the fjord and how they came to be retrieved.

Bert arrives back at the Kristensens' homestead to receive a bit of messdeck banter. "Back at the house I was greeted with some peculiar looks and remarks, regarding my dress; 'Where the bloody hell did you get that "rig out" from?' 'Why didn't you tell us you had found a posh clothes shop?' 'Trust you!' They were to learn later.

"But then Stoker Bowden and myself were called to go up to the pay table and get paid. A small bit of furniture had been rigged up and every lower deck man received something. The first in the queue received a one-pound note and two-shilling pieces, the others a 10-shilling note and two-shilling pieces each. 'Stokes' and myself being last, received the smaller amount. Then it struck me where the money had come from. Gunner McCracken, after he had collected it from the ship's safe, had handed it in. My estimation and respect for him changed instantly!"

Stan Robinson: "We were in her house for about four hours. A chap called Jenkins from Cornwall came running in, and said to the Lieutenant in charge, the Germans are seven miles away. They're coming after us. Seeing as this man was a known rumour monger, the Torpedo Officer said, 'If you're telling lies, I'll shoot you.' He said, 'No Sir, I am telling the truth, the Germans are around the corner, it has just been broadcast around the village."

George Heppel was as diligent as ever. "I again went round the houses to see how everyone was getting on and from one of these I saw that the dinghy was still afloat and drifted clear of the ship. I was just about to fit out a second expedition to fetch it, when I heard that the First Lieutenant had decided to start the march to Ballangen. It was a pity that we lost the dinghy because the medical chest was badly needed later."

Bill Pulford was ready for moving on, although similarly to others he realised he was not exactly dressed for mountain climbing or going on a rambling trip. "A little conference was held about what was going to happen now; we could stay where we were, we could live off the Norwegians that were there. Narvik was taken by the Germans, the Norwegians told us that Ballangen was free and hadn't been taken yet. Right! We would march off to Ballangen.

"Well to combat the cold, best as we could, speaking for myself and quite a few others who followed suit, we wrapped our legs in brown paper, newspaper, anything we could get our hands on. Boots, we didn't have any, so we cut up our lifebelts and wrapped them around our feet; because the snow was about three feet deep. So we were going to do this hike to Ballangen. We thought we would stick to the centre of the road, where the traffic was, what traffic there was because we were almost in the Arctic Circle, and it had compressed the snow down into ruts."

The following BBC Radio News Bulletin, the first of a series, is of authentic transcripts sent to Elizabeth Warburton-Lee and are now kept in the family's documents.

BBC 'WORLD SERVICE'.
WEDNESDAY 10th APRIL AT 1.00 P.M.

The Admiralty communiqué says that the destroyers engaged in the Narvik action at dawn today, met with strong opposition. During the fighting H.M.S. HUNTER was sunk and H.M.S. HARDY ran ashore. The action was broken off. No details of casualties in these ships are yet available, but, says the communiqué, complete lists will be published as soon as possible, and the next of kin may be assured that they will be informed by telegram without delay.

The survivors are now ready to move on from the possible threat of capture by the enemy. Their ship, aided by the tide, is also about to move on from where it had grounded, taking with it the remaining bodies of the crew on board. Able Seaman Billy Wearen, the young adopted man whose adoptive family still do not know 'when or why', was probably one of those bodies.

Billy's great niece, Jacqui Harris, says, "All we have are his Service records and a photograph. My search is to try and find someone who had known him to find some information on who he was and why my Great Grandmother adopted him. Sadly none of the family, apart from my mother who was born in 1942 survive."

Bill Sanders' wife Bjorg-Anna comes from the Ballangen area and therefore Bill as an ex Royal Navy man had a personal interest. He explained to Jacqui, "Later in the day of the battle, at high tide, the abandoned 'Hardy', listing heavy to starboard, lifted off the 'Vidrek' beach. The ship drifted two miles up the fjord, eventually grounding at her final resting place at 'Skjomen'. The water here at extreme low tide is only six to ten feet deep. Therefore, 'Hardy' standing out of the water was too accessible to intruders to be classified as a war grave. The late Cyril Cope told me that twelve bodies were recovered from the wreck and taken for burial at 'Hakvik' cemetery. If so then your Great Uncle will be one of the thirty-two graves marked 'A Sailor Of The Second World War – HMS Hardy'. Although, twenty of them should have been marked 'HMS Hunter'."

Jacqui has the final words, "My Great Grandmother Priscilla must have been very fond of Billy. On 'Remembrance

Sunday' she always wore his medals. She also travelled from Manchester for the unveiling of the Plymouth Naval Memorial in 1954 by Princess Margaret." Priscilla died in 1978, but the search goes on.

There was another family who made visits to the Plymouth Naval Memorial.

You will remember Jack Hay, the proficient boxer who at the age of twenty-one was tragically killed when a shell hit No 2 Gun. Unknown to his parents Lawrence and Mary, Jack had become married just prior to Narvik. David Taylor, Jack's nephew, continues the story. "As I understand it, Uncle Jack's parents knew nothing about either the wedding or Violet Ruby. That is until she turned up on their doorstep in Liverpool after he was killed at Narvik. Unfortunately I am not sure she was well received and I don't believe there was any further contact.

"My Grandmother did not take the news of Uncle Jack's death well. I believe that he was reported as missing and because his body was never identified it allowed her to 'not accept' his death. Indeed, she used visits to 'Spiritualists' to further this denial and somehow see Jack as living on the bottom of the sea. My mother, Hilda, had been very close to Jack and always got upset when the subject of his death was raised. My mother accompanied my Grandmother to one of the spiritualist meetings. She always said it scared her to death and she never went near one again."

19

The Saga of the Secret Codes

Before returning back to the survivors and their intentions to 'move on', into the unknown, including the reception at the town of Ballangen and the potential threats from the enemy, I believe there is an important issue to be examined. Namely, some of the officers' thoughts may have returned to whether the confidential material on board the ship had been adequately dealt with. Obviously, if such documents found their way into the hands of the enemy, it could have serious implications for the war effort.

There appears to be contradictory accounts as to who actually disposed of the secret codes and papers that were on the 'Hardy' during the Battle of Narvik. As such, sufficient gathering of evidence is required before making any kind of valid judgement.

Initially the first confusion arises in knowing how many safes were actually on board: as HMS Hardy was the flotilla leader it seems reasonable to conclude that, rather than having the usual three, the ship contained four safes. Access to such safes would be allocated to officers including those of Warrant Officer rank. These personnel would be the custodians of the keys: this was a precaution so that in times of battle or other unexpected circumstances there would be at least one other delegated custodian.

On board the 'Hardy', Paymaster Lieutenant Geoffrey Stanning would have been the main custodian for the safe in the ship's office and, as verified by Bert Mason, Warrant Officer McCracken was the second custodian. This safe was where the cash was kept, for both the ships' companies' pay and any other incidental bills that needed to be paid (for example, victuals when the ship went into harbour, home or abroad).

However, there are two accounts spanning approximately twenty-five years which collaborate an intriguing and possible outcome of the dispatching of the 'Secret Codes'.

Extracts from the autobiography of Bernard Penrose, a RNVR officer during the war, unearthed information regarding who on board was responsible for throwing the 'Hardy''s 'secret box' over the side when beached. Known for hosting social gatherings at his home in Lambe Creek, Bernard came into contact with people from all walks of life, with one such person being the naval officer Lieutenant Commander Victor Mansell. In his notes Bernard describes how "Mansell through a mistake that he could have avoided in the heat of battle allowed secret codes to get into enemy hands with the result that the Germans could decipher naval messages for the first time in the war; a mistake that would undoubtedly cost lives. Instead of burning the secret documents Mansell threw the weighted box overboard, but in only eight feet of water which allowed the Germans to retrieve the secret codes at low tide. It appears that Mansell could not get another job after this disaster, however, brave his actions had been at Narvik. The mistake was to stay with him for life."

In order to have a better overall picture of the issues it is necessary to analyse accounts from the crew members who had been privy to information about the destruction of the secret material.

Lieutenant Stanning states his movements just before 'Hardy' had started her voyage up the fjord to Narvik, "I then went aft again and instilled into Mr McCracken that he should dump the safes aft in an oil fuel tank if anything happened. This sounds rather as if I had some premonition of disaster but that was actually not the case as I had given up trying to think what was going to happen to us and was not in the least worried. If I had stopped to think I should have remembered that disaster always overtakes me when I have no premonition of it, and never when I have."

Later, when the ship is about to be abandoned, Stanning seems to have taken it upon himself to oversee the destruction of various secret papers: "The first thing on my mind was to destroy the cyphers and the Asdic cabinet and Bridge Set (External Receiver), [...] I sent a message to Mr McCracken, by the Chief Stoker, who I thought could help him throw the safe aft into the oil fuel tank outside the Captain's cabin. I told Midshipman Pope to get the naval cyphers out of the charthouse, put them in a weighted bag and throw them overboard as far aft as he could. Mansell then came up and said that the Asdic cabinet had been blown out of the ship and he confirmed that the set on the Bridge had been destroyed."

To corroborate, in Mansell's report for the Admiralty (which is kept in the National Archives Kew), he states how he witnessed Stanning "organising the destruction of the books which were put in a weighted bag and put over the stern, which was probably in deep water." Mansell also describes how "Mr McCracken (the Gunner) and I had been ordered by the Secretary (Stanning) to dispose of the secret chest in the office aft and this he did by dropping the contents into an oil tank under the Captain's cabin."

Les Smale recalled how, after getting the injured Captain off the ship, "We then got the Navigator clear of the Bridge and destroyed what books we thought might be of use to the enemy before finally leaving the Bridge ourselves."

In his account Bert Mason states that "Gunner McCracken collared me and said he wanted me to help him inside the ship's office. […] Pointing to an oil fuel tank cover he said that he wanted it opened which was no trouble…He then handed me a bunch of keys, he said one fitted the ship's safe and I was to go through them one at a time until I got the safe open. We succeeded and then he told me to hold out my arms carefully and take every single paper as he got them out and dumped them in the fuel tank. Midway through the operation he came across some money, £1 notes, ten shilling notes, two shilling pieces and then put them in his pockets. I remember thinking he could have given some of it to me. But under the circumstances it didn't seem much use. The job completed he banged the safe lid shut whilst I dropped the lid on the tank."

Interestingly, there is no mention from Mason of Mansell having being present at the time. As such, it could be that there were two safes to contend with, and that McCracken enlisted Mason into helping him with the second one.

Bill Pulford, according to his account, was also involved in the task of dealing with the confidential material. However his was a different version to that of Bert Mason. Gunner Mr McCracken shouted, "Give us a hand you chaps." He had the remainder of the confidential books and wanted them thrown over the side. So Torps (Heppel) and I got together and pitched what was left of them over the side so that they wouldn't get into the hands of the enemy."

Although Lieutenant Heppel did not mention his involvement in this episode in his report to the Admiralty, he did outline his involvement in destroying safes after the ship was finally abandoned when he had cause to return to it to rescue the Pilot and Navigator: "The Navigator was lowered into the float and Leading Seaman Mason and I went below to the Captain's cabin with a nine pound TNT charge to destroy the safes. When we had placed it I sent Mason on deck and after a couple of minutes lit the fuse and followed. [...] We had to get clear quickly because explosive charges had been set behind the safes, so that any confidential papers would be destroyed."

In this way, it would seem that these 'safes' or so called secret chests had either not been dealt with prior to the order to abandon ship, or had been dealt with insufficiently by simply filling them with oil soaked rags before closing. Further detail as to this episode comes from Mason, albeit almost forty years later: "I was now back on the raft with Heppel on board, saying he was going to destroy the Captain's safe with an explosive charge and we were to be ready to push off as soon as he came over the side. He was going to attach a TNT charge and fire it with a length of slow burning 'bickfords' safety fuse, giving us time to push off as soon as he came over the side for the last time [...] the charge detonated blowing a huge hole in the starboard side of the ship."

Based on this evidence, valid conjecture could be that once Mansell, Stanning and Heppel were reunited at Petra Kristensen's homestead, concerns were raised about whether or not all of the safes and confidential material had been dealt with appropriately. Certainly, with time to analyse the situation on board and confirm who had carried out the tasks, it may have been decided that whilst Heppel was going to rescue the Navigator, he should also do a proper job of destroying the safe in question.

However, confusingly there was another safe in the Captain's 'Sea' cabin. Before abandoning ship, Stoker Gordon Avery from Plymouth was ordered to take the keys to the ship's safe and remove all coded books and documents. On finding the safe damaged he decided to put oily rags inside, re-locked it and threw the keys over the side.

Much later, after the war, Gordon's son John Avery made a visit to the National Archives at Kew, where he discovered a file recording the eventual outcome of the above mentioned safe. According to John, the file recording describes how "some locals went on board 'Hardy' before she finally sank and with great effort managed to get the safe ashore. Later one of them buried it in the ground. At the end of the war, the local chap disclosed his secret to a visiting Royal Naval ship.

"A long wrangle ensued, as the Norwegian was looking for a reward. His argument was that he would probably have been shot by the enemy if they had found out. The Admiralty put the case that it was British Government property that had been illegally removed from the ship." As John says with tongue in cheek, "In a typical Civil Service fashion, the file got bigger as both sides argued their case."

In 1947, a submarine was dispatched to bring the safe back to Chatham. It took two locksmiths to gain entry. To John's amusement the report concluded: 'There was a most obnoxious smell and thick oil stains made all the contents unreadable'. John adds, "My father died in 1974 and it was after that time that I made the discovery at Kew. But I am sure that he would have enjoyed the ending to the story of the 'safe'."

Yet, for all this, such evidence does not explain Bernard Penrose's comments concerning Victor Mansell's 'mistake'. Indeed, from the above accounts it would seem that there was not one individual who was solely responsible for the disposing of confidential information. However, upon making a visit to his former First Lieutenant in 1971, my Dad, Cyril, learnt that since retiring from the Navy, Victor had problems securing appropriate employment. What is more, unlike fellow officers, and irrespective of his long service, Victor neither received an award nor was he promoted after the Battle: after the traumatic experience of Narvik, he had shore appointments for two years from September 1940 as a Port Anti-Submarine Officer in Devonport. He then left the Navy in 1945.

Therefore, it could be concluded that, as a senior officer Victor Mansell took the blame for the secret documents which, although allegedly destroyed, were actually thrown overboard into shallow water, allowing the Germans to retrieve them later. Such negligence would help to explain why Victor was not commended by the Admiralty in the same way as his comrades, despite his bravery being equal to that of the other men.

However, it could easily be argued that, even though the enemy gained access to confidential documents which were not disposed of properly at the Battle of Narvik, the Germans had already broken the Royal Navy codes a long time before. In his book, 'Very Special Admiral', Patrick Beesly states that "Aided by British security failures during the Abyssinian crisis they had, by 1939, penetrated some of the Royal Navy's operational and administrative cyphers. This, combined with other forms of radio intelligence, such as direction finding, traffic analysis and study of call signs (which they themselves had abandoned), enabled the xB Dienst to supply Admiral Raeder with much useful information about Naval dispositions during the first ten months of the war. British submarine losses in the Heligoland Bight were largely made possible by German knowledge of their patrol areas and during the Norwegian Campaign the location and movements of the Home Fleet were accurately deduced."

To conclude, I believe that the actions of the men in regard to the destruction (or indeed lack of destruction) of confidential material and secret codes on board the 'Hardy' is understandable. Certainly, in a frightening, fast-moving and constantly developing situation, self-preservation is a natural, human instinct. With the fight having been completed, it was time for flight. Also, as the command had been wiped out early on, the remaining, injured, non-seamen officer and ratings could only do their best under the circumstances. It was not until all of the surviving crew members managed to re-group ashore that some normality was established. Regardless of the failings (in regard to some of the confidential material entering German hands), the constant bravery of these men is undeniable.

20

Ready for Moving On

I now return to Petra Kristensen's final memories, before the sailors had to make well their escape into the unknown.

"The Chief Stoker died and was covered in a snow heap outside the house. Later in the day Mr Ravn came from Ballangen with others in cars and fetched the men. It was then that we had time to notice what the survivors were wearing, some had ladies' pants, others had embroidered tablecloths over their shoulders and one ran across the snow drifts in my 'wedding dress' complete with sequins and all.

"Several times we had to go out and cover the body of the dead man. It was spring and the sun soon melted the snow. After the living had been attended to, Mr Ravn came back and took the body to Ballangen for burial."

A long time passed before Cyril found out that many weeks after these events, a covert courier turned up at the Kristensens' home, handing them an envelope on behalf of the British Government, to reimburse them for their caring assistance. Also of course it covered the mess that the sailors had made, in the few short hours that they were there, sundry items of clothing and other personal belongings which were taken from the chalet. I would like to think that Petra's wedding dress once discarded by the sailor in Ballangen, found its way back to her in one piece.

Lt Paymaster Geoffrey Stanning, although naturally desperate to have hospital treatment for his badly injured foot, still had time to think about the well being of other crew members. "Then a lorry and a car drew up outside and I was sure that it must be Germans come to fetch us but could not see which way the vehicles were facing. A small man in spectacles came up the path and someone said perhaps he's a doctor. He came up to me and said I ought to put some clothes on and he would take me to hospital.

Petra with Cyril and Ron having attended 50th Anniversary Service at Ballangen. 1990. *Ron Cope Collection.*

"He said he had a cottage hospital about fifteen miles away at Ballangen and that he had room for all our wounded. I asked him to go into the house and help with Chief Stoker 'Stiles', who I knew was in a very bad way with a fractured skull. He said 'Stiles' was too bad to be moved and in fact dying but he would take some of the wounded to his hospital straight away. The worst cases were taken out and put in the lorry and we felt extremely thankful to have them off our hands."

The surviving crew had re-grouped and were ready to go, as felt by Bert Mason. "By now everyone was in a more cheerful mood, thoughts of being captured by the enemy had gone and some organisation was in hand. We were to make our way to Ballangen which was about twenty-four kilometres distant following the coast road. Norwegians with vehicles had volunteered to transport the wounded but for those uninjured and able to walk it was 'Shanks' pony'."

Cyril Cope was also desperate to get under way. "At last a decision was reached, the wounded would travel in the Doctor's car, some to the village of Ballangen and the three serious cases to a place called 'Harstad'. (These three sailors could have been Able Seamen Geoff Bailey, Hugh Argent, Robert Clarke; all part of Gun Crews.) The order to move was given by the First Lieutenant. We said goodbye to Chief Stoker Stiles, who at this time was lying on a stretcher outside the chalet and who we knew would not live much longer than an hour if that. We also said our goodbyes to the lady and her daughter who had done so much for our wounded comrades."

Anna Reid mentions that her Granddad Jack Good and about six of the other wounded sailors, having been helped by the two women, were dressed in women's clothing. Anna indicates that Jack was transported to Ballangen hospital "by sledge".

Stan Robinson, obviously still suffering from his experience: "I cut my lifebelt in half and put half on each foot. I can't remember wearing any clothes. But Douglas Bourton and me kept knocking each other about all the way."

Bill Pulford indicates that Lieutenant Heppel finally got his way by volunteering him (and Bert Mason again) to an important task. "Torps said, to go off in small groups because going en-mass if there are any prying eyes, they may think we were 'Jews' getting out of the way of the Germans; before the Gestapo started sending them back to Germany. Go in small groups so as not to form any suspicions, which we did. He called me to one side with Mason, his two Leading Seaman LTOs. He said, while you are going down there keep your eyes open for anything that might be of use to the enemy, we might be here for some time and don't forget we're still at war. We've got to do what we can to impede his progress.

"Well, being a typical matelot, I said, 'If we find any explosives, what the hell are we going to do with them?' He said, 'You can keep some of them under your skirt so they don't see.' Tongue in cheek! 'Anyway, I want you two to take up the rear, apart from keeping your eyes open, you can also be the rear guard, keep everybody moving, don't let anybody straggle behind you, when you get to Ballangen or wherever we are. When you arrive I know everyone else has got in. At the same time should the Germans be coming up, you can at least give a warning to everybody up front of you.' We started off at a brisk pace but after about a mile, these snow ruts had been frozen. They were like sharp icicles or knives and they had pierced the rubber on our makeshift boots and my feet were bleeding. Then we didn't walk we limped and shuffled, that's how it was!"

Dougy Bourton: "We were told then that all those who could make their way should go South to Ballangen. We didn't know what or where Ballangen was, but we had to follow the coast road. There was only one road, so we took out a party of four particular friends. Conditions were bad, the snow was quite deep, what wasn't deep was wet and icy and we walked and walked."

Cyril: "We set out at 1300 hours, in twos and threes with the Torpedo Officer leading the way. When we had picked our partners prior to setting out, I had picked a chap from my mess, an AB Torpedoman called Bowman, we called him 'Birdy'. He was older than I and a very reliable chap, just the type if I tried to quit, to make me keep going. The sun at this time was shining very brightly and felt quite warm to our near naked bodies. We were thankful for this but knew it would not last long, certainly not all the way to the village we were making for. Long before then it would get very cold; still it was a nice warm start to our journey. On our feet we had used our rubber lifebelts in place of socks and shoes, cutting them in half and putting each half on each foot, tying the tapes round our ankles. This was all right for the first few miles but then they began to wear through and slip off. So we threw them away and carried on in our bare feet."

Geoffrey Stanning: "After what seemed ages, we heard that the lorry was coming back. I must admit I was longing to go to hospital myself as I could not seem to get dry and my foot was aching almost unbearably. Then we heard that Heppel was on his way ashore with 'Gordon-Smith' which was very good news. About a dozen of us went down and got into the lorry and I understood that was all the wounded there were except for Pilot who was brought up a few minutes later and put in the lorry. He was still a terrible sight but was smoking a cigarette quite contentedly. So we set out for Ballangen in this very general purpose lorry which was evidently used in normal times for taking to market people, pigs, chickens or whatever wanted to go.

"The road was deep in snow, trodden in the middle by pedestrians and car tracks at the sides. There were deep potholes where the snow was soft and the road was especially hilly and lopsided where it kept close to the shore of the fjord. I was sitting on a bench at the fore end of the back part of the lorry and so could see out through the glass behind the driver's seat as there was no other window. The lorry bumped along at twelve miles an hour stopping every few hundred yards to pass people or vehicles or negotiate apparently insurmountable blockages of snow. It seemed an endless journey though I could not tell how long it lasted as my watch had stopped at twelve minutes past seven which was presumably when I jumped into the sea."

Bert and his group, similar to others, were finding the trek a considerable challenge under such conditions. "We set off in small groups along the snow bound road, the top layer becoming quite slushy due to the spring thaw setting in. Our group consisted of Torpedomen in various rigs of attire which included items of female clothes and a variety of footwear. One poor devil struggling along with his feet bound in old newspapers.

"One of the 'heroines' of the whole episode, the good lady Mrs Kristensen, was at the door of her house, with her daughter waving goodbye and good luck to the motley throng of ship-wrecked mariners who had so suddenly descended on them that morning. Tired and hungry we traipsed on, occasionally being overtaken by vehicles carrying the wounded, their tyres wrapped in chains. It was some time before I remembered the 'Ensign' left behind hidden in snow. It was too late to go back, but I was certainly peeved after all the trouble I had gone to bringing it off the ship!"

Bill 'Ned' Sparkes had a good memory as seen in his previously mentioned letter to my father. "He [Bert Mason] said he would need to hide it so he said later that he had stuck it under the floor of – here's where I can't remember either a house or a hut or barn. One thing I can recall quite well, even though I never wrote it down, is the name of the house. If this was the same one or not, I'm not sure and the owner. It was:

AXEL. F. NILSEN OR NEILSEN
DRONNINGS GT 50
NARVIK

Bill Pulford trudging onwards. "We passed various houses, no Norwegians offered to give us a lift but everybody said, 'The wounded first'. Mason and I overtook one chap, well people who had to fall out or dropped out due to wounds were propped up alongside the road with a group of Norwegians to keep watch and so they were not left on their own. We came up to one chap – he was a 'Stoker' – and there was ten or eleven staying with him. This Stoker had just about had it. He'd been hit in both legs or burnt, whatever the case may be. He couldn't go on any further, he was propped up against a wall, smoking a cigarette. As we passed we had a few words of cheerfulness as best we could with him. He said, 'Oh don't worry about me, it could be worse, it could have been raining, whilst I have been stood here. She's been looking after me- meaning a little girl. They were waiting for a sledge so someone could take him to Ballangen."

Geoffrey Stanning and the other wounded are slowly making their way towards their final destination, albeit having to endure a very uncomfortable ride in the lorry. "There were about twelve wounded in the back and three or four in the front. Pilot lay patiently on the floor with his feet against the back door. I was amazed at the patience of all these men most of whom were in much more pain than I was, though I was praying for the end of the journey as every bump of the lorry jarred my foot. I could not imagine what was wrong with it but thought there must be a fairly large splinter inside as there was a hole in the very middle of my heel which was bleeding steadily and I could not imagine a hole being made in that tough skin any other way than by something going in.

"After we had gone what I thought must be about twelve miles I asked one of the two Norwegians who were in the back with us how much further there was to go and he said about seven kilometres. We were going through occasional villages and seemingly getting further and further from civilisation. At last I was told we were coming to Ballangen and my heart sank as there seemed to be no large houses and my hopes of a proper hospital began to fade. Not having slept at all for the last three nights I was desperately tired but could not rest my mind for thinking what to do next and above all how on earth to let anyone in England know where we were or what had happened to us."

Back to Bert Mason and his memories of the immediate ordeal. "At one point where the road neared the edge of the fjord we stopped to look at a huge blackened crater on the shore line and came to the conclusion that a torpedo (probably an enemy one) had tore into the beach and exploded. After a while we sighted what seemed like a small farmstead just off the road. We were determined to try our luck for a mouthful to eat. We knocked on the door and were immediately taken inside and sat down while the farmer's wife set to make hot coffee. A few minutes later we were feasting on hard boiled eggs and bread and butter. Some of the lads were having a twiddle on a small radio to see if they could pick up any 'English' broadcasts but not having much luck."

Bill Pulford gives his version of the hospitality provided by the farmer and his wife. "Another place we passed, an old lady was standing at the gate. She had pity written all over her face. She saw my feet bleeding and asked us in. So she gave me a cup of coffee and something to eat. She took the rubber strips and newspapers off my feet which were now sodden red with blood, washed them and put linen around best she could. Then I was given a pair of ski boots. They were about two or three sizes too big for me - apparently they were her husband's. But she was quite insistent that I took them. When I put them on, Mason said to me, 'God you do look like a bloody duck have you seen yourself?'

"Well, this was first time I had had a chance to see myself in a mirror, she had also given me a Norwegian ski cap, I was wearing a ladies' jumper, ladies' skirt, legs wrapped in paper and ski boots. I know when I got to Ballangen 'Torps' came to see us and he just took one look at me and all he could say was 'Christ' and he walked away with a grin on his face."

Bert: "It was soon time to continue our journey but before we went we had a whip round for the household. We did not know what he could do with the 'English' money but out came the recently paid out two shilling pieces; there was a look of surprise on his face when we made him accept them. At the door he noticed the lad with the shredded newspaper around his feet and pointing down he immediately whipped off his own shoes, indicating that he should put them on, which he did. Just one of the gestures of the kindly Norwegians."

Before recalling the rest of the surviving sailors' trek, hopefully to an improved position of safety, the 'man of the house' at their last port of call, Hakon Kristensen, arrives back home. "Returning from fishing in 'Lofoten', I met the English warships coming out of the fjord (presumably 'Hostile' and 'Havock' towing 'Hotspur') and after landing in Ballangen I met cars coming from Skogseth. I remember my family were very glad to see me."

Cyril, even under the desperate circumstances, remembers that they kept their sense of humour. "Here we were on a good long hike over snow and an icy road. We did not at that time know how far the village was or if there were any Germans in the vicinity or where we could go if we met any on the road. Because to our right, a hell of a long way down the cliffs was the fjord, while on the left, reaching a hell of a way up were more steep mountains. Both sides covered by snow and ice, with no footholds for us to climb up or down and certainly no shelter to hide if we met the enemy."

Dougy and his pals are also finding the going tough and just when they think they have found a temporary haven they come across what appears to be unwelcoming locals. "We got a little bit tired along the way and we saw a Norwegian farmhouse, some distance away from the side of the fjord. So we went up there and knocked on the door. We couldn't understand the Norwegians, because they were saying 'Tiske, Tiske'. We knew what they meant, we thought it was Norwegian for 'Go away, Go away'. But it turned out that the 'Tiske' was the word for German. They thought we were Germans and they didn't want anything to do with us."

Walter Mitchell: "Although a lot of us were half naked, half frozen and nearly fagged out, the chaps would not let their spirits drop and we sang such songs as 'Roll out the Barrel' and 'Somewhere in France – the Lilies Grow'. You can't kill the spirit of the British Navy."

Cyril: "It took many weary hours to reach Ballangen. On the way some Norwegians asked us into their homes to have a cup of coffee and pieces of bread with honey or treacle. Some chaps received clothing from them. It was quite dark when we reached the village but I found my way to the hospital. I was only wearing the girl's knickers and still nothing on my feet. I was frozen stiff, barely able to walk."

Stan Robinson wearing hardly any clothes starts to suffer. "I was about half a mile from Ballangen, staggering about, I didn't know where I was. A Norwegian came out of a house, picked me up over his back, put me in an empty bath and covered me with snow. They gradually warmed up the snow and I thawed out. They gave me a skiing suit to wear. So I sat down and they asked me where I had come from. 'Was I German or was I English, Deutsch or whatever?' I said, give me a pencil and paper and I'll draw you, so I drew a picture of the British Isles and put a dot where Port Talbot was. He exclaimed 'Ah Celtic, Celtic.' I said, 'Yes, Welsh, Welsh.' So I had a bit of a smile about that, you see. After he gave me coffee and cakes, I followed the rest of the boys, who were trudging up and we helped the wounded."

Bert Mason and his group were also near to their goal. "Late that afternoon we were within kilometres of our destination in Ballangen, a wooden school building. We passed two girls by a gateway, well and truly muffed up in their winter outfits and wearing skis. We did a friendly grin and amazingly one of them, a young fair haired girl, called out in perfect English 'That is where you are going!' and pointed to the school on some high ground. We chatted for a few moments and asked her what she thought of the Germans invading her country and our intrusion at Narvik, but we didn't think she fully understood the situation then."

Bill Pulford: "Anyhow we kicked off again from this little shack. We got to Ballangen about 6 to 7 o'clock at night. Just before we went into Ballangen there was a small group of girls and boys waiting at the roadside. They walked with us the rest of the way, cheering us on, giving us a helping hand. They guided us into a school house at the top of the hill."

BBC 'WORLD SERVICE'.10th APRIL AT 6.00 P.M.

"Mr Chamberlain announced the British achievements. He said, 'I do not propose today to make any general statement on the naval aspect of the war as I hope it will be possible for one to be made by the First Lord of the Admiralty tomorrow.

But the House will probably wish to hear an account I have just received of the fierce action fought by British destroyers against the German forces in Narvik. Five British destroyers steamed up the Fjord and engaged six German destroyers of the latest and largest type, which were also supported by shore guns and batteries with newly mounted guns.' The Prime Minister said, that H.M.S. HUNTER was sunk and HARDY was so severely injured that she had to be run ashore and became a wreck. The HUNTER a thirteen hundred ton destroyer, has a normal complement of one hundred and forty five. That HARDY, a flotilla leader, is slightly larger and normally carried a crew of one hundred and seventy five.

"The Prime Minister continued: 'After a most determined action against a superior force, and larger and more modern ships, and in face of gun-fire from the shore, the damaged HOTSPUR withdrew, covered by the two destroyers. The enemy appeared in no condition to attempt pursuit. A sixteen hundred ton German destroyer was torpedoed and believed sunk, and three were left heavily hit and burning.'

In the House of Lords, Earl Stanhope made a statement similar to that of Mr Chamberlain. He said that the British action at Narvik was brilliantly executed, and carried out against overwhelming odds. The tradition of the British Navy had been upheld most fully."

Dougy Bourton and pals have finally made it together and in one piece. "We continued making our way down to the village of Ballangen. When we came there, the village children were there to meet us. We were weary by now, having been on our feet for several days. We had fought action with all the shock and trauma, abandoned ship, dragged the wounded and dead about, we were tired! I will always remember the young Norwegians taking us up the hill to the school."

21

Saviours of Ballangen

During the 'Hardy' survivors' trek to Ballangen the remaining three ships of the flotilla 'Havock', 'Hostile' and the badly damaged 'Hotspur' had made good their escape out of the Vestfjord. Signals between the ships and the Admiralty continued. Here are the last of those copied by 'Havock' from the W/T Log found in my father's documents.

> 1639 – Second Destroyer Flotilla from Admiralty. – Their Lordships congratulate all concerned on your determined action against superior forces and on the successful result you achieved despite severe losses.

Times for the next signals are not recorded.

Havock Hostile from Hotspur – The gallant manner in which Havock and Hostile returned and covered their sister Chatham ship out of Narvik resulted in the saving of the ship and many lives and is highly appreciated.

Hotspur from Havock – Many thanks for your kind message, after three years together even the Germans cannot part us.

All Concerned from Admiralty – Following has been received from the Governor, Government and peoples of Malta. Deepest regards and admiration on the successful operation just completed especially to ships of the Mediterranean Fleet.

The end was in sight for Geoffrey Stanning and the rest of the wounded. "We went right through the village of Ballangen and my hopes of a proper hospital sank entirely. But suddenly we turned off the road to the left and stopped in front of a largish square building on three floors and were told we were there. This did not look too bad. Some of us were taken inside and then they said that some of the worst cases must go on to 'Harstad' where there was a better fitted hospital. I was extremely sorry for them. Inside the hospital there was a marvellous smell of cleanness and antiseptics, there were plenty of nurses hurrying about and I really felt we were in good hands.

"We were all put on benches in the passage way until the doctor could see us and when I had settled everyone down I went hopping to see who was in the hospital already. I was rather disgusted to find that several of our ratings had got to the hospital in the first loads on the ground that they had frostbite when I knew there was nothing wrong with them at all. Also in the hospital were quite a number of English merchant seamen who had come from ships sunk in Narvik. They were only suffering from exposure and were being sent from the hospital to board at houses in the village."

Harry Rogers was one of those wounded who were provided with lorry transportation. He had been unconscious, probably through the wound in his back and loss of blood, as the next thing he remembers clearly was "waking up in what looked to be a school hall and being attended by a local girl". The 'bite' turned out to be a piece of shrapnel about the size of a 50 pence piece which lodged itself very close to his lungs and heart. It appears the icy water of the fjord prevented him from losing too much blood. You will hear more about Harry's recovery from the injury and his ongoing exploits in WW2 in the latter chapters.

Before continuing the other accounts of 'Hardy''s crew members on arrival at Ballangen, I would like to introduce readers to Fred Evans from Plymouth. In Cyril's memorabilia I found a copy of a letter written in 1973 from Fred to the Mayor of Ballangen. Fred Evans wrote the letter because out of all the Hardy survivors he recalls an incident in Ballangen that he alone experienced. For years this had been troubling him because it could not be substantiated by any of the other crew members. I leave Fred to tell the story of his determination to verify what he saw was fact. Here is the first part of his letter, the remainder will follow:

Dear Sir,
12th April 1973

I am one of the survivors from H.M.S. Hardy who swam ashore at Vidrik, and were given shelter at Mrs Kristenson's house, and then provided with such wonderful hospitality by the people of Ballangen. I am encouraged to write to you after hearing from Mr Cope of the welcome you gave to him and his daughter when they visited Ballangen. I now wish to relate what I can remember of what happened to me from 10th April 1940.

I was brought out of Mrs Kristenson's house and taken by motor-van to Ballangen Hospital with other wounded men. After being X-rayed I was passed as a convalescent by the doctor. A *wound in my knee turned out to be not very serious. I was taken to a house with another shipmate. (I have tried to place the position of the house on the enclosed map, but this is no more than guess work.) At this house we were treated as members of the family. We enjoyed nice meals; although I realised now that food at the time was scarce. We were given a lovely large bed with a soft mattress. We must have stayed there three nights, because on the Saturday morning, it was realised that it was not safe for this good family to shelter us any longer, and we had to move out.*

Lieutenant George Heppel arrives at their destination. "At Ballangen, we found that some of our men had already arrived and that the wounded were in a little hospital. I first went up to the school where arrangements had been made to house the main body. The school was a big wooden building, with central heating but otherwise scarcely completed, and mattresses and hay were provided as bedding. [...] The hospital was working wonders. All the wounded with the exception of three very bad cases which had been sent on to Harstad, had been made comfortable; either in the hospital or its overflow or in private houses; where the owners had volunteered to put up the less serious cases. While I was there the last three bad cases arrived on sleigh. They had had a very bad journey indeed, although the First Lieutenant and other officers had done their best for them. The three men were Able Seaman Clark and Signalmen Turner and Brigginshaw."

Les Smale has also completed his gruelling trek. "We were treated with many kindnesses by Norwegians, in the way of food, clothing. Eventually, at about 7 pm we reached a village called Ballangen, where they opened a big centrally heated school for us and gave us tea, rye bread and some sausages to eat. It didn't take long to get off to sleep that night but it took a bit more effort to get us up next morning. All that day the people were bringing up bedding, clothes and food. They treated us well and the only way we could help them by way of payment was to give a hand at clearing away the snow which we all willingly did."

Dougy Bourton: "The school in a short time had been made into the second naval establishment for HMS Hardy. We all very quickly became organised and were given a scratch meal of some sort of biscuits, odds and ends. But anyway we just collapsed on the wooden deck and slept. The school incidentally was still standing in 1980, it had been preserved, I don't know whether it was a monument or what. Although it was boarded up, we could go inside. We had a photograph taken on the steps of the school that had sheltered all of us."

George Heppel: "I did not visit the 'out patients' because by now it was dark, but returned to the school, where I found that a party of merchant seamen from British ships at Narvik, under Captain Evans of the 'North Cornwall' had joined us."

Captain Evans told the 'Hardy' survivors that his ship the 'North Cornwall' was seized on 9th of April when the German destroyers entered Narvik. He and his seamen were taken as prisoners and placed on the 'Jan Wellem'. In fact, by the time the British destroyers had come in for the third attack, Captain Evans, having put his life at risk, managed to get to the upper deck on the temporary prison ship. Where to his delight, he was able to see the damage done, leaving him with a feeling of pride for the Royal Navy. Shortly after, the Captain of the 'Jan Wellem' made the order to abandon his ship and was sufficiently courteous to allow and assist Captain Evans and his men to leave on one of the life boats."

However, there is more to Captain Evans' story which he was able to relate to Peter Dickens thirty years later. "Captain Evans and his Chief Engineer having made their way to 'Jan Wellem's' boat deck were able to watch the attack by their compatriots and the devastation they left behind. The Captain of 'Jan Wellem' being amongst the melee, would probably have been thanking his luck that his vessel was still afloat and no lives lost. However, he and Evans both, were also concerned about their future prospects."

This is Captain Evans' version as described by Dickens. "The whaler's Captain was equally apprehensive and asked Evans what he thought of the situation; Evans replied staunchly that knowing the Royal Navy as he did they would assuredly not rest until the 'Jan Wellem' had been accounted for. That started a train of thought, and when the Captain asked Evans what he would do were he in command, he responded readily that he would give the prisoners a chance to get away while they still might. There the matter rested while the Captain digested the proposal."

School House at Ballangen. Circa 1983. *Provided by Bill and Borg-Anna Sanders.*

Subsequently, Captain Evans with forty-six crew and their two armed guards decided to go the opposite way from Narvik town and crossed to the Southwest side of the fjord. Arriving cold on a snowy shore the Captain guided his men into a close and intimidating circle around the two guards, and not surprisingly persuaded them to drop their firearms. This was on the basis that they were now on 'neutral territory' and could not be held any longer as prisoners of war. With advice from some nearby Norwegians they made for Ballangen.

Returning to George Heppel at the school and his conversation with Captain. "One sidelight on their experiences, was their report of the extreme cheerfulness and confidence of the Germans in the success of their part of the Norwegian campaign. This was so marked that it even tended to shake the confidence of the prisoners in our ability to rescue them and re-take Narvik. But the most interesting point of all was the manner in which the German confidence gave way almost to panic, with desperate cries of 'Englanders komm' when our attack started. [...] I listened a little longer to their adventures and turned in; it was late, nearly midnight I think, and so ended twenty-four hours, which I shall never forget."

In the meantime Cyril Cope is now suffering physically from the ordeal. "Somebody came out of the hospital and assisted me up the steps, taking me inside they laid me on a bed. Then two nurses came to attend to me, they wrapped me up in blankets and gave me some hot soup and started to massage my feet and legs with some kind of oil. I am sure this treatment saved me from getting frostbite like some other chaps did. They next massaged my arms and tried to unclench my left hand which was closed tight and had been for the whole of the journey. This was because I had my two shillings in it. I hadn't wanted to lose it and due to the intense cold, the joints of my fingers had seized up. When they eventually opened up my hand they both had a good laugh on seeing what I had in it. I am sure they thought I had been trying to hide it from them. By this time I was feeling much warmer. I had been given some 'Red Cross' shorts, socks and a vest. Then the younger of the two nurses called in a boy aged about twelve. She told him to give me his overcoat and rubber boots, and then told another boy to take me to her house."

Bill Pulford and Bert Mason having arrived had differing priorities. First, Bill explains, "There was a pile of clothes and I saw a pair of trousers and an old jacket. Without further ado I grabbed these, they were mine! I discarded the skirt and kept the jumper of course. I realised then I still had the 'White Ensign' with me. I'd taken it out of my overall pocket when I had got ashore and stuck it in the waistband of my underpants and taking the skirt off, I realised I had it. I cut away the lining of the jacket, which I had purloined - it was only a small boats 'ensign'. I thought that would be my life line maybe. If we get to wherever we're going if I showed this ensign it would prove I'm British. If I show it to Germans it proves I am a naval man because I am in 'civvies'. I don't want to be shot as a spy. It will prove we are who we say we are. So I stuck it in the lining of the jacket, did a few 'homeward bounders' in the forming of sewing and kept it there and forgot all about it again."

Bert describes a feeling of great relief. "The haven of the school at last, we were the last to arrive. There was nothing much left in the way of food and the sleeping blankets had long been taken. A nurse came over to ask if we had any injuries and I suddenly thought of the blow I had received when abandoning the ship. I went to pull my trousers down and she said I had better see the doctor! I had a good look myself and saw that I had received a nasty smack just inside my left knee; no skin was broken but from my knee downwards to my ankle was a huge bruise. I came to the conclusion I had been hit by a flat piece of metal, probably shrapnel, but funnily enough it had not bothered me. Although dead tired and lying on bare boards I couldn't sleep. I just went over the events of the past few days and wondered about the future. Here we were trapped in Norway inside the 'Arctic' circle. I wondered what was going to happen next."

Geoffrey Stanning: "There seemed to be plenty of nurses in the hospital and any amount of voluntary helpers. After about 20 minutes we were called into the kitchen and given a good meal of stew followed by preserved fruit. Then we were seen one by one by the doctors of whom there were three, two belonging to the hospital and one who had escaped from the hospital in Narvik. I was not seen until about 4 o'clock and my foot was very painful. I was taken upstairs and put in a small room by myself, given some morphia and I went to sleep."

KARL SMIDT

APRIL 10 1940. AT 0500 ENGLISH DESTROYERS BROKE THROUGH ALARMING THE GERMAN DESTROYERS IN NARVIK HARBOUR 2 GERMAN DESTROYERS WERE OUT OF ACTION. THE REST OF THE GERMANS JOINED ACTION WITH THE BRITISH. THE BRITISH DESTROYERS 'HARDY' AND 'HUNTER' WERE PUT OUT OF ACTION; 'HARDY' ENDED UP ON THE REEFS OF NARVIK HARBOUR. 'HUNTER' WAS SUNK. THE REMAINING 3 BRITISH DESTROYERS ESCAPED BADLY DAMAGED. 'GIESE' RESCUED SURVIVORS FROM THE 'HUNTER', THEY WERE FOUND SWIMMING IN THE FJORD. 16 SEAMEN WERE PUT ONBOARD THE 'BARKASS', 8 OF THEM DIED FROM EXPOSURE.

AT 2040 HOURS AN ESCAPE ATTEMPT WAS MADE BY 2 BATTLE READY DESTROYERS 'WOLFGANG ZENKER' AND 'ERICH GIESE'. NEAR BARO A BRITISH DESTROYER AND 1 CRUISER WERE SIGHTED. ESCAPE ATTEMPT WAS HOPELESS. NEAR RUCKKEHR ON RETURN IT WAS NOTICED THAT THE BOILER OF THE 'GIESE' WAS LEAKING SALT IN THE CONDENSER!

It is interesting to note, if Karl Smidt's figures are correct, that this is evidence of the 'Giese' picking up 'Hunter' survivors, which I knew, but that eight died on board of 'exposure'. However, a photograph taken by the German crew shows more than eight men in the 'Barkass'. This raises the question did Karl mean there was sixteen who survived and eight died?

This will be fully covered further in my following book, dedicated to the loss of HMS Hunter and her ship's company.

Returning back to the 'Hardy' survivors, with the assistance of their newly found Norwegian friends, beginning with Dougy Bourton, continuing their recollections. "We formed into working parties, woke up in the morning, had 'Divisions', as if we were onboard ship. Some helped the chefs, some went scrounging for firewood and all sorts. Typical naval routine, grab a shovel and clear the thick snow around the schools steps. Our wounded had now been brought to the village hospital, we put sentries there and on the jetty. It was run as a naval establishment no doubt at all."

Bert wakes up wondering what the day would hold for them. "Next morning we were told to make our way down to a local community hall to get a meal; boiled potatoes and boiled white fish. It was very satisfying but nowhere near enough to appease our starving pangs of hunger. We lived on this fare, more or less, during our stay in Ballangen. The Norwegians were at their wits end as to how to feed us and to increase the problem a large number of British Merchantmen had joined us making a total of over 200 men."

Geoffrey Stanning: "Dr Waind was brought in with me the next morning and I was very glad to have someone to talk to. The hospital had no books which we could read and there was absolutely nothing to do but look out of the window at a magpie's nest in front of the window. We were thankful for the visitors who came at all hours of the day, both townspeople and our own ship's company."

Anthony Ronayne, the crewman from Malta, eventually went on to have a long and distinguished career in the Royal Navy until 1964. I will mention more about this later in the book. However, Anthony was also befriended by a local family.

"Everyone was in agony with frostbite, as very few of us had shoes on. We had many wounded. The Norwegians were good to us, they put us in a school and we all lay on the wooden floor. The women came and brought hot water and bandages and they took good care of us. I was lucky, as the woman who bandaged my leg, next day she took me to her house. She also tried to hide me so that I stayed there for good, but the Officer knew that I was staying in that house."

When I visited Anthony's family in Malta in 2010 (Anthony having passed away in 2007), from what they told me it became clearer that the Norwegian family were relatively wealthy and ran their own small iron ore or other type of natural resource mine. It appears they had an above average size house with a cellar, where Anthony was able to be kept hidden in case the Germans arrived.

It is easy to forget the young age of most of the sailors at the time, having read their experiences so far. Les Smale like Anthony Ronayne was twenty years of age. Les was the only survivor from the First Battle of Narvik to have the foresight to write down his experiences shortly after the event. "During the day we visited the wounded in the hospital and they were as glad to see us as we were to see them. We could all now find time enough to spare a moment or two for those, some of whom were very close friends, who were not just lucky enough to share our good fortune to have survived the battle of yesterday."

Charles Cheshire: "When we got to Ballangen, I think he may have been the Mayor took us down to a 'Man's Outfitters', and got us dressed in suits, boots and socks, the lot. I was dressed in a two piece suit, a sweater, a ski cap and ski boots. I did feel the cold, not that it bothered me really. It was very cold in the water but there were other things to think about, rather than being cold. We ate boiled cod with potatoes and Ryvitas."

Cyril is moved on. "On arriving at the nurse's home I was met by her son and daughter, two blonde beauties. The boy, who could speak English enough for me to understand him, was aged twelve and his sister was five. After a while I found out that the boy's name was 'Torrod Haugland'. By this time some of his pals had come around to see the 'English shipwrecked sailor' and Torrod sent one of them home to fetch his father's razor so that I could have a shave. This I had, after a good wash, the first for thirty-six hours. We sat talking while we waited for Mrs Haugland to come home. The children wanted to know all about the battle, so with Torrod translating for me, I told them a bit of what had happened during the fighting; as much as I could about our ship and the crew, and tried to find out what the people in the village thought about the Germans."

Bill Pulford and the majority of the crew members had not got access to the niceties of life which those moved to family homes had. "We only had three razors and two blades to keep ourselves shaved with. When it was my turn to shave for instance, there had been thirty before me. So you can imagine what it felt like, especially going out in the cold, it felt like it had taken all the flesh off my cheeks."

Cyril is now feeling much fresher and comfortable in his newly acquired surroundings. "When Mrs Haugland arrived home, she made me a meal of fish, cheese, bread (which was like our Ryvita) and coffee with goat's milk. Then came the task of finding some clothes for me. Her husband was away at the time either on business or he had been called up to the Army because of the emergency. I couldn't make out which. Anyway she fixed me up with a navy blue suit, white shirt, black shoes, black overcoat and a tie. They fitted me perfectly. After putting on the clothing we sat around the fire and with Torrod once again acting as interpreter we had a good chat. They wanted to know all about me, what part of England I came from; my family and my life in the Navy. Then we discussed the Battle and the war in general. We tried to get the BBC News on their radio but interference was too great.

"It had just turned midnight and I was feeling a bit uneasy about what might be happening to the remainder of the survivors. Mrs Haugland asked me if I would like to stay there for the night. She said that I could have Torrod's bed. I thanked her for the offer but said I would have to refuse. I explained that I would have to find out what my shipmates were doing and wherever they were sleeping, I would have to sleep. Because if the Germans came during the night and an order was given to move out I did not want to be left behind. After asking me to return for breakfast the following morning, if all went well, she then told Torrod to take me to the village school. Away I went with the overcoat over my arm, well shaved, hair brushed, looking like a 'Toff'.

"At the school, which was the lower of the two village schools, Torrod said goodbye and left me. I walked through the doorway into a noisy, smoke filled room. At long tables sat groups of scruffy half clad sailors eating fish and bread and drinking cups of coffee which was being served by several teenagers at tables fixed up as counters. These teenagers had come from all over the district to give their help. Some, from far up the mountains, had come down on their skis. What a wonderful lot they were.

"As I approached the table at which some of my pals were sitting they looked at me without recognising me for a few seconds, then the penny dropped. They gaped at me, then, with one voice they shouted, 'Where the hell did you get fixed up like that?' (using much stronger language of course). 'Oh', said I very seriously and quietly, 'I'm a native now, I'm living here.' That started it, from all sides came good natured abuse in typical nautical language, most of them saying what a lucky so and so I was. Others making terrible suggestions, as to how I came to get spruced up, all in fun of course and it was good for a laugh. Leaving them to enjoy the joke, I walked over to the table where the coffee was being served and asked for a cup. They wouldn't serve me because they did not believe I was a survivor. I had to get one of my mates to fetch me a cup."

In the meantime, Bert is getting back to being his 'well organised self'. "As my Wellingtons were drawing my feet badly and other lads needed items of clothing, several of us visited the local shops. I managed to purchase a heavy pair of ski boots and was quite taken aback when the young lady assistant accepted my last ten shilling note as payment! The boots were eventually given away by my mother to a chap named 'Tom Swannick' in the village where I was born! Other men were kitted up in Norwegian ski suits, complete with cap.

"My mate Joe Sweetland was extremely proud of his new outfit. I did not need any change of clothes as my smart ex T.L.'s outfit (Torpedo Lieutenant) would pass anywhere. The whole idea was disguise, as no one was certain where the Germans were but by the end of the first day in Ballangen we resembled and could pass for any of the locals. That is until we were spoken to in Norwegian. I met the girl again who spoke English to us on our way in, she said she had been evacuated from Narvik and was staying with her grandfather. She rooted around for any of his old clothes and handed them to us."

Cyril goes on to describe the diversionary tactics to be employed should the enemy forces (potentially the well equipped and trained German Alpine Troops) come looking for them. "It had been decided that we would take over a much larger school on top of the cliffs overlooking the fjord. This was called the top school and here we would all sleep on the floor in one large room. If the Germans attacked the village, we could all be warned at the same time, giving us the chance to get out and make off in the opposite direction from which the attack was being launched. To help us to receive a good warning of the approach of the enemy, it was decided we would have lookouts posted.

"Our chaps took on the job at the school, and Boy Scouts with trumpets, at the end of the village where the road came in from Narvik; this being the direction from which we thought the Germans would most likely make their attack. Fortunately there was only the one main road through the village, so if they came in at the end we expected them to, we would run like hell to the other end and hope that we could out run them. If of course they attacked from both ends, we would have to go straight up the mountain side, over the top and try to reach Sweden, which was about twelve to fifteen miles away. I don't think many of us would have made it in the conditions prevailing at that time. The lack of food, clothing and proper equipment with maps and guides would have taken a terrible toll on us; but I am sure that each and every one of us would have had a good try."

KARL SMIDT

APRIL 11 1940. ENTERED NARVIK ON REMAINING GOOD ENGINE. OBTAINED TECHNICAL HELP FROM THE TANKER 'JAN WELLEM' WHICH WAS THERE AND REPAIRS WERE MADE.

Cyril: "We 'turned in' the early hours of Thursday morning, prepared for anything. As I said earlier we had to sleep on the floor. We had nothing in the way of bed clothes to cover ourselves up and the central heating wasn't very good. So we spent a cold, uncomfortable night but at least we were alive and had a roof over our heads, also the promise of a cup of hot coffee and something to eat the next morning."

George Heppel: "Our chief worry the next day was to discover some method of sending a message out to our own ships. The Norwegians were in a peculiar state; their main concern was that we were a bait to the Germans and that the village would be likely to suffer if they came to round us up. In addition there was a faint atmosphere of distrust among the inhabitants themselves. Those who looked after us, however, were exceptionally kind over food, clothing and shelter: but they would not let us use the telephone and were very much against us detaching any expedition. They also insisted that we should discard any clothing identifiable as uniforms and replace it with a variety of clothes from the village shop and elsewhere.

"One amusing incident in this connection was that I had collected the whole Ship's Company together and delivered an impassioned appeal to them not to 'kit up' with unnecessary stuff because the demand was rather a strain on the little village. I had scarcely finished when three other officers came mincing down the road in the most beautiful ski suits I had ever seen!"

Cyril: "During that morning while I had been at the Haugland household, a number of British merchant sailors arrived in the village. Among these merchant sailors was a Captain. He was Captain of the 'North Cornwall' and his name was 'Evans'. He had his Chief Steward with him and these two gave valuable assistance to the members of our party who were concerned with the messing arrangements."

Bill Pulford remembers the merchant seamen joining in with pride. "Around fifty or more men came down, they were all British merchant seamen, who due to our action in the harbour, they had managed to free themselves. They were held prisoner on a ship in Narvik harbour and told us 'Where the Royal Navy goes we're going' and they followed us to Ballangen. In the meantime CPO 'Tubby' Cock, the Chief Buffer had organised us into four watches, we were going to maintain a strict naval routine all the time we were ashore. The merchant men said they would look out for the billets ashore, if we would do the naval routine. We weren't going to be caught by the 'Jerry', so we did the 'look out' watches. Myself, I was detailed off by Chief Cock to look out for the 'darken ship' side of life. The building had to be completely dark by ten o'clock at night. Although, there was little light then at that time in the Arctic Circle.

"Every morning there would be a crowd of Norwegians who had scoured the countryside to feed us. Captain Evans from the 'North Cornwall' with his Chief Steward and two or three other merchant seamen took it in their heads to act as mess men. They collected all this food, cooked it and supplied it as rations. They saw to it that everybody had equal shares per day."

Cyril: "The following morning, Thursday April 11th, after a night of little sleep but at least no alarms from the lookouts, I returned to the 'Haugland' household where I found another lady waiting to greet me. This lady was a sister-in-law of Mrs Haugland and lived in the flat above. It was the first time any of them had mentioned that the house was split into two flats and I hadn't noticed it myself the evening before. The first thing this other lady said to me was, 'Being an English sailor I know what you could do with'. I wondered what was coming next, but thought it best not to ask what, then she said, 'A nice cup of English tea!' Without waiting for a reply off she went to her own flat to make the tea. After her return and with large cups of lovely tea in our hands we settled down to a good chat.

"She told me that she had recently returned from London, hence the tea. She, like Torrod, could speak English enough for us to have a reasonable conversation. So after giving details of the battle and telling her about me and my home, we got down to more serious business. I had been thinking very hard of what I would do if the Germans came looking for us. I didn't relish the thought of capture with the possibility of a long trip to Germany followed by God knows how long in a prison camp. I had come to the conclusion that a planned escape was necessary. With one partner, some food and a map with a likely route drawn on it, it might be possible for me to get away.

"With this in mind, I asked Torrod if he had any school maps of Norway and Sweden. He brought out his school atlas and sure enough there was the map I required. We spent some time picking the routes which would be easiest for us to travel over. I say easiest, but actually at that time of the year with snow and ice filled roads, very cold weather, especially at night and with no proper equipment or clothing; any route would be hard for men who had lived in ships for as long as 'Birdy' Bowman and myself had lived. Yes, 'Birdy' was to be my partner in the venture if it became necessary although at that moment he did not know about it.

"One of the routes would take us over the mountains to Sweden. This was the most difficult and it was suggested that Torrod should give me some lessons in how to walk on skis. The other route would take us to the town of 'Bodo' which lay in the opposite direction to' Narvik' and at that moment the enemy had not occupied. At least that was what the locals told us. We had no means of finding out for certain, so we would just have to take a chance and make for there.

"Our little 'council of war' over, we had dinner, listened to the one o'clock news on their radio; the BBC News I must add. Some details of our Battle were given out but obviously news of it and the survivors was taking a long time to reach London. Our only means of getting information through was via the French Consul in a town across the other side of the fjord. He evidently had a radio transmitter and it was he who first sent the list of our dead and wounded to the Admiralty. I then wanted to hurry back to the school to pass on to the other chaps what I had heard on the radio. On the way Torrod started the skiing lessons. I can't remember how many times I fell flat on my face but I know he had quite a few laughs at my expense.

"As you can well realise, the addition of nearly two hundred more people, to those already living in the village, put a great strain on the food supply in Ballangen. To make matters worse the Germans had put a destroyer on patrol at the entrance of the small creek leading to the village and which normally the fishing boats would use when they went out to fish for what was the staple food of the people in that part of Norway. The patrol of the destroyer was primarily to prevent us taking any of the boats in the village and so escape down the fjord to the open sea. However, it also prevented the fishing boats from going out and this created a serious food shortage because the Norwegians had no stocks of food put by.

"While I was at the school, I explained my plan for escaping from the village to Birdy Bowman. He was all for it and we decided that as much as possible we would stay close to each other and that at the first sign of alarm we would be off. Our plans were this: if the Germans approached the village from the direction of Narvik, we would make off in the opposite direction along the road leading to 'Bodo'. If they made their approach from the 'Bodo' end or from both ends at the same time, we would go over the mountains in the direction of Sweden and take our chance with the snow, ice and cold winds. It was decided that we would try to get a supply of food to take with us on the journey. With this in mind, I returned during the afternoon to the Haugland house. Once again I had some lessons from Torrod on the use of the skis. We also went over the routes and names of places my pal and I would be passing through.

"Torrod and his Aunt tried to teach me the names of the towns and villages in Norwegian. They also wrote down many words in Norwegian with their English translations alongside. It is surprising how much one can learn in a short time when the need is pressing. We really got stuck in and the time flew. After having an evening meal with them, at which I ate very little, pleading that I was off my food because of worrying about the situation and after once again listening to the BBC News, I said goodnight to them all promising to see them the next morning. I made it clear that I would not be coming for any more meals as they had so little for themselves with not much hope of getting any more while we stayed in the village.

BBC 'WORLD SERVICE'. THURSDAY 11th APRIL AT 6.00 P.M.

"Here is an Extract from Mr Churchill's statement: Off Narvik on Tuesday morning the battle-cruiser RENOWN saw SCHARNHORST and a ten thousand ton Hipper class cruiser. Our battle-cruiser opened fire at 18-thousand yards and after three minutes, the enemy replied. The enemy almost immediately turned away and after nine minutes the RENOWN observed hits on the forward structure of the German battle-cruiser. Thereafter, her armaments stopped firing and later her after turret began firing on local control.

"On Tuesday night, he continued, orders were given to our destroyers blockading the West Fjord leading to Narvik to attack the enemy. But after a submarine had reported the presence of six destroyers, the Admiralty thought the operation so hazardous that they told the Captain of the Destroyer Flotilla that he must be the sole judge of whether to attack and he would be supported whatever he did and whatever happened.

"The five destroyers entered and attacked the six enemy. The fighting was worthy of any British Naval records."

Down at the Victoria Inn in Gloucester Place, landlord Maggs and family, with early customers were listening to the above news bulletin and their ears must have pricked up. "We were informed that there had been a successful engagement [...] HMS Hardy was named." They listened out for more bulletins and no doubt the news got round very quickly and probably more customers arrived. "Ominously, added was a statement to the effect that the Royal Naval unit had suffered losses. Then, at nine o'clock came the announcement that HMS Hardy had been sunk. It's not difficult to imagine the effect on the locals! Was Alec OK?"

However, as Alec's family and friends were soon to be informed Alec was not OK. The Captain of Number 2 Gun killed as described by the only survivor, Geoff Bailey, was in fact Leading Seaman 'Gunner' Alec Hunt, the "handsome young man with a ready smile and wit to match".

Cyril continues, "That night we got our first alarm from the Boy Scouts who were at the Narvik end of the village. We were turned in at the top school trying to sleep when all of a sudden our own sentries heard the trumpets sound off. They roused us all and out of the school we flew. It was all right if we kept to the path which sloped down from the door, but if we strayed off the path we ended up in deep snow flat on our faces. That's what happened to me. I tripped over the over-coat I was carrying and ended up buried in the snow away from the path. My mate Birdy stopped to grab me and pull me up. The other chaps were by now streaming past us.

"We got going again and off down the road to 'Bodo' we went, overtaking everyone else because we knew where we were making for while they had to stop and think. Just clear of the village and well out in front we heard our pals shouting to us to stop and it sounded as though they were telling us to come back. We stopped and listened, they were waving their arms and still shouting so we walked back to the nearest of them. They told us it had been a false alarm and that everyone had to return to the school, which we started to do.

"Birdy said, 'How were we fixed for food if we had to keep on going', I replied: 'I have got two pieces of bread and half a bar of chocolate which my friends the Haugland family gave me. That was all they could spare.' He said, 'We were lucky it was a false alarm then, because I have got nothing, there was only coffee for our evening meal at the school. They have run out of grub because of the blockade and because of the extra mouths to feed.' It was at that moment that I realised that our stay in Ballangen would be ending very soon. Whatever happened we could not possibly stay there without food and we could not allow the villagers to suffer because of our presence. But for the present, it was back to the school to lie once more on the floor and try to get some sleep.

"During Thursday, another thing that had brought home to us the seriousness of our situation was the swooping over the village by German planes. We took it for granted they were searching for us and the order went out for every one of us to wear Norwegian clothes and if caught out in the open when the planes came over, to act as much as possible like villagers. Also anyone who had saved items of uniform after drying them had to bury them in the deep snow. The only thing we were allowed to keep were our identity discs which we had to keep hidden, unless we were captured. Then of course, we would have to show our captors these to prove our identity."

George Heppel: "Captain Evans and his Chief Steward were very helpful and a good working organisation was started. The main difficulty was to discover how long the food they let us have was to last. We gathered that supplies were limited but they gave us no idea of a regular maximum which they were prepared to let us have. For a period of our stay, however, everyone had enough. [...] The wounded were getting on well there and enquired about Able Seaman Trigger, for many months my valet, office keeper and friend; and was told that he had been one of the three who had been taken to Harstad where he had since died. I had last seen him in the ambulance bus and had thought that he was only slightly hit, so this news gave me a shock and made me very sad. But all was well, they had made a mistake, and the next smiling individual I met on the road was 'Trigger', in a beautiful plain clothes suit, with his hair neatly brushed and his arm in a sling! He had been boarded out in one of the private houses where he was living in luxury.

"I listened to the news that night in the house of one Rolfe Steen of whom there is more to say later. The next day, Friday, we insisted that something should be done and told the Norwegian authorities that our expedition was going to set out. Under this threat and after a long argument they got through to the French Consul at 'Bodo'. I spoke to him and gave him the message that there were a number of 'Hardy' and Merchant Service seamen at Ballangen. We learnt afterwards that this message was taken off to HMS Penelope by a fishing boat."

Cyril: "On Friday morning I went as promised to the Haugland home, where I had a cup of tea but would not except any food. I did not stay long because I had told Birdy that I would meet him at the village barber's shop. Taking Torrod along as my interpreter, I went to have my hair cut. Seems daft doesn't it? If I remember correctly Birdy had his hair cut as well. From there we returned to the top school and Torrod left us to go home. Once again the planes swooped over the village. We stayed indoors. Just as the planes disappeared the trumpet sounded at the Narvik end of the village. Out we flew and this time there was no falling down. Birdy and I once again took the lead and once again we were well on the way to 'Bodo', when the recall sounded. Believe me; we were done in with all this running. What with the cold, rare atmosphere, no food and no proper sleep we had just about had it by the time we reached the outskirts of the village and I don't think that was anywhere near a mile.

"Anyway back we came. This time it was refugees from Narvik who had caused the false alarm. There they were old men and women pushing carts or prams with their belongings in. Some even had little children with them. We all rushed to help them through the snow. It was a terrible sight to see them like this and we felt very badly about it, especially as we knew there was nothing we could do to help them in their plight. We had nothing with which to help them or ourselves, so we had to leave their welfare to their fellow countrymen."

Interestingly, around this time a somewhat peculiar news bulletin was released. It is a concern, that this could have triggered an immediate response by the German command in Berlin to send any available Alpine Troops searching for the Hardy survivors.

BBC 'WORLD SERVICE'.
FRIDAY 12th APRIL AT 12 NOON.

"It was learnt in London today that forty or fifty men of the HARDY, which went aground at Narvik, rowed ashore fully armed. When they were last seen in their boats, it is said, they were making for the Norwegian shore as though 'they were starting off on a little military expedition of their own'. Nothing has been heard of them since."

KARL SMIDT

APRIL 12 1940. AIR RAID BY BRITISH PLANES; 'GIESE' SUSTAINED NO DAMAGE.

22

The Germans Arrive

The 'Hardy' survivors seeing more convoys arriving got an unexpected shock. Cyril recounts, "Early in the afternoon another long line of what we thought were refugees approached the village from the direction of Narvik, but this time it was our enemies. They came in a very odd assortment of vehicles; horse drawn carts, old cars and vans, lorries, anything with wheels that would move but they had not come to attack us or the village. Oh, what a sight: some had legs off, some arms off. They were all badly wounded, cold and dirty. It was impossible to get the vehicles near enough to the hospital because of the deep snow. We had had quite a lot of heavy falls since we had arrived in the village and the road to the hospital was blocked.

"Our First Lieutenant asked the Mayor of the village to collect all the shovels and spades they possessed. He then had us all mustered near the school and set us to work clearing the way through to the hospital, which we did. Although, there was one or two that thought it wrong that we should aid our enemies in this way. One 'Stoker', who was more outspoken than anyone else, got a punch in the eye off one of his own mates for working a one man go slow strike. This caused a bit of laughter when we returned home, because a reporter thought that his black eye had been done in Battle and that he was one of the wounded. He asked him for an account of how it had happened, and the 'Stoker' let him believe it had been done by the enemy."

Here are Dougy's recollections of the incident. "One thing that amused me was a Stoker, of the less enthusiastic type was given an instruction from Lt Fallwell to grab a shovel and get shovelling. He told him what he could do with the shovel in words of one syllable, all obscene. He said he was no longer on a ship and he didn't want any orders. Whereupon we persuaded him to drop his shovel, took him round the shed, showed him the errors of his ways and delivered him back. We wiped the blood off, and said, 'He's ready to shovel now Sir'. The Lieutenant replied, 'Aye, Aye carry on then.'

"It was the only breakdown in discipline I saw the whole time I was there. I did see him on Horse Guards Parade. He had the most beautiful black eyes you'd ever seen, which I thought was a bit incongruous because we'd been left behind. (Dougy Bourton did not return to Britain with the first group, it was not until he did, that he then saw the film footage of his shipmates being welcomed home on Horse Guards Parade.)

Dougy, like Cyril and some of the other survivors, was befriended by members of the Ballangen community. Dougy explains how for him this came about. "During the time we were there, I formed a friendship with a Norwegian, Magnus Erick Petersen who was a student. He was hoping to gain entry into the Oslo University and could speak a fair bit of German. I also having taken it (as a subject) for four years at grammar school. So the strange thing was, we spoke in German and I translated it into English. He then translated it into Norwegian for his people. So the common tongue was that of the enemy. But I went to his house, visiting his family and friends.

"However, we were under strict orders not to eat their food because they were not wealthy. So we virtually starved, it was the only time I had ever had to trisect an ordinary 'Crawford's' type biscuit into three for distribution by two mates and me. We didn't fight over the crumbs but food was that tight."

Cyril: "With the coming of the German wounded I realised more than ever before that the time for our capture or hurried departure could not be far away. So with a feeling of guilt about the good clothes I was wearing I made my way to the Haugland home for which was to prove to be my last visit. On entering I realised that something was wrong. They all looked at me sheepishly and hardly spoke. Then a man came down the stairs. He was introduced to me as Mr Haugland. We shook hands but I knew things were not right.

Torrod Haugland with mother and sister. *Cyril Cope Collection.*

"He looked so serious and stern and although I knew I had done nothing wrong at his house, it had me worried for a moment. He said, 'While you are here you are the boss but if the Germans come you will have to go. I have to think of my family.' I replied, 'If you will please find me some old clothes to wear I will give you these good ones back. I have no wish to see you or your family get into any trouble with the Germans or your own people for helping me, but I want to thank all your family for what they have done for me. They have been wonderful and if I am fortunate enough to get back to England alive I will never forget the Haugland family.'

"They searched around and found a full Norwegian skiing outfit which they gave me. I said goodbye to them. There were tears in the eyes of the little girl, Mrs Haugland and the sister-in-law as I shook hands with them. Then I was out of the house and on my way back to the school accompanied by Torrod, who had to take the good clothes back after I had got changed. He also had tears in his eyes when he left me. I promised him I would one day get in touch if we both survived the war. I still have a postcard photograph of the village with their house clearly shown. Torrod marked it with a cross and wrote his name and address on the back. In the twenty-four hours or more that I was still to remain in Ballangen I did not visit their house or even see any of them again." As promised Cyril and Torrod were to meet up again forty years later. Although the young Torrod managed to survive the war, later, he had to endure a devastating episode in his life.

Note: Cyril kept his promise and made contact again with Torrod and his family in Norway. In 1980 Torrod, his wife Lisa and their teenage son visited Cyril and our family in Devon. A number of years later we received the sad news that Torrod and Lisa's son, who had become a pilot in the Royal Norwegian Air Force, was killed in an air accident. Ironically, this occurred not far from Narvik. To add to the tragedy he left behind a young wife and baby daughter.

Now follows the next part of Fred Evans' letter to the Mayor of Ballangen in 1973. He and his shipmate are well looked after by the Norwegian family.

My companion was quite well by now but I developed severe frost-bite and was being treated by the doctor. As I could not walk unaided I was taken to an emergency hospital. Now this is the main part of the story I am relating. None of the British sailors knew anything of this emergency hospital, and in order that you may be able to identify it, I have drawn a sketch of its interior separately. It was built as a fairly large concert hall with a stage at one end and main entrance at the opposite left end corner. The whole floor space being filled with freshly prepared beds, with not one occupant. There were only Red Cross nurses, apparently waiting to receive expected casualties. (I did not know then of the second Narvik battle which was taking place about that time.)"

Cyril: "Once the job of snow clearing was finished, and believe me it was hard work on an empty stomach, in that energy sapping, fresh cold air, I went into the hospital to visit our wounded comrades. The first room I went into was a small one with a bed in one corner. I could just see the face of its occupant. It was a grey face full of shrapnel wounds but I recognised the owner. It was Lieutenant Commander Gordon- Smith, our Navigating officer, who had so efficiently guided our little band of ships up the fjord and who had been so terribly wounded during the fight. I went close to the bed and realising he was awake and fully conscious, I said, 'We will soon have you home again Sir and you will be as right as rain.' The words choked me.

I was filled with deep emotion and could say no more. He smiled but said nothing. Just then a nurse came in so I left. That was the last I ever saw of that gallant gentleman. Months later I read in the paper that he had died after a relapse and this after getting home and receiving the DSO from H.M. The King. What a sad loss to his family and to the Royal Navy."

Bill Pulford: "One morning, these girls came up (school house) with haversacks full of food. It wasn't much for two hundred of us, but it was plenty for them to carry. They said there are other ships down in the mouth of the fjord. Well, we knew they couldn't be Germans, so we got a little excited about this. The 'Crusher' said 'keep calm!' He took the over excited ones to one side and pointed out, 'Keep calm we have to ascertain who they are, what they are and what's going to happen."

The 'Crusher' is a Petty Officer or Leading Rate trained in 'disciplinary techniques' for ships smaller than a cruiser. Interestingly, the nickname devolved from one of their duties on board ship, which was to check around the ship for any illegal activities or breaches of 'ship's orders'. To enable the 'Crusher' to do this, he would sneak around in soft soled footwear. The ship's company would only know if he was in their vicinity when he happened to 'crush' a cockroach in his path.

Cyril, back with his shipmates, is beginning to become despondent and emotional about his own family back home. "That night as I lay on the school room floor, I thought of all that happened in the past few days. It seemed a lifetime, I'd seen so much, done so much and met so many new people in circumstances which before would have seemed impossible. I wondered what was happening back home. Was my wife all right, was I a father yet? And if so, when, if ever, would I get back home to see her and the baby. At that moment England seemed very far away and I felt a bit depressed."

I now return to the next part of Fred Evans' letter.

I appeared to be the only person requiring to be accommodated, and when I was advised I was to get into bed I had a free choice as to which I should occupy. I chose one in front of the stage so that I would not be surrounded by other patients (probably strangers). They were indeed strangers. A few seconds after I had got undressed and into bed I saw through the windows on the right of the stage, a procession of wounded men in uniform; in ones, twos and threes, carrying their rifles. Where one man was so injured that he could not carry a rifle, an extra rifle was being carried by his companion. Some were blinded, some had body injuries, and others had various limb injuries.

All were really severe casualties. I felt quite fit by comparison. The procession continued past the windows of the side wall, round the right hand corner of the building, and past the window opposite the stage. It was like watching scenes from films, as the men moved past each of the windows. When they began to reach the entrance to the hall at the left hand corner from the stage, where the nurses were ready to receive them, I suddenly realised that they were all Germans. I couldn't decide what to do, being undressed in bed and not aware if there could be another exit. I could not seek advice from one of the nurses because the Germans would not enter the hall and were becoming congested around the entrance.

Bill Pulford, seemingly as relaxed as ever: "Three days after the action (Saturday the 13th of April), 'Torps' came puffing and panting from the town where he went in the mornings to find out any passing news. He sorted out the First Lieutenant, we could see there was a bit of excitement in the air, but we kept ourselves a reasonable distance. If there was anything for us to know they would tell us. 'Torps' had finished his little 'pow wow' with 'The Jimmy' (First Lieutenant) and they came across to us. 'Torps' said he had heard from the Town Council Clerk, that there had been a little excitement at the mouth of the fjord and would like us to act like Norwegians and help clear the snow from the roads. 'Torps' had agreed to that, he couldn't do anything else."

George Heppel: "The First Lieutenant and I went to the Police Station to see if there was any result from our telephone message. There was none but there was a message from another village giving numbers of the two ships on patrol off 'Baroy'. These identified as 'Bedouin' and 'Eskimo' and it was the first confirmation that the patrol was British.

"As it was still uncertain that our message through 'Bodo' had got out, we insisted on fitting out our expedition and for the first time the Norwegian Police gave way and even helped us. They arranged a boat at 'Forsa' by telephone and a sleigh to be by the hospital at 1200."

Meanwhile, Fred Evans is in a quandary as to what to do next, visualising he was soon to be surrounded in his hospital bed by armed enemy.

I then realised that the delay was being caused by nurses trying to relieve the men of their rifles which they would not relinquish. Naturally the nurses felt that hospital patients should not be armed while the men wished to retain their ability to defend themselves against the danger of attack by the British. It seemed there could be no solution to the impasse, with the congestion outside increasing as the wounded men were still walking around past the windows.

Stan Robinson (I.W.M.) confirms the hospital arrangements at the Ballangen hospital, when asked "Do you think the Norwegians would have given the Germans as good a treatment as yourselves?" He answered, "Yes, they rigged up a school as a hospital and our wounded and the German wounded were in the same place. I had always had the greatest respect for the German sailors because I had drunk with them before the war, and after the war at Cuxhaven in 1946. I thought they were very nice fellows and had no ill feeling towards us. I mean they had a cause and we had a cause. They prayed to the same God as we did at sea in morning prayers."

Once more the mist of time can result in differing dates of past events. Although, from my research only Stan Robinson actually states this was the case. Therefore Evans' story, supported in Bill Pulford's account that many German wounded arrived on the Saturday 13th April is probably correct. In which case, the local authorities must have had prior warning to expect them. Hence the Red Cross had to rapidly make arrangements for the 'emergency hospital'. For whatever reasons, their actions were not made known to the British survivors. It was therefore fortunate that the British sailors were evacuated on the 13th April, otherwise one wonders what would have been the outcome. Especially, when one takes into account that the Germans' discarded weapons could possibly have been accessed by the 'Hardy' crew, to make good their escape. However, the Germans, irrespective of their injuries, may have been able to put up a fight. Perhaps the local police anticipated this scenario and as mentioned by Lieutenant George Heppel, this was the reason for the police changing their minds and allowing and assisting the expedition to go ahead.

Geoffrey Stanning tried to stem the boredom of a hospital bed by keeping up with regular updates and considering escape options. "That four days is a confused memory for me of a good deal of pain, never being able to sleep even with the morphia and trying to think of ways to escape. After a time I got a map and studied it all day long trying to think how we could get away before the Germans arrived from Narvik. There were rumours each day that the Germans were on their way and we were most anxious to know where any of our own ships might be. On Saturday morning I gave a nurse who was going to 'Bodo' a note to give to any destroyer she might see and then a few minutes afterwards came the most definite rumour we had had of British ships in the offing (ready or likely to happen). However, I did not really believe all these rumours."

Saturday morning had arrived, Cyril begins to describe the eventful day. "We all went down to the lower school for a cup of coffee. There was nothing to eat but I still had my two pieces of bread and half a bar of chocolate but as it would have to be shared with my partner if we had to make a run for it, I decided not to eat it. While we were in the lower school the planes swooped down over the village. It was decided that we would make for the top school in twos and threes and stay indoors. We had not been there long when we heard the trumpet sound off again. This time we hardly got going before we found out it was a false alarm. There were more refugees from Narvik coming to the village. "The place was certainly filling up and the hospital was having a busy time. We wondered how much longer this could go on without something happening to shatter the peacefulness of it all, because regardless of what had been happening in the place, the village was so quiet and peaceful, everybody so calm and confident; the war might have been miles away instead of on their doorstep. What could you expect, these were a peace loving people and to be otherwise was against their nature. We were used to being at war after seven months of it. They had had only four days."

Fred Evans explains how his dilemma is eventually resolved.

Suddenly, a middle aged, largish Norwegian appeared through the doorway. I think I understood later that he would have been the 'Burgo-Master' of the village. He took immediate action by shouting in a commanding German voice to the wounded Germans. He must have ordered them to give up their rifles at once. All I recognised were the words 'Deutsch Reich', and finally 'Heil Hitler'. It seemed obvious that he had assumed the authority of a German commanding officer and ordered the men to 'ground arms', because immediately there was the rattle of rifles hitting the cemented floor, and the men commenced trooping into the hall. I had happened to catch the word 'sailors' by one of the nurses and so I quite believed that they were men from the sunken or damaged German ships. Although they wore military type uniform (field-grey) I could have thought they were similar to our Royal Marines. (Probably Alpine Troops.)

By this time I had managed to gain the attention of one of the nurses, explaining that as I was British I didn't think that I should be there. She quite agreed with me and immediately helped me out of bed, and after helping me to dress in some fashion, I was bundled out through another door which I think was on the left of the stage.

Bill Pulford now provides his version of that fateful day the 13th of April 1940. "We were all now dressed like Norwegians best we could. So we went out to the roads and helped clear the snow. We were in the main road, if you could call it that, which came from the fjord to Ballangen. We were clearing the snow when one of the 'lookouts' called out 'There's a Stingbag'. We all looked round and thought 'he's wrong because we couldn't see any aircraft. But we could hear them, so naturally we thought it was an aircraft we had seen earlier in the day from the German base. We called him all the names under creation and someone said, 'What the hell would a "Swordfish" be doing flying around Ballangen at that time of the morning'. But he persisted it was a 'Stingbag' and then we heard gun fire, first, the whip cracker of 4.7 inch then the rubble of a 15 inch. We thought that must be 'Renown' which was in action with us four days ago."

A 'Stingbag' is the slang for the Swordfish a Fleet Air Arm torpedo carrying aircraft flown from an aircraft carrier.

George Heppel, adrenalin flowing at the prospect of completing his task, fast moving events have preceded him. "I went back to the school to get all my clothes and my expedition were within a quarter of an hour of starting when the news came of an attack by ten of our ships and we soon heard the first gunfire. This, of course, altered the situation altogether and so we cancelled the sleigh and I went as fast as I could down to the fishing harbour to get a motor boat with the threefold purpose of making contact with our ships, acting as a lifeboat and watching the battle."

23

"Come on Jack. You're rescued. It's Time to go Home"

Cyril: "At about 12 o'clock noon on that Saturday 13th April, we were about to go down to the lower school. We knew there would be nothing to eat as supplies had run out. Suddenly we heard the whine of shells passing overhead. Thinking we were under attack from German ships, we all rushed outside expecting the school to go up at any moment. More shells whistled overhead and we realised they were not meant for us. They were going in the direction of Narvik. P.O. Neal, our gunnery expert said, 'There is only one place they can be coming from, the deck of a British Battleship or Battle Cruiser, because the Germans have not got any ships with guns that large.'

"The thought of going for coffee was forgotten, as we all lined the top of the cliff overlooking the fjord, which at this point opened out like a lake, with the small inlet which led to Ballangen away to our right and at the mouth of which patrolled the German destroyer ('Georg Thiele'). It had been there since our arrival in the village and it had certainly done a good job in cutting off the food supplies of the villagers, besides ensuring that we did not try to escape in fishing boats down the fjord."

At this moment in time, Dougy Bourton was spending some time with his newly found Norwegian friends. "Early on the Saturday I was with Erick at his Grandmother's house further along the fjord. We were out near the fjord walking around and we heard this tremendous rumble. We said straight away that's a 15 inch, then a big explosion. We got to the end of the fjord (Ballangen Bay), it was only a small indentation, we saw destroyers; which we recognised as 'Tribal Class' and old 'F' boats. We also saw a stack of destroyers going up with the 'Warspite' and actually saw her fire a salvo from the forward guns as she passed us. It was the most tremendous sight I have ever seen in my life. That the Navy as we expected would come, it was just a question of when and who."

Cyril: "As we looked down from our vantage point high above the fjord we saw German destroyers coming at full speed from the direction of Narvik. ('Wolfgang Zenker', 'Erich Koellner' and 'Erich Giese'). Their guns were blazing at targets which at that moment we still could not see. The scene changed very rapidly. The enemy ships were backing away. Some began to take punishment. Then into our view came the most wonderful sight that any of us could have wished for, two lines of destroyers in 'V' formation with the good old 'Warspite' in the centre. The destroyers were 'Hero', 'Forester', 'Eskimo', 'Bedouin', 'Foxhound', 'Kimberly', 'Icarus', 'Punjabi' and 'Cossack'.

"The enemy destroyer which lay below us at the entrance to the inlet had by now turned broadside on to the fjord, with its torpedo tubes facing the direction from which 'Warspite' and her attendant destroyer screen would come. The enemy's intention was plain to see; a torpedo attack without warning. Because of the curve in the coastline, our ships would not see this lurking destroyer until after the torpedoes were fired."

Some of the other survivors saw the action from another vantage point, including Les Smale. "This battle we were able to see from the attic of the school and it was a grand sight; to see the 'Tribal Class' destroyers driving 'Jerry' step by step back up the fjord. It must have had a great de-moralising effect on the German destroyer crews."

Cyril continues with his observations of a second historical naval event in the fjord. "To us Torpedomen, who were well versed in the art of torpedo attacks, the situation was clear: the enemy would set their torpedoes to run at a depth suitable for an attack on a battleship. 'Warspite' was obviously the more valuable target, and the torpedoes would pass under the escorting destroyers which were acting as a screen for her. As we fretted and fumed at what we thought was going to be a disaster for 'Warspite' and as we called the Germans some nasty nautical names, a 'Walrus' plane catapulted from the deck of the battleship."

In fact it was a 'Swordfish' and the air crew consisted of Lieutenant Commander W.L.M. Brown who was the Observer and the Petty Officer Airman Pat Rice the pilot. For those readers who would like more information about these two brave airmen's involvement, it can be found in Peter Dickens' book 'Narvik: Battles in the Fjords', Chapter Six.

Geoffrey Stanning recalls, "Tallboys and Heppel continued their plans for escaping towards Tranoy. About noon they were both in my room when excited people rushed in and said there were British ships coming up the fjord. This time it was really true and we could hear firing. Then (Carmelo) Aquilina the Maltese cook rushed in and said he could see a German battleship coming and down went my heart into my feet. In came someone else and said it was certainly the 'Warspite' and at that moment she opened fire with a terrific crash on a German destroyer in Ballangen Bay. All this firing went on the whole afternoon and rumours began to drift in about German ships being sunk and also a story of a British ship aground further up the fjord. About 4 o'clock a message was sent up asking me what the man was to do who was looking after the horse and sledge which Heppel and Tallboys were going to escape in. They had to rush out to look at the battle and had forgotten all about plans for escape so I told the man he would not be wanted – ever I hoped."

Returning to Cyril and his shipmates' 'heart thumping' moments on the top of the cliff, with great expectations of a possible rescue. Depressingly, cheers turned to tears. "It flew over our heads. Obviously it was on its way to serve as a spotter plane for directing the gunfire from our ships to the enemy ships and to Narvik harbour. We waved like mad at the two men crew, hoping to attract their attention to the German destroyer down below. If they saw us they probably thought we were Norwegian villagers cheering them on their way. They certainly wouldn't expect to see a gang of British sailors on the top of the fjord dressed like we were.

"As things turned out we had no cause for alarm: the crew of the plane must have spotted the lurking enemy ship. We saw the observer flash a message to 'Warspite' with their Aldis lamp. One of the escorting destroyers detached from the line of ships nearest to our side of the fjord, hugged the coast until it reached the bend. Then with all guns blazing, it came full speed at the enemy destroyer. It badly damaged it setting it on fire, forcing it to run on to the beach. That was the end of that one.

"The other enemy ships were fleeing from the accurate gunfire of 'Warspite' and our other eight destroyers as fast as they could go. Soon they passed from our sight, followed relentlessly by the ships of the Royal Navy, whose crews were determined to avenge the sinking of 'Hardy' and 'Hunter'. Who were also determined to drive the Germans out of Narvik and Norway?

Or at least to make sure that they stayed there forever, either at the bottom of the fjord or under solid earth on land. The battle although beyond our view was still within hearing distance and it was obvious to us that our ships were dictating the fight. We could tell that most of the gunfire was coming from them. Very soon the sound of the guns receded in the distance. It became very quiet up there on top of the fjord. We stood around in groups, our eyes focused up the fjord in the direction in which the two opposing naval forces had disappeared.

"We then began to chatter excitedly about what we had been privileged to witness; the second Battle of Narvik. One of the three real naval battles of the war up to that date. The others of course being: The Battle of the River Plate and our own battle of three days ago. It seemed more like three months to us. We had packed in such a lot of incidents, done so much and met such a lot of new people in the short time since entering the fjord which led to Narvik. A town which was to go down in history as one of the vital focal points of the Second World War. A town which so few British or German people had ever heard of, but was such a vital asset to the war potential of both combatants because of the iron ore which could be shipped from the port.

"This then was Narvik, the place where already many good men had died in battle, and where many, many more would die before the end of the Second World War in Europe. Men and women of different nationalities would lay down their lives for Narvik and Norway."

Bill Pulford, as only he could, describes those moments. "Well, we just all grouped up together about a hundred of us and as we watched this lot, we couldn't say a word. I had a rock in my throat as big as Gibraltar, no one mentioned anything, I am sure everyone felt the same. My eyes were really wet with tears. 'At last relief.' "

Cyril describes the emotional 'highs and lows' that were to follow. "We spent the rest of the afternoon looking out over the fjord, hoping and praying that our comrades in the little armada would find out somehow that we were ashore awaiting rescue. As evening approached we were delighted to see the lines of victorious ships coming back down the fjord from Narvik. Once again we clapped and cheered. We waved to them but of course it was hopeless and impossible for them to recognise us or to hear us at such a great distance. Our cheers turned to near tears as we sadly watched them disappear from our sight round the bend in the fjord's coastline. At that moment we gave up all hope of getting out of Norway. We were feeling very despondent as we all went back to the school, to then sit around and talk about our chances of escape."

KARL SMIDT

APRIL 13 1940. AT 1215 HOURS ALARM! BREAKTHROUGH OF 1 HEAVY BRITISH DESTROYER UNDER THE COMMAND OF 'WARSPITE'. AT 1352 HOURS TRIED TO START UP THE 'GIESE', BUT 12 KNOTS WAS THE MAXIMUM SPEED. IN THE MEANTIME THE REST OF THE GERMAN DESTROYERS JOINED THE BATTLE. FINALLY 'GIESE' LEFT NARVIK HARBOUR, WAS ATTACKED BY ONE BRITISH AIRCRAFT AT THE ENTRANCE BUT IT WAS SHOT DOWN INTO THE SEA 100 METRES IN FRONT OF THE 'GIESE' IN OFOTENFJORD, 5 OR 6 BRITISH DESTROYERS WERE SIGHTED. THE 'GIESE' CAME UNDER FIRE. THE BATTLE OF THE 'GIESE' AGAINST OVERWHELMING ODDS LASTED 15 MINUTES. THE BATTLE PICTURE CHANGED RAPIDLY. THE REMAINDER OF THE

AMMUNITION WAS RAPIDLY USED UP, AS WELL AS THE TORPEDOES . ONE BRITISH DESTROYER 'PUNJABI' HAD TO WITHDRAW FROM ACTION BECAUSE OF DAMAGE.

DURING THE SHORT BATTLE THE 'GIESE' WAS HIT 22 TIMES. ENGINES AND ELECTRICAL INSTRUMENTS WERE PUT OUT OF ORDER. LAST BATTLE DISTANCE WAS 1000 METRES. COMMANDER ORDERED EVERYONE TO ABANDON SHIP.

ALL SURVIVORS WERE GIVEN THE CHOICE OF RESCUE AT LAND OR TO GIVE THEMSELVES UP AS PRISONERS. WITH THE AID OF LIFEJACKETS THEY REACHED LAND. MOST MEN SURVIVED AFTER DIFFICULTIES WITH THE COLD 3 DEGREE WATER. NINE MEN WERE TAKEN PRISONER.

The German POWs, as you will read, were taken to Britain by the RMS Franconia with survivors of 'Hardy'.

Little did most of the despondent sailors know that efforts were already being taken to reach the departing ships. Lieutenant George Heppel had reached the fishing harbour, accompanied by Captain Evans. Here George puts the record straight about the attempt to let their fellow sailors know that the survivors needed rescuing. "Unfortunately, there was some delay in getting the boat because the Norwegians were not keen on lending it and certainly not in favour of coming with us. It was unfortunate too that the first boat we went out to, had an engine which would not start.

"Eventually two Norwegians came out to us and even they could not start the engine, so we went to another boat which we got going. All this delay meant that we missed the battle. Although a destroyer came down the fjord at high

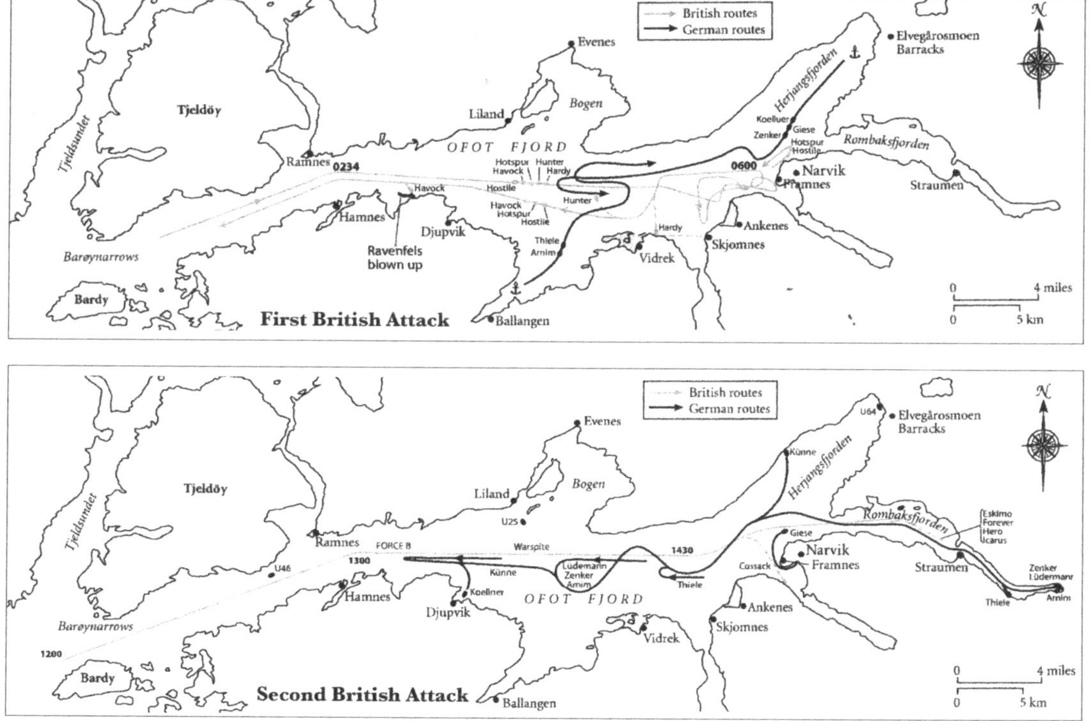

Maps of First and Second British Battles of Narvik. *G. Haarr Collection.*

speed, turned and went up again, we could not make contact. So, as nothing was in sight we returned rather sadly towards Ballangen; picking up a few souvenirs in the form of cartridge cases and a German medical chest etc., debris from the attack.

"As we got back we fell in with another expedition which had followed us out and had been successful, in that they had discovered a large German boat, brand new, and with a beautiful diesel engine in it, which they were towing back to Ballangen. Its new owner was Rolfe Steen by virtue of having been the first on board. It was much faster and superior to the fishing boat in every way and I suggested that we should try it out at once and if it worked that we should take it out to meet one of our ships. Steen refused at first and we compromised by agreeing to take it back to the jetty before trying it out."

In the meantime Fred Evans is struggling to get away from the emergency hospital.

Dusk was falling by this time and I do not remember the direction I took, I may have been supported on foot or on some kind of wheeled chair. For the first time since my arrival at Ballangen I came into contact with other of my shipmates. I think it was a school building and I was put to lie down with others slightly wounded on an upstairs floor. We were required to maintain care lest we were discovered by Germans who were known to be penetrating the district. Later that night, the 'Burgo-Master', who I saw at the emergency hospital appeared amongst us. I recognised him mainly by his voice. He was not speaking to me, but to a group a few yards away. He was describing how he had had to pretend that he had received orders from the 'German High Command' that the men entering the hospitals in Norway were to hand over their arms and ammunition.

George Heppel is naturally becoming impatient with more unnecessary delays. "I was sorry afterwards that I had given way because by doing so we missed getting into touch with 'Warspite' herself. Once alongside the jetty further difficulties were put in the way by a shabby looking policeman who started to remove the fuses of the electrical system. I protested to Steen and reminded him of his promise to try the boat out; he interpreted to the policeman that I wanted to take the boat out and after saying that I required it in the name of the 'Admiralty', they agreed. I could give no guarantee that we would return but invited the policeman to come too. He declined but Steen said he would and so we set off, with Captain Evans, one of his officers and Signalman Kennedy."

BBC 'WORLD SERVICE'
SATURDAY 13th APRIL AT 9.00 P.M.

"British destroyers sank altogether three German destroyers in the Battle of Narvik Fjord on Wednesday morning, according to the crew of the Swedish steamer BODEN, which was in the Narvik Roads at the time. They have now reached Sweden, and they state that fifteen cargo boats belonging to Britain, Sweden, Norway and Germany were sunk during the battle. They described the scene in Narvik harbour as one of complete chaos. When the British destroyers made their daring attack the Germans took possession of the BODEN, which was sinking, and launched the boats to rescue survivors of the three sinking German destroyers. One of the German destroyers had been cut in half."

George Heppel: "Our objective was to stop one of our ships, or, if none could be found, I intended to go up to Narvik to find out what the situation was there. Soon after we started it began to get dark and very soon we were overtaken by a destroyer coming up from seaward. We recognised her as one of the minelayers from Monday's operation and called her up using Hardy's pendants. She answered, closed us and stopped. We went alongside and were taken on board."

As mentioned above, one of the five crew in the recovered German boat was Signalman Bernard Kennedy. His son Lance, before I had access to Lt Heppel's account, informed me, "Later, when a British destroyer was spotted, Bernard signalled a message with a small torch. In a borrowed boat they were pulled out to the ship, which turned out to be HMS Ivanhoe and were taken aboard." I am sure that Lance now feels appreciative and proud, that what the family had been told by his father has now been confirmed by Lt Heppel.

Geoffrey Stanning: "About 6 o'clock one of the doctors said a German destroyer had been sunk in Ballangen Bay and that the wounded were being brought into the hospital. The unwounded survivors had been put in an empty house and told they could escape if they liked but none of them seemed to want to escape naked into the Arctic night. Pilot was then put in with me to make room for the Germans but when he arrived he didn't seem like talking very much. About 9 o'clock Heppel came in again and said he had been on board 'Ivanhoe', that he was going on board with the unwounded members of the ship's company that night and that we would be taken on board in the morning."

Cyril tried to sleep but his thoughts were of home. "At about ten o'clock we turned in to sleep in the classroom of the school wondering what the next day would bring. Our bellies were empty; our bodies cold and aching through lying on the bare boards of the classroom floor. I am sure that I can speak for all that were there, our thoughts before sleep overtook us, were all of home. What would our families be thinking about after hearing the news on the radio of our battle and the sinking, or perhaps reading about it in the newspapers. Would they know for sure which of us were safe. At that time we did not know if any news of our casualties had reached England or if anybody knew that there were so many of us ashore waiting to be rescued.

"What a terrible blow it would be to the families of our dead and seriously wounded when they learned of the tragedy that had struck them. What a burden of grief for them to bear. We shared their tragic loss because those gallant men who had passed on to a more peaceful world and the ones who were so badly wounded during the heat of the battle had been our comrades for a long time. Members of a family of men, thrown together by the contingency of war, in a ship which had been our home as well as a weapon of war, our home for ten months. Now she was gone and so had many of our pals. Why had we been chosen to survive when others had perished. With these thoughts, prayers for our loved ones at home and for an early and satisfactory solution to our plight, we fell into a deep and troubled sleep; which was to be our shortest and our last on Norwegian soil."

What Cyril was not to know was that by then telegrams with bad news were being formulated for sending, to the 'Hardy', 'Hunter' and 'Hotspur' crew members' next of kin.

Cyril, like his shipmates, was in a despondent and melancholy state. "Not one of us had the slightest inkling of what was to happen two hours ahead or what two courageous officers had been doing to achieve it during the past few hours. If we had known I am sure there would have been no turning in, never mind sleeping that night. When I said we fell into a deep sleep, it really was. With so many of us in such a small room, all the windows closed because of the cold, the atmosphere was terrible. It reminded me in a way of the story of the 'Black Hole of Calcutta'. At least we could go outside for a breath of fresh air if we wanted to, but whilst in the room we were in a stupefied state of sleep because of the stinking air.

"During the battle in the afternoon, while we had been watching from our grandstand viewpoint, Lt Heppel and Captain Evans of the RMS North Cornwall had gone down to the jetty in the village; hoping to find a boat in which they could go out into the fjord to try and contact one of our ships. They were allowed on board and taken up to the Bridge to see the Captain. When they reported that there were so many survivors from 'Hardy' plus the merchant seamen ashore waiting to be rescued, a loud cheer rang around the ship. The Captain signalled Admiral Whitworth in 'Warspite' giving him the good news. Cheering also broke out in 'Warspite' when the crew received the news. Their journey up the fjord had not been in vain. The German ships had been wiped out and now they could rescue men who they had thought were lost forever.

"The Admiral signalled for two of the destroyers to return up the fjord to Ballangen that night to take on board all the survivors of 'Hardy' and the merchant seamen. Those ships were HMS Ivanhoe and HMS Kimberley. There was a suggestion that whilst Evans and Heppel were on the jetty sorting out how to get out to the retreating destroyers, a boatload of German survivors from one of their sunken destroyers came to the jetty. The German sailors were taken prisoner, having given up the fight and were locked in a shed by Norwegian civilians. This led to the makeshift guards being supplied with rifles which they had to be shown how to load and fire."

Bill Pulford recalls that moment for reasons which could be seen as that of either 'in the line of duty' or a potential 'Court Martial' offence. "Chief Cock the 'Buffer' said to me,

'Don't forget to do your rounds, because we don't want any surprise attacks.' We had heard the Germans were five miles away and still looking for us. Come 10 o'clock, I did my job and made sure everything was darkened. Tubby Cock called me by name, 'Keep outside "Scouse" let us know if anyone is coming up that shouldn't be!' So as I was walking around at about twenty to twelve, I was suddenly grasped from behind by the left arm. Out of the corner of my eye I saw what looked like a peaked hat. Cursing, I just lashed out – and caught this bloke straight in the face. I didn't know if I had smashed his nose or what. Anyway, I caught him, knocked him down and I was just about to kick him in the crutch, where it hurts most, when a voice from out of the shadows, bawled out, 'It's all right sir, leave him, he's one of 'Hardy''s.

"I heard a rifle cocked, stopped still and this chap got up and said, 'Who are you?' I told him I had challenged him. He proved his identity by producing an I.D. card. This other chap, now out of the shadows, said again, 'He's one of Hardy's, Sir, because only a matelot would have used language like that when they're caught.' That is how I was identified. I said, 'What time is it?' He said, 'Why?' 'Just like to know Sir." He replied, 'I am Lieutenant (so and so), it is now twenty to twelve midnight.' I replied, 'Oh what a pity.' His next words were, 'What is the significance?' I said, 'Well, today is the 13th April and tomorrow is my birthday.' His reply, 'Well on behalf of the Royal Navy, Leading Seaman Pulford, "Many happy returns", now "sod off" and get me your First Lieutenant!'"

Cyril: "Back at the school we were unaware of what had been taking place between Lt Heppel, Captain Evans and our ships further down the fjord and as I have already mentioned we were asleep. At about midnight I was awakened by a rough hand shaking me. I looked up but all I could see were two rows of white shiny teeth. I thought I was having a nightmare and blamed the lack of food and the atmosphere in the room. Then a gruff voice said, 'Come on Jack. You're rescued!' I could not move. I just stared, then my eyes must have started to focus properly or perhaps I was at last fully awake. I could just make out a large hairy face. Suddenly it dawned on me, it was a sailor with a beard of jet black hair and when he opened his mouth his teeth shone like pearls. Once again, in a gruff cockney voice, he said, 'Come on Jack. You're rescued. It's time to go home.' I got up off the floor, as he moved around the room shaking others, telling them to move outside and follow another of our rescuers down to the village jetty.

"Outside the school and all the way down to the jetty, we saw fully armed sailors guarding the route. We learned that they were an armed landing party from the destroyers previously mentioned and that more of them had gone to the hospital in the village to fetch our wounded. What a wonderful awakening it had turned out to be for all of us. When we thought that all hope of rescue had gone, with the passing of our ships down the fjord, we had been in the depths of despair. Now the picture had changed. We were elated and eager to get on board the German launch which was being put to good use ferrying us to the rescue ships.

"We formed a happy and jubilant queue on the little fishing jetty waiting patiently for our turn to jump into the launch. I don't think any of us gave a passing thought to the fact that the Germans in Narvik might take it into their heads to attack us as we embarked. We knew their ships had all been sunk and that the troops occupying the town must have taken a terrible pounding from 'Warspite' and the destroyers; so really they could not be in great shape to interfere with us or our rescuers.

"There was quite a good crowd of Norwegians on the jetty to see us off but in the darkness it was impossible to recognise any of our new found friends. We just waved and shouted goodbye to them all hoping that all would go well for them in the dark days ahead. In the years that followed, I often wondered if those Norwegians were satisfied with our conduct whilst among them and with our efforts to stop the Germans holding Narvik. We had done our best but the odds had been against us and at least most of us were alive to carry on the fight. There would be many more Narviks for some of us before the enemy was finally beaten."

In Bill Pulford's interview with the I.W.M., he appears to substantiate Fred Evans' written version in his letter, that in fact there were wounded soldiers being brought to Ballangen on the 13th of April. The same night the survivors were evacuated. Here Bill describes what he recalls after the Second Battle. "Eventually, when the destroyers had passed up the harbour and clear out of our vision, 'Warspite' followed letting fire with shells. Then we let go, we just couldn't contain ourselves any longer. As far as we were concerned that was the end of troubles in Ballangen.

"Without a further ado, we started getting ready to go back but then before we started to move back there was a convoy coming up the road, so we stood to one side to let it pass. No one said a word, deathly quiet, they were German lorries bringing the wounded from the first encounter in the fjord. We knew they were injured because as the last lorry passed, a slight breeze lifted up the tail flap of the canvas, we could see stretchers inside and a German orderly. We had mixed feelings, there was the enemy a matter of feet away from us and we couldn't do a thing about it and on the other hand the enemy were only feet away from us and didn't do anything about it. It was a strange experience."

On their way home, this is Fred Evans' final part of his letter to the Mayor of Ballangen, written in April 1973, where he hopes to verify his account for personal curiosity.

About midnight we were all led out of the building down to a boat at a nearby jetty for evacuation to the destroyer 'Ivanhoe'. I remember being transported by some of my comrades on a sledge, so I should imagine the journey was downhill, and not by a proper road or path.

When I returned to my normal naval life, after two or three months in hospital at Plymouth (my frostbite having turned septic), I realised that I must be the only British person who could know of my narrow escape from contact with German sailors. The reason I have remembered the event so vividly is the difference in the type of discipline between British and German seaman. I have been reluctant to have much to say of my experience fearing that the listener might well think that it was a story to be taken with a 'pinch of salt', as the saying goes in England.

But last weekend, under the leadership of Cyril Cope, the British Narvik veterans were guests of the German Narvik veterans at Kiel, and I thought it would be a wonderful opportunity for me to confirm the story. But, to my immense dismay, from over one hundred German Narvik veterans I could obtain not the slightest verification. Indeed 'Captain Kurt Reitsch' practically convinced me that the Germans that I saw with rifles were not the German Navy. We managed to compromise however in that it is possible that the men were soldiers, maybe 'Alpine Troops'.*

* *Note:* Captain Rechel is the correct spelling. He was in command of 'Bernd von Arnim'.

Captain Reitsch also said that there was no official record of any Germans landing at Narvik on 13/4/40 with rifles and that he would be very pleased if I could present him with anymore verification than I can give at present. I feel that it is a challenge that I prove that I have not imagined that it was a true happening, and feel forced to write to you to confirm that I am not just a victim of one of those war-time hallucinations. Please don't refrain from telling me if it has been only my imagination, as such a reply would really be worth hearing. I have always considered myself to be quite a sober minded person.

Again I must apologise for taking so much of your valuable time and trusting that in Ballangen there should be someone who would remember something. It would be too much to hope for that the Burgomaster I have mentioned is still with us, but I am hoping that one of the nurses will be able to remember. I am very grateful to you and to all the good people of Ballangen (and Vidrik) for all that you did for me and my comrades. I have often thought how wonderful it would be if I and my wife were able to offer our thanks personally.

I Remain,
Yours Sincerely
Signed Fred Evans.

I have never found out if Fred Evans received a reply from the Mayor of Ballangen. Perhaps now the book is published more information will be forthcoming to be included in any future reprints.

Not all of the physically fit survivors went with their shipmates to 'Ivanhoe'. John Avery describes how his father Gordon Avery took a much more risky option. "My father was not in that group. He volunteered to stay and support the wounded and help to move them inland. As the villagers would face reprisals if caught assisting British troops, this meant several demanding trips, carrying or supporting their wounded colleagues over icy frozen ground while German aircraft were constantly flying over the area.

A rescue was mounted the following month and one of the ships HMS Jaguar received several hits during the mission. But all of the surviving crew were successfully recovered. Although, William Joyce (Lord Haw-Haw) did announce on the wireless that my father was one of the sailors killed in action. Fortunately, my father survived and proved him wrong. He lived undercover for ten days, then by moving along the coast he boarded a neutral ship and was handed over to the 'Red Cross' in Sweden.

As a boy I used to dress up using the ski cap, woolly jacket and long stockings that he had used during his time in Norway. But at the time, I was too young to understand the significance. My father had missed the triumphant march through Horse Guards Parade where Churchill had made one of his memorable speeches in praise of the battle."

Hardy's - final resting place at Skjomnes.
G.Haarr Collection

Narvik Iron Ore Train Depot before the battles. *G. Haarr Collection.*

After the First and Second Battles. *G. Haarr Collection.*

With regards to the wounded 'Hardy' men, they were finally taken by Norwegian fishermen to the Lofoten Islands. The only version I have of the voyage is that of Jack Good, described here by his granddaughter Anna. "My Granddad was hidden from the Germans by two local ladies (Ballangen) then transported to a hospital. On the boat Granddad was naked with a blanket over him. He had no tag, so that if they were captured, they would have nothing to identify him. The crew members kept covering his face with the blanket but Granddad kept pushing it back, thinking it was because they thought he was dead, not because his eye was unsightly."

Note: Kirsten Amundsen, who lives in Norway contacted me about her great aunt Ingeborg Sandsvik. She had been the head nurse at the hospital in Ballangen. Ingeborg, sometime after the War was given a gold finger ring. Here Kirsten explains, "As a small girl in 1960 I was told she had got this ring from the Captain of HMS Hardy. As the Captain had died in the battle the ring must have been given by someone else, who was not connected to the boat. I have happened to inherit the ring." The intriguing gift was inscribed 'OFOTEN-10.04.1940', and an engraving of a destroyer.

I offered a possible solution. There had been two other ships named 'Hardy'. The first was sunk by a German U-boat in 1944 and the second commissioned in 1955. During the latter ship's service she would have visited Narvik, for a memorial ceremony in the 1950s. It may be that the then captain, Commander Peter Drummond Alan, presented the gold ring to Ingeborg. This would have been in recognition of her and the other nurses devoted care of the 'Hardy' survivors.

24

Back Home, for Some

Back to the 'Oystermouth Parish Journal', "Sunday morning, a brown enveloped telegram was delivered to Alec's home in Park Street. It carried the worst possible news. 'The Admiralty regrets [...] Leading Seaman A.P. Hunt (D/JX138336) [...] 'Killed in Action [...]'."

I am informed by Alec's great nephew Keith Greenslade that Alec's 'Mam', on the same day the telegram was delivered, also received the moving letter from Alec. Optimistic that she would give her consent to the marriage of a lady he had met in Plymouth.

The journal author continues, "Mumbles was stunned, Alec was only the second Mumbles boy to have been killed in action in World War Two. [...] It wasn't long before someone pointed out Alec's chalked name on the wall and suggested its preservation. First move was made by the Borough Engineer's Department. He sprayed the, now precious, letters with a sealant and later fitted an overall transparent plastic sheet. And, as such, it stayed for many, many years. [...] Landlords came and went and somewhere along the line, during a period of refurbishing, the names were lost. There were no contemporaries left amongst the customers to voice an opinion. They'd all gone, too."

As a footnote, there is a story behind how the original letter that Alec wrote to his Mam and the telegram amongst other mementoes came into the possession of Keith. I will let Keith tell his story. "Alec and my mum were the best of mates as well as being brother and sister. Mum followed his career in the Navy very closely. He came home on leave at Christmas 1939, [...] he was best man at my mum's wedding, which he regarded a great honour.

"Well after the war, I grew up not knowing much about Alec, but I was always interested in the sea and began to find snippets about Alec around. One day I was up in the loft of the house, nobody had been up there for years and I found an old small case. As kids are, I wanted to know what was in it. It was bound with a belt to tie it together and I found lots of family stuff inside. But what I was about to find sent me numb. It was a letter that Alec had sent to his mum, my Gran, just before he left harbour to Norway on that fateful mission. It did not have the name of the woman on it, so to this day she is a mystery."

Paymaster Geoffrey Stanning, on awakening the next morning, was becoming restless. "About 9 o'clock the following morning, Sunday the 14th of April the doctors came in discussing whether I should be allowed to go in 'Ivanhoe' or not. I joined in energetically and said I had every intention of going so they decided to put my leg in plaster and let me go. About 10 o'clock we were taken down and put in our old friend the lorry and after waiting there about half an hour, driven down to the pier. 'Ivanhoe's' boat was there but it was a long trip out to the ship and very uncomfortable. When we got there, the boat was hoisted and I was taken and put in the Captain's sleeping cabin aft where I was very comfortable.

"We got under way a few minutes later and there was an air raid alarm which came to nothing. I slept that afternoon but was told afterwards that the ship had been up to Narvik: but with deadlights down I should have seen nothing in any case. The idea was to transfer the wounded to 'Warspite' the following day and I must admit I was anxious to get to a larger ship as it was such hell lying there with no means of seeing what was happening. If there was a submarine alarm – as there were several times – I could tell roughly what was happening from the engine movements but naturally it was irksome."

Meanwhile amongst those being rescued on 'Ivanhoe was Stan Robinson who began to enjoy the hospitality aboard, not knowing he and a large number of his shipmates would soon be moving on to other warships. Not only going back towards Norway but spending another ten days at sea. On board the 'Ivanhoe' we had a corned beef sandwich about one inch thick, cup of Pussers 'Kye', which is cocoa, you can stand a spoon up in that. It was the most delicious I ever had."

Here are Bert Mason's recollections of the rescue. "A few men had to be left behind in hospital, but later were spirited across the fjord by Norwegians to Harstad, Lofoten Islands. One I remember was a young signalman Ralph Brigginshaw. Leaving an excited Norwegian crowd on the jetty, over 200 of us were taken on board and then put to sea in the commandeered German lifeboat. We were badly over crowded, so in the night we went alongside the destroyer 'Ivanhoe' and a large number of us were transferred to her. On board we were told to occupy the same messes we had on 'Hardy', so our little gang finished up in the Torpedoman's mess. The next day 'Ivanhoe' and the other naval vessels steamed up and around the fjord. Passed the 'Hardy' wreck, stood off

Narvik, sailed into Rombaksfjord and Herjangsfjord and out again into Ofotfjord; to survey the wrecks of the German destroyers. It was dead quiet like a graveyard, which of course it was.

"We were treated to an excellent meal of 'fish and chips' on 'Ivanhoe'. We asked where they had got such beautiful fish. They replied that they had done some bartering with Norwegian fishermen, whilst patrolling, after laying the minefield a few days earlier. We were then told we were going home."

However, this was not the case for their unfortunate wounded shipmates, who had to undergo urgent medical attention. Signalman Ralph Brigginshaw, then aged nineteen, who had received wounds to his arm, described his experience to me in 2010. "It was planned that the more seriously wounded men would be taken to the Lofoten Islands, to be picked up by HMS Penelope, a cruiser. This was instead of the destroyers. However, previously 'Penelope' had hit a rock and was then needed to be towed by HMS Eskimo. When the two ships arrived, the 'Penelope' would not take us onboard, and after a few discussions it was decided, we wounded men should go to a hospital ashore. This was the Gravdal Hospital (Gravdal Skyehus) on the island of Vestvagey in the Lofotens." I will return to Ralph's story describing how after six weeks' recuperation, he was given little notice to get ready to go back home. Although, even after his return to Britain his was still not a smooth recovery.

Jack Good and Geoff Bailey also needed immediate medical attention. Geoff had the remainder of his hand amputated. However, this did not deter him from eventually having a successful career back in his home surroundings, serving his local community with distinction.

With regard to Jack, his granddaughter Anna explains the attention Jack received from the Norwegian hospital staff.

"They worked miracles in the operating theatre, saving the tear-ducts of the socket of the lost eye and one knuckle of the three fingers lost. This skill meant a lot to his future life, as it enabled him to lubricate a false eye and still write with his right hand. They may sound trivial things, but not to him."

In Geoff Bailey's case, as told in the book 'Torfaen Heroes of World War Two', I quote, "For awhile he was posted as missing in action. It was several weeks later that his anxious father received notification that his son was off the danger list and on his way home. While convalescing in an English hospital the 19 year old seaman received numerous letters. One he would particularly treasure was from the widow of his skipper, Mrs Warburton-Lee."

Cyril was also enjoying the some well earned treats, "Once aboard 'Ivanhoe', we were soon distributed among the various messes. Our new hosts had prepared hot tea and soup for us. We also received a tot of rum. The next job was to find somewhere to sleep. On small destroyers there was never much room for the normal complement of men on the messdecks. Finding room for our large number of extra men posed a problem. We did find room though on lockers, tables and mess stools. Our hosts provided blankets and something to use as a pillow. As their hammocks were slung above us we could only hope that they would not forget we were there and step on us next morning when they climbed out of them."

Bill Pulford was tired and still feeling the emotions of the previous week's events. "I had a typical naval fare, slice of bread about one inch thick and corn beef about two inches thick. I don't think we were able to eat much, as we were too full up with emotion. However, we drank the tea, there wasn't enough there to supply us, because we hadn't had a decent cup for five days. They just left us on the messdeck where we bedded down for the night, anywhere, anyhow. But we just felt, we're all right here, we were safe, we just slept. The following morning the 'chef' made a decent breakfast for us, 'trainsmashers' we called them. All red, slices of bacon and tinned tomatoes. To a matelot's humour that's a 'train smash'. We enjoyed that hot meal and more tea. I think we must have cleared out the messdeck issue of tea before we left."

Cyril continues, "The ship stayed at anchor in the middle of the fjord for the rest of the night but early next morning, Sunday 14th, it set off up the fjord in the direction of Narvik. The Captain of 'Ivanhoe' wanted to show us the extent of the damage in the harbour and to give us a last look at the position where our ship had met her sad end. On passing the spot, the 'Ensign' on 'Ivanhoe' was lowered to half mast. We lined the rails and saluted our dead comrades. Then we came back down the fjord for the last time heading for the open sea, leaving a chapter of British Naval History behind us; but more important to us were the officers and men of 'Hardy' and 'Hunter' who would never leave the fjord."

BBC 'WORLD SERVICE'.
SUNDAY 14th APRIL AT MIDNIGHT.

"The British Navy's entry into Narvik Fjord yesterday, and the sinking of the seven German destroyers, was front-page news in all the Paris newspapers today. French gratification has been expressed in many ways, notably by M. Reynaud, the French Prime Minister, who has sent a telegram to Mr Chamberlain saying 'The French nation shares Britain's feelings of admiration and gratitude for the Royal Navy, which has added a page of glory to its records, and has inflicted on the enemy a wound that will never heal'.

"It is estimated this morning by an official of the French War Office that as a result of the action, at least a third and probably half of the German Navy is at the bottom of the sea. He pointed out that the victory would have an enormous lead to interesting military developments. For Germany it was a bitter blow.

"An Admiralty casualty list issued tonight shows that Captain Warburton-Lee, commander of H.M.S. HARDY lost his life during the gallant action at Narvik Fjord last Wednesday. Another officer and fourteen ratings of the destroyer were also killed and three officers seriously wounded. Two ratings, listed as missing, are believed to have been drowned, and six are seriously injured. Captain Warburton-Lee, who had spent most of his thirty two years' service in destroyers, led his flotilla into Narvik against overwhelming odds. Knowing that superior enemy forces were in the Fjord, he sent a radio message to the Admiralty, asking: "Shall I go in?" As Mr Churchill has since told the House of Commons, the Admiralty replied that he must be the sole judge. Back came the message: 'Going into action!'"

I am informed by families of 'Hardy' and 'Hunter' crew members that it was not until the 18th of April 1940 that they received a letter from the Royal Naval Barracks Devonport. This stated, "It appears very unlikely that there are any survivors from the loss of HMS Hunter", or HMS Hardy if applicable. However, having talked to my Auntie Vera (Cyril's younger sister, married name Parkin), regarding the above BBC announcement, it appears, from her memories, that a telegram must have arrived at the Cope's family home much earlier than 18th April 1940.

Here are Auntie Vera's recollections. At the time she was twelve years of age. "I came home from school at dinner time and saw our stepmother Annie upset and I was not sure why. However, I finally found out that a telegram had arrived which I believed said, 'It is with regret I have to inform you that your son Cyril Cope is missing and presumed drowned'.

"We all thought about Edie, who was pregnant, so we all walked down to St Stephen's Street, Salford 3, to give her our support."

Les Smale's arrival on the rescuing ships did not last long as he relates hereafter, "The following morning we were transferred to different ships. I went on board the 'Hero', who was soon on the move down the fjord to open sea. Orders were then received to join with 'Warspite' in patrolling an area which we thought to be in the vicinity of the entrance to the Vestfjord."

Charles Cheshire mentions being given options, "Ivanhoe was running short of food, we went back near Narvik, from there we were given choices of staying on 'Ivanhoe' or one of the other ships. It only had one gun turret, so I thought I'd go on one which had a few more. So I went on the 'Hero', she had four guns and I thought I'd be better off on there. If I'd have stayed on the 'Ivanhoe' I'd have been home in a few days."

Dougy Bourton also quickly found himself on another ship. However, even after having to endure the previous eventful week, he still seemed happy to stay at sea. "The next morning we were split up amongst the fleet. I was unlucky! Some went on board the 'Forester', who were almost out of ammunition and fuel, just enough to get home. But I was sent to the 'Havock', which was part of the old flotilla. I wasn't unhappy about that, it was commanded by Commander Courage, tremendous man, a fine 'fighter' and quite a character. We did a seven day patrol with the fleet, the others went home."

Bill Pulford: "I was transferred later in the forenoon to 'Hero'. Obviously, 200 extra men on a destroyer only made to fit 150, well she couldn't take it. 'Ivanhoe' went around dispersing us to various ships of the 2nd Destroyer Flotilla ships. That was my own doing, because while all the other ships were sent home, myself and thirty men with me were detailed to remain in Norwegian waters."

Geoffrey Stanning: "On Monday afternoon we arrived in 'Skjel Fjord' and they fetched all the wounded away and then came to take me, as I thought to 'Warspite'. Luckily I asked where we were being taken and found that we were to be taken to another shore hospital. So I said I would prefer to stay where I was, at my own risk. 'Ivanhoe' soon got under way again and we were going to screen 'Rodney' on her way back to Scapa. I lifted up the deadlight and had a look at Skjel Fjord which had 'Penelope', the oiler, and the captured German ship 'Alster' in it as well as several damaged destroyers.

"By Monday evening we had made our rendezvous with 'Rodney' and were formed on her screen. The following day signals began to come from C-in-C (Commander in Chief) in 'Rodney' asking for personal accounts of what had happened and also for a story to give the press. With the help of Briggs, the Chief who typed them, I made up both but it was a bit of an effort. We were very lucky to be screening 'Rodney' as the destroyers screening the other large ships did not get back till days later for one reason and another."

Stan Robinson: "We were going home to Scapa Flow in a South Westerly direction, when 'Hero' came alongside. The orders were that fifty of us had to jump across from 'Ivanhoe' to 'Hero', so I stood on a guardrail, hanging onto a davit, waiting for the ship to come up, so I could jump at the proper time, and as I jumped a Lieutenant Commander had a camera and was whirring away with the camera and I nearly jumped on top of him." The man with the movie camera will feature again shortly.

'Hardy' survivors transferring from 'Ivanhoe' to 'Hero'. *Cyril Cope Collection.*

It appeared that those survivors on the 'Ivanhoe', having been temporarily accommodated in various parts of the ship, were probably in such a 'compos mentis' state that they didn't know of the latest 'buzzes' going around the ship. Including the unconfirmed reports of other ships about to disperse and return back to home waters. However, either by chance or wisdom there were some who heard the rumours and thought that they could take advantage of their newly acquired information. Alas, this eventually led to disappointment.

A national newspaper having interviewed LTO Bill Pulford on arriving back in Britain reported that, "Pulford with a few others, was later transferred to HMS Hero; which was an unfortunate move for them, as the ship was ordered to remain in Norwegian waters until further notice. Whilst on board they had the galling experience of listening on the radio to the London welcome by Winston Churchill himself to the men from 'Hardy'."

Cyril reflected back on the traumatic events he had experienced in the battle and their attempts to survive. "Our hearts were heavy with grief, because we were leaving good friends behind. Our thoughts were filled with memories of last moments spent with them. One such memory of mine was about Bill Pimlett. Known as 'Popeye' to his mates because of the good impersonations of that character he used to perform when we were closed up at action stations on the torpedo tubes.

"After we had fired all the torpedoes from our tubes and after helping the other tubes crew to get their tubes on the starboard beam, Bill and I remained near our tubes. We had turned away from the harbour after the third attack and were now under fire from the first group of enemy ships outside the harbour. Bill suddenly said, 'Let's go forward for a cup of char.' The ship had not been hit up to that point. He had just finished speaking when shells started to pass over our heads. They were close. We both dropped to the iron deck. He said 'I'm off forward for that cup of char. Are you coming?' I replied, 'No, I will hang on here with the headphones on in case I get an order to make smoke.' He slithered away on his belly heading forward. I never saw him again.

"Then, there was another memory of Chief Stoker Stiles, who passed away slowly in front of my eyes. For, this to happen so far away from home and loved ones; a good man like 'Chiefy' Stiles didn't deserve to end his life like that. What a waste and what a tragedy. I am sure that all of us must have turned our thoughts finally to our gallant Captain Warburton-Lee. What a momentous decision he had to make when he decided to attack the enemy under the terrible conditions prevailing at the time. Blinding snowstorms, a treacherous narrow fjord, an unknown quantity of enemy ships, the fjord probably mined. Last but not least, I remember the crews in each ship who had not tasted action, except of course for the short running battle with 'Scharnhorst' and 'Gneisenau' on the morning of the ninth."

Returning to Edward Stiles' family, his wife Violet, as previously explained had three young children and a mortgage to pay on their new home. Daughter, June, at the time was nine years old, recalls, "It obviously all came as a shock to hear my father had been killed at Narvik. More so the effect on my mother who shut herself away for three days. But realised she had to keep things going for us children. She took on lodgers and had three jobs, one was at the British Legion serving teas and another as a cleaner. She also found night shift work in the dockyard I think working in an ammunition department. Eventually, she married one of the lodgers. I think probably for security. Mum died aged eighty-seven in 1991."

Cyril continues his thoughts and feelings regarding the last few days. "Oh yes, we had done quite a lot of hard training in the few months we had been together. However, doing things in practice was a different kettle of fish to doing them whilst under attack from the enemy. When we entered that fjord we knew we had still to prove ourselves under those conditions. That then was the position when Warburton-Lee sent his signal 'Going into action!' There was never any doubt in our minds as to whether he had made the right decision. Both before the attack and after we were knocked out, we backed him to the limit. He was right in taking the calculated risk and we in 'Hardy' would not have had it otherwise. I am sure the crews in the other four ships felt the same.

"I remember talking to one of my messmates, 'Jimmy Lee' about the situation at Narvik as we found it. The disposition of the German destroyers was very fortunate for them, unfortunate for us. With a bit of luck on our side we might have found all ten enemy destroyers inside the harbour instead of half in, half out. In that case, we could have sunk the lot and taken the port. On entering the harbour, surprise was on our side and if there had been more destroyers inside, I think that our skipper would have brought our other four ships in much sooner, therefore doing more damage to more enemy ships. As things turned out, it was the Germans who were able to take us by surprise outside the harbour, forcing us to engage two separate targets in different directions. That and the very small area in which we had to manoeuvre was our undoing.

"Jimmy and I both agreed that it would have been a big victory if only those ten ships had stayed in the harbour but wars are not won on ifs. We had done a good job under trying conditions and paved the way for the ships taking part in the Second Battle. For many of us the action in which we had taken part would prove very valuable during other battles, in other ships in other theatres of war, as the months and years of struggle went on. However, as we steamed down Vestfjord, heading for the open sea and home none of us could have guessed just how long the war was going to last or just how serious things would be for Great Britain before victory at last came our way.

"On reaching the open sea we set course for Scapa Flow and home, escorted by a large fleet. Unfortunately, for some of our ship's company, this was not to be. It happened like this. We were approximately half way between Norway and Scapa when a signal was received by the Admiral in command of the fleet. It came from one of our cruisers. This ship had been under constant bombing attack for over twelve hours; she was running short of ammunition, was under water from stern to midships and required assistance.

Left: Surviving 'Hardy' officers on 'Ivanhoe'. L – R. Unknown, Fallwell, Mansell, McCracken and Pope. *Cyril Cope Collection.*

Below: The lucky 'Hardy' survivors on 'Ivanhoe' going straight back home. *Cyril Cope Collection.*

"The Admiral despatched several ships to go to her aid and among these was the 'Kimberely', which had on board some of our ship's company and the merchant seamen. This diversion in the journey home prevented a large number of 'Hardy' survivors from travelling to London and taking part in the wonderful reception we were to have when we arrived there. It also caused great anxiety to their relatives, who of course expected to see us all arrive home together.

"As we in 'Ivanhoe' ploughed on to Scapa Flow, we were unaware of what had happened to our shipmates in 'Kimberely'. It was like a cruise to us. No work to do, no action stations or watches to keep. The weather had improved as we left the Arctic Circle and we were able to spend a lot of time on the upper deck. There was the usual crop of U-boat contacts on the 'Asdic'. Depth charges were dropped by some of the destroyers but if there were any results we didn't see them. Neither did we see any signs of enemy planes or ships. I think that their losses of the past few days had put them off.

"The most memorable sight during our trip was seeing the 'Eskimo" being towed stern first. She had been very badly damaged during the second battle, having a good part of her bows blown off and it looked queer to see her moving through the water stern first; because at a distance it was impossible to see the towing hawsers but she was doing fine."

Many years later in his interview with the curator from the Imperial War Museum, Cyril continued, "We noticed, some of the ships turned around and went back towards Norway, from whence they had come. The reason that the Admiral had received a signal from the cruiser 'Suffolk' was because she had been dive bombed for about 12 hours, was running out of ammunition and sinking from the stern. She wanted someone to come to her assistance. So part of the fleet had to go back to help 'Suffolk', and the 'Kimberely' was one of those ships."

25

Surprise Welcome

The Warburton-Lees' family memorabilia, including letters and photographs, offer not only a glimpse of the great Captain's life, but are important documents of World War Two naval history. When it was announced that Bernard Warburton-Lee had been killed, as you expect, over the following weeks, his wife Elizabeth was overwhelmed with letters of condolence.

Geoffrey Stanning: "We were lucky enough to get to Scapa about 7 o'clock on Wednesday evening and went straight alongside the oiler. After we had oiled and 'Ivanhoe' was just getting under way again, the hospital drifter came to me, to take me to HMS Woolwich for the night. It took about an hour to get there which I rather enjoyed as I lay on my stretcher on the warm engine room casing and could look about me, but by the time we got to 'Woolwich' I was a bit cold and by the time I had dangled on the end of 'Woolwich's' crane for 20 minutes I was completely fed up. After an uncomfortable night in 'Woolwich's' sick bay, I was taken to the 'Isle of Jersey', the hospital carrier and thence to Kingseat Hospital, Aberdeen." By now this was eight days after the first battle.

Cyril Cope and some of his co-survivors finally returned to British soil. "On our arrival at Scapa Flow we were greeted by cheering from the ship's companies of some of the ships anchored there and by ships' sirens sounding off. We were taken to the depot ship HMS Forth where we were warmly welcomed by her Captain, Officers and Ship's Company. Here we were able to have a hot bath, given clean underwear, a good hot meal and a medical inspection. Late afternoon we left by tender for Thurso, the little Scottish port which was the link between the Navy at 'Scapa' and the rest of the British Isles.

"At last we were really on our way home. By this time we realised that many of our shipmates would not be travelling down the line. The destroyer bringing them back had still not arrived home. By this time we realised that many of our shipmates would not be travelling down the line. The destroyer bringing them back had still not arrived at 'Scapa' and we were all upset about it even at that period when we did not know what lay in store for us at the end of our journey. As far as we knew it was just a matter of returning to Devonport barracks, kitting out with new uniforms, a spot of survivors' leave, then back to the 'War at Sea'. Our arrival on shore at

Thurso did not create any excitement. I am sure that nobody had been told who we were, which led to an amusing incident.

"All our chaps and the crew of the destroyer 'Eclipse', which had been damaged by a bomb, had to go to a large hotel in Thurso for a dinner before catching a train. (The Lion Hotel) Petty Officer West, myself and another rating were late reaching the road in which the hotel was situated. We did not know where the rest of the party had disappeared, because we did not know the name of the hotel. We eventually found ourselves outside a large hotel. Near the door stood a police Sergeant talking to a civilian. As we looked around, hoping to see a trace of our shipmates, I heard the Sergeant say, 'I wonder what they want. I would ask them, but they look like foreigners and perhaps they do not understand English.' 'Foreigners be damned,' I said to him. 'We are survivors from the "Hardy"; we're looking for the rest of our ship's company.' 'They are all in here,' the civilian said. They had seen the crew of the 'Eclipse' go in and they were in naval uniform, but they had not been there soon enough to see our chaps go in; and of course we were all in our Norwegian clothes, so we did look like foreigners.

"Once inside the hotel we sat down to a wonderful dinner. The waiters and waitresses were fussing around us. It was a good start to our homecoming. After dinner we made our way to the little railway station to board the train which would take us on the next stage of our journey. As we looked out of the carriage windows we saw some German sailors coming into the station guarded by soldiers. They marched to our train and word got around very quickly that they were survivors from a U-boat. Some of our chaps went raving mad and rushed onto the platform to have a go at the prisoners. It took the Army escort and some of us all our time to restrain our mates. The Germans looked scared to death and were glad when they reached the compartments in which they were locked. Where they left the train I do not know. It must have been at one of the stopping places during the night while we were asleep. Our first big stop was at Inverness, where we were allowed out of the train and given cups of tea; but we were not allowed to talk to anybody, especially reporters.

"The next stop was Carlisle and by this time it was daylight. The ban on talking to reporters was lifted. On the station there was quite a crowd to welcome us including a lot of reporters and photographers. We received tea, sandwiches and cakes from welfare workers, while the reporters and photographers questioned us and took photographs. Then on once more to our next stopping place which was Preston. By now word had spread that we were on our way and we found much larger crowds waiting for us as we stepped off the train. Everyone wanted to shake our hands. We were given cigarettes, money, playing cards and newspapers. Lots of young girls from church organisations came around with trays of minerals and biscuits. It was a fantastic reception.

"A reporter from the 'Daily Mirror' came to me and asked for a story. I said, 'I will give you one if you will do something for me in return. When you leave the station will you send a telegram to my wife saying I have arrived safely in England, am on my way home and that I am all right?' I explained to him about my wife expecting our first baby and that she would have been worried if she had no positive news about me. He said, 'Yes I will send it straight away' and he did. That was the first news that my wife received about me being safe. The telegram was delivered that afternoon.

"We continued our journey south passing through countryside with open farmland and forests of trees. My mate, Jimmy Lee, who came from Plymouth said, 'I didn't know that they had fields and farms in this part of the country. I thought it was full of coal mines and dirty mills.' He was serious about it. The next stop was Crewe. We did not draw into a platform but stopped between two of them with a set of rails separating us from the crowd of people who had come to look at us. The place was absolutely packed. We opened the carriage windows and chatted to the sightseers. They threw cigarettes, chocolates, and money through the windows to us. Below us on the tracks, some railway policemen patrolled backwards and forwards.

"Obviously they were there to keep the crowd from getting down onto the track to reach us. One of these policemen said 'Where do you think you are going lads?' We replied, 'To Plymouth and then home on survivors' leave.' He said, 'You're not. It has just been announced on the one o'clock news that you have to go to London to be presented to Winston Churchill on the Horse Guards Parade.' All the chaps that lived in Plymouth moaned like hell on hearing this but the rest of us were delighted. When the train pulled out of Crewe and after we had all settled down in our seats, one of the Officers came around the compartments to tell us officially that we were indeed going to London to meet Winston Churchill and the First Sea Lord Admiral, Sir Dudley Pound.

"Our arrival at Euston Station was an occasion which none of us will ever forget. The station was packed with people waiting to greet us. Among them were relatives of some of the men, a Royal Marine Band and a Blue Jacket guard of honour. The Band struck up with 'See, the Conquering Hero Comes'. Dozens of reporters and photographers mobbed us as we stepped off the train. After many photographs had been taken and some of the men had been greeted by their relatives, we were marched to a number of double decker buses, which were to take us to the Horse Guards Parade. We moved off in the buses, which were well decorated with flags and bunting. The pace was slow as we had to move through lines of well-wishers. Some came to the bus handing out cigarettes, chocolates, sweets and money. It was a fantastic drive through the streets of London.

"At Horse Guards Parade we were met with similar scenes to Euston with thousands of people clapping and cheering. We formed into lines of three and marched to the doors of the Admiralty. Here we formed three sides of a square. All the we were met with similar scenes to Euston with thousands of people clapping and cheering. We formed into ' cameras and the whirling of newsreel cameras Mr Winston Churchill came out of the Admiralty with other members of the Government and Admirals. He walked around the ranks, chatting to some of us and accompanied by Lt Commander Mansell, our First Lieutenant, who like the rest of us was dressed in a Norwegian skiing outfit. After the inspection Mr Churchill spoke to us, welcoming us on behalf of the Government, telling us what a good job we had done."

Hardy' survivors being inspected by Winston Churchill. Able Seaman Walter Mitchell is the one with book in pocket. *Cyril Cope Collection.*

MR WINSTON CHURCHILL'S SPEECH WAS AS FOLLOWS:

"Your countrymen are well content with the manner in which you have discharged your duties. You have shown the courage and the readiness to take opportunities by the hand and make your way through the difficult situations which are always associated with the flotillas of our destroyer force. The Board of Admiralty welcomes you for yourselves, and also because you represent the flotillas of the destroyer forces, numbering scores and scores, who are serving every night and day on all the coasts of our country and on other coasts as well. The hard service demanded of the flotillas has been freely given, and it has played a notable, and indeed an indispensable part in securing the safety of the country during the opening months of this hard and obstinate war. Therefore, in paying our tribute to the officers and men present, the Londoners gathered here are also paying a tribute to the whole of the Royal Navy.

Your gallant captain, Captain Warburton-Lee, took the responsibility of ordering that determined attack, and sealed his great decision with his life.

"You are the vanguard of the army which we and our French allies will use this summer to purge and cleanse the soil of the Vikings, the soil of Norway, from the filthy pollution of Nazi tyranny. Therefore we welcome you home, and we know that after a short rest you will be anxious to resume your duties in this conflict. In the name of the Board of the Admiralty, I wish you good fortune and success."

A London 'welcome home' Churchill addressing the survivors of 'Hardy' and Eclipse'. *Cyril Cope Collection.*

A reporter for the 'Daily Mail' in the following day's edition adequately described the scene from an eye witnesses perspective of the event. His report was a front page news feature. I have left out the mention of Winston Churchill's speech so as not to duplicate the content.

'DAILY MAIL'
(SATURDAY APRIL 20th 1940 EDITION NO 13725)
THE HARDY'S LITTLE B.E.F. COMES HOME.

[Note. British Expeditionary Force]

They are home again, the men of HMS Hardy ... back from 'the heart of hell', as one of them described the fight at Narvik. But the Navy spirit is still there. Tour through

London with them in these pictures, and join in the reception, gay and serious.

TO-DAY, the Daily Mail presents a graphic series of British fighting men. Men of Hardy – here and on the back page.

YOUR COUNTRYMEN ARE WELL CONTENT.

Mr Winston Churchill stood deeply moved, on Horse Guards Parade last night and talked to the survivors of HMS Hardy – which led the attack on Narvik ... plus men from the destroyer 'Eclipse', now back in its base after being damaged by a bomb which exploded alongside. "Your countrymen are well content", he told them, "with the manner in which you have discharged your duty".

The 60 Hardy survivors wore Norwegian ski suits of all colours from blue to canary yellow, fur hats, mittens, ski shoes – given to them by the Norwegians, when they swam ashore from their grounded ship. There were 70 men from 'Eclipse'. The cheering rose and died and Mr Churchill went on speaking, especially to the men of Hardy. "You are actually our vanguard......". Again the cheers – and again, louder and longer when he declared, "......to the Nazi tyranny".

THEY WAITED IN VAIN.

"From the parade ground the men who had come through streets lined with cheering crowds from Euston past the watching eye of Nelson in Trafalgar Square, went on to the Union Jack Club in Waterloo Road for a meal and a rest. Everywhere they had been dazed by the cheering, the shouting. But at Euston there had been those who watched the joy with set lips.

"For many with no definite news of their menfolk, had gone there in the hope that they might see them among the survivors. They scanned every face as the men stepped from the train but failing to see the ones for whom they waited, turned quietly away. But even for those, there was heartening news, for they were told that other survivors were on the way and might reach London in a day or so.

"THANK GOD. HE'S SAFE.

All was noise around these wordless little groups. The Royal Marine Band playing, 'See, the Conquering Hero Comes' as if it were the last piece they would ever play; the hiss of escaping steam, the clatter and din of a big railway terminus and the cheers – loudest of all; the cheers. Beside me stood two middle-aged women and a schoolboy – sisters and nephew of CPO George W. Cock of Hardy. "We shan't believe he's safe until we see him", one told me. "We haven't heard from him since Christmas". I had in my pocket a photograph of him taken before the Hardy men left Scotland for London, as I pulled it out, "Yes that's him! Thank God he's safe".

BUFFER – THE ROCK

And then the train came in and there she noticed the figure of CPO Cock coming down the platform. You couldn't have missed him ... particularly as he wore a canary yellow ski suit. How they hugged him, how they cheered.

Another newspaper covering the event read as follows: "At the Union Jack Club – sailors sang 'roll out the barrel' and the crowd outside joined in. 'On parade was 181 bottles of beer' said

Back Home. Chief 'Tubby' Cock with Cyril on his right shoulder. *Cyril Cope Collection.*

Bill (Ned) Sparkes wearing a ski cap and bright blue jumper with a pretty flowered collar. Bill was asked by a London pressman how he got the jumper. 'As we were hiking we met a girl', he said, 'She could see that I was feeling cold – I only had a vest and a pair of slacks – and she took off her jumper and gave it to me'."

Cyril, like rest of the sailors, although having enjoyed and been overwhelmed by their surprise reception now just wanted to go back home. Whilst remaining in London for a few more hours they looked forward to celebrating their arrival. "The speeches over, the photographers, reporters and film cameramen were having a field day, we marched to our buses for the journey to the Union Jack Club where we were to have a big dinner.

"One bus refused to move. Several of our chaps got out and pushed it, but the crowd and photographers loved that. Eventually we moved off through the throng of onlookers who still clapped and cheered us. At the entrance to the Union Jack Club thousands more people waited to greet us. We had a hard job getting through them to the door, but once inside we were able to relax and have a refreshing wash before settling down to a wonderful dinner with bottles of beer to wash it down. This was our first good meal since the dinner at Thurso, so we really got stuck into it. After dinner there were quite a lot of speeches from Admirals, the President of the Union Jack Club, and I think a message from His Majesty King George VI welcoming us back to England."

There was another group of survivors welcomed onto Horse Guards Parade. These were the brave survivors from the destroyer HMS Eclipse (H08). On the 11th of April 1940 she had been escort for the minelaying ships in the 'Leads' off Norway. Whilst awaiting further orders, she was attacked by 'Luftwaffe' aircraft, which led to major flooding and four of the crew killed. Fortunately, sister ship HMS Escort was in the vicinity and managed to tow 'Eclipse' to Scotland. Whist undergoing repairs, her crew were dispatched back south to barracks, via London and the surprise celebrations."

Cyril continues, "When at last we were free to leave we were given a few hours on the town before reporting back at the Club to rejoin our buses for the drive to Waterloo Station. As we walked through the doors of the Club we were met once again by crowds of people. The whole street was packed. Then the fun started. They mobbed us trying to take our Norwegian clothes off us for souvenirs. What a job we had stopping them and trying to keep on our feet. Everybody wanted to shake our hands, or slap us on the back.

"Eventually I fought my way clear without losing anything. Invitations to go with some of the people, especially the girls, for a night on the town, were being given freely. I stood on the opposite pavement being pestered by several young and not so young ladies to go for a drink, when a little cockney lad came up to me and said, 'Come on Jack, I'll take you to my local for a drink, nobody will know you're there so you can relax and enjoy yourself for a few hours.' I agreed and off we went, my little friend almost running to keep up with my long strides.

Leading Telegraphists Vernon Rees and Bill Sparkes. *A Central Press photo.*

"When we reached the pub he said, 'Keep quiet about who you are and then you won't be pestered by people wanting to shake your hand, or asking questions about the battle. We will have a few games of darts, a few pints and then I will take you back to the Club in time to catch the Bus'. We entered the pub. He ordered two pints of beer. The landlord brought them. My new found friend turned, pint pot in hand and said to a crowded room, 'Folks, I want you to meet one of the boys from the "Hardy". He's got a few hours leave before returning to Plymouth, so let's make them happy ones, and show him how proud we Londoners are of him and his fellow survivors.'

"Everyone clapped and cheered, then the back slapping and hand shaking started all over again. Pints of beer were ordered for me, more than I knew I would be able to drink. When I was able to talk to my friend, I whispered, 'I thought we were going to keep quiet about who I was.' He replied, 'I had to tell them. They might have thought you were a foreigner in those clothes.'

"I had a good time, in spite of having to be introduced to every newcomer and closing time soon came round. Saying goodbye to the landlord, his wife and all the customers who had shown me such grand 'Cockney' hospitality, I set off with my chirpy, we inebriated friend to return to the Union Jack Club. Hoping he could find his way after so much drink, because I hadn't a clue where it was.

"On the way I said to him, 'Why did you go to the trouble of taking me along to your local and giving me a good time?' He said, 'Because I have a brother in the Navy and he served in the "Ajax" during the battle of the "River Plate". When he came home he was given a good time by somebody, so I am repaying it for him. Another thing, I am a NAAFI Canteen Manager and will soon be going to sea. I hope that I can serve with men like you and your shipmates from the

"Hardy", and if I am unlucky enough to lose my ship, perhaps I might have to rely on somebody like you to save me.' I have always been sorry I did not get his name or address. I would have liked to know how he went on during the war, because after saying goodbye to him on reaching our destination, I never saw or heard from him again.

"We were soon on our way to Waterloo Station. Some of the lads had been drinking a bit too deep but everybody was in a good jolly mood. Even the Naval Patrol, who had the task of seeing that we all got onto the Plymouth bound train, treated it as one big skylark, even though they had to carry one or two of our chaps from the bus and throw them into the compartments. So off we went on the last leg of our journey to Plymouth. To a place, to which we were returning, much sooner than we thought possible, when we left there in the February. In contrast to our arrival at other places during our long trip which had started in the Arctic Circle at Narvik, we were met with profound silence at the Devonport Barracks train station."

Bert Mason's recollected that episode, "We arrived in Plymouth, our coaches were shunted into the platform at RN Barracks station, where we disgorged, a sleepy dishevelled crowd with perhaps a few with a mammoth hangover! Now it was back to naval discipline we thought, but not quite so! We lined up four deep to march to 'Jagos' for breakfast."

Note: Prior to World War Two, Royal Naval barracks accommodation and meal facilities, similar to warships, were conducted on a 'messdeck' basis. This at least assisted new recruits to become familiarised with the system prior to joining their ship. However, Alphonso Jago, a Warrant Officer Cook, for more efficiency in serving food, came up with the idea of changing the arrangements in barracks. This resulted in the introduction of a 'General Messing System' where the lower deck sailors would come together to have their meals in a dining hall. Hence, the naval slang 'Jagos Mansion'.

Cyril described the moment. "The only person there was a Commander, who greeted our Officers. We marched off the platform, round a corner, then up a slope to reach the barracks. As the front ranks reached the top of the slope they stopped abruptly. We behind wondered what was the matter. We were soon to know. A thunderous roar of cheering and clapping broke out ahead, and as we marched on we were confronted with two packed ranks of Sailors, Marines, Wrens, NAAFI girls and even dockyard workers. The sides of the road down which we had to march were absolutely packed with them, and this was at six-thirty on Saturday morning.

"By now, ships' sirens in the dockyard were sounding a welcome. It was one of the most nerve racking experiences I have ever had. What a climax to our journey! As friends or old shipmates in the crowd spotted anybody they knew, they shouted to them. What a din! We finally reached one of the mess halls where we were to have breakfast, but first a wash to get the sleep out of our eyes. During the meal, Officers of all ranks came round asking us for our autographs for their children, some even paid with packets of twenty cigarettes. It was gradually building up to something one only dreams about, but never expects to come true."

Bert, being a relatively experienced 'sea dog', gave his slightly cynical opinion. "On our way the Barracks had cleared 'lower deck' and led by the Officers they shouted 'Three cheers for the Hardy survivors!' The mind boggled! For breakfast, which consisted of the previous day's supper – fish and chips, again; but we were not complaining. Whilst in the gym, I witnessed to me, an unbelievable sight. A 'Master of Arms' walking jauntily amongst us, smile like a full moon, carrying a basket containing packets of the best brands of cigarettes. He was throwing them out with complete abandon, like a pretty country maid dishing out bunches of flowers at a country fair! I remembered him from a few years earlier as a R.P.O. (Regulating Petty Officer) on HMS Rodney. He was nicknamed 'Dillinger' after that infamous American gangster of the thirties. He would sneak around the messdecks after 'pipe down', hoping to catch some unwary matelot having a final puff on his pipe before 'turning in'. It took a war to alter things a bit!"

Returning back to my Auntie Vera's recollections. "Out of the blue a photograph came, of women sat on a railway station with mountains in the background. We looked and looked again – 'That's our Cyril in a ladies' skirt!' We thought 150 (Hardy survivors) had taken to the mountains."

Actually the skirts were pantaloon type trousers provided by the Norwegians. It may have been a photograph taken by a war correspondent at the time in Thurso, with the Scottish mountains in the background. It appears, as you would probably expect, that the newspapers and the BBC were more able to keep families informed, albeit by chance, than the Navy who had a much larger job with many ships throughout the world to deal with.

26

Survivors' Leave

Cyril only had thoughts of going home. "After breakfast we went to the supply stores to be kitted out with a complete outfit of new uniform. Then to the pay office, ration card, travelling warrant and a pass for two weeks' leave. At eleven o'clock we mustered in the gymnasium. Once more we formed into a three sided square and again batteries of cameras were focused on us. This time it was the Commander in Chief of Plymouth Command and the Commodore of the Barracks who inspected us and then gave us a speech of welcome. Time seemed to be flying. I watched the gymnasium clock and hoped the speech making would finish in time for me to catch the one o'clock train for Manchester. At twelve o'clock we were free to leave Barracks.

"As we approached the main gate, we could see the road outside packed with people. This time there was no chance to push through them because quite a lot were relatives of either our own shipmates or the men from 'Hunter', which like our ship had been manned by the men from the Plymouth Command. These relatives required information about their men folk. We could say nothing about the 'Hunter' ship's company because at that time we knew nothing about them. Although any of us who saw her being so badly hit knew there would not be many coming back; we kept quiet."

Bert Mason was also on his way home on survivors' leave when he encountered some unexpected greetings. "Outside the gates there were quite a crowd of people, mostly women. They were eagerly enquiring of husbands, sons and relatives – namely the 'Hardy' ships company who were not with us. We told the waiting women that some of their men had unfortunately 'missed the bus' and would be along in due course. Back in the fjord where we were rescued at Ballangen, those that did not get on board 'Ivanhoe' found themselves in an isolated place among the fjords called Cripple Creek; temporary home for all our wrecked and disabled ships. These men did not get home until nearly three weeks after us and had the chagrin experience of listening to the radio telling how we were whooping it up in London and elsewhere. I believe some of them did arrive back in Liverpool aboard the troopship 'Franconia'; with not so much as a Cornish pastie to welcome them home!"

Cyril tried hard to placate the confronting crowd. "Of our own shipmates who had not returned with us, we could only say they were safe and on their way home in another ship. It was hard trying to convince some of the people that this was so, but the worse moment for me was when some relatives enquired about one of our comrades who had been killed. They wanted to know how and if he had suffered. Would he be buried in Norway? It was a distressing moment for me but I tried my best to reply in words that would hardly come out. I told them what they wanted to know, said how sorry I and the rest of the chaps were that their loved one had not returned. After replying to questions from other relatives packed around me, I managed to squeeze through the crowd to the bus stop where I was then surrounded by small children asking for my autograph."

Outside Devonport Barracks going on survivors leave. On the right Able Seaman Bobby McAtamney with shrapnel wound to lip.

Both Cyril and Bert were not to know that one woman amongst the crowd outside the barracks was the wife of their messmate Bill Pulford. You will read shortly about Bill's wife's endeavour to get news of her husband and its emotional outcome. Cyril was feeling guilty for not being able to supply the families with more concrete information, especially as he was now making his own way home. "It was a relief to get on the No. 14 bus for North Road Station. By this time I was feeling the strain of my long journey from London, the hectic routine in barracks and the emotional experiences outside the barrack gate. Added to this was the fact that I had not had a good night's sleep in a bed or a hammock since 7th April. It was now 20th April, where in thirteen nights, I had either been at action stations, sleeping on a floor, a table, or in a train compartment. Also, of course I had the added worry of thinking about my wife, who for all I knew then may have had the baby, or still be waiting for it to be born."

Leading Torpedoman Bert Mason confronted by anxious families wanting news of their loved ones.

Cyril eventually felt more relaxed and finally settled into his journey home. "I caught the one o'clock train with five minutes to spare, sharing the compartment with several Petty Officers going home to Wales on leave after a commission abroad. They asked me about the Norwegian clothes I was carrying. When I told them who I was and the name of my ship, out came the bottles of beer. They really looked after me. Two of them had to get out at Bristol, so I asked them would they send a telegram to my wife giving the time of my arrival in Manchester. They sent it and unbeknown to me another one to the Manchester Evening Newspaper. So that when the train arrived at London Road Station at 9 p.m., I was met not only by my wife Edie, my father, stepmother and one of my brothers but also by a large crowd of people. This was obviously a surprise, I thought I was just going to get on a bus and go home. [Cyril became emotional on I.W.M. tape – last sentence sounds like]

"Everybody started waving and clapping their hands. People getting off the train with me were looking round and saying, 'What's it all about?', someone said, 'Oh he's a chap off the "Hardy". So then I had these passengers coming up to me, shaking my hand and wishing me well. There were reporters and photographers; and once again relatives of members of the 'Hardy' ship's company."

One of the survivors who missed his train home was Able Seaman Walter White; fortunately, as you will remember, he only lived a short distance away in Exeter. Moving forward through the years to 2010, his sister Lily, now aged 97, explained to the local newspaper 'Echo and Express' that she had gone to St David's train station to meet Walter but he had missed his train from Plymouth – because he was speaking to reporters. However, once he had made it back home, like many others his return was celebrated. Walter and his family were greeted by the Mayor of Exeter at the Guildhall. Lily said, "We were all very proud of him, especially father, who was a Royal Navy man and had served in the First World War."

As a matter of interest, Walter had told reporters, "I helped to throw timber over the side of the ship to help the lads get ashore, and eventually I got on a raft and reached the shore. It was extremely cold, but the excitement kept me warm." It would not be long before Walter White was back at sea again but this time facing a different enemy.

Bert Mason finally got on his train going north. "Then it was to North Road railway station to catch the Penzance–Liverpool Express and home for a fortnight's rest. A letter I had pencilled to my mother when we were in 'Scapa' was late being delivered and my parents and all the residents of Maesbury village were in a state of uneasy anxiety, wondering what had happened to me."

Cyril, on the Manchester station platform, was again confronted by desperate people wanting news of their loved ones. "The parents of 'Stoker Brown' were the first I spoke to. All I could say was that he was safe and would be home later. I explained that for security reasons I could not tell them why he would be late but told them not to worry. Other relatives I told the same. I think that only two of us from the North West arrived home that Saturday night. The other lad was Harold Davenport who had assisted in getting Captain Warburton-Lee ashore. He was a youngster like me and he had undergone his baptism of action with the same courage and fortitude as had all the youngsters on 'Hardy'.

"My home was only a short taxi ride from the station. We were then living with my mother in law Sarah-Ann. So after photographs had been taken and a few words given to the reporters, off I went with my wife, Edie, who had not yet had the baby. Off, on what was really the last leg of a journey which had been long, tiring but very exciting. I looked forward to a nice rest among relatives and friends who would understand my reticence to talk about what had happened there in Norway. I needed time to think, to get incidents and people in their correct places, to go over the many ifs and buts of what might have happened. Since leaving 'Ivanhoe' in Scapa I had not found much time for thought. Events had crowded in on top of each other and in the mad whirl of our trip to London and Plymouth thoughts of our ship and the battle had been pushed to the back of our minds. We were entering a new phase of our lives. The past seemed to be an age away.

"The street where I lived had been decorated with flags and streamers, 'Welcome Home' notices on some doors and windows. A party had been laid on for me at my home. It was a happy occasion with everybody enjoying themselves for the first time since news of the action had reached them. I joined in as best I could but reaction to my long, tiring journey was setting in and I was glad when the time came for me to go to bed.

"On the following day, Sunday 21st, what I had expected, happened. I was besieged by more reporters and photographers from several newspapers all wanting a story. All enquiring about when the baby would be born. Would I name it after 'Warburton-Lee'? They called it the 'Narvik Baby' in the stories in their papers. This went on every day I was home. They were getting impatient because the baby was late in arriving. Edie thought she was OK and so did I.

"A very sad event took place on that first Sunday. I was having a rest after a morning of being questioned by reporters and posing for photographs. My wife woke me up saying that a man and a woman from another town had come enquiring about one of my shipmates who was a relative of theirs. They had seen his name among those killed but wanted to confirm it, because they did not know what ship he had been on, and had neither seen nor heard from him for years. On hearing his name I knew who he was and that he had indeed been killed. I told my wife to let them come in.

"They were the sister and brother-in-law of the chap. His name was Leading Seaman Hunt (Alec) and he had been the 'Captain' of Number 2 Gun which had as its crew a lot of young sailors, who were on their first ship since finishing their training. The majority of them got killed, the remainder wounded. Leading Seaman Hunt died alongside those of his crew. His relatives had a photograph with a group of sailors on it. They said 'Can you see him on there?' I did not have to look twice. He was there all right. So I pointed him out to them. It was very upsetting to me to have to confirm their fears. I have always hoped it was some consolation to them when I explained how he had died at his gun, and how brave he and his young crew had been."

Another younger sister of Cyril, Marion, was "thrilled and relieved" to have her brother back home. Auntie Marion, now in her nineties, recalls, "I remember on his return he came to see me at my works and was wearing his uniform. He had been invited by the bosses as a Salford 'Hero'. He told us of his amazing story of how they had escaped and was cared for by a Norwegian family."

Cyril was also invited back to his former employers, where he had been an apprentice electrician, where they had had a collection for him. Cyril and Edie, with Cyril's parents, were honoured guests at a Manchester theatre.

It was now time for Cyril to return back to naval life and the ongoing war but it would not be long before he was back home again. "So it was with some misgivings that I left home to catch the train. My wife had still not had the baby. At the time we wondered why it was taking so long, but of course we had to have patience. I had to report to the Torpedo and Electrical School HMS Defiance to complete courses for promotion to Leading Torpedo Operator, which would take about seven months."

Able Seaman 'Gunner' Austin McNamara returned to his home town of Bolton, having kept the clothing he had received from a local fisherman. His younger sister Josie remembers, she was playing marbles outside the front of their house with the boy next door. Someone walking past asked why all of the houses in the street had flags hanging out of their windows. Josie replied proudly, "Because my brother Austin is coming home today!"

Those of Hardy's crew who had been fortunate enough to reach home at that stage had had a unique and tremendous welcoming by the public and their families and friends. However, no doubt in the back of their minds, they still had a thought for their comrades who had not yet reached the safety of their home land. To recap, of those whose accounts I had gathered, Robinson, Pulford, Cheshire and Smale, had been transferred to HMS Hero, whilst Bourton had been sent to HMS Havock, and Ronayne, whose whereabouts had not been established, all finally came back together on the requisitioned RMS Franconia, now a troopship.

Les Smale: "Here we were, still out in the North Sea, somewhere. Just twenty minutes after this announcement, the 'Hero' turned about and once more made a heading for the Narvik area; where we arrived on Sunday 21st April, in the afternoon. I can't express how we felt but anyone who reads this may well imagine. Hardly had we dropped anchor then along came three German planes and dropped bombs. Fifteen minutes later, back they came to drop more and shortly after, this was followed by yet another attack. No damage was suffered in any of the raids.

"That is until another fearful event occurred, a reminder of two weeks before on 'Hardy'. That same night, we, the 'Hardy' survivors, were transferred to the troopship 'Franconia', who also re-embarked six hundred troops, whom it seemed she had transported to Norway earlier. We sailed again for home at 0800 on Tuesday the 23rd April. We had one escort for a little way and then were left to proceed on our own.

"All went well until 0200 on Friday morning when we were all awakened by a terrific explosion. I was out and had my lifebelt on in no time, and then there was another explosion. I just stood there in the cabin, and well, I was quite surprised when the ship didn't heel over or feel as though she may be sinking. We made our way up toward the upper decks but were stopped by the she may be sinking. We made out that we had been met by an escort during the night and they had been dropping depth charges. The explanation sounded feasible, so we made our way back down to our bunks and sleep again. The next morning, the Captain passed a message to us all saying that during the night we had been attacked by torpedoes from a submarine; and that they had exploded either in the ship's wake or at the end of their run."

Charles Cheshire was also in 'Hero': "We were in action most of the time, against enemy aircraft. They had their own gun crew members, so we had such jobs as 'look outs' and supplying ammunition. Planes would fly over and did drops, but we were not hit. Eventually, we went back into Norway, where there were a few 'Liners'. I went on one called 'Franconia'.

"There were a number of captured German sailors on board. The Captain said, all sailors, it didn't matter if they were German or not, had cabins and the troops they were down in the hold somewhere. I know they didn't go much on it. We set off for Greenock, I suppose we must have been about 24 hours out, early in the morning, there were two or three loud explosions. Of course there was panic amongst these soldiers, we didn't know what it was. It turned out to be torpedoes which exploded prior to hitting the ship, they had magnetic heads on, so either they didn't go off or were some way away.

"It was while I was on the 'Franconia' that I met up with my stepbrother, the one I had joined up with. Of course they had adopted me by then. He was on the 'Eskimo', which was torpedoed."

I have no more information on Charles Cheshire than that which I had access to from the Imperial War Museum's audio recordings dated 1985. From the list of 'Association Members', it shows Charles then lived in the Doncaster area.

Bill Pulford: "For another ten days on 'Hero' we did patrols, the weather was still filthy. On our last day out we came into harbour, where the 'Franconia' was, an old 'Cunard' liner. On board were all the soldiers who had been evacuated from Norway, which it had been decided was 'too big a project'. We had thirty there, plus some of the wounded from other ships who had survived the 2nd Battle of Narvik and were being sent home for hospital treatment.

"Myself and one other Leading Hand, being in good health, apart from a shrapnel wound to my leg, were put in charge of the German naval prisoners. There were quite a number of them. The 'codes' (protocol) was that Navy looked after Navy and so forth. I don't know whether it was a matter of revenge, because they were all in uniform and I was dressed in 'God knows what'; Norwegian ski cap, old jacket which was far too big, trousers that looked like 'plus fours' down to my shins and an oversized pair of ski boots. Anyhow, they were nice chaps and of course 'Jack', me included, we never finished ribbing their backs about Narvik. Where they had ten destroyers and we only had five. As 'Torps' said to me, 'We had to take them on, to give them a sporting chance, to knock us out.'

"They didn't take the ribbing very well, still thinking they had won at Narvik, but we managed to convince them that they hadn't. But not one of them admitted to being a 'Nazi', they were all German 'Kreigmarines'! Even after that, throughout the war I never met a self-confessed 'Nazi'. When we got to Greenock, they were the first taken off, they shook hands with us and we gave them a couple of cigarettes each. After all was said and done, they were Navy as we were. We parted in the best of spirits. It was only later in the war we met the 'Gestapo' and the 'bully boys' of the German people. You have to bear in mind that at the beginning of the war we didn't have any 'Hostilities Only' men on board and they didn't have the 'SS Gestapo'. We were all seamen and treated each other as such. It was just the unfortunate part of it that made us fight each other."

Anthony Ronayne had a different and eventful route back to Britain as described in his local Maltese newspaper. "Anthony stated that when he boarded the 'Ivanhoe' he met the other Maltese and they were delighted to see one another once again and all of them expressed their joy at being so lucky to be still alive." Anthony recalls, "We then went to the Lofoten Island and I was transferred to a troop ship 'Franconia'. We had many air attacks until we came to Scotland, Greenock. We arrived at 7 p.m."

Many years later, Dougy Bourton formed a deep affection for life in the Navy and the sea, but now started to feel it was time to go home. "We then heard they had received a welcoming home on Horse Guards Parade, whilst we were still clogging around doing a seven day patrol. This we weren't pleased about. The 'Forester' was very low on provisions, although we got food, we only had what they could manage. Don't forget by now we had been at sea for several weeks. Eventually, our patrol was finished and we were taken to Harstad and put on the 'Franconia'. I'll never forget it.

"They took us into the dining room, now don't forget we were literally starving. We must have looked a right bunch, because we were dressed in all sorts. We went straight into the saloon, in amongst all of the troops there. The tables were prepared for six with the knives and forks set out. The 'dish of the night' was 'Cod à la Espaniola', it was unforgettable, consisting of steamed cod, slices of tomatoes and onions. I'm sure that in 'Franconia', which was one of the Cunard Cruise Liners, it was the first time the dish had ever been eaten without waiting, with fingers stuffed in sailors' mouths. We just attacked it, well not polite at all, but we were hungry so that's my excuse."

27

Last of Survivors Arrive Home

Cyril receives bad news: "On the evening of my second day on 'Defiance' I received an urgent telephone call from home. My wife had lost the baby and I was required at home. It was night-time so I had to go before the Master At Arms to tell him. He took me to the Officer of the Day, Lieutenant George Pappin, a well known character on 'Defiance', who was very sympathetic. The M.A.A. said, 'This chap is one of the survivors from "Hardy", he has just come back off survivors' leave and they have lost their first baby. They suspect it was over the loss of the "Hardy".' The O.O.D. said, 'Right, don't worry about it, get all your things together, and catch the first train in the morning.' They arranged compassionate leave, a travel warrant, a ration card and leave pass made out and I was on my way home.

"On my arrival home the family doctor explained what had happened. My wife had kept the shock of hearing the news about the ship bottled up inside, instead of crying and being outwardly upset. The baby was fully formed [Cyril became emotional on I.W.M. tape – in this sentence it sounds like] she was in a cot laying there on the settee, you would have just thought she was asleep. Except for where the shock had struck her on the temple."

Cyril's sister Vera, then aged 12, remembered, "Our 'Baby Cope' had beautiful auburn hair, all curls, on the left side near her ear it was just turning black – she just looked as though she was asleep."

Cyril: "We had our funeral, my wife's mother, Sarah-Ann, carried the little coffin. She was put in a grave with my mother, who'd died when I was 10 years of age.

"For us personally, this was a tragic ending to the Battle of Narvik. Not only had I lost my seagoing home, my comrades who had been killed in action, my personal possessions, uniform, wedding photographs, all the usual things sailors carry around in their 'ditty boxes' from ship to ship, eighteen pounds that I had saved to buy a pram and other necessities for the baby, but my wife and I had also suffered a worse blow, and it would take us a long, long time to get over it.

"I recall the family doctor saying to my wife, "You can always have another baby, but you could not have got another Cyril, if he had been lost at Narvik."

The remaining fit 'Hardy' survivors having arrived in Scotland are well received and provided with a feast of a meal. Unfortunately, although someone remembered to issue them with a train warrant, they forgot that they might also need a few pounds in their pockets.

However, Dougy Bourton, penniless, found a surprising benefactor, "We came back to Greenock and were met by the Flag Officer, Scotland. They gave us a marvellous dinner at the Central Station Hotel in Glasgow. I can discount any story that all Scotsmen are mean, because I went to the Post Office at the platform there. Of course we had no money and nothing but the clothes we stood up in. I went up to a Scotsman, who didn't look particularly wealthy. I said

'Excuse me Sir', I explained I was a survivor and asked him if he could lend me some money, which I would return to him, so I could send a telegram home. He replied, 'Not to worry, come on, we'll do it together." So we wrote the telegram and he paid for it. He said, 'Best of luck kid' and gave me half a crown; which bought me a pint at the station bar. I still have the telegram now after fifty years."

It is worth mentioning for younger readers, that in those days, other than newspapers or radio, the other main source of news was at the cinema. Unlike today, where we have the advantage of almost instantaneous news reports on television with action recordings, this was probably the nearest you could get. Although shown a number of days or weeks after the event, credit must be given to providers of the 'newsreels' and their reporters and camera men. They obviously had to be in the thick of the action and return their filming as soon as was possible. These would be shown for five minutes on screen prior to the main feature. It was also a good propaganda method for the Government to inform the public of mainly the ongoing successes in the Second World War.

Stan Robinson was another transferred to the 'Franconia' who did not know if his family knew whether or not he was alive. "My mother and father had received a telegram saying that in no doubt, 'Your son is believed lost and killed in action'. My father wouldn't believe it. They were at a cinema 3 or 4 days after, and who should be jumping across from one ship to another, but me. My brother and sister happened to be in the cinema and they shouted out 'That's our Stan'. So they all went round the village, Llanviry, up in the valleys, calling out 'He's alive, he's alive!' As it turned out the Lieutenant Commander with the camera was in fact a 'War Correspondent' (the officer whom he nearly jumped on)."

Anthony Ronayne: "As soon as we landed we were taken to the Guildhall for dinner, the Admiral gave us a speech and how nice it was to be back in the UK. The first chance I had I ran to a telegram office and made a telegram home, 'Tony is safe', I had no money for it but everyone in the office wanted to pay. I was dressed in rags and they thought that I was a student, as on that day the students were having a Carnival Day. We left Greenock next day for Plymouth. We arrived at Drake Barracks, Devonport at 2.30 p.m. We'd been medically tested and given new uniforms and a complete kit. We stayed in the barracks for a few weeks."

By the time Anthony arrived back home in Malta, many months later, he had initially been presumed killed in action at Narvik. As was then the Maltese 'Roman Catholic' custom, a service of remembrance 'Mass' had already taken place, with 'special prayers said for the repose of his soul'. This had been paid from money raised by his family and friends. So the telegram Anthony had sent from Scotland was a blessing to all who knew him.

Les Smale recounts his experience of being back home. "The next morning, Saturday 27th April, we arrived safely in Greenock and were soon on our way to Plymouth. The Barracks' staff then re-kitted, paid and generally processed us, so that I was home on leave by 8 p.m. on Sunday the 28th April. Much to the relief of my family who were really without a word of our well being since the events on the 10th April and the First Battle of Narvik."

Another survivor who returned home to Thornton in Lancashire, approximately two weeks later, was Telegraphist Victor Gould. Prior to this, his family and friends had had grave concerns for his welfare. The headlines of the 'Fleetwood Chronicle' on the 19th April 1940, began, "Grammar School Old Boy Was In HMS Hardy". The newspaper went on to report, "It was hopeful news to his many friends to find that his name was not in the casualty list published this week". The feature continued with, "He is the only son of Mrs Gould and the late Mr Gould. Mr Gould's father also served in the Navy". Adding that Victor, "was last at Thornton during his leave shortly after Christmas. Mrs Gould told the reporter that she had no idea what had happened to her son. The first she knew about the ship's adventure was when news came through on the wireless, and it was a big shock to her."

The 'Fleetwood Chronicle' edition of 3rd May 1940 went on to report, "When Victor Gould, Thornton's 20 year old 'hero' of the destroyer 'Hardy's' exploit at Narvik arrived at Thornton station on Monday on leave, he learned that Longton Avenue, where his home is, was decked out with flags by the neighbours, who were waiting to give him a big welcome. Feeling shy, he asked a milkman to take him home in his milk van, so that he could dodge his admirers. The milkman obliged and the moment the van pulled up at Victor's front gate, he dashed indoors, where his mother was waiting to greet him."

Bert Mason, much to the relief of his family and the village community of Maesbury, returned to his naval duties, and learnt that his conduct in battle was rewarded. "After my leave I was drafted to HMS Defiance, the Torpedo School, to await another Torpedo Course. Whilst there, I received a copy of the 'London Gazette' and a letter from Mrs Warburton-Lee, congratulating me on being awarded the Distinguished Service Medal (DSM). I presumed it was for helping to rescue the Navigating Officer, Lieutenant Commander Gordon-Smith. Stoker Bowden was also decorated with the DSM.

"In my opinion, there is no doubt about it, the hero of the whole chain of events after we lost our ship was Lieutenant

George Heppel DSO RN. He took complete charge when we were stranded and showed great determination, leadership and courage in adverse conditions.

"Another Officer to receive the DSO was Paymaster Lieutenant G.H. Stanning. He took over the ship's wheel after the cox'n had been killed. He prevented the 'Hardy' careering across the fjord out of control. Somewhere, since the War ended I read an account by him telling how he was rescued from the water. He stated, 'Two ratings assisted me to reach the house.' Yes, two ratings all right; Able Seaman Joe Sweetland and Leading Seaman 'Bert' Mason. I wonder if he ever realised how near he was to being left to struggle on his own!

"It is well known that the Hardy's Captain, Captain Bernard Armitage Warburton-Lee, was posthumously awarded the 'Victoria Cross'. I believe it was the first to be awarded in World War Two. It was certainly listed in the 'London Gazette', Friday 7th June 1940."

Bert Mason has mentioned his friend Joe Sweetland a number of times in his account. In 1971 Joe's sister Molly wrote to my Dad:

Dear Mr Cope,

Your letter which was published in 'The South Wales Post' on March 30th 1971, was sent to me by my sister who lives in Llanelli. She has recently sent me another cutting, stating that you have now been able to contact 180 survivors of the First Battle of Narvik, and that relatives of men lost in the Battle had also written to you.

My brother, Leading Seaman H. Sweetland (a Torpedoman) was serving in the Hardy during this time, and was among those *cared for with great kindness by the Norwegian people afterwards. Unfortunately my brother was killed in action in HMS Hecla in November 1942.*

My family and I are very pleased that you have had such success in tracing the survivors, also the German survivors and the Norwegians from Ballangen, and we would like to send you all the very best wishes for an interesting and enjoyable Reunion at the Victory Services Club next April.

With kindest regards.
Molly, Mrs. K. M. Wyld.

Joe Sweetland, having been through the Battle of Narvik, was unfortunate not to survive a torpedo attack off the coast of Morocco. HMS Hecla was a Destroyer Depot Ship with a complement of 838 of which twelve were killed and 273 reported 'Missing Presumed Killed'. This was ironically on 'Armistice Day'. One of the rescue ships was HMS Marne, which shortly after picking up survivors had a torpedo "blew off her stern" but she managed to make her way to Gibraltar for major repairs.

Meanwhile, Stan Robinson finally arrived at Devonport Barracks. "They dealt with us as sharply as they could. They dished us all with uniforms to go on leave. When I went ashore in Devonport we changed out of that into our Norwegian civilian suits. Unfortunately when we got into Fore Street in Devonport, we didn't recognise the place: it was bombed flat. I was with Douglas Bourton and we came home together to Newport. But of course the Battle of Narvik was on everybody's lips then. We were chatting to this old lady and gent in this hostel, where we stopped for the night. (This was 'Aggie Weston''s in Plymouth, which was a convenient and low cost accommodation for sailors or those staying with their families.)

"In the meantime, I sent a telegram to tell them to expect me home. So I got away the following morning and was home about 11 o'clock in the forenoon on 7th May. I was greeted at the station in Llanviry by a big 'Silver Band' playing 'Rule Britannia' and all that sort of thing. I was hoisted shoulder high for one and a half miles from one end of the village to the other."

Bill Pulford: "We arrived in the barracks about 12 noon and the first thing they did was give us lunch in 'Jago's'. I think we were the only matelots, ever, to be allowed to smoke in the dining hall. This was whilst we awaited the Commodore (Barracks) to come down and talk to us. We were then taken down to the 'Slop Room' as we called it, where we were re-kitted out with naval uniforms again.

"The 'Wrens' (Women's Royal Naval Service) were not very pleased to have to 'turn to' on a Sunday afternoon. We were not very pleased to being refused in a sense, but everything went very well and we were kitted up with enough clothing to last us for about a month. Next was the gymnasium, where they opened up all the baths and showers for us. Once dried, we went into the main gym hall where a pay table was erected. We were given leave tickets, a prompt payment and victualling money for the fourteen days survivors' leave. On top of which the Great Western Train Company had sent down four clerks to give us our railway tickets, should anyone need to travel. At 4 o'clock we all mustered, were paid, kitted up and the last of the 'Hardy' men marched out of the barracks."

Les Smale was welcomed home as another hero, although because of his natural modesty, it would be a while before the crucial role that he had played at the demise of 'Hardy' became known. "The people of the home village of Stoke Canon (four miles from Exeter) gave me a great welcome home; and presented me with a Gold watch engraved as follows:- 'Presented to Leslie. J. Smale; as an appreciation of services rendered on H.M.S. Hardy at Narvik April 10th, 1940. From friends at Stoke Canon' In addition to this, they used the balance of the village collection to buy five War Savings Certificates' in my name."

Bill Pulford's wife had a similar experience to that of Stan Robinson's family. "At that time I lived in Devonport and after the 'Hardy's' action my wife had been going to the barracks, morning and night to see if there was any news. Because I was in the 'land of the living' having had to go around the Norwegian fjord for a further ten days; she had seen all the first of 'Hardy' survivors coming home and I wasn't with them. Nobody knew anything about us. It so happened one day when she had been to the barracks, she came home and the landlady said, 'You had better come with us to the pictures, it will help pull yourself out of it for a while and try to cheer you up.' So she went and on the Gaumont British News there was this newsreel of the 'Battle of Narvik' and the remainder of the survivors which was taken by an officer on 'Ivanhoe'."

This emotional surprise was recorded in both the national and the local Plymouth newspapers: "Pulford's wife made daily enquiries at the Royal Naval Barracks Devonport but was continuously told 'sorry no news'. Until one evening, when hopes were fading, she was persuaded to go to the cinema and there she recognised her husband on 'Movietone News' as one of a party being transferred to 'Franconia' for passage home."

Back to Bill: "Without further ado she shot out of there, went back to the barracks and told the 'Officer of the Day' what she had just seen at the cinema. They then contacted the manager of the theatre and he agreed that the following morning, if a contingent from the barracks with my wife went to the theatre, he would re-run the film and stop at that particular spot. From that they identified a further twenty men who they thought were in the 'land of the missing'. It was the first indication that the barracks had of us being safe. I came back off leave and went to HMS Defiance to qualify at a higher level of 'Torpedo Rating'."

Bill Pulford, having gone through the same barracks procedure of being transformed from a 'ship wrecked' mariner to a 'smart as a guardsman' naval rating, finally went home to his relieved wife nearby in Devonport. "When I got back to Devonport I took all this old clothing home with me. I told my wife to get rid of it but she said, 'There's something in here' and she pulled out the 'White Ensign'. I thought 'my God' so I kept it." The final outcome of the 'White Ensign' you will be able to read in a later chapter.

Dougy Bourton: "Fourteen days of survivors' leave came and went. It was then back into the 'sausage machine'. I was already recommended to a higher Gunnery Rate (promotion), so I went straight into the Gunnery School. I always wanted to be a 'Gunner', basically a Gunnery Officer." However, what Dougy omitted to mention was the reception he received on returning to his home town of Ebbw Vale, where he was "hailed as a hero". As told to me by Dougy's daughter Lesley Bourton-Hood. Dougy was invited back to his Grammar School, which he had only left a few years previously, to give a 'talk'. Finally, the headmaster asked Dougy "if there was something he would like to have to commemorate his achievement of being awarded the Distinguished Service Medal. The story goes that Dad asked the headmaster to award the pupils a half day holiday – to which there was an almighty cheer. The headmaster had no option but to agree. Many years later, the inhabitants of Ebbw Vale still talked about the day 'Dougy Burton' (he was often referred to as Burton, rather than Bourton) gave the Grammar School a half day holiday."

You will remember young Signalman Ralph Brigginshaw who was badly injured and sent to a hospital on the Lofoten Islands. "I remained a patient there for six weeks. I was then cared for by a local family. Later, some of the lads came along and suddenly told me to get ready for transport in a local fishing boat. I spent my 20th birthday cruising up the fjord. I then arrived at Tromso just in time to catch the last Hospital ship 'Atlantis', leaving for Britain. I arrived at Liverpool about the 9th June, but because of a relapse I needed to be stretchered ashore."

However, Ralph's journey was not quite over having still to endure a train journey to a hospital near Glasgow. Ralph continues, "Then two and half years changing from hospital to hospital, including Winwick Hospital, near Warrington in Lancashire, I had another hiccup there. They used a bone from one leg to patch up the arm and when the plaster was taken off, sent me to a hospital near Bristol for recuperation. Unfortunately they left me alone on the station with a full kitbag. As I lifted the bag to put it on the rack in the train, I heard and felt a big crack. On arriving in the hospital they confirmed the arm had been broken again. So within 48 hours I was back at Warrington. They then took a bit of bone from the other leg and patched me up again."

By July 1940, Ralph had lost touch with his shipmate 'Ginger' Turner. So he decided to write to him.

Sadly, Ralph received a reply from Ginger's mother to say that a week before his own discharge from hospital he had gone sailing nearby with a nurse. Tragically the boat had overturned and he had drowned.

Stan Robinson, after his homecoming experience, returned for duty, only to become involved in another eventful incident, albeit on home ground. "When I came back from survivors' leave I went into the 'Depot Guard'. (Devonport Barracks.) I was turned in till three in the morning. We had a sudden shout to get out, get hold of our rifles, ten rounds of ammunition each and 'fall in' outside sharpish. It turned out that 'Paris' was there, a sixteen year old French battleship. The 'Paris' had trained her guns on Plymouth, was ready to fire, because we had taken over the whole of her ships."

To slightly expand on the background to this controversial event, in June 1940 with the invasion of France by the Germans irrespective of assurances by the Nazis, an attack was made on the French Fleet by the Royal Navy. Apprehended French warships were dispersed to Plymouth, Portsmouth and Gibraltar. The 'Paris' had come into Plymouth on 3rd July 1940. The ship having been forcibly taken over by British military units was kept in Plymouth for the remainder of the war.

Able Seamen Walter White from Exeter and Charles Stocks, a Yorkshire man, both previously mentioned, went on to serve in another ship together but in a different theatre of war. HMS Prince of Wales was commissioned in March 1941 when Walter joined the battleship and in June he was followed by Charles. With the Japanese swiftly advancing through Asia both 'Prince of Wales' and another battleship 'Repulse' were sent out to the Far Eastern station. For whatever reasons Charles left the ship after six months. Initially his luck held out by missing the epic event when the 'Prince of Wales' was attacked by Japanese bombs and torpedoes. Both battleships were sunk in the South China Sea.

The Exeter newspaper 'Express and Echo' reported that although Walter was injured he still had to endure time in shark infested seas. To quote the final part of the feature in the newspaper, "Picked up by a naval ship. That ship was en route to the safety of Australia when it was torpedoed by a Japanese submarine, and Walter was lost at sea."

Sadly, Charles Stocks fared no better, as the Commonwealth War Graves Commission records show that from 1st January 1942, Charles was sent to the Singapore Naval Base, where on the 16th February 1942 he was listed as 'Killed on War Service'.

I would add that another crew member on the 'Prince of Wales' was Stoker Harry Rogers from Middlesbrough, who believed joining up saved his life from his day job at the 'Iron and Steel Works'. He also survived the sinking and along with another previous death defying incident during the 'Dunkirk' evacuations. Harry's survival accounts at Dunkirk and subsequently on the 'Prince of Wales' are featured in a later chapter.

An additional crew member on 'Hardy' who was also drafted to the 'Prince of Wales' was Cyril Cope but the outcome for him was different. His story is a little closer to home and will be told later. It appears for reasons unknown former 'Hardy' survivors' names were on the Drafting Officer's list for the 'Prince of Wales'. Perhaps having been sunk once, the officer thought they would have a better chance of survival on a battleship in warmer climes. However, it may have been that other veterans from the Battle of Narvik who were part of the five ships in the 2nd Destroyer Flotilla were subsequently drafted to the two battleships.

Ron Cockayne's wife, Sarah Ann, gave birth to another daughter, Jill, who was born eleven days after Ron died. It was Jill, never knowing her father, who contacted me seventy years after the battle. A friend had sent her a cutting from my local newspaper the 'Shropshire Star' which featured the story of the book I was writing on the subject.

Sarah Ann had passed on stories of her father, memorabilia and photographs to Jill. Jill also mentions that a number of weeks after the battle, her mother had received a very meaningful letter and parcel containing baby clothes and tins of Ovaltine from Mrs Elizabeth Warburton-Lee.

Jill, the daughter Ron never saw, sent me additional memorabilia left by her mother Sarah Ann, including this telegram sent on the 3rd of May 1940 from Elizabeth Warburton-Lee.

"I wanted to write to tell you how much I sympathise with you in your sorrow, which I understand so well from my own loss. Our comfort must be in the pride we all feel in the magnificent action of the 'Hardy' and of all she achieved. Will you let me know when you feel able to write, if there is anything I can tell you about or any advice I could give you."

There was also a eulogy featured in Ron's church, where he was known as Harry. He and his wife Sarah Ann not only attended but also Ron gave his own time to the younger members of the community.

My Dad, Cyril, on being the Founder of the Narvik Association, enjoyed visits from various Association members, German veterans and families of those 'Hardy' crew members. One such family was that of Chief Stoker Edward Stiles.

Charlie Stiles was Edward's older brother who had set up home in Canada. Charlie with his wife decided to travel to Narvik for the 45th Anniversary in 1985. Charlie's son Ted tells the remainder of the story. "Whilst on a train (from Oslo to Narvik), my Dad met a young lady, Christen, to which he told the story about his Uncle Edward and HMS Hardy in the Battle. Christen said, 'You're talking about my Great Aunt Petra Kristensen.' Dad thereby met this wonderful woman. When he showed Petra a photograph of Edward, she immediately replied, 'The Propeller Man'."

I would point out that Stokers' insignia was, as it is still today, the three blades of a ship's propeller. Depending on the rank this would include a star or two, then a crown above. For Edward as a senior Chief Stoker it was a crown and a star below. In his case the badge would be displayed on the front of his working shirt to stand out for identification because of his important role on board ship. This was particularly crucial when at 'action stations' so that other crew members, especially from other departments, knew the authority he held. Therefore it appears that as Edward was critically ill and needing special attention, Petra for the next forty-five years never forgot the man she would always remember as 'The Propeller Man'.

On Charlie Stiles' and his wife's return from Narvik, they made a detour and visited Cyril and Edith at their home in Exeter. This led to them forming a close relationship, reciprocating the occasion by a visit to the Stiles' home in Canada. A trip they never forgot.

In the final part of Bert Mason's superb 'down to earth' account he goes on to tell the story of the eventual finding of Lt George Heppel's Naval Sword. The outcome of which I will leave to George to tell, at the latter end of the book.

Bert Mason was to become involved in more action during the rest of the war. His next ship would be 'Broadwater' and in less than eighteen months the ship would be torpedoed by a U-boat in the Atlantic off Ireland. Once more luck was with him, and he survived for another day.

In May 1943, whilst serving on the destroyer 'Aldenham' in the Mediterranean, Bert, now a Petty Officer, became involved in taking enemy sailors as prisoners. The incident is described by Bert in the book he was to write in 1988 called 'The Last Destroyer'. "Next morning the prisoners were brought up again to use the toilets and wash, then out onto the upper deck for exercise and fresh air. In the bright morning sunshine and calm sea, they looked better than when we first saw them on the beach. They were chatting among themselves, pointing to various equipment on board, probably comparing it with what they had on their own ships."

Bert's attention was drawn to one man who was wearing a brass-type amulet with the word 'Narvik' on it. He approached the man, pointed to his badge saying, "You at Narvik?" The German quickly looked up. "Ja, ja," he said, and when Bert said, "So was I" the POW enquired what ship. When told 'Hardy', he started to draw a rough map on the deck with his foot, marking off the position where 'Hardy' was grounded and his own ship, the 'Anton Schmitt' was sunk. Surprisingly, out there in the Mediterranean, thousands of miles from where the event occurred, two men from opposite sides found something in common after their short tête-à-tête. However, their reverie was suddenly cut short by a loud voice from somewhere in the Bridge area, yelling out, "Petty Officer Mason! How dare you fraternise with the enemy! Come up here at once!"

Later the ship docked in Malta and the POWs were off loaded into Army enclosed trucks, "unceremoniously helped on their way by a huge, bullying 'Red Cap' sergeant". Bert, finishes by saying that, "Several of us watched them and inwardly resented the treatment they were receiving. They were sailors the same as us – enemy or not – and all over the world there is a close comradeship and fairness between seafaring men, no matter what nationality or creed."

After Captain Bernard Warburton-Lee's death, his wife Elizabeth experienced a period of deep mourning, so much so that it wasn't until 1944, that she told their son, Philip, then aged sixteen, more about his father. In a series of touching letters, Elizabeth recalled how "The moment I met Daddy, I knew he was the man I wanted to marry. [...] he always had those smiling lines at the corner of his eyes. I think Daddy was happier in Malta than anywhere because he got all the exercise he could possibly want, [...] we were fearfully gay, dancing nearly every night, he was a beautiful dancer. [...] He was a very good host and loved a party."

After giving birth to Philip, Elizabeth remembered how "I was supposed to be having my afternoon nap and I heard him coming down the street – he had a real athlete's step – spring – he came into the room with an enormous bunch of Lillies of the Valley – it was a wonderful moment." Such a sentimental recollection reveals how the energetic and athletic Captain of HMS Hardy was also a deeply family-orientated man. Elizabeth also wrote that "He was not a person who talked much about his feelings but I had always sensed his tremendous love for his job."

Further testaments to Captain Warburton-Lee's character and skill as a Captain come from Captains of other ships. One such man was Captain Baillie Graham of HMS Ramillies. He remembered how Bernard "always seemed to me so perfect in every way [...] I loved him as a brother and know of no one else to compare with him –so genial, so humorous, so able in all he did, so dashing, and yet with such good judgement, so kind and friendly, so modest and loveable in every way."

Moreover, Captain Rafe Courage of HMS Hostile stated how Bernard's "rapidity of decision, clearness of thought and conciseness of orders were masterly [...] His attack on Narvik was a masterpiece [...] Certainly boldness was never better repaid".

Captain Hilary Biggs, HMS Hero: "what success that I have made of my life in the service has been very largely due to his tuition, example and inspiration."

Less than a week after the Battle, Elizabeth received a letter from Captain, Lord Louis Mountbatten.

HMS KELLY
THIRD DESTROYER FLOTILLA
C/O G.P.O. LONDON
16th April 1940

My dear Elizabeth,

How heartbroken you must be over Wash's tragic death and yet how proud at the glorious manner in which he met it.

In offering you my most heart felt and sincere sympathy I should like to say that I share your grief for I have lost a friend whom I admired and looked up to and whom I am the better for having known.

It was such a pleasure dining with Wash in the 'Hardy' and seeing him again, so full of enthusiasm and ideas of how the war should be fought. He was the grandest leader any man could wish to serve under: a certain C-in-C and 1st Sea Lord of the future, had he survived.

I do not know if young Wash is destined for the Navy to follow in his father's footsteps, but if he does go into the service please remember it would be a pleasure and a privilege for us to do any of the little things Wash would so easily have been able to fix, like making sure he goes to a good ship and gets among friends he wants to be with.

Don't bother to answer this letter in the midst of all your grief and worries. Edwina joins us in all our sympathy.

Yours ever,
Dickie

Vice Admiral (D)'s Office
Mediterranean
c/o. G.P.O. London
18. 4. 40

Dear Mrs Warburton-Lee,

Please allow me to offer you the deepest and most sincere sympathy of my wife and myself in your terrible loss.

When your Husband was first appointed to the 'Hardy' I was more delighted than I can say that we should be working together again.

As you will easily understand, I have always had an intense admiration for him, both as one of the best officers I have ever served with and as one of the finest men I have ever known. He was a born leader whose example was an inspiration and whom men loved to serve and would follow anywhere.

If consolation is possible you have it in that he gave his life in as gallant an action as has ever been fought in our Naval history, the result of which will have a great influence in helping us to achieve victory in that theatre of the War.

I mourn the loss of a wonderful friend and a magnificent officer.

Yours very sincerely
Jack C. Tovey.

A tribute from Bernard's past commanding officer and mentor, who went on to become Admiral of the Fleet and 1st Baron Tovey.

Last but not least, another letter to Elizabeth from a surviving crew member on 'Hardy'.

I am writing these few lines asking you please to oblige me with a small photo of your husband.

I would like a photo to remember him because he was the best captain I ever seen.

Stoker William L. Jones. HMS Hardy.

I end the chapter aptly with Elizabeth Warburton-Lee's reminisces of her husband, the man who was awarded the first 'Victoria Cross' of the Second World War. These are the remaining paragraphs in the letter to her son Philip.

"We were married for fifteen happy years. We had endless miserable partings and happy reunions. We never got in the least tired or bored with each other. He could be moody if he didn't get enough exercise; I think he over did exercise and then felt ill if he didn't get it.

"He had a very fine brain but the most remarkable thing about it was the breadth of his knowledge, I put this down to his immense interest in everything he came across or read about. He always wanted to know the inner workings of everything and he never seemed to forget. He didn't read very much; he led too active a life but I never had any fears of his being bored in old age, as so many athletes are. He would merely have turned to other things and so kept alive his interest in life.

"He was always interested in people – what they did and why they did it. He had absolutely no use for anyone that wasn't dead straight and had a particular contempt for the 'Yes man' of whom there are many in all walks of life.

"He had plenty of push when he chose to use it but was not in the least ambitious. I don't think he ever pictured himself as Commander-in-Chief but he always wanted to do the particular job in hand better than anybody else; whether it was his naval work or playing games.

"As you know he had a great love of the country and considerable knowledge of farming and country things. Much of this he must have picked up as a boy from his father who was a land agent.

"His brain worked like a lawyer's, he used to say if he had not gone into the navy he would have been a barrister. He adored an argument and was always ready to argue against his conviction for the sake of a mental rough and tumble. He had enormous charm and took as much trouble over the old and boring as he did over someone he liked."

28

Malta and the Royal Navy in World War Two

I believe there has been insufficient acknowledgement in Britain since the war ended to the loyalty given and the human costs endured by the Maltese people. Hopefully, this chapter will serve to remind those of my own generation as well as the following generations of this fact.

During World War Two, Malta, situated in the narrows of the Mediterranean, was an important strategic British base. Crucially it was just over 50 miles from Sicily. Here, there was not only the historical Royal Naval dockyard but also three airfields able to monitor and swiftly attack enemy shipping.

During a six week period in the spring of 1942 Malta had to endure an extremely intensive assault by Axis aircraft. This resulted in the island being renowned at the time as the most bombed place on the planet. When an attempt was made by the Italians and later the German Luftwaffe to totally destroy the island's infrastructure and starve the population into submission, the brave people of Malta kept their nerve and miraculously survived the onslaught, which inspired King George VI to present the 'George Cross' to the island. This was the highest award that could be given to a civilian and equated to the Victoria Cross for military personnel. It was unique in that the award was presented to a nation rather than an individual.

The Maltese people for many years had served the Royal Navy and the British Empire with distinction; in more ways than one. For such a small island, despite the attempt at annihilation by the Axis' aircraft, a relatively large amount of her citizens joined the Allied forces during WW2. Unfortunately, I have to say that this fact is now a fading memory to the younger generations of both Malta and the United Kingdom. Hence, I feel that the Maltese people's war effort should be retold for posterity, if only in a brief summary of the cost in their lives and livelihood.

As an Island race they were natural mariners for many centuries. With the men folk serving on board other countries' ships. It appears they fought for both the British and the French sides in the Napoleonic Wars. To quote Carmel Vassallo's essay on the subject:

"The censuses for Malta and Gozo between 1891 and 1931 give detailed tables of the officers and men serving on board HM ships at Malta, divided into English and Maltese. Based on these and Admiralty sources, it would seem that the Maltese may have constituted between 4.7% and 9.9% of total RN personnel in the Mediterranean in this epoch."

During both WW1 and WW2 there were approximately 2000 Maltese sailors contracted in the RN, with duties at sea or based ashore. Whilst serving overseas, as many as a quarter of these were killed in action in WW1. In that time they were predominantly firemen, trimmers and stokers with a lesser number of stewards, cooks and bandsmen. (Carmel Vassallo.)

However, with regard to WW2 fatalities of Maltese crew members in the RN, the balance had changed to becoming mostly stewards and cooks. This is due to the fact that between the wars there was a move towards an increased recruitment of Maltese personnel into the so called 'Domestic Branch'. Whilst the introduction of oil from coal fired boilers resulted in a reduction in the numbers of 'Stokers' required.

Returning to the enemy's attempt to bomb the Maltese people into submission, the first attacks began in June 1940 and lasted until August 1944. There were a total of 3,340 alerts which peaked in the first half of 1942, when as many as 300 Axis bombers took part in single raids.

The Maltese inhabitants' response was typical of their natural flair for self preservation and resourcefulness. They constructed sandstone shelters. Living in an environment with virtually no trees meant there were fewer wooden buildings which the enemy aircraft could target with incendiary bombs. However, by April 1942 in the populous areas around Valletta, many homes were either destroyed or damaged. This left the occupants no alternative but to find other accommodation in relatively secluded areas on the island.

Throughout the siege between June 1940 and December 1943 it is recorded that 1190 civilians were killed, 296 died from wounds and 54 were missing presumed dead. In addition there were 1846 seriously injured and 1932 slightly injured. From the total of 1540 who lost their lives, 703 were men, 433 were women and 404 were children.

There were many attempts by the Allied forces to reinforce and re-supply the 'Fortress of Malta' which are adequately described in other books. This included on numerous occasions the sending of replacement British fighter aircraft by an aircraft carrier. Here, on his arrival in May 1942, on being immediately sent into action, one of the RAF Spitfire Pilots wrote, "One lives here only to destroy the 'Hun'.....living conditions, sleep, food, have gone by the board.....It makes the Battle of Britain.....seem like child's play." The RAF lost 547 planes in the air and 160 on the ground.

With regard to Royal Navy casualties in WW2 there were approximately 50,000 killed in action, of which there were 198 Maltese sailors. This totals 10% of those enlisted against 5% of their British comrades.

I will end with the words of Carmel Vassallo: "The World Wars, but particularly the second one, were a watershed. Fire and blood seem to have bonded the British and the Maltese in a manner which it is difficult to conceive nowadays. In 1946, there were 1736 Maltese men in the RN, probably an all-time record in peace time. After the war, the RN eventually offered the Maltese both the opportunity to serve in Malta within the Malta Port Division with local conditions of service or to join the RN or Royal Marines in the UK under exactly the same conditions as other people recruited in the UK. The first batch of recruits joined up in 1952 and eventually proceeded to the UK for further training on HMS Ganges. The Malta Port Division was disbanded in 1979, when the British forces finally took their leave."

On a personal note, I remember on my first ship HMS Devonshire in 1964 there were numerous Maltese crewmen on board. They were employed predominantly in the wardroom from the Chief Petty Officer (Steward) in charge down in rank to Assistant Stewards and Cooks. However, there were others employed elsewhere. I recall that you could not have had a friendlier and more diligent bunch of shipmates on board.

WORTH READING:

'Fortress Malta. An Island Under Siege 1940–1943'. James Holland.

'A Century of the Royal Navy at Malta'. Joseph Bonnici / Michael Cassar.

'The Cross and Ensign. A Naval History of Malta. 1798–1979'. Peter Elliott.

An Essay by Carmelo Vassallo. 'Servants of Empire: The Maltese in the Royal Navy'.

29

The War is not Over for Cyril

It was my father Cyril's accounts that first inspired me to start writing the book, not thinking for one moment it would lead to my gathering all the other stories from his fellow comrades and their families. I must have been about eight years old when I was able to completely understand his experience at Narvik. Dad would then have been the age of thirty-five, and in my opinion a very organised and worldly wise man, whom I had no problems respecting as a father. However, in developing the book, I had to keep reminding myself that at the time of the historical event, he was just twenty-one years old.

Cyril went through the rest of the war unscathed, although he had two near misses. However, irrespective of his and my mam, Edie's, earlier loss, in March 1942 they celebrated the birth of another daughter, Edith. Then later Edith became literally the 'Big Sister' to Cyril born in 1945, myself in 1946 and a late arrival Linda in 1954.

During Cyril's home leave, shortly after returning from Narvik, the family doctor thought it would be wise for him to have a medical examination. Cyril describes how the doctor told him that, due to his body being frozen in the water and then a long walk over the ice, he would very soon have trouble with bronchitis. "Sure enough within a few months, the following winter I had bronchitis. However, bronchitis saved my life!"

After Cyril had completed his Leading Torpedo Operators qualification course, he eventually had a draft to a seconded American destroyer being converted and modified in Devonport for service in the Far East. "One day I was walking through Williams Street in Devonport and I met a chap, Tubby Fell from Newton Abbott, who I had served with before the war in the 2nd Submarine Flotilla. (HMS Maidstone Submarine Depot Ship.) I said, 'What are you doing here?' he replied, 'Oh! I am in the barracks waiting to join the American destroyer.' 'That's funny I'm waiting to go on her as well, we're going out to the Far East.'

"So we agreed once we got on board we would 'mate up' again, like we did on 'Lucia'. I had to go through the usual routine, including seeing the dentist, doctor and having inoculations. When I got to the doctor, he looked at my medical sheet, and said, 'No you can't go to that ship, not with bronchitis and there is no doctor on board. They are not good ships to serve in and besides it's going to the Far East.' He stamped, 'Not fit for draft'. So I returned to barracks waiting for another draft.

"Eventually, I got one, to a seaplane carrier HMS Albatross stationed in Freetown, West Africa, where I had been with the 'Hardy'. But in them days it was hard to get men out, you had to wait for a troopship, and the troopship would have to wait for a convoy. So you had delays longer than what you would normally have to do in peace time to get out to these places. I was in barracks about three months. One Saturday afternoon, I was going up the same street in

Devonport, who should I bump into but Tubby Fell again. I looked at him and he looked at me. He said, 'Where the hell did you get to? I thought you were coming to the St James.' I explained the reasons and said, 'You've never been out to the Far East and come back in such a short time.' He replied, 'We never got to the Far East, we were off the West Coast of Africa and we got just one torpedo midships. The ship just went over.'

"If you can't go to a ship then someone has to take your place, I knew the lad, he had been in my class. I said to Tubby, 'What happened to such and such?' He replied, 'When we climbed up the nets on the destroyer that saved us, an officer and rating from the Bridge got up first, I followed and the next was that chap who took your place. But he wouldn't climb up, so they put a boat hook down for him to hold onto, whilst they pulled him up. Then the Captain noticed he had both his legs off being severed by sharks. So the Captain said it was no use bringing him on board, let him go, which they did.'

"Whilst waiting for the draft to the seaplane carrier I managed to get a week's 'foreign service' leave and went home. I had only been on leave two days when I got a telegram, ordering me to come back to barracks immediately – You are wanted for the 'Prince of Wales'. The 'P of W' had come into Plymouth on its way to Singapore, and a Leading T.O. had been put ashore in hospital and they wanted someone else to replace him. I was the next one in line. I had to catch the next train to Plymouth, but rather than an eight hour journey it took sixteen hours. This was because Bristol station had been bombed and put out of commission, we had to do a detour as far as Woking to the Waterloo line. By the time I reached Plymouth the 'Prince of Wales' had 'up anchor' and gone without me. You know what happened to her, she was sunk in December 1941."

In September 1941, for three months, similarly to Stan Robinson, as you will have read, Cyril was attached to the impounded French battleship 'Paris'. By now known as HMS Paris, used as a floating barracks in Devonport for Polish Naval personnel. He went on to serve on the sloop 'Eaglet' moored in the River Mersey, the base for the Commander in Chief 'Western Approaches'. Then HMS Ludlow, an old US destroyer which was stationed at Rosyth for coastal defence duties.

Cyril joined HMS Rodney in October 1942, which the previous year had developed major structural problems and was sent to Boston, USA for repairs. However, because they could not be rectified she sailed back home. But the 'old girl' was not finished yet and continued to make a major contribution to the war at sea. Cyril had only been on board for two days when 'Lower deck was Cleared' and the crew assembled on the quarterdeck. Once more Cyril was present for another stirring speech given by Winston Churchill, who visited the ship at Scapa Flow.

Cyril remained on 'Rodney' for two and half years until the war in Europe ended. During his time on board, the battleship saw action in the Sicilian, Italian, North African and Russian campaigns. Finally, the ship's 16 inch guns were utilised for bombardment of the German positions in support of the troops at the 'D Day' landings in Normandy.

Originally, Cyril volunteered for a seven year active engagement and five years' reserve service. However, now having two children, Edith and Cyril, nobody could blame him for thinking, "I've had enough excitement to last a life time, it is now time to go home to look after my family." So in December 1945, having completed over nine years' 'very active' service, and been given his 'War Gratuity', off he went back to Edie and dear old Salford.

It was not long before Cyril, with his much needed skills and life experiences gained from his Naval background, secured employment. So he returned to his previous trade as an electrical engineer at the 'Greengate and Irwell' company owned by an appreciative Jewish gentleman. In 1954, having saved sufficient funds, he was able to purchase a new property for the family in Flixton. He went on to work for other manufacturing firms in Trafford Park, Manchester. In 1964 most of the family moved to Exwick in Exeter. By now I had been accepted for what became a long career in the Royal Navy.

In 2000 family and friends from far and wide all joined together to celebrate Cyril and Edie's 'Diamond Anniversary' at a hotel just outside Exeter. Most guests stayed overnight at the hotel so it was a long day and an old fashioned evening's 'knees up'. During the evening Cyril, still with his well known melodious voice, sang to Edie the following song from the '40s, "Don't Sit under the Apple Tree with Anyone Else but Me, Anyone Else but Me, ...". I am sure that everyone present will always remember the event with great affection.

Over the years Cyril had many 'Association' members or their families calling in on their way on holidays in Devon or Cornwall. In the end he had to set up his own museum in the garage, with memorabilia presented to him from far and wide, books, photographs and newspaper cuttings placed in cardboard frames. Every time we visited, my son James would go into the garage with Granddad to look at the display. James never tired of it, as Granddad would tell him another story of his time in the Navy.

Cyril intended to write his own book but was never able to do so. In 1971 he wrote to film companies in the hope that his story would be accepted.

COLUMBIA (BRITISH) PRODUCTIONS LIMITED
10 WELLS STREET, LONDON W1P 3FP
17th April 1971

Dear Mr Cope,

I am sure you will appreciate that we have a great number of War Stories submitted to us for potential filming, and I would agree that in this particular case the idea has definite possibilities.

Yours sincerely,
MAX GOODLEFF. STORY EDITOR.

Sadly, in May 2003 Edie passed away when taken ill and was hospitalised. Followed four months later by Cyril. Both their funerals were well attended by many family and friends from far and wide.

Reunion in London. 1972. Petra with her "Hardy Boys". *Ron Cope Collection.*

Edie and Cyril loved their large family and were always very excited when another addition came into the fold. The last to come along before they died was my son James' daughter Naomi Cope, our granddaughter. Therefore at the time of Edie and Cyril's passing away there were four children, ten grandchildren and one great grandchild (our granddaughter Naomi). Here are some dedications provided by family members.

Edith, the eldest of Cyril and Edie's children: "I now live in Plymouth and have seen for myself the ensign brought back from HMS Hardy. The great Navy tradition of my family is being carried on by my two sons and my granddaughter. As a little tot, I was once a welcomed visitor down on the messdeck of HMS Rodney, when they were in port here in Plymouth. We owe a debt to all who have fallen in all wars, so that we may live today and might I add in peace. I now have the privilege of being the custodian of the medals my Dad was honoured with during his time in the Royal Navy."

Caron Barker is Edith's eldest daughter: "I was privileged to have listened to the stories of this battle told by my grandfather, since being a child. It was quite an emotional journey reading through these accounts again. I am so very proud of all he achieved and humbled by all he endured alongside his comrades so that we could all live in freedom today. God bless you my beautiful grandfather, until we meet again.

Brian Dash, grandson: My Granddad was my hero and I miss him every day. I never got bored of hearing his war stories. I am privileged to have known him and we cannot thank him and my nan enough for all the sacrifices they made for the good of our country. They will never be forgotten and are always in our hearts. God bless them."

Nichola Royle: "I am the proud granddaughter of Cyril Cope. I miss my Granddad's stories but most of all I miss him. All the above heroes will live on in our children and will never be forgotten."

The naval tradition remains in the family, so far through four generations.

30

Norwegian Participation Medal

Despite the bravery of all those involved in the Battles of Narvik, it would seem that not everyone received the recognition which they deserved. As has been mentioned, Lieutenant Commander Victor Mansell received neither an award nor a promotion after the battle, despite his long service in the Navy and unfaltering bravery. However, as Dougy Bourton explains, lack of recognition after Narvik extended beyond this.

Dougy: "It always saddens me that when we went to Narvik in 1980 we were wearing our medals and we were called to task by a Norwegian Commander, who asked why we were not wearing the Norwegian Participation Medal. I pointed out that we had never been given it. He said: 'You were, because I was one of the officers who arranged for the presentation of the medals.' I said: 'Well we haven't got them.' He pointed out: 'Well your officers have got them.' Which surprised us, and it turned out that the Admiralty had refused us to be granted this medal against the wishes of the Norwegian people, for some reason best known to themselves.

"When it was taken up by the Norwegian Embassy again, they made provision for the presentation at a service in 1982 at Westminster Abbey, when the Norwegians who took part in Narvik came over to visit us. Arrangements had been made for the medals to be presented by the Norwegian Ambassador and again it was refused!"

In a letter to King Olav of Norway, which was dated the 10th of April, 1989 (probably because of it being the anniversary day of the Battle), it triggered my Dad back into action. Cyril Cope describes how he had "not found any ordinary Sailor or Soldier who was notified of its [the Norwegian Participation Medal] existence by our Government after the end of W.W.2". The reasons for this are unclear. To make matters more confusing, after completing long negotiations, working towards the belated presentation of the medals in 1982, Cyril was informed that the medals "could not be awarded". This is something which he describes as having consisted of "many feeble and lame excuses" from the British Government. One of these "lame excuses" was based upon a decree (renewed by George VI in 1952) from the reign of Elizabeth I which stated that no British serviceman could be awarded a medal by a foreign power if the battle had taken place over five years before the application. Yet, a valid point to contradict this decree would be how could the men have applied to receive a medal which they did not even know existed?

Such bureaucratic confusions and contradictions could be regarded as the Admiralty covering up an ulterior motive. After all, as Dougy states in his account, officers involved in the battle were awarded the medal. Indeed, at the 40th Anniversary celebrations held in Oslo, six British participants were presented with the Norwegian Participation Medal. This is something which Keith Speed (Minister of State) from the House of Commons in 1982 described as an "embarrassment". Moreover, the Minister at the Foreign and Commonwealth Office at the time, Lord Belstead, wrote to Cyril explaining how "Although the Officers who received the medal did not have the permission from the Queen to do so, they are being allowed to keep them as a Souvenir with the understanding they will never receive permission to wear them." One cannot help but wonder why Senior and Junior ratings could not have been given the medal as a "Souvenir" also.

To make matters worse, not only were British officers awarded the medal, but servicemen from France and Poland too. Indeed, Cyril wrote in his letter that as these new members joined they were also able to apply up to this day (letter 1982). If this was true, then surely their British counterparts should be able to receive their medals also. In this matter, it is not entirely inconceivable that Her Majesty could have superseded existing legislation from the 1500s to make sure that her servicemen received the recognition which they deserved. Moreover, in Cyril's documents there are letters from former comrades in Australia, New Zealand and Canada. These confirmed that their governments had eventually given permission for the medal to be received.

As it stands, this matter is still unresolved. However, to end this unfortunate subject, an extract from a letter from the Norwegian Royal Ministry of Defence states how although they "deeply regret that it is not possible to accommodate your [Cyril's] request for decoration [...] the Norwegian people will always remember the British soldiers for their sacrifice and strong contribution to Norway's freedom." Certainly, a physical remembrance of the brave men's involvement in the Battles of Narvik would be a fitting tribute, particularly for surviving family members and future generations. Yet, for all of its meaning, a simple piece of metal in a shape of a medal cannot replace the knowledge, memories and emotional links to the battles which still exist to this day. These men and their sacrifices will never be forgotten.

Carole Knowles, the daughter of John Hague, a survivor on HMS Hunter, wrote to me.

"In a chance conversation with a friend, who happened to be a 'Medal Collector', we mentioned to him that we had heard Dad had been awarded another medal. The friend looked up Dad's name and found an article in the 'London Gazette' stating he had been awarded the Norwegian War Medal. Subsequently, I e-mailed everybody 'below God', including the Queen. At first I was told he was not able to receive a Medal from another country, a rule brought about in 1952. I pointed out that Dad was awarded the medal before this ruling, so more e-mails were sent."

In November 2008, the Royal Navy made contact with John, then aged eighty-eight. Carole's determined hard work paid off, when Colonel Knut the Norwegian Military Attaché, arrived from London. So it was that John Hague, BEM, with his proud family in attendance, received the medal at the 'Trafford Branch' of the Royal Naval Association.

John Hague's and his shipmates' stories of how they survived the sinking of HMS Hunter, sent into internment to Sweden, and their methods of escape will be featured in my next book.

31

Recollections of the Reunions in Germany

In 1973 the '2nd Destroyer Flotilla of Narvik 10th April 1940 Association' members were invited by their former adversaries to a joint reunion at Kiel, then in West Germany. This gave Dougy Bourton an opportunity to vent his feelings and state his opinion to a distinguished guest who had also been invited.

"I met Captain Dickens when he was writing his book. I don't think he gave sufficient credit to the Gunnery people in any way for the number of hits. I think we scored far more hits than were announced by the Germans. They tended to play down the amount of damage done. But the fact is the evidence they found afterwards for the second battle proved that the damage we did was colossal at the time.

"I am quite certain in my own mind, that had we used 'Direct Action Impact' ammunition (nosed fuelled shell) I am sure that the damage would have been much greater. Certainly, the explosive nature of the shell would have done more damage than the 'Semi Armoured Piercing', which was usually for destroyers firing at similar craft. But the 'base fuse' on the shells takes a little time to warm up in passage through the air to actually come into action. This is because it has to go through steel plated armour before it explodes but unfortunately I don't think the fuses had gained sufficient heat. So by the time they had gone through both sides of the ship, they were away. The holes were not as big and therefore the damage was half as much as it could have been. Although we hit, I don't think we hit with the right things. The Germans when they hit had used 'High Explosive Direct Impact' and the damage was colossal.

"We did two attacks. We hit everything that resembled a German ship, either destroyer or merchant ship. The amount of return fire was negligible. I expect the odd army gun was firing but generally speaking the Germans took off. Most troops ashore headed up the railway line on their way to Sweden. They didn't want to know!"

Bill Pulford was also one of the veterans attending the reunion. "It was not until I went to Kiel, that we understood another torpedo hit that was considered to be a merchant ship but in fact it was a 'troop transport' with 3000 German 'Alpine Troops', all of which went down with the ship."

The second reunion in Germany was at Bremerhaven. It was well organised by the hosts and attended by many veterans. For the British, their hosts made every effort to make them feel most welcome. Here Dougy Bourton again looks back to the event this time in 1979. "They told me that they were in Willemshaven aboard their ships when they heard that Britain had declared war on Germany. They said there were some in tears on the messdeck, because they knew that from 'day one' they were never going to beat us and that we would just keep coming and coming, until they just couldn't do it any more. The sailors were quite convinced that there was no way that the German Navy could win. Some of their officers may have had different ideas, I don't know.

"They didn't really like us or the thought that they were trained by us and beaten by us. Generally speaking I found the German naval ratings were people I admired one hundred per cent. Their ships were bigger than ours but very poor sea boats. The conditions that they lived under compared to us were rough. They were not intended for long voyages or to live aboard. When their ships came into harbour they completely closed down, leaving only watch keepers aboard. Then connected up to all the dockyard supplies; no Stokers or engineers. They put all services onto shore lines, so they were not intended to be lived on, consequently comfort on board was virtually nil.

"We were expected to take a destroyer around the world for two and half years commissions, with just a kitbag and a hammock. So this was a different Navy. But, we had deep respect, great admiration and a liking for them.

"The German sailors did what they could do to save their ships. They were in a hell of a state. They told me afterwards that 'Anton Schmitt' and 'Hermann Kunne' lost a tremendous number of men. These men to give them credit, had been on their feet for days on end. They had fought very heavy seas and the German ships were not good sea boats, top heavy, not intended for ocean going as ours were. They took a fair old battering, by the time they had gone up there, they were exhausted (the passage from German ports to Narvik).

"The Captain of the 'Anton Schmitt' (Commander Fritz Bohme) told me himself, that it was the first time he had taken his clothes off for the best part of a week. He had turned in when he heard this mighty roar, when the torpedo hit them. He then ran up the companion way and the sea came in to meet him and washed him down again through the opening in the deck leading to the staircase to the cabins. He got away with it. Captain Bohme was a very nice man and a fine sailor and very good company. He and his wife Tilly became good friends of ours.

"One of the sailors that I met was Heindrick Palmer, who was on the 'Erich Giese'. He sent me his Narvik shield (show picture). He is now a Police Captain on the German 'Water ways'. He sent it as a memento. He carried it either in the seat of his trousers or at the bottom of his kitbag from the time he was taken prisoner on a 'German Blockade' runner which was sunk off the coast of South America by the US Air Force. He sent me this Narvik shield, as I said he had to fight hard to keep it. He actually ended up at a POW Camp in Manchester and still thinks Manchester United are the greatest. A fine man, and I met him, and I have also been to his house and met his wife.

"I also have this other shield here. This came about in a strange way. It shows Herbert Riese who was on board 'Wolfgang Zender'. He's got his destroyer badge on the left breast. The Narvik shield and Iron Cross he was awarded for laying mines off the Thames Estuary in 1939. We both had heart attacks in the same week, and wrote to each other and commiserated that we couldn't attend. He sent a present of these badges mounted on an oak shield and sent them to me to pass on to my family. As he said he lost his wife during the Russian occupation. The shield shows a destroyer cutting through the gold ring of laurel. And the Narvik shields shows an 'Anchor' for the Seamen – Propeller for the Stokers and the Edelweiss with the Swastika above it. This was because every one of the ten destroyers took 250 German 'Crack' troops up to Narvik. So altogether a total of 2500 soldiers were on board those ships.

"They thought enough of us to send these mementos as a token of their admiration, that we got up to Narvik at all under the conditions that existed at the time. Snow, darkness on arriving and proceeding to carry out the damage that we did, the five of us – not the 'Warspite'."

32

What Happened to 'Hardy' Survivors after Narvik

FREDERICK 'GORDON' AVERY

Gordon was the strong swimmer from Plymouth who saved Jack Good's life and later forged a long friendship between their families. Gordon's son John describes his father's career path for the remainder of the war and during his later years: "My father continued his service on the minesweeper HMS Bangor, Russian convoy escorts, then HMS Unicorn the aircraft repair carrier. His brother Reginald William Avery was a Chief Yeoman of Signals and for two periods they served on the same ship but this was against Admiralty policy as casualties would badly affect a single family.

"After the war he served on the aircraft carrier HMS Illustrious. In 1952 he joined HMS Euralyus on a two and half year commission based in Simonstown in South Africa. Gordon married Olive on his return.

"He ended his RN career in the Navy with the rank of Chief Petty Officer in 1954. He then became part of the HMS Drake barracks civilian staff as a watch keeping boiler attendant."

Gordon became Jack Good's granddaughter Anna Reid's godfather. Anna says that "Gordon was a lovely man and life-long friend until his untimely death a couple of weeks before his daughter's wedding in 1974."

GEOFFREY BAILEY DSM

Geoff Bailey, having been taken to safety, received immediate surgery in a Norwegian hospital. On his eventual return to his home town Pontnewynydd, he was deservedly given a 'feted' reception. The community organised a special evening event where Geoff was presented with an inscribed gold watch and War Loan Bonds. The school that he had attended a few years previously gave him a silver cigarette case.

Geoff, on medical grounds, was discharged from the Navy, but this did not stop him, still in a war time environment, from considering other employment opportunities. His staunch approach to forging a new life away from the Navy led to him attending evening classes at the local technical college.

In September 1941, his well-deserved moment came, when he was finally able to attend an investiture at Buckingham Palace, in order to receive the Distinguished Service Medal, presented to him by King George VI. Geoff's father, Wilfred, who for many weeks had been anxious for news about his young son's wellbeing, proudly witnessed the occasion: "I shall never forget this moment for as long as I live." Without doubt, Geoff would always remember every part of the event.

Geoff quickly settled back into 'civvy street'. His studies led to him obtaining employment at the Royal Ordnance Factory at Glascoed. It was there that he met Doreen Meredith and they were married in December 1942. They had two sons, Brian and Christopher. Geoff remained at ROF for a further nineteen years. Having passed civil service exams, he was appointed onto the Ministry of Social Security, where he eventually became the Executive Officer.

Mrs Gytha Lane-Morrow was a previous colleague of Geoffrey: "He was my boss when I worked in Social Security in Blaenavon. [...] He was a truly rare person."

Mike Tanner who initially made contact with me explains, "I lived a few doors away from Geoff and Doreen. As a child I used to call on their eldest son, Brian. We had great times playing in their garden, which was on the edge of the Brecon Beacons. We used to watch Geoff gardening and were amazed at the various extensions he used to fit onto his injured arm as he dug the soil. Looking back it appears quite morbid but we were about 8 years old and he was our hero. He never allowed his disablement to interfere with his life and had a great sense of humour."

Geoff continued to have an eventful life, not only as husband and father. He became Chairman for the local branch of the Royal British Legion, treasurer of the local Labour Party and Chairman of the Council. However, between his busy schedule, he did have some leisure time to relax by enjoying lawn bowls and an interest in various sports. In 1966 Geoff was appointed to the magistracy and his final honour was to become the Mayor of Blaenavon.

Geoffrey Bailey passed away in 1972 at the age of fifty-one.

The following tribute to this brave man comes from the National Archives, entitled 'The First Battle of Narvik Recommendations for Decorations and Awards': "The courage and endurance of the rating after swimming ashore with one hand shot away, and whilst waiting two hours for medical assistance was a fine example to officers and men."

DOUGLAS BOURTON DSM

Approximately one month after the Battles of Narvik, the Admiralty made their recommendations to the Government's 'Committee for Decorations and Awards' who in turn passed on their verdict to King George VI. The process once completed resulted in a number of officers and men receiving various decorations or awards. However, from the records held in the National Archives at Kew it was shown that it was not until ten days afterwards that 'Hardy' officers set in motion a recommendation, stating that Able Seaman Douglas Aubrey Bourton should be put forward for a medal. This was accepted which resulted in him deservedly receiving the Distinguished Service Medal (DSM). The citation outlined how: "Able Seaman Bourton remained behind at his gun and fired one more round on his own initiative. [...] The bearing and discipline shown by this rating both at this time, and during subsequent events, was of the highest order and an example to all."

Further insight into Dougy comes from his daughter Lesley Hood-Bourton. She describes how: "All the time my sister and I were growing up we would frequently go to the seaside but Dad never ever went in the sea with us, not even for a paddle on a hot summer's day. When we'd tried to drag him in with us, he'd frequently say, 'I did all the swimming I ever wanted to on April 10th 1940. That'll do me", and left it at that.

"He never lost his profound love of the sea, of literature about the sea, whether poetry or fiction, of watching films about the sea, but he never set foot in it again.

"[...] They were so young and unworldly by today's standards, yet so incredibly brave, all of those young men. I find it all very poignant and am so immensely proud of him."

Dougy Bourton DSM went on to have further eventful wartime experiences such as that recorded by the Imperial War Museum. However, as a Petty Officer the job he enjoyed unexpectedly came to an abrupt end. Whilst serving with the Motor Torpedo Boats section a shell hit his vessel and as one of the casualties he suffered a spinal injury. This resulted in Dougy being discharged for medical reasons.

In 1958 he volunteered for the Sea Cadet Corps as an instructor with 'T.S. Forward' in Ellesmere Port. He eventually became the Commanding Officer with the rank of Lieutenant Commander. He committed himself to the Corps for two nights a week without fail for the following thirty years.

Former cadet Paul Downie sums up Dougy's commitment and the loyalty he received within the Corps: "I had the privilege of being a Marine cadet and I was fortunate enough to have Lieutenant Commander Dougy Boulton DSM RNR as my commanding officer. Later in life I had the opportunity to sit and listen to Doug retell his story. For all those who read this and to his family I would just like to say, as a person my life is richer for having met him. A true gentleman and a hero for all the young cadets to truly look up to, sadly missed but he left a very big legacy."

During Dougy's time with the Corps he enrolled his two daughters Hazel and Lesley at an early age. Lesley explains: "As a child of five or six I became fully competent at marching whilst throwing (and catching!) the mace [...] My sister and I were also fully competent in using semaphore flags to signal from the top of the air-raid shelter (which still existed in our garden) into the house, to send messages. I mustn't forget the 'Morse code', tapping away with the little machine and its dots and dashes. Our father was remarkable and much loved."

Dougy 'Gunner' Bourton DSM passed away in his adopted town Ellesmere Port in 1997. I leave the last words to his daughter Lesley: "Dad never lost his love of the Navy, his shipmates and the sea itself. Right up until he died, if I took him a cup of tea, he would always ask me to 'put it on the deck'. His 'Jackspeak' was part of him and always remained so."

RALPH BRIGGINSHAW

Ralph was finally discharged from hospital in October 1942 and sent back to Devonport barracks.

Signalman Ralph Brigginshaw repatriated and recuperating at hospital in 1940.

He was very pleased to be drafted to a ship within a month. Ralph tells me that "I was sent to a new 'Sloop' HMS Cygnet which had just been built at Birkenhead. We did our 'acceptance trials' in the Clyde and then sailed to Tobermory for our final sea trials. Unfortunately, she ran aground on entering the harbour." He was then loaned to the 'Black Swan' for the North African 'Landings'. After a while he returned to 'Cygnet' in time for the Sicily 'Landings'. From then he had a few months in the North Atlantic before going to HMS Mercury for the 'Yeomans' course. On completion, whilst waiting for transport to Canada to pick up a new 'Algerine' minesweeper he spent a spell on a Polish destroyer at 'Slapton Sands' in South Devon. This was in readiness for the D Day landings.

Ralph remained in the Royal Navy until 1950 leaving as a 'Yeoman of Signals'. However, he still had problems with his back injury. On his release to 'civvy street' initially he was a manager in a Radio and Electrical Shop in Brighton. He was later transferred by the firm to Crawley, during which time he completed a correspondence course in electronics. Once having attained his qualifications he secured employment at Gatwick Airport as a 'Radio and Radar Engineer'. In 1957 he married Betty.

Ralph retired after twenty-four years in the aviation industry. He and Betty are still living in Crawley. Ralph is now well into his nineties.

GEORGE 'TUBBY' COCK.

If, as suggested by a number of the 'Hardy' crew, Lieutenant George Heppel was the main man after the ship was abandoned, then the next in line must be the man with a personality to fit his size, namely the irrepressible, bubbly and resilient

Chief Petty Officer George 'Tubby' Cock. As mentioned, Captain Warburton-Lee, whilst initially having doubts about Tubby's physical fitness to be part of his crew, relented and allowed him to join his crew. From the time he joined the ship he became well respected and had good personal management skills. He had a great sense of humour which was needed once the survivors scrambled ashore. Because of his size he was the only one who could not find any suitable attire to replace his own soggy seaman a jumper and working trousers. Hence, as you see in the photograph on Horse Guards Parade, he was still wearing the same.

The news of the success of the 'First Battle of Narvik' and the unique welcome the survivors received back in London rapidly spread around the world. You will remember the 'Daily Mail' newspaper reporter's front page column of the event. One of the main features picked up in colonial newspapers was the picture of 'Tubby' leading his young sailors, with a smile and 'thumbs up'. He led from the front with compassion, a great sense of humour and held remarkable respect from all on 'Hardy'. Here is just one newspaper report by the 'Daily News' (Perth, Western Australia) dated 2nd May 1940, with the heading, "Roll out the Barrel".

"Chief Petty Officer Cock hurled every pound of his 24 stone as his destroyer HMS Hardy fought her way up the fjord and led the attack against superior enemy forces. Later 120 men were returned to England, many still wearing clothes that Norwegians had given them. In this picture the hefty sailor in a massive sweater and with his trousers splitting near the pocket, gives the thumbs-up salute during a London inspection by Mr Winston Churchill."

Remembering when the survivors had to endure the long march into the unknown from Petra's home Bert Mason mentions the BBC's 'People's War': "To keep our spirits up, there was a lot of larking about and light hearted banter. The Chief Bosun's Mate, Tubby Cock, a man who weighed twenty-four stones, really made us all laugh. He sat on a small chair which was on runners. It was only meant for a child to use as a sleigh, but some of the lads had pushed him up the slopes and he glided down the other side. He then had to wait for his helpers to catch up with him. [...] He took it all in good part, and was a tower of strength to us all."

In August 1961 'Tubby' was admitted into hospital for nine months which resulted in him having a leg amputation. He returned home to sister Jessie's care but passed away after a heart attack on the 20th of June, 1965. As Jessie went on to explain: "He always kept cheerful and had a wonderful sense of humour, and I know he would have liked to have met ex-members of the crew. He spoke highly of them all and greatly admired the Norwegian people."

HAROLD DAVENPORT

Harold Davenport was another crew member to arrive in Manchester on survivors' leave. On Harold's return home from Narvik he served briefly on HMS Devonshire but was later diagnosed with Crohn's disease. This eventually led to him being medically discharged in 1941. However, similar to many service men in the war who had to leave prematurely he did not dwell on his predicament and quickly found a way to become re-employed and to fend for his family.

Danielle, Harold's granddaughter, takes up the story: "Granddad set up his own business as a carpenter making furniture to order but due to his ill health he then went into Retail Management. I always remember him making things when my brothers and I were children. He always made the boys go-carts with pram wheels and bits of wood. I remember a rocking chair he made for my 11th birthday, he painted it green and hand painted my name on it. It was beautiful."

Interestingly, Danielle's brother, Craig, also continued the family's naval tradition serving first in the Royal Navy, then in the Royal Fleet Auxiliary Service.

Danielle ends with this tribute: "He was a true hero, as are all service men and women in my eyes. My Granddad passed away on June 1997 and we still greatly miss him to this day."

FRANK JOHN GOOD

Once more I had to rely on Jack's granddaughter Anna Reid to provide details of how Jack managed to adapt back into 'civvy street' with the injuries that he had sustained during the war. Having served in both world wars, he was finally discharged, due to his services no longer being required on medical grounds.

Anna explains, "In a bid to better himself and his family's prospects, he could not go back to his old job in the Science Laboratory at Brentwood hospital. Having lost his fingers his dexterity was affected and with the loss of his eye this meant he could no longer judge perspective properly. Imagine trying to pour something, accurately, into a test tube with one eye shut. He also couldn't work in the laundry either, as he wasn't well enough. So the hospital put him on the 'Gate'. They had to give him work but he hated it, it was shift work and not what he wanted to do.

"However, Granddad put up with it until in 1941, when he met a friend who'd gone into the pub trade. His friend had been called up into the services but was worried about leaving his wife and children with a stranger. So Granddad offered to be his relief and took over the running of the 'Bush Hotel' in

Shepherd's Bush, London. He remained there until mid-1945, when he got a pub management position with Clarke & Baker at Herne Hill, London. The first pub he managed in his own right was the 'Commercial Hotel', also at Herne Hill. He then went on to have the 'Tenancy' at the 'Railway Inn' in New Barnet.

"Granddad knew, contrary to Chamberlain's speech, that there would still be a war, because there were warships in all of south of England ports. In 1939 when 'Hardy' went off before the war to places like Malta and Sierra Leone, then chasing the 'Graf Spee'; in letters written home he obviously couldn't divulge where they were going. So he signed them off with kisses, putting at the end, either North, South, East or West to show which direction he was from home.

"He often praised the spirit and compassion of the Norwegians and expressed his gratitude for his life. I cruised into Narvik in 2001 on a small ferry from Svolvaer in order to see the fjord and imagine its history. I visited the museum at Narvik and I was very impressed.

"Granddad died in 1968 after a few strokes and heart attacks aged sixty-eight. A tough man but the Narvik battle had taken its toll."

GEORGE 'TORPS' HEPPEL, DSO

You will recall George Heppel's efforts to rescue the Navigating Officer from the burning wreck of 'Hardy'. As you know Lieutenant Commander Gordon-Smith was saved. However, due to Bert Mason's hands suffering from the icy cold waters, this led to an insufficiently secured rope.

Here, almost forty years later, George tells a fascinating anecdotal story of what actually happened, to a National Newspaper reporter:

"I remember that just before I left the ship, I thought I would grab my sword and silver cigarette case. I put them in the dinghy and asked one of the men if it was properly fastened. He said it was. We had to get clear quickly because explosive charges had been set behind the safes so that any confidential papers would be destroyed. But we suddenly noticed that the dinghy had broken loose. There was nothing we could do except watch it float away with all our personal effects. I never thought that I would see my things again, but apparently they were found by a man called 'Svenson'."

It so turns out that the Norwegian man had kept the naval sword as a souvenir, leaving it to his son to contact the British Naval Attaché after his death.

George describes how "It was strange seeing them again after all those years. The sword was a bit rusted and pockmarked and at first I thought I would have it cleaned. But someone suggested that I should leave it as it is – to commemorate its story."

London Reunion 1972. Lt Heppel middle and on his right the Mayor of Ballangen.

For his brave actions at Narvik, in July 1940, Lieutenant George Heppel was awarded the Distinguished Service Order. Prior to this in June 1940 he went on to be the Torpedo Officer on the cruiser HMS Hermione, where he was 'Mentioned in Dispatches'. In 1942 he was promoted to Lieutenant Commander. Between 1945 and 1957 he served on other ships as a Squadron Torpedo Officer until he had his own command on HMS Gorregan. This resulted in his promotion to Acting Commander. At the latter end of his naval career, he had appointments which involved Torpedo Sea Trials and Development and the Admiralty. He retired to Cornwall in 1958 aged forty-six.

Here, rightly so, Bert Mason has the last word: "In my opinion, there is no doubt about it, the hero of the whole chain of events after we lost our ship, was Lieutenant George Heppel DSO, RN. He took complete charge when we were stranded and showed great determination, leadership and courage in adverse conditions."

George Heppel, a truly remarkable naval officer, died in 1985.

BERNARD FRANCIS MOSTYN KENNEDY, BEM

Bernard Kennedy from Cwmbran was the young signalman who not only assisted his pal Geoff Bailey, but also made a contribution in alerting the retreating warships by using a torch. This probably saved his shipmates from at best a delayed escape from Narvik, or at worse a disastrous outcome.

In the remaining years of the war, he once more became involved in another death deifying incident. As reported by a local newspaper, "His heroism did not end with the escape. During other actions, he saved others in distress, including a doctor and a nurse, when their rafts tumbled in angry

Mediterranean waters." Regarding this incident, Bernard's parents said that the story only reached them through his shipmates. When it came to telling them of his exploits, his parents described him thus, "He is like an oyster."

After the war, Bernard decided to make a career in the Navy. He was promoted to Petty Officer 'Yeoman of Signals' and married Betty (maiden name Cranfield) from Newton Abbot, Devon, who was an ex-Wren Petty Officer. Gill O'Rourke, Bernard's daughter, takes up the story. "My father married Mum on 22nd January 1943 and a few days later he left on his ship and she didn't see him for several years. I was born in 1947 and Lance 1952. I know from conversations with our mum and relatives that he was very much in love with our mother and very proud of both his children. Sadly we didn't get to know him as adults.

"In 1949, my Dad was posted to Ceylon [Sri Lanka] and my mum and I (aged 2) went with him on a troop ship. Of which I have no memory at all. According to Mum they had a wonderful time, as in those days it wasn't often that postings came up that enabled wives and families to go. It was while we were in Ceylon that he heard he had been awarded the BEM. He was a fairly modest man and he had the choice of waiting until they came back to be presented in London by the King or to receive the award in Ceylon by the Governor. He chose the latter."

Once more Bernard's home town newspaper reported: "The reticent Petty Officer Bernard Kennedy has an outstanding record in the Royal Navy, and his British Empire Medal could mean recognition of more than one case of his gallant deeds."

Gill continues, "When we came back from Ceylon we lived with our mum's sister in Newton Abbot until we moved to a home of our own in the same town. Our Dad sometimes talked about the Battle of Narvik and one of the cousins, Pat Ofield, remembered him using the salt and pepper pot along with other kitchen pieces to show them the battle on the kitchen table.

"Dad's plans for after the Navy were to move to Canada to join his two sisters and he was in the throes of laying a path for emigrating, with the assistance of his sister. He was very keen to know about the qualifications needed and what type of work would be available; as he had another 8 years of Naval Service to complete in which to get it right."

In 1956 Bernard had joined HMS Triumph, a maintenance depot ship, which went on a three month deployment from Plymouth to Scotland.

Gill: "During Dad's free time, he went out as a pillion with another sailor. They were involved in an accident and both were killed. He was only a week or so short of the ship coming back to Plymouth. He wrote his last letter to Mum two days before he died and sadly she received it after hearing of his death."

My wife Alison and I met up with Lance and his wife Sandy in 2013. Lance, an ex police officer in Devon, had moved to live in Cornwall. Lance was now a Cornwall County Councillor and had brought along his father Bernard's war medals which very much resembled my own father's collection.

The loss of one of their comrades whether in battle or otherwise is always an extremely sad occasion, as it would have been on HMS Triumph. A number of his close shipmates, led by the Padre, travelled from Scotland to Newton Abbot to attend Bernard's funeral. They brought with them a small white marble anchor for his grave. Unfortunately, a sad coincidence occurred, as explained by his son, Lance. "With regard to the small white anchor, it was subsequently stolen in 1971 and was the first crime I investigated as a newly trained police officer, sadly not one I was able to solve."

As you can appreciate, Bernard Kennedy BEM was a modest man, who gave eighteen years of his life to the service of his country. After all his achievements, with a new stage of his life ahead to look forward to, he was prematurely taken from his young family at the age of thirty-three.

ROBERT 'BOBBY' MCATAMNEY

As previously mentioned, Bobby was one of the six 'Fighting McAtamneys' from the town of Carrickfergus. Although three were wounded, they all survived the war. Bobby received a shrapnel wound to the lip which could have easily been to other more serious parts of the head.

The McAtamneys were a well-liked family in Carrickfergus. When the news of the Battle became known, everybody was worried for Bobby and kept on asking his parents for any news. When he eventually returned home, the town was decorated with flags and bunting, and the town's people lined the streets to welcome him home and a special ceremony was put on at the Town Hall. When Bobby was presented with a watch and a ring, he told the audience that "I will look back on this day with pride."

Bobby remained in the Navy till 1960 and rose to the rank of Petty Officer. As Kate, Bobby's daughter, says: "He loved the life but by now he had married two years earlier and one year later they had my brother, Roy. It was then that he found the long separations a bit too much to bear. So he left the Navy and went to work at Courtaulds the giant textile company. It was at the factory in 1974 that Dad suffered a massive heart attack and died. He was only fifty-four years old. He left a son, Roy and a daughter [Kate] and was sadly missed by many in the town, as he was liked so much."

I leave the final words to Bill Cameron a nephew of Bobby who writes: "My Uncle Bobby was a quiet and select person. I remember reading a story about him in an old 'Belfast Telegraph', my mother [Bobby's sister] used to keep. The story told of Bobby coming home to a heroes' welcome in his home town of Carrickfergus, after his ordeal in the sea. Indeed, he was a hero in my eyes and the whole family circle, and also one of the best tenors one could listen to. Rest in Peace, hero."

AUSTIN MCNAMARA

You will remember Austin receiving a 'heroes'' welcome home to Bolton, where his family and neighbours had decorated their street with flags hung from windows. His sister Josie, obviously excited by Austin's imminent arrival, kept calm by playing marbles with the boy next door. Many years later Josie and her husband Jim and their daughter Jo emigrated to Australia. However, Josie made sure she also took with them treasured memorabilia signifying her brother's involvement in the First Battle of Narvik.

I am very grateful to Leo Styles for his ongoing support and the massive amount of information he has continued gather and send to me over the last five years. Leo writes, "This is the story that my 12 year old son Patrick gave as part of a school class presentation in his first year of secondary education. The human interest story obviously is related to Austin McNamara of Bolton, and coincidentally my son delivered the presentation on 1 March 2004."

"On the 60th anniversary of Austin's untimely death during the war in 1944.

"I'd like to share with you an artefact that has historical significance to my family. This is a pair of sea boot stockings.

They belonged to my great uncle, Austin McNamara, who was my Grandmother's brother. He received them from some Norwegian fishermen who rescued him from his naval ship, the HMS Hardy when it was sunk while in action against German destroyers at Narvik on the coast of Norway, on the 10th April, 1940. They would have been cold and wet from being in the water so the fishermen gave them some of their clothing. When he returned to England he was issued with a new naval uniform but he kept the sea boot stockings, a hat, a scarf and gloves. The survivors were inspected and addressed by Winston Churchill on the 19th April 1940. In these photos, Austin is still wearing the fisherman's clothing.

"Almost 4 years later Austin was on the HMS Gould which was torpedoed and sunk by a German submarine in an area between Ireland and the Azores (west of Portugal). Half an hour later, this German submarine was in turn sunk by other British ships with only one German survivor! The Ministry of Defence's Naval Historical Branch's records show that the cause of death of Able Seaman Austin McNamara was 'Missing – Death on War Service Presumed', the assumption being that he lost his life as a result of the action that day, 1st of March 1944. He was 23 years of age.

"When my Grandmother married my grandfather, they came out from England to live in Australia. My Grandmother brought Austin's scarf, gloves, cap and the sea boot stockings with her. My grandfather used to ride a motorbike to work so he used the scarf and gloves until they wore out.

"My Grandmother can't remember what happened to his cap. A few years ago, she asked if we would like to keep the sea boot stockings.

"My artefact has some historical value due to its age, more than 64 years old and due to its link with the Second World War. It is obviously of great sentimental value to our family.

As far as monetary value goes, they would cost about 50 (Australian) dollars to make today but this does not take into account any value given for their historical worth."

Patrick's moving presentation illustrates perfectly not only the historical, but also the sentimental and human impact of the Battle of Narvik: the stories of these men are still deeply ingrained in the lives of their families today.

VICTOR GEORGE MANSELL

Subsequent to his traumatic experiences at Narvik, Victor was given a shore appointment for two years from September 1940 in the position of the Port Anti-Submarine Officer at Devonport. This was followed by similar duties at Scottish bases, including his last appointment as an Inspector of Anti-Submarine Equipment. He retired from the Navy after the war in 1945. It appears that Victor was married in 1950 to Ms Dennis at Abergavenny.

As you have previously read in the chapter 'The Saga of the Secret Codes', Cyril visited Victor at his home near Exeter. I recall Dad telling me they had an enjoyable reunion reminiscing about the times on 'Hardy'. One story previously unknown to Cyril, recalled by Victor, was an incident during the early days of the war. This was when 'Hardy' was in Freetown, West Africa for maintenance and a rest period. Victor's brother lived in the area and either he had his own plane or had access to one. Victor described the occasion: "Whilst we were there at anchor in the harbour, my brother's plane came diving down to the ship and was buzzing away." Consequently, Captain Warburton-Lee sent for Mansell. "I got a right bollocking from him in his cabin, saying the next time they might not think he was a friendly pilot and could shoot him down."

Eventually, Victor moved to the Somerset area, where he died at the age of seventy.

FREDERICK 'BERT' ARTHUR MASON, DSM

During my research, I found Arthur 'Bert' Mason's account on the BBC 'WW2 People's War' website. It was contributed by Olwen George, Bert's niece. It took a while to make contact with Bert's sister, Catherine Mason. I was in luck because Catherine and neice Olwen lived only half an hour from my home in Shropshire. As you have read, Bert's personal story was well written and helped to bring alive the events at Narvik. I have to thank both Catherine and Olwen, because their contact and enthusiasm at the early stages of writing this book gave me a much needed boost to continue my task.

After Narvik, Bert went on to serve on HMS Broadwater until October 1941, when she was torpedoed by a U-boat in the Atlantic off Ireland. Once more he survived and the Navy must have taken this into account because his next draft was nearer to home in Birkenhead. Here he was part of the standby crew whilst the new 'Hunt Class' destroyer HMS Aldenham was completed at the Cammel Laird's shipyard. The newly appointed commanding officer was Lieutenant Alex Stuart-Menteth. (Incidentally, he was the First Lieutenant on HMS Hunter.)

Bert reminisces, "In March 1942 Stuart-Menteth was in command of the 'Berkley', a 'Hunt Class' destroyer which was having a boiler clean. He was whisked away to take command of the 'Aldenham'. The following day she set sail for the Mediterranean. I served under Lieutenant Stuart-Menteth on the 'Aldenham' for about twenty-one months and a better 'skipper' one could not wish to have had."

Bert went on to serve on 'Aldenham' in the Mediterranean until May 1944. He then returned to Plymouth where he became an instructor at the Torpedo and Electrical School HMS Defiance. Later he transferred to the submarine maintenance and repair ship HMS Forth. He left the Navy in 1946 and became an electrician. He finally joined the British Oxygen Company in the construction department.

Bert became one of the founder members of the 2nd Destroyer Flotilla of Narvik Association, where he met up once more with Gunner Dougy Bourton. Having found they lived near each other it enabled them to keep in close contact.

Although born in Maesbury, Shropshire, Bert settled in the Deeside area with his wife Lily. They had no children but Bert had a close knit family with sisters Catherine and Annie and brothers, Edward and William, who was also a Royal Naval man. Bert's legacy remains for future generations in his book, 'The Last Destroyer'.

'Bert' Mason, DSM, a brave and remarkable man, passed away in 2005 aged ninety-two.

WALTER MITCHELL

After coming back to Britain and attending the ceremony on Horse Guards Parade, Walter, similar to his fellow shipmates, returned to his home town and a grand welcome. As referenced in an earlier chapter, his local newspaper the 'Evesham Journal' wrote a feature on Walter's experience at Narvik. The article concludes with the lines: "They reached their base on Wednesday last week and it is doubtful if there was one who did not feel relieved; 'Oh! To be in England.......' Mitchell paid a fine tribute to Captain Warburton-Lee and his fellow-members of the crew."

Subsequent to a spell in barracks, Walter's next ship was HMS Offa. Within two months, his ship took part in one of the early Russian convoys PQ-4 from Iceland to Archangel. There were eight merchant ships escorted by eight Royal Naval vessels; all arrived safely with their much needed cargoes. During his time on 'Offa' he was promoted to Leading Seaman.

In 1943 Walter returned to Devonport to complete various courses and his next two drafts were on the minesweepers 'Worthing' and Lysander' respectively. The former becoming involved in the clearing of mines prior to 'Operation Neptune', alternatively known as D Day. By the end of the war it seems that Walter had become attached to a life in the Navy. He had passed exams as a Torpedoman and volunteered for submarine service. Yet, in September 1946, now an Acting Petty Officer at the age of twenty-five, because of his father's ill health, Walter decided to leave the Navy.

Here, Walter's daughter Norma explains, "Dad's parents lived in a 'tied cottage' in Grafton, Gloucestershire. Dad, being the only single man in the family had to return to live with his parents and take over his father's job. This enabled the family to retain their home." However, Walter's affinity with the Navy continued and he became a Petty Officer in the Royal Naval Reserve. "Dad worked on the land for a while where he met Cicely (maiden name, Hyde) from Brierley Hill, Staffordshire. At the time my mum was in the local 'Land Army' and she and Walter married in June 1947."

Walter's connection with the Navy ended in 1951 when he was discharged from the RNR. That is until twenty years later when he became a founding member of the 2nd Destroyer Flotilla of Narvik Association.

Walter and Cicely raised four children: Norma, Marion, Michael and Diane. "My Dad eventually joined a company that manufactured aeronautical instruments where he worked as an engineer until he retired. All during his life he had a great love of sport, especially cricket, which he played until he was no longer able. Then he became an Umpire."

Norma also describes how her aunt had "fond memories" of Walter: "She thought it very sad that Dad had to leave the Navy, as he loved the life."

Walter 'Mick' Mitchell died in March 1997 at the age of seventy-six.

DESMOND POPE

Desmond, aged nineteen at Narvik, was another young crew member who was able to relate his first experience in battle. He went on to be promoted to Sub Lieutenant in October 1941. His next ship was HMS Chitral an armed merchant cruiser previously a P&O passenger liner requisitioned by the Admiralty. Promoted to Lieutenant in 1943, between 1944 and 45, he served on the submarine HMS Unseen. Subsequent to 'VE' day, in July 1945 he was appointed to the Royal Navy Air Station HMS Seaborn in Halifax, Canada. Shortly afterwards he joined the captured German U-boat 190 which was re-commissioned into the Royal Canadian Navy. The only further information I have is that Desmond left the Royal Navy in 1950.

WILLIAM J. PULFORD

During his interview with the Imperial War Museum in 1989, Bill Pulford was able to explain the outcome of the 'White Ensign' he had managed to hide away in his coat until his return to the UK: "When my first wife died, I told my daughter, this would have been fifteen years ago now [1974], 'There's a "White Ensign" in my case [Ditty box] with other stuff, when I die I want that put in my coffin. It goes with me.' She said, 'I promise you Dad.'

"Anyhow, March this year [1989] my grandson was at HMS Raleigh and on his 'passing out parade', I saw an establishment Warrant Officer who happened to be a friend of mine. He later took me around the Raleigh Museum which was full of models and wartime stuff. I said to him, 'Would you like a "White Ensign" which was in the Battle of Narvik." He jumped at the chance and so it was passed on to Warrant Officer Mr Smith at HMS Raleigh. So it is now for the Trainees to see they have 'a bit of Narvik' there."

The small boats 'White Ensign' can still be seen in the foyer of the theatre at HMS Raleigh. *Photograph taken by Warrant Officer Antony Royle, grandson of Cyril Cope.*

Bill was also an active member of the 2nd Destroyer Flotilla of Narvik Association. Here he relays the story that as part of the British Veterans entourage representing the 'Association' he went to their counterpart's reunion at Kiel in Germany in 1979. "I was introduced to the nephew of Kommodore Bonte. I found out then that Kommodore Bonte had gone down to his cabin to sleep, not knowing our ships had arrived. I told him that I was a torpedoman on 'Hardy' that had fired the first torpedo. Kommodore Bonte's nephew, who was then a Korvettenkapitan, or a three ringed equivalent to a British Commander, said, 'Well war is war, we would have done the same to your Captain, if we had had the chance. It's just one of the unfortunate systems that war brings about."

GEORGE J. QUINN

As the Petty Officer 'Writer', George was given the responsibilities of encryption and decryption of signals passed to him by Lt Paymaster Stanning. His son Tony contacted me to tell me what he knew about his father's involvement during the battle.

"My brother Michael told me that they were aware of him meeting Churchill on Horse Guards Parade. He also mentioned seeing a picture in a magazine. Local news reporters came to our house in Plymouth, trying to get a story. But my grandfather, George's father in law, was told to send them packing! My father never attended the 'Narvik Reunions'. He was quite a reserved man, who didn't enjoy such occasions too much. I think he was trying to remove the 'horrors of the war' from his mind."

George became another of the 'Hardy' crew who continued his service in the Royal Navy. He had obviously impressed his superiors during the battle because he was promoted to Chief Petty Officer just seven months later. For the remainder of the war he went on to serve with other ships between spells at Drake barracks in Plymouth, which was his home town. In 1948 there were significant changes made in the Warrant Officers' ranks and they became known as Commissioned Officers. Subsequently, four months later, George was further promoted and became a 'Commissioned Officer Writer'.

Following this, George was given appointments to other ships as well as shore bases in Aden and Sasebo in Japan. The latter naval base was used by the Royal Navy during the Korean War for logistic purposes, including the resupplying of fuel, ammunition and spare parts. By a seemingly coincidence, Geoffrey Stanning was also based there. Perhaps he had taken George along as a proven and trusted part of his staff. In 1955, he was promoted to Senior Commissioned Officer and then three years later Lieutenant Commander. At the age of 50, in 1964 he took voluntary retirement.

His son, Tony, tells of his father's move back into a life outside the naval environment. "He was a very private person, who enjoyed the company of his shipmates but didn't join in everything. However, he played the piano in the mess and enjoyed a drink. He was a practising Catholic, whose prayers were important to him in times of battle and adversity. After his naval career, he joined the Barclays Bank as a cashier and retired at sixty-four, when my mother died of cancer. He lasted another ten years, grieving a lot of the time."

George Quinn after a long and exemplary service to the Royal Navy died in 1991. The brave part he played in the Battle of Narvik will never be forgotten by future generations of his family.

STANLEY GEORGE ROBINSON

Stanley was another South Walian from Port Talbot. You will remember his struggle on the march to Ballangen; when almost there he was picked up and thrown over the shoulders of a friendly Norwegian. I had little information about Stanley's fortunes after 'Narvik' until Peter Kerswell, the son of 'Jake' Kerswell on 'Hunter', re-contacted me in 2012. Peter lived near Stanley and saw an obituary notice in the local newspaper. It described how Stanley George Robinson passed away "Peacefully, on 23rd May 2012 at Neath Port Talbot, in his 94th year, Stan (Ex Petty Officer, Royal Navy), dearly beloved husband of the late Mary, devoted father to all his children, grandchildren, great and great great grandchildren. He will be sadly missed by his sister and brothers together with all his family and friends."

I made an unsuccessful attempt to make contact with Stan's family to pass on my belated condolences. I was not sure whether his family were aware of his contribution to the Imperial War Museum's archives left for future generations.

HARRY ROGERS

Stoker Harry Rogers believed that joining up saved his life from his day job at the 'Iron and Steel Works'. However, you would not blame him if after his first four years in the Navy he had had second thoughts. Even more so, because in the following two years it did not get any better!

Harry was one of the crew who had tried to lower the Captain's wounded body onto a boat, when a salvo came in, causing more death and destruction. He remember at that moment receiving a 'bite' to his back. It appears that when it was later attended to in Ballangen, it was decided that his injuries required no ongoing everyday treatment. Subsequently, he was able to join his other shipmates who were going back to the UK on HMS Ivanhoe. On Harry's eventual arrival in London, further investigations by medical staff showed that in fact the 'bite' was caused by a piece of shrapnel, which it was decided was best left untouched. The disappointing outcome was that he was unable to attend the great welcome by crowds on Horse Guard Parade and witness Mr Winston Churchill's historical speech.

Approximately a year later, during a routine X-ray the shrapnel was found; lodged precariously close to his lungs and heart. Fortunately it seems that the icy waters of the fjord had prevented him from losing too much blood. Apparently the surgeon decided not to operate because the shrapnel was too near to his heart.

The story does not end there. Shortly afterwards Harry was diagnosed fit to continue his naval duties. As recorded in a special feature on Harry by the Middlesborough 'Evening Gazette' from 1973: "For 33 years Mr Harry Rogers has kept close to his heart a grim souvenir of the three times he cheated death. It is an old half penny sized piece [or a fifty pence piece] of shrapnel lodged an inch above his heart".

Harry was soon back in action not many weeks later in time for the Dunkirk evacuation. In a desperate attempt to repatriate our armed forces back home safely, virtually any sea worthy vessel was acquired to cross the English Channel. Hence Harry was detailed to an ageing tug boat. This resulted in Harry Rogers' 'second great escape'.

The tug was returning from the fourth trip to the Dunkirk beaches. Harry, as a Stoker, was in his usual part of the ship, the boiler room. As part of the age old naval tradition, midday became 'tot' time. Harry was relieved for a short spell to go up top to consume his rum. At that moment there was a bomb blast, which "capsized the tug like a toy". Whilst he was flung into the water, his boiler room relief was killed. Unbelievably, 'stranger than fiction', the warship which picked up Harry and the other crew members was none other than the HMS Ivanhoe. Ironically, 'Ivanhoe' herself was sunk soon after having landed the survivors.

As you have read there were two crewmen on HMS Prince of Wales, Walter White and Charles Stock, both of whom never returned home. Another of their shipmates on 'Hardy' was Harry Rogers.

Returning back to the 'Evening Gazette': "[...] Mr Rogers was in the engine room of the Prince of Wales when the first of nine torpedoes hit. A handful of others had fought their way to the deck, the huge ship had begun to keel over and they were left sitting on the upturned stern.

"'Then she just begun to sink beneath us' said Mr Rogers. 'We were drawn down with her and I was rolling over and over in the inky darkness. My lungs were bursting then suddenly I was on the surface and gulping air before going down again.' He went up and down a third time before finding himself in the oily sea surrounded by hundreds of others. For hours he managed to stay afloat as sharks savaged their victims all around him. He was eventually picked up and taken to Singapore. There he found himself enlisted by the Army fighting against the Japanese, who were sweeping down through Malaya.

"A letter written by Rogers in Capetown, was received yesterday by his mother. Mr and Mrs Rogers told an 'Evening Gazette' reporter that their son was a marvellous swimmer and when they heard the news that the Prince of Wales had sunk, they felt sure he would be saved.

"But he got back to Britain in time to go out on the African campaign landings in Sicily, Salerno and Anzio. Then he was in the first wave of the D-Day landings. 'Nothing much happened after that third escape' said Mr Rogers philosophically. 'I've never had a twinge from this bit of old iron in me and fortunately have enjoyed the best of health.'"

It was normal practice in the Royal Navy that sailors are given nick names. It would not be a surprise if Harry Rogers in the remaining years of his naval career would have become known as 'Harry Houdini', after the famous escapologist.

Harry left the Royal Navy as a Chief Petty Officer after fourteen years' service. He went on to work for the industrial chemical company I.C.I. as a foreman until he retired in 1979. One of his work mates, with much affection, recalls that on the night shift meal breaks Harry's team would listen in awe, as he told them some of this wartime experiences.

Harry, married to Eileen, had five children and the family home was in Redcar. His son Keith also went on to become a Chief Petty Officer. Harry's eldest grandson, Alex Kopsahilis, a serving officer whilst on HMS Ocean, visited Narvik and was proud to visit the local war museum. In a moving tribute, on behalf of his grandfather, Alex laid a wreath on Captain Warburton-Lee's grave. I have to thank Harry's other son, Tony, his daughter Fidelma and Alex for their contribution in making sure their much loved father and grandfather's astonishing naval career would never be forgotten.

Harry Rogers passed away on the 12th of October, 2010.

ANTHONY RONAYNE, BEM

Anthony, not deterred by his experiences at Narvik, was soon in action again. Here, Anthony's eldest daughter, Lucy, explains: "I persuaded my father to give me the account of his service days in the Navy. Besides the account of the Battle of Narvik, he also managed to write about the Battle of Bari [Italy], where for a short time he was blinded by mustard gas."

This occurred on 2nd December 1943 when the British and Allied Forces used the port of Bari for logistical purposes in the Italian Campaign. The Germans made an air attack to cut off supplies and twenty-seven transport ships were sunk. One of the ships had a 'secret' supply of 'Mustard Gas Bombs' on board, for retaliatory purposes. This was because the Germans had threatened to use chemical warfare in their attempt to avoid a possible defeat in Italy. Some of the liquid sulphur mustard evaporated into the surrounding smoke. It was this poisoned vapour that Anthony and other men suffered blindness and chemical burns. In fact there was over 600 hospitalised and within three weeks eighty-three victims had died. There were even more civilian victims affected and lost their lives.

During the action, irrespective of Anthony's temporary disablement, through his own initiative he managed to assist colleagues around him. For his bravery, almost a year later, he was awarded the British Empire Medal (BEM). By the end of the war he had been awarded ten medals, which are proudly held for future generations. He served on ten warships of varying types. In 1944, Anthony had met Mary and they were married in July 1947. They then had three daughters, Lucy, Margaret and Miriam.

After the war Anthony continued his Royal Naval service at HMS St Angelo in Malta, as a Training Officer for 'New Entries' and those developing their careers in the 'Steward' branch. He was promoted to the rank of Chief Petty Officer in 1960. At one stage he was offered a prodigious posting in London. However, he turned this down due to family reasons. He finally retired from the Royal Navy after twenty-five years of service in 1964.

Chief Petty Officer Anthony Ronayne R.N. *Kind permission of daughter, Lucy Tirchett.*

In 1992, at a special ceremony at the Presidential Palace in Valletta, Anthony received the 'Memorial George Cross' medal from the then President of Malta, Dr Vincent Tabone. This was presented for Anthony's contribution on behalf of Malta to the fight against 'Nazism'.

Anthony Ronayne passed away in 2007, but his close family remember him with much love and respect. Here is a tribute provided by his granddaughter, Gertrude: "I feel that I was so privileged to have listened to the stories of the Battles of Narvik and that of Bari told by my dear grandpa, since I was a little girl. Today I felt very emotional as I was reading through this account again but I can say that I am so proud of my grandpa more than ever!"

In 2010 I visited Malta and had the privilege of meeting and receiving a warm welcome from Anthony's extended family. It was a memorable occasion for me, where Lucy,

Lorry and their daughter Gertrude showed me around the places in Malta I had visited with the Royal Navy many years before. However, a special moment came when they arranged for me to visit Mary, then aged 83. However, I must not miss mentioning Margaret with whom Mary lived, as well as Gertrude's children Lara Marie and Owen.

I leave the final words to Anthony's grandchildren. "As Maltese children we are very proud of our great grandpa because with his actions he managed to save other people's lives in a foreign country. We miss him so much. Lara Marie and Owen Azzopardi."

LESLIE JOHN SMALE, BEM

Les Smale was described by Peter Dickens in his book as 'Man Friday'. This was when Les arrived in time to help the wounded Paymaster Lieutenant Stanning who needed someone to take over the dead helmsman's wheel. It could be argued that Les should have received more recognition for the relatively calm manner in which he carried out the task under the intense pressure of battle. However, a month after the battle on the 8th of May, 1940, Lieutenant Stanning, whilst recovering from his wounds, took time to write to the Chairman of Stoke Canon Parish Council. Unfortunately, this was after Les had attended his previous school award ceremony when he had received his engraved gold watch and 'War Savings Certificates'.

Lieutenant Stanning wrote, "I had a good deal to do with Smale in the 'Hardy' and knew him fairly well. I liked him very much indeed and thought very highly of him, as did all the officers. He was considered one of the most hard working and steady seamen in the ship. [...] he appeared in the wheelhouse at a most critical moment [...] he was the first unwounded man in there to come to his senses after the explosion and have the courage to see what there was to be done." Lieutenant Stanning concluded his letter with the following words: "I would like his Mother to read this letter if possible. She must be a very proud woman."

Les and Barbara married in 1944. He served at sea throughout the war and after thirty years' service retired in 1965 as a Chief Petty Officer. One of his last ships, in 1960, was HMS Cavalier, the oldest remaining destroyer from the Second World War. She now rests at the museum in Chatham Dockyard.

Les Smale at his old school for the presentation. At his right shoulder is the fourteen year old Barbara, he eventually married.

Les spent the latter years of service as a Chief Instructor at 'New Entry' training establishments. He was finally rewarded for service to his country, when in 1965, he received the British Empire Medal. It seems even after a long distinguished career in the Royal Navy, Les still had an affinity with the sea. Hence, he joined the HM Coastguard Service for the remainder of his working life.

I visited Les and Barbara at their home in Crediton, during which Les was able to provide his account of Narvik as if it was yesterday. Les described how "I relive the events of early April 1940 every year. The popular song in those days was 'It's a Lovely Day Tomorrow' sung by Vera Lynn – for years I would avoid listening to it." On asking Les as to whether he would allow me to use his account in my book, he took a short while to think before he said, "You will have to ask Barbara". Such a modest man, who during the battle, being one of the younger crew members, remained calm under perilous circumstances.

Barry Knell, who served with Les on HMS Cavalier in the 1960s: "Les was my Chief 'Buffer' on 'Cavalier', a finer Englishman you will never find."

Leslie John Smale passed away on the 11th of June, 2011 whilst I was writing this book.

Bill Sanders, a family friend, ends with a fitting tribute: "Les Smale was one of the most interesting old 'Sailors' I ever met. God Bless Him."

GEOFFREY STANNING, DSO

Lieutenant Paymaster Geoffrey Stanning was awarded the DSO at Buckingham Palace in June 1940. Although discharged from hospital, he still needed to have a walking stick to meet the King.

Geoffrey was to suffer from back pain for the rest of his life. In 1942 he married Mary and had a son and two daughters.

His daughter Rosemary Barnes remembers her father recounting to her that when he woke up in the Ballangen hospital, "He called a nurse and asked her if he had had one or two legs amputated, as he had been warned that amputation might be necessary. The nurse replied, 'I don't know, I'll go into the office and see'!"

Despite his injuries, he was to continue duties in the war. Geoffrey was attached to the planning staff for 'Operation Neptune' prior to the Normandy landings where he received a commendation for his work. This led to his promotion to Commander. He was appointed to HMS Bermuda part of the Pacific fleet in advance of the Japanese surrender.

Subsequently, Geoffrey served in the Korean War joining HMS Belfast to become secretary to the Flag Officer Second-in-Command, Far East Fleet. He was 'Mentioned in Despatches'. This was for his efficient planning of logistics when the Royal Navy was quickly required to control the sea lanes on the west coast of Korea. He followed the Admiral as his secretary, firstly in command of the West Indies station and then at NATO Headquarters in Norfolk, Virginia. After completing a spell on an aircraft carrier, he was seconded to the Royal New Zealand Navy, where he was responsible for the personnel department.

Geoffrey Stanning was promoted to Captain rank in 1956 and returned for UK duties in 1958. He then became the 'Appointee' for appointments and careers for all officers in the Supply Officers branch. His last employment in the Navy was at the Ministry of Defence, as Director of Administrative Planning, where he was described as an "innovative thinker". In civilian life he went full circle by returning to his old school Marlborough College as the Bursar. He and Mary became involved in all school activities and he made many improvements.

Lieutenant Paymaster Geoffrey Stanning. As seen reached the rank of Captain. 'The Times' newspaper.

Somewhere along the way Geoffrey nurtured a hobby in carpentry in which he became highly skilled.

Captain Geoffrey Stanning RN DSO, after a very eventful and fulfilling life, passed away in 1997 at the age of eighty-five.

Rosemary tells me, "My father was never sure that he had done the right thing in beaching HMS Hardy, but I am convinced that his actions saved many lives."

WHAT ABOUT THE 2nd DESTROYER FLOTILLA.

Having explained what eventually happened to some of the crew members, it would only be appropriate to mention what became of the remaining ships in the 2nd Destroyer Flotilla.

Hostile. Having escaped down the Ofotfjord to live again the ship was struck by a mine between Cape Bon and Pantellaria and eventually had to be sunk by a torpedo from 'Hero' on August 26th 1940.

Hyperion was also struck by a mine in the Mediterranean and was also sunk by our own forces in January 1941.

Havock was bombed and ran aground off Cape Bon on April 6th 1942.

Hotspur was transferred to the Dominion Republic Navy in 1948 and renamed 'Trujillo' until 1962 when she became known as to the 'Duarte'. She was eventually withdrawn from service in 1972, not bad for a ship built in 1936.

Hero was transferred to the Royal Canadian Navy in 1943 and scrapped in 1946. Her ship's bell is on display at Meon Stoke in Hampshire.

Hasty was sunk by an E-boat in June 1942 whilst taking part in 'Operation Pedestal'.

Hereward was sunk by aircraft off Crete May 28/29th 1941.

Epilogue

I finally return back to the very beginning of the book, to the 'Prologue'. Tragedy in warfare extends beyond the side which you fight for. Nothing illustrates this more clearly than the two bodies – one of a young British sailor, one of a young German sailor – which were found washed up on the rocks in the fjord. Although the German sailor remains nameless, his sacrifice is equal to that of his British counterpart, Seaman 'Gunner' Hugh Morris Mantle. Both men's lives were prematurely taken away in the cause of duty to their country: arguably, more united these two men than ever separated them.

Hugh was probably the youngest crew member on 'Hardy'. After the battle, his family were made aware that Hugh had been wounded by a single piece of shrapnel to the temple. Then, tragically he was washed overboard. In consequence, decades passed with the whereabouts of Hugh's body remaining a mystery to the loved ones he left behind.

However, in 2005, the week before the 65th Anniversary of the Battle, Hugh's sister Lillian, her daughter Rosemarie and son in law, Daryl, made a memorial visit to Narvik. This was also an attempt to finally put matters to rest. Previously, similarly to other families' experiences of searching for their loved ones, they had had difficulties ascertaining the whereabouts of Hugh's grave.

Daryl explains how "On our arrival, fate and the Narvik police sent us on a wild goose chase from Narvik to Harvik, Ballangen and all villages between, only to be unsuccessful in our quest. On our return to Narvik cemetery, even though we had been told there were no HMS Hardy graves there. Lo and behold the only 'Hardy' grave there was the one we sought. I strongly believe fate needed us to record all other cemetery details before allowing us to find our own."

To end this story, it is interesting to note that standing by her brother's grave, Lillian could look up and see her hotel bedroom window. As though by fate, just as Lillian's quest came to an end, she was shown her destination by the chance stroke of the hotel clerk's pen: the room she had reserved had placed her window right above Hugh's grave.

Lillian, the younger sister of Hugh, having finally found her brother's grave. Kindly provided by Daryl Harries on behalf of the Mantle family.

IN MEMORY.
FOR YOUR FREEDOM THEY GAVE THEIR LIVES.

Leading Seaman Harold Cockayne
Lieutenant Edward Clark
Lieutenant Charles Cross
Leading Seaman Frank Edwards
Lieutenant Commander Russell Gordon-Smith (Died of Wounds)
Able Seaman John Hay
Chief Petty Officer Leonard Heal
Able Seaman Charles Hillier
Leading Seaman Alexander Hunt
Able Seaman Henry Lang
Ordinary Seaman Hugh Mantle
Stoker 1st Class Henry Maxfield
Ordinary Seaman George Matthews
Able seaman William Pimblett
Leading Seaman Edward Plant
Chief Stoker Edward Stiles
Captain Bernard Warburton-Lee
Ordinary Seaman Cyril Watson
Able Seaman William Wearen
Able Seaman Andrew Whearty

As well as those who died on HMS Hunter, HMS Hotspur and the Norwegian Coastal Defence Ships 'Eidswold' and 'Norge'.

Bibliography

The German Invasion of Norway. April 1940. Geirr Haarr. ISBN 9781 84832 0321

Narvik: Battles in the Fjords. Peter Dickens. ISBN 0 7110 0484 6

History of the Second World War. The War at Sea Volume 1. S.W.Roskill. HMSO.

Narvik. Donald Macintyre. ISBN 0330 02708 5.

Jackspeak. Rick Jolly. ISBN 0 9514305-2-1.

Destroyer Actions. Harry Plevy ISBN 978-1-86227-483-9.

Jack's War. G.C Connell. ISBN 0-7183-0565-5.

Fortress Malta: An Island under Siege.1940 James Holland ISBN 978-0-3043-6654 -5

The Author

Ron Cope was born in Salford in 1946 before his family moved to Flixton on the outskirts of Manchester. On joining the Royal Navy in 1964 in the radio and radar maintenance branch, his first ship was a new guided missile destroyer HMS Devonshire. He was then aged eighteen and this gave him not only his first experience of travelling the world but also involvement in a conflict zone. During the following years having been quickly promoted to Petty Officer he served on the aircraft carriers 'Eagle' and 'Ark Royal', as well as overseas postings to Singapore and Gibraltar, accompanied by his wife Alison.

In 1976, Ron had a one year spell on the staff of Dartmouth Naval College. As a Chief Petty Officer he served on the frigates 'Naiad' and 'Galatea', in charge of radar and communication systems and in the role of training officer. He retired from the navy in 1986 to complete a full time two year Home Office sponsored Probation Officer qualifying course at Plymouth Polytechnic. This led to him gaining employment with the Shropshire Probation Service in Telford.

Over the following twenty years Ron was employed as a generic caseworker and lead facilitator for 'offending behaviour' groups. His last appointment was at a 'Young Offenders Institution' in Shropshire. He says that moving from a naval environment, where his training responsibilities were predominantly with junior ratings, this gave him the necessary experience to work with other young men having social and lifestyle difficulties. Whilst presenting a different challenge, it was also very rewarding.

Ron retired from the Probation Service in 2008 moving to the private sector. This was with Telford Training Consultants (TTC 2000) in a part time role counselling substance misuse offenders with West Midlands Probation Area. During which time, having been given his father Cyril Cope's documents and memorabilia, he began researching for this book.

Ron Cope

CPSIA information can be obtained
at www.ICGtesting.com
Printed in the USA
BVHW081022020123
655389BV00003B/623